Muslim Sources
of the
Crusader Period

)( )( )(

An Anthology

MUSLIM SOURCES
OF THE
CRUSADER PERIOD

)( )( )(

An Anthology

Edited and Translated, with an Introduction, by

James E. Lindsay & Suleiman A. Mourad

Hackett Publishing Company, Inc.
Indianapolis/Cambridge

For our teachers
R. Stephen Humphreys & Tarif Khalidi

Copyright © 2021 by Hackett Publishing Company, Inc.

All rights reserved
Printed in the United States of America

24 23 22 21   1 2 3 4 5 6 7

For further information, please address
    Hackett Publishing Company, Inc.
    P.O. Box 44937
    Indianapolis, Indiana 46244-0937

    www.hackettpublishing.com

Cover design by E. L. Wilson
Interior design by Elana Rosenthal
Maps by Beehive Mapping
Composition by Aptara, Inc.

Library of Congress Control Number: 2021933147

ISBN-13: 978-1-62466-996-5 (cloth)
ISBN-13: 978-1-62466-984-2 (pbk.)
ISBN-13: 978-1-62466-997-2 (PDF ebook)

The paper used in this publication meets the minimum requirements of American National Standard for Information Sciences—Permanence of Paper for Printed Library Materials, ANSI Z39.48–1984.

∞

Contents

Acknowledgments — xi

Introduction — xiii

Maps — xxiv

Chapter 1: Travel Literature and Geographical Guides — 1

1. Al-Harawi on Antioch, Tiberias and its surroundings, Acre, Jerusalem, Bethlehem, Hebron, and Ascalon — 1
2. Ibn Jubayr on the Christians of Mount Lebanon and trade between Muslims and Franks — 15
3. Ibn Jubayr on the cities of Banyas, Acre, Tyre, and the Muslims under Frankish rule — 17
4. Yaqut al-Hamawi on Ascalon, Jaffa, Caesarea, Atlit, Acre, Tyre, Margat, Saône, and Kerak — 28

Chapter 2: Jihad Books and Juridical Directives — 41

1. Ibn 'Asakir on Jihad — 41
2. Al-'Izz son of 'Abd al-Salam on Jihad — 48
3. Al-Subki's account of al-'Izz son of 'Abd al-Salam's juridical directive banning the sale of arms to the Franks — 50
4. Ibn Taymiyya's juridical directive against the Shi'is — 54

Chapter 3: Chronicles, Memoirs, and Poetry — 59

1. Ibn al-Athir on the emergence of the Franks — 59
2. Ibn al-Qalanisi on the capture of Antioch, Ma'arrat al-Nu'man, and Jerusalem, and the attack against Ascalon in 1098–1099 — 62
3. Ibn al-Athir on the capture of Jerusalem and the attack against Ascalon — 66
4. Al-'Azimi on the Battle of the Field of Blood (1119) and several events between 1108 and 1141 — 71

Contents

5. Hamdan al-Atharibi on receiving a land tenure from the Frankish lord of al-Atharib — 76
6. Al-Qaysarani's poems about the Frankish and Greek women in Antioch — 78
7. Ibn al-Qalanisi on the siege of Damascus in 1148 — 80
8. Ibn al-Athir on the siege of Damascus — 85
9. Ibn 'Asakir's poem about Nur al-Din in honor of his forces taking Egypt in 1169 — 89
10. Ibn al-Athir on the defeat of the Franks at Hattin in 1187 — 91
11. 'Imad al-Din al-Isfahani on the seizure of the Relic of the True Cross, the capture of Tiberias, and the execution of the Frankish prisoners — 94
12. Rashid al-Din al-Nabulusi's poem on Saladin's liberation of Jerusalem in 1187 — 97
13. Ibn Shaddad on the expedition of the German emperor and the letter of the Armenian catholicos to Saladin in 1190 — 99
14. Ibn al-Athir on the Franks' capture of Acre in 1191 — 104
15. Sibt Ibn al-Jawzi on al-Mu'azzam's destruction of the wall of Jerusalem in 1219 — 107
16. Sibt Ibn al-Jawzi on the Franks' capture of Damietta in 1219 and their defeat in 1221 — 109
17. Sibt Ibn al-Jawzi on the envoys of Frederick to al-Mu'azzam in 1226 — 115
18. Ibn Wasil on Frederick arriving in Acre in September 1228 — 116
19. Sibt Ibn al-Jawzi on Frederick's visit to the Noble Sanctuary of Jerusalem in March 1229 — 119
20. Ibn Wasil on the negotiations between al-Kamil and Frederick, and the emperor's visit to the Haram of Jerusalem — 121
21. Ibn Wasil on the handing over of Jerusalem to the Franks in 1243 — 128
22. Al-Yunini on a local Christian ransoming a Muslim captive from a Frank — 130
23. Jamal al-Din Ibn Matruh's poem on the defeat of King Louis IX near Damietta in 1250 — 132
24. Abu Shama on the Mongols' capture of Damascus in 1260 — 134
25. Ibn Wasil on the battle of 'Ayn Jalut in 1260 and related events — 137
26. Ibn Wasil on a Muslim embassy to Emperor Manfred in 1262 — 143

27. Baybars al-Mansuri on the capture of Crac des Chevaliers (1271); the death of the Sultan Baybars (1278); and the capture of Tyre, Sidon, Atlit, Beirut, and Haifa (1291)   144

28. Al-Nuwayri al-Iskandarani on Peter of Cyprus's sack of Alexandria in 1365   149

Chapter 4: Biographies   157

1. Ibn 'Asakir on Jesus   158
2. Ibn 'Asakir on al-Findalawi   162
3. Ibn 'Asakir on Nur al-Din   165
4. Sibt Ibn al-Jawzi on al-Mu'azzam   174
5. Al-Dhahabi on al-Mu'azzam   184
6. Ibn Abu Usaybi'a on the Christian physician Ya'qub son of Siqlab   186
7. Al-Dhahabi on the Christian physician Ya'qub son of Siqlab   190

Chapter 5: Correspondences, Treaties, and Truces   191

1. Al-Qalqashandi's account of Saladin's letter of condolence to King Baldwin IV in 1174   191
2. Ibn Shaddad on Saladin's negotiations with Richard the Lionheart in 1191 and the latter's proposal that al-'Adil marry Richard's sister Joan   194
3. Ibn Nazif al-Hamawi's account of Frederick's letter to commander Fakhr al-Din son of Shaykh al-Shuyukh   196
4. Al-Qalqashandi's account of the oaths of the truce between Sultan Qalawun and the Franks of Acre, Sidon, and Atlit   200

Chapter 6: Inscriptions   205

1. Fatimid inscription on a tower fortification in Ascalon (1150)   205
2. Inscription on the pulpit that Nur al-Din commissioned for the Aqsa Mosque in Jerusalem (1168–1169)   206
3. Inscription panel marking the foundation of a trench around the fortification wall of the old city of Jerusalem during the reign of Saladin (1191)   206
4. Inscription above the entrance to St. Anne's Church in Jerusalem, transformed into a college of Shafi'i law and named after Saladin—al-Madrasa al-Salihiyya (1192)   207

Contents

5. Inscription above the main entrance gate to the shrine in Hebron housing the cenotaphs of Isaac and Rebecca (1215) — 207
6. Foundation inscription on the wall of the Fortress of Subayba (Nimrod's Fortress) on the hills overlooking Banyas (1228) — 208
7. Inscription above the arch of the gate to the northwest tower of the Fortress of Subayba (1230) — 209
8. Inscription on a mosque in the village of Bayt Hanun (1239) — 209
9. Inscription on the mausoleum of Khalid son of al-Walid in Hims (1266) — 210
10. Inscription on the shrine of Salman al-Farisi in Ashdod (1269) — 210
11. Inscription commemorating Baybars's renovations of Crac des Chevaliers (1271) — 211
12. Inscription commemorating Baybars's renovations of the Fortress of Subayba (1275) — 211
13. Inscription on a hospice in Hebron for visitors to the shrine of Abraham (1280) — 212
14. Inscription on a hospice for pilgrims in Jerusalem (1282) — 213
15. Inscription on the top and the bottom of the two doors of the gate that leads to the shrine housing the cenotaphs of Abraham and Sarah (1286) — 213

Appendix A: Islamic Calendar — 215

Appendix B: Quranic Verses on War and Peace — 219

Appendix C: Bibliographic Overview of the Major Muslim Sources of the Crusader Period — 225

Appendix D: Glossary of Dynasties, Persons, Sects, Terms, etc. — 243

Bibliography — 257

Index A: Honorific Titles — 270

Index B: Names — 273

Index C: Place Names — 283

Index D: Terms and Events — 288

Index E: Quranic and Biblical References — 290

Acknowledgments

Many of our joint projects, stimulated by common research interests, started with a conversation at a conference or during a visit. This time, however, it was not around Scottish tea or some other libation. The conversations were over Skype or WhatsApp or Zoom, and the common interest was pedagogical: how best to teach our students about the complexity of the interactions between Franks and Muslims in the broader context of Islamic history. Therefore, we decided that we should simply collect and translate the kinds of sources that we would want to use ourselves in our classes. *Muslim Sources of the Crusader Period: An Anthology* is the result. It is our hope that colleagues who teach courses on the Crusades as well as courses on the premodern Islamic Near East will find this anthology useful in their own teaching. We equally hope that this anthology will be useful to researchers who seek a better understanding of the contemporary Islamic perspectives on the Crusades and the period in general, and who might encounter for the first time some of the sources that we included.

There are several people we want to thank for their help in bringing this project to fruition. Rick Todhunter, our editor at Hackett, for his interest in and his willingness to take on such a project and especially for his patient prodding along the way. The discussions with him have been very constructive and allowed us to make the anthology accessible to a wide audience of students and researchers. Elana Rosenthal, our project manager, and her team for shepherding the anthology through the different production stages. Our students at Colorado State University and Smith College who were the first to read and analyze some of these translations in our classes. The three outstanding reviewers for Hackett for their insightful comments. The meticulous care with which they read the text and their valuable suggestions stimulated us to rearrange some of the material, and helped us revise and finalize the anthology in a much better way. Of course, any infelicities or errors are our own.

Finally, we thank our families for their love and support. This project took time and attention away from them. They even had to put up with our constant musings about the texts we have translated, and grandiose claims about the importance of the anthology. They received all of that with tremendous wisdom and graciously offered in return smiles and encouragement.

INTRODUCTION

In popular literature and films, the period of the Crusades has traditionally been defined as beginning in 1095, when Pope Urban II made his famous address in the town of Clermont in which he called upon the knights of western Europe to undertake an armed pilgrimage to liberate Jerusalem and the Holy Land, and ending in 1291, when the Crusaders lost their last holdings along the coast of the eastern Mediterranean to the Mamluk Sultan al-Ashraf Khalil's forces. Few specialists in Crusades history today accept this narrow time frame, even though it remains popular among non-specialists and the public. More problematic is that the 1095 to 1291 time frame tends to restrict the focus of the period solely to the clash between Western Christendom and the Islamic lands of the eastern Mediterranean. Studies in the last three decades have demonstrated that Crusader campaigns continued long after 1291, that they targeted areas elsewhere throughout Europe and the Mediterranean, and that they were not exclusively against Muslims.[1]

Nevertheless, the clash between the Muslims and the Franks (as Western Europeans were collectively referred to in Muslim literature) remains the focus of Crusades scholarship. Additionally, religion is invariably the lens through which the period is historically analyzed. Other forms of interactions between Muslims and Crusaders or categories of analysis for the period tend to be secondary and have not resulted in serious alterations to the general narrative of Christian–Muslim conflict. While evidence of conflict is abundant, there is also a great deal of evidence of amicable Muslim–Crusader interactions. Moreover, because the period is riven with internal animosities and rivalries among Muslims and among Crusaders, limiting ourselves to "Muslims" and "Crusaders" as analytical categories that reflect unvariegated unity, cohesion, common approach, and so on within each group simply is not feasible. Rather, while these groupings can be used as

---

1. See, for example, Helen Nicholson, *The Crusades* (Indianapolis: Hackett Publishing, 2009), xxxix–xlx; Jonathan Riley-Smith, *The Crusades: A Short History* (New Haven: Yale University Press, 2005), xxvii–xxx; Thomas Madden, *The New Concise History of the Crusades* (New York: Rowman & Littlefield, 2014), 173–195; Norman Housley, *Contesting the Crusades* (Malden: Blackwell, 2006), 1–23. See also Andrew Jotischky, *Crusading and the Crusader States* (Harlow: Pearson, 2004), 1–22.

Introduction

terms of convenience to simplify the discussion, we should be careful not to infuse them with assumptions that convey meanings that do not reflect the complicated realities of the actual situation among the various actors and communities in Syria and Egypt.[2]

Historians of the Crusades have at their disposal a large corpus of Muslim sources, which reflect a variety of views on what unfolded in the eastern Mediterranean and the Near East between the eleventh and fourteenth centuries. Written in greater Syria, northern Mesopotamia,[3] and Egypt, they provide eyewitness and contemporary historical accounts of the period, as well as secondary testimonies on the variety of Muslim responses to and interactions with the Franks. They also register how the events and main figures involved in them were remembered in later years and subsequent centuries, allowing the historian to gauge the impact of the Crusades on Islamic history, culture, and society, as well as their legacy and how it was exploited in intra-Muslim dynamics as well as Muslim–European relations.

Despite their importance, the Muslim sources remain relatively marginal in the way the general history of the Crusader period is written as most Crusades historians are understandably trained in the numerous requisite European languages and not Arabic. Consequently, the European sources tend to dominate the narrative apart from the relatively few Arabic chronicles that have been translated into English or other European languages. This anthology is an attempt to bring to light a disparate selection of sources that in our assessment introduce the student of Crusades history to a more complex understanding of the Crusades and the interactions between Franks and Muslims—which ranged from animosity to amity—in the broader context of Islamic history.

The Franks' earliest military successes, which culminated in the capture of Jerusalem in 1099, are often dubbed the First Crusade. Their direct consequence on the region is that they exposed a major area of the Islamic heartland to non-Islamic rule for the first time since the Arabian–Islamic conquests in the seventh century. Nevertheless, the Franks were received by

---

2. For historical surveys of the Crusader period from the Islamic point of view, see Carole Hillenbrand, *The Crusades: Islamic Perspectives* (Edinburgh: Edinburgh University Press, 1999); Paul M. Cobb, *The Race for Paradise: An Islamic History of the Crusades* (Oxford: Oxford University Press, 2014); and Niall Christie, *Muslims and Crusaders: Christianity's Wars in the Middle East, 1095–1382, from the Islamic Sources* (Farnham: Routledge, 2014). For reasons of space, we have limited our focus to the Islamic lands of the eastern Mediterranean. See the bibliographies in Hillenbrand, Cobb, and Christie for references to Muslim sources that address the central and western Mediterranean.

3. Northern Mesopotamia (*al-Jazira* in Arabic) is the region between the rivers Euphrates and Tigris, and today comprises most of northern Iraq, northeast Syria, and southeast Turkey.

Introduction

the Muslims in the Near East with attitudes ranging from indifference, to collaboration, to complete rejection. While some Muslims raised the alarm about what they considered to be an orchestrated Christian onslaught against Islam, many others saw the Franks as merely another regional player and forged alliances with them against their local foes. In other words, Muslims generally became accustomed to the Crusaders' presence as part of the political and military landscape of the region; some Muslim leaders even actively sought to take advantage of the Franks' military capabilities to enhance their respective positions vis-à-vis fellow Muslim opponents.

From the perspective of some of the Muslim authors included in this anthology, the early victories of the Franks in northern Mesopotamia and Syria did not represent the beginnings of anything new. Rather, the Franks' campaigns were seen as merely another episode of a long-standing religious and military conflict between Christendom and Islamdom that had waxed and waned since the initial Muslim conquests of the Byzantine and other Christian territories in Syria, Iraq, Egypt, North Africa, and Spain during the seventh and eighth centuries.[4] In fact, these Muslim authors viewed the Frankish encroachment into northwestern Mesopotamia and coastal Syria as part of a much larger Christian campaign on multiple fronts around the Mediterranean, which included the Christian Reconquista in Spain and the Norman conquests of Sicily and southern Italy.[5] Indeed, the rapid success with which the Franks established themselves generated loud, though at first ineffectual, calls for jihad from some members of the Syrian Sunni religious establishment who believed that the Frankish invasion was only successful because Muslim political and military leaders had failed to attend to their religious obligation to wage jihad against the Christian infidels.

Jihad

Before we proceed: a few comments on the frequently misunderstood word jihad and how it was employed by the authors of the Muslim sources in this

---

4. For a survey of some of the major conflicts prior to the First Crusade, see Paul F. Crawford, "The First Crusade: Unprovoked Offense or Overdue Defense?" in Alfred J. Andrea and Andrew Holt, eds., *Seven Myths of the Crusades* (Indianapolis: Hackett Publishing, 2015), 1–28.

5. In his geographic work *The Excursion of One Who Is Eager to Traverse the Regions of the World* (also known as *The Book of Roger*), Muhammad al-Idrisi (1100–1165) included a circular map that reflects the medieval Islamic conception of the world with south at the top and Arabia at the center. See front cover. *The Excursion* was composed for the Norman ruler Roger II of Sicily (r. 1105–1154), whom al-Idrisi served during the Crusader period. See Jean-Charles Ducène, "al-Idrisi, Abu Abdallah," in Kate Fleet, Gudrun Krämer, Denis Matringe, John Nawas, and Everett Rowson, eds. *Encyclopaedia of Islam, Third Edition* (Leiden: Brill, 2007–in progress).

Introduction

anthology. According to the celebrated thirteenth-century Arabic lexicographer Ibn Manzur (1232–1311), the basic meaning of the word jihad (from the root *j-h-d*) is to struggle against something or to exert one's effort toward an objective.[6] In a specifically religious context, and as understood and articulated by nearly every premodern Muslim religious scholar, including Ibn Manzur, jihad has one meaning: to exert one's effort in fighting the enemies of God by deeds or by words. The rather obvious parallelism between two quranic phrases—*jihad fi sabil Allah* (waging jihad in the path of God) and *qital fi sabil Allah* (fighting/slaying in the path of God)—cemented the equation in Islamic religious thought between jihad and religious warfare. In fact, the phrase *jihad fi sabil Allah* came to mean "warfare against infidels." It is important to note that it has become common practice among modern apologists to argue that the traditional Islamic position on jihad is that the "greater" spiritual jihad is superior to the "lesser" military jihad and that spiritual jihad is sufficient in and of itself—even to the exclusion of military jihad. Such a position is without foundation in the classical sources (e.g., Qur'an, canonical Hadith[7] collections, treatises on jihad, etc.). When the authors of the Muslim sources in this anthology used the word jihad, they invariably meant warfare against the enemies of God and the Muslims.[8]

Authors and Sources

Some of the authors in this anthology wrote to rally their fellow Muslims against the Franks and other enemies of Islam.[9] Others limited their literary efforts to chronicling specific aspects of the twelfth, thirteenth, and fourteenth centuries,[10] while still others were concerned with far larger historiographical and religious projects.[11] Add to this the authors who focused on straightforward political propaganda and personal aggrandizement

---

6. See Ibn Manzur, *Lisan al-'arab*, 15 vols. (Beirut: Dar Sadir, 1990), 3: 135 (*j-h-d*).

7. Hadith is the corpus of statements or traditions attributed to or anecdotes about Muhammad and his deeds. Hadith is also the name of the individual statement or tradition. They were transmitted by many of Muhammad's Companions and are preserved in a wide variety of books. They form one of the foundations of Islamic law and practice. We are using Hadith to refer to the entire corpus, and hadith to mean a specific report.

8. See Suleiman A. Mourad and James E. Lindsay, *The Intensification and Reorientation of Sunni Jihad Ideology in the Crusader Period: Ibn 'Asakir (1105–1176) of Damascus and His Age* (Leiden: Brill, 2013). See also Appendix B, p. 223 (footnote 2).

9. Ibn 'Asakir, al-'Izz son of 'Abd al-Salam, and Ibn Taymiyya.

10. Ibn al-Qalanisi, Ibn Wasil, and Ibn al-Shaddad.

11. Ibn 'Asakir, Ibn al-Athir, and Sibt Ibn al-Jawzi.

Introduction

of rulers.[12] At the same time, some in the Muslim society were fascinated with the Franks. They developed friendships with some of them and were impressed with those who adjusted to the local culture.[13] There is also a record of continuous diplomatic channels between Muslims and Crusaders that led to lasting friendships.[14] One important perspective, however, is lacking a direct representation: the voice of the uneducated Muslim masses. Our sources tell us about them and their reactions to and interactions with the Franks, but it is not their voices that are expressed, but rather that of the authors, albeit in some cases we can still grasp their general attitudes to what was unfolding around them.[15]

Whatever their particular motives for writing, each of the authors viewed himself as participating in a well-established Arabic-language tradition that conceived of Islamic history (the history that mattered) as a kind of sacred history that stretched back to the beginning of human time—a historiography that recounted tales of the creation of the world; Adam and Eve; the many biblical prophets, especially those noted in the Qur'an; the unique sanctity of the Holy Land (*al-Ard al-Muqaddasa*; Palestine); the prophetic, political, and military career of Muhammad; and the political, military, and religious history of his community after his death in 632. The Crusades, then, fit into this scheme as yet another episode—this time an episode of tribulation—that once again demonstrated God's special relationship with his chosen community of the Muslim faithful.

Content and Structure of the Anthology

A few comments on some of the choices we have made regarding the content and structure of the anthology are in order. Given the necessary size limitations of an anthology like this, we had to make some difficult choices about what to include and what to leave out. Generally, we opted to forgo material from sources that are widely used and for which there are excellent recent English translations; for example, al-Sulami's *The Book of the Jihad* and Usama Ibn Munqidh's *The Book of Contemplation*.[16] That is not

---

12. 'Imad al-Din al-Isfahani, Rashid al-Din al-Nabulusi, Ibn Shaddad, and al-Subki.
13. Hamdan al-Atharibi and al-Qaysarani.
14. Ibn Wasil.
15. Ibn Jubayr, Sibt Ibn al-Jawzi, and al-Nuwayri al-Iskandarani.
16. Niall Christie, *The Book of the Jihad of 'Ali ibn Tahir al-Sulami (d. 1106): Text, Translation, and Commentary* (Farnham: Ashgate, 2015); and Usama Ibn Munqidh, *The Book of Contemplation: Islam and the Crusades*, trans. P. M. Cobb (London: Penguin, 2008). In the anthology, we only

Introduction

to say that we have ignored works on the ideology of jihad or texts that include personal memoirs. Rather, we have included material on these subjects from sources that are less readily available in recent English translations. Additionally, we have prioritized eyewitness or near-eyewitness accounts. With that in mind, because al-Maqrizi (1364–1442), who is an overused source, lived long after the main events of the Crusader period, and because all the information about the period that he included in his many works was lifted from works well before his time, we have opted not to include excerpts from his works. Finally, rather than merely constructing a sustained narrative based on selections from familiar chronicles, many of which focus on Saladin and the Third Crusade and are already available in English,[17] we prioritized representative examples of the many disparate types of Muslim sources that we believe provide a more complete picture of the Islamic Near East in the Crusader period, many translated here into English for the first time.[18]

We have also included study questions throughout the anthology to help guide readers and to assist them in making the most out of the material. Obviously, these only begin to address the many kinds of questions that the texts can help us answer. The choice of study questions is based on principles we encourage our students to bear in mind as they read these or any Muslim texts from this period. First, accept as a given that authors were not passive reporters of events. Each author had his particular point of view and agenda for crafting his narrative, his poem, his juridical text, his monumental inscription, and so on, in the way in which he did. Second, accept as a given that each of these texts made implicit sense to its author and his intended audience. Consequently, the job of the historian is to learn how and why this is the case, and by extension to grasp the complexity of

---

provide the English titles of the Arabic sources. For the Arabic titles, see Appendix C or the Bibliography.

17. The most notable include Ibn Shaddad, *The Rare and Excellent History of Saladin*, trans. D. S. Richards (Aldershot: Ashgate, 2002); and Ibn al-Athir, *The Chronicle of Ibn al-Athir for the Crusading Period from al-Kamil fi'l-Ta'rikh of Ibn al-Athir*, 3 parts, trans. D. S. Richards (Farnham: Ashgate, 2006–2008).

18. In an effort to provide a more chronologically balanced perspective, we have included extensive material on the thirteenth century, which is often given short shrift but in fact represented the climax and ultimate failure of the Crusading enterprise. Saladin's victories in 1187–1188 were indeed impressive and important, but they merely set the stage for a century-long war of attrition, in which new Frankish expeditions against Egypt in 1218–1221 (Fifth Crusade) and 1248–1250 (Seventh Crusade) almost succeeded. In addition, although the Frankish states after Saladin's victories and the Third Crusade (1189–1192) were significantly reduced to areas primarily along the eastern Mediterranean coast, they proved very durable indeed.

Introduction

the historical sources. In other words, the historian's job is to seek to understand these texts on *their* terms and in *their* historical contexts—not according to our modern presuppositions and expectations of what is normal or righteous.

Chapter 1 provides a geographical overview of Frankish coastal Syria and Palestine from the perspective of three renowned travelers and scholars who traveled throughout the Islamic world (including Syria and Palestine) in the late twelfth and early thirteenth centuries. Al-Harawi (d. 1215) was born in Mosul to a family that hailed from Herat, Afghanistan. His *A Lonely Wayfarer's Guide to Pilgrimage* is a guide to Islamic sacred sites and shrines, many of which were shared with Jews and Christians. Ibn Jubayr (1145–1217) hailed from Valencia, Spain. His *Travel Narrative* provides a detailed account of his experiences and keen observations of daily life while on his two-year pilgrimage journey from Granada to Mecca and back to Spain (1183–1185). Yaqut (1179–1229) was born in the Byzantine lands and was enslaved as a boy. When he was approximately six years old, his master took him to Baghdad where he was given an Islamic education. His *Dictionary of Countries* is an extremely valuable compendium of geographical and toponymic information on cities, towns, and villages in the Islamic Near East and many of the notable Muslim scholars who hailed from these places. These three texts—a pilgrimage guide, a travel narrative, and a geographic gazette—provide us with three different perspectives on the social and religious life in Syria at the time, as well as eyewitness accounts of the conditions of cities, villages, and Islamic sacred places that were either in Frankish hands or had recently been restored to Muslim control when the authors visited them. As such, they shed light on a wide range of interactions between Muslims and Franks in some localities.

Chapter 2 includes two jihad texts and two juridical directives[19] on important issues of the day. Ibn 'Asakir's *The Forty Hadiths for Inciting Jihad* is an important jihad manual composed at the behest of the Zangid ruler of Damascus, Nur al-Din. The brief introduction to al-'Izz son of 'Abd al-Salam's *On the Laws of Jihad and Its Merits* clarifies in no uncertain terms

---

19. *Fatwa* in Arabic. A *fatwa* is a non-binding juridical directive on a point of Islamic law given by a qualified jurist in response to a question posed by an individual, a judge, or a sovereign. Depending on the status of or respect for a particular jurist, the juridical directive may or may not have received wide acceptance by the public. Because Ibn Taymiyya was (and still is) a giant in Hanbali jurisprudence, his juridical directives often did (and still do). In principle, a juridical directive was non-binding because the jurist who issued it did not have state enforcement powers to compel acceptance. Of course, sovereigns from time to time chose to use a juridical directive by a respected jurist to legitimate a policy for pragmatic reasons of state.

Introduction

his views on the obligation to wage jihad in the path of God and the rewards for doing so. The mere fact that al-'Izz son of 'Abd al-Salam also deemed it important to issue his juridical directive banning the sale of arms to the Franks illustrates a significant level of economic interchange between Muslims and Franks. It also reinforces his concern that the Muslims should be engaging in jihad against the enemies of God—and certainly not entering into economic alliances that would necessarily redound to the detriment of the Muslims. Ibn Taymiyya's juridical directive against the Shi'is is vintage Ibn Taymiyya. It clearly articulates his own Sunni supremacism as well as his view that the various Shi'i sects in his day were not Muslims and were collaborators with the enemies of Islam (Franks and Mongols). In fact, his anti-Shi'i animus led him to participate in the 1305 jihad campaign of the governor of Damascus against the Druzes and Shi'is of the coastal region and mountain range of modern-day Lebanon.

Chapter 3 is the longest chapter in this anthology. We have arranged the material according to the chronological order of the events the works describe. Taken together, these texts provide an overall narrative of important events and insider assessments of some of the key Muslim personalities of the Crusader period. As noted above, we have prioritized eyewitness or near-eyewitness accounts. While the chronicles and memoirs may appear to be straightforward narratives of events, as noted above as well, each author had his particular point of view and agenda for crafting his narrative in the way in which he did. An often-overlooked Arabic source for the history of the Crusader period in this regard (as well as for the pre-modern Islamic Near East in general) is poetry. We have included the poems that the authors incorporated as part of their narratives, but which are often deleted in English translations. We have also included several stand-alone poems that reflect the values and concerns of their authors as well. We conclude this chapter with al-Nuwayri al-Iskandarani's account of Peter of Cyprus's sack of Alexandria in 1365 to illustrate that neither economic nor military encounters between the Franks and the Muslims in the eastern Mediterranean concluded in 1291.

Chapter 4 draws on material from one of the most important biographical dictionaries in the Muslim literary tradition—Ibn 'Asakir of Damascus's *History of Damascus*. Ibn 'Asakir's biography of Jesus illustrates the important role that Jesus played (and continues to play) in the Islamic theological and apocalyptic imagination, specifically with respect to his role (and that of all the biblical prophets) in contributing to the merits of the Holy Land, and by extension Syria more broadly. Ibn 'Asakir's biography of al-Findalawi provides insight into this aged North African cleric's role in advocating for

Introduction

the cause of jihad, illustrated most vividly by his own martyrdom during the Second Crusade when the Franks laid siege to Damascus in 1148. Ibn ʿAsakir's biography of Nur al-Din is a moving encomium to the Sunni champion that he and other scholars had long hoped would arise to unite the Sunnis of Syria against Islam's enemies—Franks and Shiʿis—and restore Sunnism to its proper place. The two biographies of al-Muʿazzam by Sibt Ibn al-Jawzi and al-Dhahabi illuminate the career and character of this important Ayyubid sovereign. Finally, Ibn Abu Usaybiʿa's and al-Dhahabi's biographies of the physician Yaʿqub illustrate the important role played by Christian physicians at the courts of Muslim sovereigns.

Chapter 5 includes four examples of the formal diplomacy that Ayyubid and Mamluk sovereigns engaged in with the Franks. Despite the elevated and formulaic prose, each conveys a genuine fondness and respect between sovereigns. Saladin's letter to King Baldwin IV reflects his heartfelt condolences for the newly crowned boy king upon the death of his father, Amalric, whom Saladin considered an honorable adversary and friend. Ibn Shaddad's account of the negotiations between Saladin and Richard the Lionheart, specifically Richard's proposal that Saladin's brother, al-ʿAdil, marry his sister, Joan, to cement an alliance between the two houses is intriguing—not only because of Richard's proposal, but also because of Saladin's enthusiastic and positive response to it. However, Joan, whose entire future was being negotiated unbeknownst to her, was less than pleased when her brother informed her of his nuptial plans for her. Not surprisingly, this well-laid plan did not come to fruition. Frederick II's letter to the Ayyubid commander, Fakhr al-Din, not only conveys Frederick's fondness for Fakhr al-Din, it also illustrates his fondness for Arabic culture, customs, and mores as he cited Arabic verses, including a couplet by the celebrated tenth-century poet al-Mutanabbi. Finally, the oaths of truce between the Mamluk Sultan Qalawun and the Franks of Acre, Sidon, and Atlit vividly illustrate the importance that both Muslim and Frankish sovereigns placed on oaths, the respective Islamic and Christian sacred language and symbols invoked to guarantee oaths, and the onerous penalties for failing to keep one's word.

Chapter 6 consists of Fatimid, Zangid, Ayyubid, and Mamluk inscriptions on a wide array of monuments: mosques, shrines, colleges, fortresses, towers, walls, gates, etc. All but one of these inscriptions commemorate the roles of Sunni Zangid, Ayyubid, and Mamluk sovereigns and officials. These inscriptions tend to follow similar protocols and language in praise of the sovereign who commissioned the building or repair of a structure. In stark contrast, the inscription on a tower fortification in Ascalon from 1150,

Introduction

when the Fatimid position in Ascalon was quite precarious, still follows the highly inflated—even pompous—protocol of inscriptions in praise of an Isma'ili Fatimid caliph.

Translations and Appendices

All translations are our own. We have endeavored to render the Arabic texts in idiomatic English. We have also used English equivalents for technical terms[20] and have avoided diacritics except for ' to indicate the consonant *'ayn* and ' to indicate the consonant *hamza*. In general, personal and place names are transliterated, except in those cases in which an already well-known Anglicized form exists, such as Saladin (not Salah al-Din), Abraham (not Ibrahim), Acre (not 'Akka), Tyre (not Sur), etc. The names of many of the characters in this anthology include a genealogy of several generations. In the Arabic naming system "Ibn" means "son of"; "Abu" means "father of." For example, Nur al-Din's full name was Abu al-Qasim Mahmud ibn Zangi ibn Aq-Sunqur; that is, Mahmud the son of Zangi the son of Aq-Sunqur. Nur al-Din (Light of the Religion) was his honorific title. Abu al-Qasim indicates that he was the father of a son named al-Qasim. To keep things simple for non-specialists, we have generally translated "Ibn" as "son of" except in those instances in which a person is already well known as Ibn so-and-so: Ibn 'Asakir, Ibn Taymiyya, Ibn Munqidh, Ibn Jubayr, etc. However, we have not translated "Abu" as "father of" because it was very common that men were simply known as Abu so-and-so: Abu Talib, Abu Bakr, Abu Hurayra, Abu 'Ubayda, etc.[21] Many of the people in this anthology were given honorific titles that indicate that they were supporters of the religion (*Din*) or the realm (*Dawla*), for example, Salah al-Din (Righteousness of the Religion), Sayf al-Din (Sword of the Religion), Iftikhar al-Dawla (Pride of the Realm), etc. See the index for a list of honorific titles (with English translations) used in this anthology.

A brief biographical sketch introduces each author the first time his work appears in the anthology. At times, an author appears not to know the name of one of the Frankish rulers and simply refers to him as the king or some other title. We have added their names in brackets to provide clarity—for

---

20. We provide clarification in a note the first time a technical term is used as well as in Appendix D: Glossary of Dynasties, Persons, Sects, Terms, etc.

21. To keep things simple for non-specialists, all transliterations of names are in the nominative case (e.g., Ibn Abu Usaybi'a instead of the grammatically correct genitive case in Arabic, Ibn Abi Usaybi'a). For bibliographic citations, we have retained the conventions of the publishers.

Introduction

example, (Conrad) the king of the Germans. We have rendered dates in the translations according to the Islamic calendar that the authors employed, followed by the dates of the Gregorian Christian calendar; for example, Jerusalem was conquered by the Franks on 22 Shaʿban 492 (15 July 1099). Otherwise, we have only used the Gregorian dates. See Appendix A for an explanation of the Islamic calendar. See Appendix B for the major quranic passages on war and peace. Qur'an translations are based on Tarif Khalidi, *The Qur'an: A New Translation* (New York: Penguin, 2009). See Appendix C for a bibliographic overview of the major Muslim sources of the Crusader period, many of which for reasons of space could not be included herein. See Appendix D for a glossary of important dynasties, persons, sects, terms, etc. that are mentioned in the text.

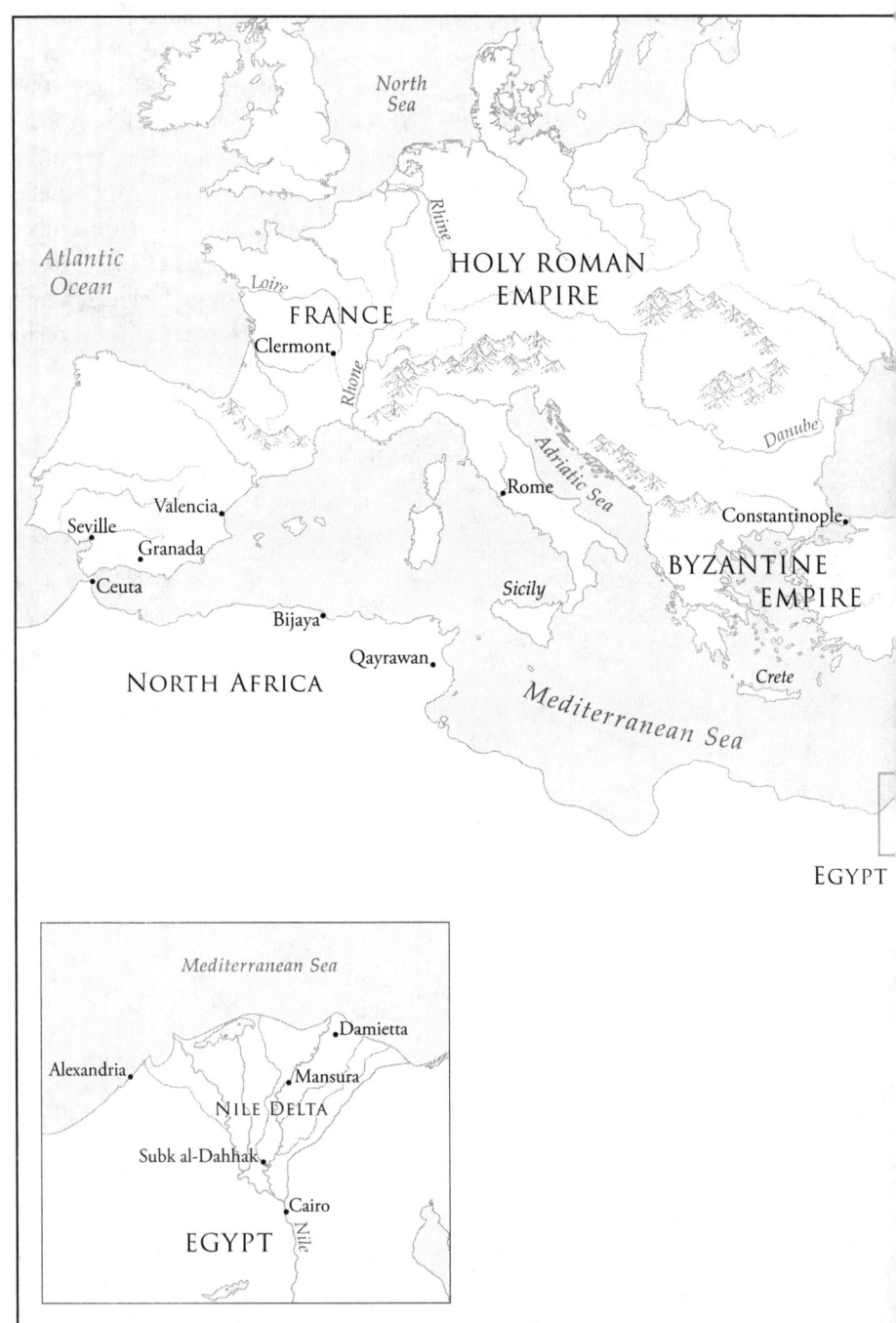

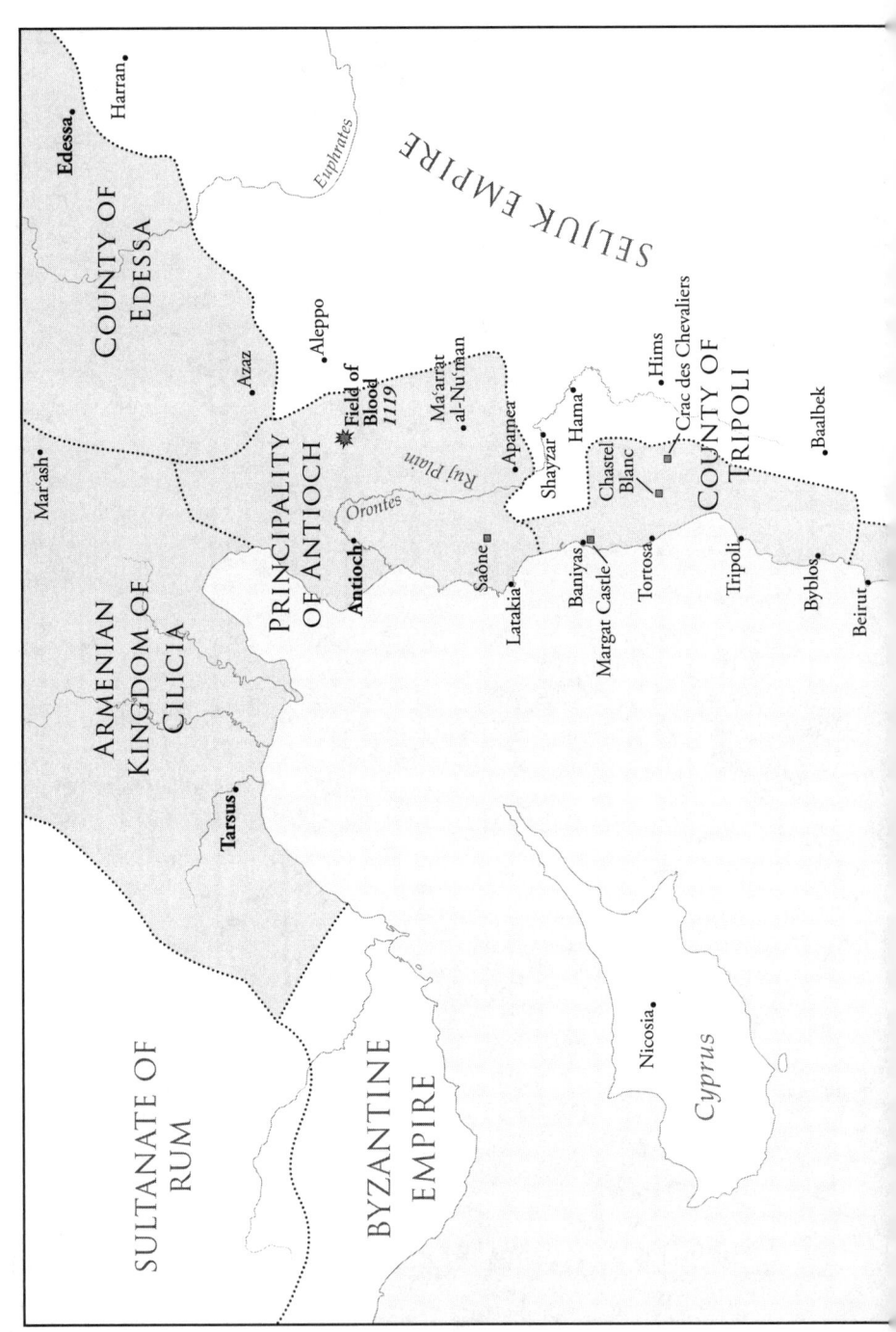

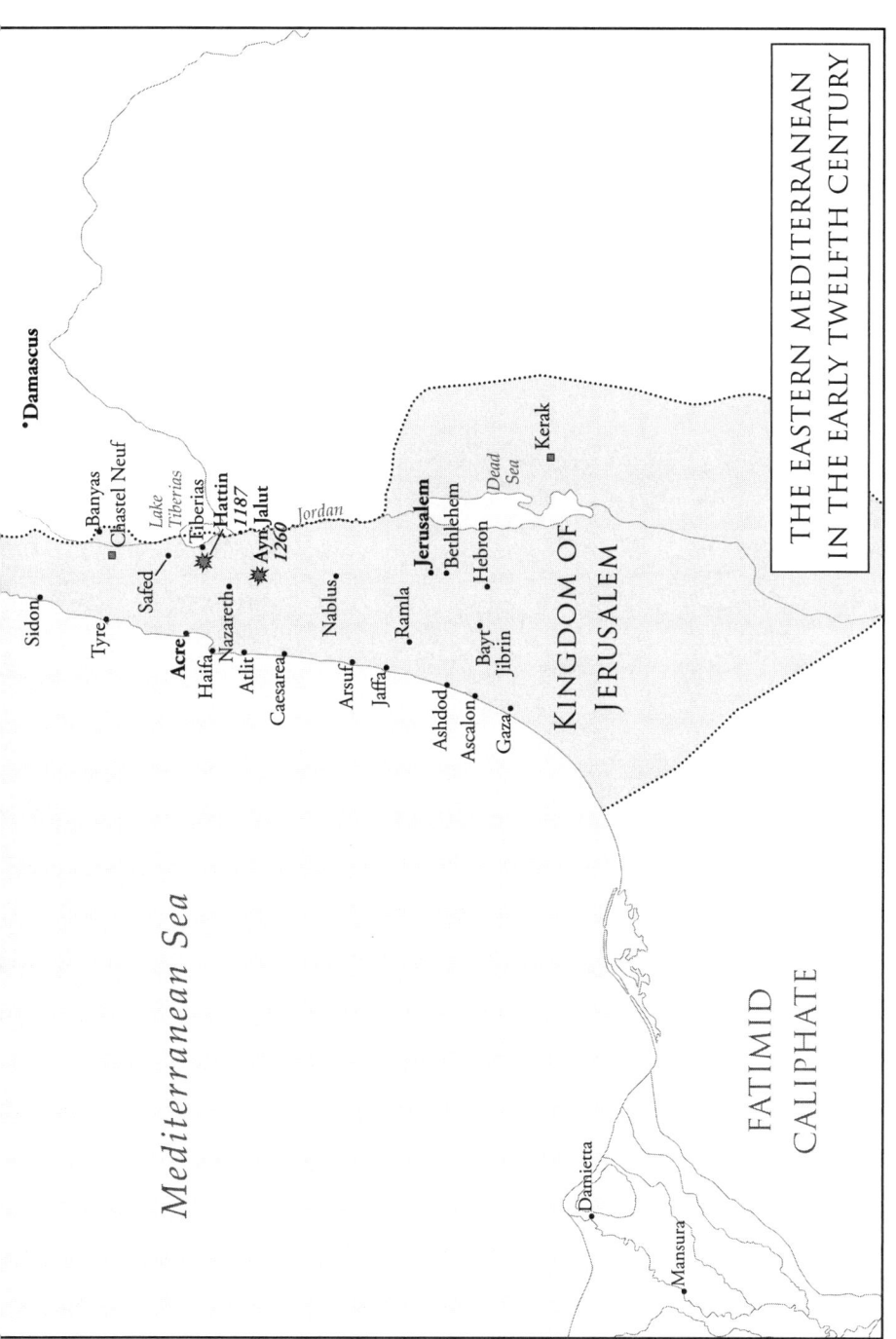

CHAPTER ONE
TRAVEL LITERATURE AND GEOGRAPHICAL GUIDES

1. Al-Harawi on Antioch, Tiberias and its surroundings, Acre, Jerusalem, Bethlehem, Hebron, and Ascalon

Abu al-Hasan 'Ali son of Abu Bakr al-Harawi (d. 1215) was born sometime in the mid-twelfth century in Mosul to a family that hailed from Herat in modern Afghanistan. He was a celebrated traveler who journeyed throughout the Islamic world and Byzantine lands. It is said that he was a bit of a graffiti artist, as he was known to write his name on the walls of places he visited. Al-Harawi is most remembered for his A Lonely Wayfarer's Guide to Pilgrimage, *a geographical guide to Islamic sacred sites and shrines, many of which were shared with Jews and Christians. The parts that deal with sites and shrines in Syria–Palestine are very useful for scholars of the Crusades as they furnish important information about social and religious life at the time, the conditions of many Islamic sacred places under Crusader control, as well as interrelations between Muslims and Franks in some localities. His reputation was so honored that the governor of Aleppo, Saladin's son, al-Zahir (r. 1183–1216), constructed a college for him there. He died in Aleppo in 1215.*[1]

The city of Antioch[2]

In it, there is the tomb of Habib al-Najjar[3] about whom God has revealed: ❦*A man came running from the other end of the city . . .*❧ (Qur'an

---

1. On al-Harawi and his *Kitab al-Isharat*, see al-Harawi, *A Lonely Wayfarer's Guide to Pilgrimage: 'Ali ibn Abi Bakr al-Harawi's Kitab al-Isharat ila Ma'rifat al-Ziyarat*, ed. and trans. Josef W. Meri (Princeton: Darwin Press, 2004), xix–xxxiv. Hereafter, al-Harawi, *Kitab al-Isharat*.
2. Al-Harawi, *Kitab al-Isharat*, 15.
3. According to Muslim legends, Habib al-Najjar, or Habib the Carpenter, was an early Christian martyr who lived in Antioch and knew some of Jesus's disciples. He is sometimes identified as St. Agabus, a prophet mentioned in Acts 11:27–28; 21:10–12. Christian tradition remembers him as one of the seventy disciples of Jesus mentioned in Luke 10:1–24.

36:20).⁴ Its mountain (Mount Silpius) was a sacred place to which people from far away came on pilgrimage. It is one of those cities where the foreigner finds comfort away from his hometown.

Tiberias and its surroundings⁵

East of Lake Tiberias is the tomb of Solomon son of David—peace be upon them—though in truth Solomon is buried next to his father David in Bethlehem in the cave where Jesus—peace be upon him—was born. Also, east of Lake Tiberias are the tombs of Luqman the Wise and his son.⁶ Luqman's tomb is also in Yemen at a mountain called La'at 'Adan, which will be mentioned later.

In Tiberias are the tombs of Abu 'Ubayda son of al-Jarrah⁷ and his wife. We visited them, as noted earlier. God knows best what is the truth. Some say that his tomb is in northern Jordan (*al-Urdunn*),⁸ others say it is in Beit Shean (*Baysan*). He died during the Plague of Emmaus.⁹ God knows best. At the foot of Mount Tiberias is the tomb of Abu Hurayra—may God be pleased with him.¹⁰ Some say that he was buried in al-Baqi',¹¹ others say in al-'Aqiq.¹² God knows best.

---

4. As was often customary for citing quranic passages, al-Harawi only mentioned the first part of this verse; his audience would have known the rest. The full verse reads: ❰*A man came running from the other end of the city, saying: 'O people, follow the messengers'*❱. Because Muslims consider the Qur'an to be the very speech of God, it was also customary to highlight quranic quotations in some fashion (e.g., a different colored ink, a different script, etc.) out of respect for the sanctity of the text. We have italicized and bracketed all quranic passages in an effort to convey a similar visual experience for the reader.

5. Al-Harawi, *Kitab al-Isharat*, 39.

6. Luqman the Wise is one of the pre-Islamic figures mentioned in the Qur'an. He counseled his son against polytheism and instructed him in proper religious observance (Qur'an 31:11–19). This passage is too long to reproduce here.

7. Abu 'Ubayda (d. 639) was the commanding general of the conquering Muslim army, and one of the most significant Companions of Muhammad. Ibn Wasil noted his role in the conquest of Damascus. See p. 138.

8. At the time, Jordan (*al-Urdunn* in Arabic) was the name of an administrative district located around Lake Tiberias and the Jordan River. It is different from the country today called Jordan.

9. An outbreak of bubonic plague, the Plague of Emmaus (*'Amwas*) occurred in Syria (638–639) during the early Islamic conquests.

10. Abu Hurayra (d. 681) was a Companion of Muhammad and his domestic servant. He was one of the most prolific transmitters of hadiths.

11. Al-Baqi' is the name of the cemetery located east of Medina in Arabia. Many Companions of Muhammad are buried there.

12. Al-'Aqiq is a valley located west of Medina in Arabia.

1. Al-Harawi on Antioch, Tiberias, etc.

In Tiberias is a spring named after Jesus son of Mary—peace be upon them—and the Church of the Tree. This is where the miracle involving Jesus son of Mary—peace be upon them—and the tanner that is mentioned in the Gospel took place. It was the first of his miracles.[13] Outside of Tiberias is the shrine of Sukayna daughter of al-Husayn[14]—peace be upon them—which we visited previously in Damascus;[15] and a shrine that some say contains the tomb of ʿAbd Allah son of al-ʿAbbas son of ʿAli son of Abu Talib[16]—may God be pleased with them all.

Hattin[17]

Also called Hutaym, Hattin is a village on the mountain where the tombs of Jethro and his wife are located.[18] It is also said that Jethro's tomb is in Mecca. God knows best. The renowned battle of Hattin took place near this village in the year 583 (1187). The kings of the Franks were taken captive and Jerusalem was conquered. So, too, the coastal and the frontier areas.

Kafar Manda[19]

The road from Tiberias to the city of Acre passes by a village called Kafar Manda, some say it is Midian. God knows best. We visited Midian east of Mount Sinai, which will be noted, God willing. In Kafar Manda is the tomb of Zipporah, the wife of Moses. In it is the well from which he removed

---

13. There is no such story in the New Testament. It could be an allusion to and a confusion with the quranic story about the miracle of the heavenly table, which in the Qurʾan (5:112–115; see p. 8, footnote 45) is attributed to Jesus, whereas in the New Testament, the story most similar to it is that of Peter's vision in Jaffa, months after Jesus's ascension (Acts 10:9–16). In the New Testament, Jesus's first miracle took place at a wedding in the village of Cana near Nazareth, where he turned water into wine (John 2:1–11).
14. Al-Husayn (d. 680) was a grandson of the Prophet Muhammad and the third Shiʿi imam. See p. 13 (footnote 72).
15. Al-Harawi, *Kitab al-isharat*, 31.
16. A grandson of ʿAli son of Abu Talib. See p. 4 (footnote 26).
17. Al-Harawi, *Kitab al-isharat*, 41.
18. Jethro the priest of Midian (*Shuʿayb* in Arabic; also known as Reuel, Exodus 2:18; and Hobab, Numbers 10:29) is the father of Moses's wife, Zippora (*Saffura* in Arabic; Exodus 2:16–21). The Druzes—a religious community spread today between Lebanon, Syria, Jordan, and Israel—claim Jethro as an ancestor, whom they revere as a spiritual founder and chief prophet.
19. Al-Harawi, *Kitab al-isharat*, 43.

the rock and watered Zipporah's and her sister's flocks.[20] The rock remains there to this day. It also has the tombs of two of Jacob's sons; some say they are Asher and Naphtali. God knows best. Near these locations is a mountain called al-Tur (Mount Gerizim) upon which some say that Moses—peace be upon him—saw the heavenly fire, and that it was there that almighty God spoke to him and sent him to Pharaoh.[21] God knows best.

Nazareth (al-Nasira)[22]

Nazareth is the city where the home of Mary daughter of 'Imran[23] was located. She was from there, and for this reason they (the Christians) are called Nazarenes.[24]

Acre[25]

The city of Acre should have been included in the section of the pilgrimage to the coastal areas, but we are mentioning it here because it is in the proximity of Tiberias. The Spring of the Cattle is located in it. They say that the cattle were created there for Adam to plow the land. Next to this spring is a shrine attributed to 'Ali son of Abu Talib[26]—may God be pleased with him. The Franks, however, made it into a church and appointed an official to oversee its construction and maintenance. On his first morning there, he reported: "I saw a man who said to me, 'I am 'Ali son of Abu Talib. Tell

---

20. ❦*Arriving at the waters of Midian, he found thereat a concourse of people drawing water and, to one side of them, two women tending flocks. He said: 'What is the matter with the two of you?' They said: 'We cannot give to drink until the shepherds have departed, and our father is an old man.' So he drew water for them and retired to the shade, saying: 'My Lord, I am in dire need of some act of goodness that You might send upon me'*❧ (Qur'an 28:23–24). See also Exodus 2:16–21 and Numbers 20:1–8.

21. Local Muslims adopted these views from the Samaritans, an ethnoreligious community with historical roots to the ancient Israelites. The Samaritans also believe that the binding of Isaac unfolded on Mount Gerizim, and consider it as the true place for the worship of God instead of the Temple in Jerusalem.

22. Al-Harawi, *Kitab al-isharat*, 43.

23. The Islamic tradition identifies Mary as the daughter of 'Imran. This confusion resulted from a misreading of the Qur'an, which uses the Arabic expression *bint 'Imran* to mean "a descendant of biblical Amram" and not the daughter of a man named 'Imran; see Suleiman A. Mourad, "Mary in the Qur'an: A Reexamination of Her Presentation," in *The Qur'an in Its Historical Context*, ed. Gabriel Said Reynolds (London: Routledge, 2008), 163–174.

24. Nazarenes (*al-Nasara*) is the word the Qur'an uses for Christians.

25. Al-Harawi, *Kitab al-isharat*, 43 and 45.

26. The fourth caliph of Islam, 'Ali son of Abu Talib (r. 556–661) was the nephew and son-in-law of the Prophet Muhammad and the first Shi'i imam.

them to restore this place as a mosque, otherwise whoever resides in it will perish.'" The Franks dismissed what he said and appointed someone else in his place. The next morning, they found his replacement dead. Then the Franks restored it as a mosque; it remains so until this day. God knows best. Some say that the tomb of Salih—peace be upon him—is in the prayer niche[27] of the mosque; however, in truth Salih's tomb is where we noted before.[28] God knows best. Some also say that Salih's tomb is in Mecca. Acre is called Acre (ʿAkka) because it is where the tomb of ʿAkk is located. Some allege that he is a prophet. Between the years 585 (1189) and 587 (1191), many people were martyred in the renowned battles and wars on the plain outside Acre. The battles and skirmishes continued day and night during this time.

The pilgrimage[29] to noble Jerusalem and its surroundings[30]

In Jerusalem is the Dome of the Rock, the place from which the Prophet Muhammad—may God bless him and grant him salvation—was made to ascend to heaven. His footprint is on the Rock from which he was made to ascend. I saw this Rock during the time of the Franks; it is on the northern side of the Dome. The part that contains the footprint is surrounded by an iron structure in the form of a house and it is currently located at the southern edge of the Rock. The iron structure is constructed atop a platform to protect it. The footprint measures a full handspan. The height of the structure is two cubits,[31] and its circumference is more than four cubits. Below the Dome of the Rock is the Cave of Spirits where it is said that God gathers the spirits of the believers. Fourteen steps lead down to this cave. They also say that the tomb of Zachariah—peace be upon him—is located in it. God knows best. On the ceiling of this Dome I read the following inscribed in gold:

---

27. The prayer niche (*mihrab*) in a mosque indicates the direction of prayer (*qibla*); that is, toward the Kaʿba structure in Mecca. Hence, in Acre, the prayer niche would be located in the southern wall.
28. In Shabwa in Yemen. Al-Harawi, *Kitab al-isharat*, 255. Salih is one of the ancient Arabian prophets mentioned in the Qurʾan.
29. *Ziyara* in Arabic. In the Islamic tradition, *ziyara* refers to a pious visitation or pilgrimage to a holy place, tomb, or shrine other than the Pilgrimage (*Hajj*) to Mecca.
30. Al-Harawi, *Kitab al-isharat*, 71, 73, 75, and 77.
31. A cubit in the medieval Arab world was a unit of length (in Arabic, *dhiraʿ*), which equaled approximately 51 centimeters or 20 inches.

Chapter 1: Travel Literature and Geographical Guides

> In the name of God, the Merciful, the Compassionate. ❧*God. There is no god but He, Living and Everlasting. Neither slumber overtakes him nor sleep. To Him belongs what is in the heavens and what is on the earth. . . .*❧ (Qur'an 2:255)[32]

The Dome of the Rock has four gates. I entered it during the time of the Franks in the year 569 (1173). Opposite the gate to the Cave of the Spirits, near the iron grill that surrounds the Rock, is an image of Solomon the son of David—peace be upon him. West of that gate is a leaded gate above which is a golden image of the Messiah adorned with jewels. Above the eastern gate, which is adjacent to the Dome of the Chain, is an arch on which is written the name of al-Qa'im bi-Amr Allah, the commander of the faithful,[33] the quranic chapter True Devotion (112:1–4), as well as other praises and exaltations of God.[34] The rest of the gates are the same; the Franks did not alter them. Next to the Dome of the Rock to the east is the Dome of the Chain where Solomon son of David—peace be upon them—used to mete out justice.[35] North of the Dome is the residence of the priests which contains pillars and other architectural wonders that I will mention when I discuss the monuments and artifacts, God willing.

In the Aqsa Mosque is the prayer niche of 'Umar son of al-Khattab[36]—may God be pleased with him. The Franks did not alter it. I read the following on the ceiling of the dome of the Aqsa Mosque.

> In the name of God, the Merciful, the Compassionate. ❧*Glory to Him who carried His servant by night from the Sacred Mosque to the Furthest Mosque, whose precincts We have blessed*❧ (Qur'an 17:1). May God give victory to his servant and vicegerent, Abu al-Hasan 'Ali, the Imam al-Zahir li-I'zaz Din Allah, the commander of the faithful.[37] Peace

---

32. Al-Harawi's audience would have known the remaining part of the verse, which reads: ❧*Who shall intercede with Him except by his leave? He knows their present affairs and their past. And they do not grasp of His knowledge except what He wills. Preserving them is no burden to Him. He is the Exalted, the Majestic.*❧

33. A reference to the 'Abbasid caliph al-Qa'im bi-Amr Allah (r. 1031–1075), who must have ordered this inscription to be placed there.

34. Here too, al-Harawi's audience would have known the chapter, which reads: ❧*He is God, One. God is the Eternal. He neither begets, nor is He begotten. And none is equal to Him.*❧

35. The Dome of the Chain was the first structure built by the Muslims atop the Temple Mount esplanade. It sits exactly in its center. Islamic traditions associate it with King Solomon as the place where he used to hold court, and also as the place where the Judgment will unfold.

36. The second caliph in Islam (r. 634–644), under whom Jerusalem was conquered in 638.

37. The seventh Fatimid caliph (r. 1021–1036).

1. Al-Harawi on Antioch, Tiberias, etc.

be upon him, his pure ancestors, and his most honorable descendants. Our lord, the august vizier, and intimate friend of the commander of the faithful, Abu al-Qasim 'Ali son of Ahmad, ordered the restoration and gilding of this dome—may God aid him and grant him victory. All of this was completed at the end of Dhu al-Qa'da in the year 426 (5 October 1035). It is the handiwork of the artisan 'Abd Allah son of al-Hasan al-Misri.

All of the inscriptions and reliefs are made of gold. The Franks did not alter any of the verses of the Noble Qur'an or the names of the Caliphs that are above the gates.

I read the following inscription on a large stone in a wall to the north of the Aqsa: "The length of the Aqsa Mosque Sanctuary is 700 cubits—the royal cubit[38]—and its width is 455."[39]

The portico of the Dome of the Rock is supported by sixteen marble columns and eight piers. The interior dome is supported by four piers and twelve columns. Surrounding the Dome are sixteen windows. The circumference of the Dome is 160 cubits. The circumference of the entire structure is 384 cubits. The circumference of everything, including the Dome of the Chain and other adjacent structures is 482 cubits. The height of the iron grill that surrounds the Rock is the measure of two standing persons. The Dome of the Rock has four iron gates: one leads to the Gate of Mercy; another to the Gate of Gabriel; a third to the South; and a fourth to the Dome of the Chain, whose circumference is 60 paces. The height of the Cave of the Spirits is the measure of a standing individual and an arm length. Its width is eleven paces from east to west, thirteen paces from north to south, and its staircase has fourteen steps. On the east side of the ceiling is an opening, the width of which is one and a half cubits. The circumference of the Cave is 50 cubits.

The Dome's portico is 15 paces wide, and its length from south to the north is 94 paces. The height of the Dome of the Rock is 60 cubits; its circumference is 96. The circumference of its square base is 160 cubits. The length of the Aqsa Mosque, from south to the north, is 148 cubits.

---

38. The royal cubit was approximately 60 centimeters or 23.5 inches, longer than the normal or commoners' cubit (see p. 5, footnote 31).

39. These measurements are clearly for the entire sanctuary, and not for the Aqsa Mosque. It is important to note that Muslim scholars consistently used the expression "Aqsa Mosque" interchangeably to mean the actual structure where the prayers are held and the entire esplanade. The measurements of the Aqsa Mosque are approximately 83 × 56 meters.

According to what the locals say, Solomon son of David's stable is beneath the Aqsa Mosque. It contains huge stones; the feed troughs are still there until today. It also includes a cave which is said to contain the cradle of Jesus son of Mary—peace be upon them. To the north of the Aqsa Mosque Sanctuary is the pool of the Children of Israel that Nebuchadnezzar is said to have filled with their heads.[40]

In Jerusalem is a Jacobite church that contains a well where it is said that the Messiah washed himself and where the Samaritan woman converted at his hand.[41] They visit it and believe in its cures. Also in Jerusalem is the Tower of David—peace be upon him—and his prayer niche, which is mentioned in the Noble Qur'an.[42]

Outside of Jerusalem, there are pilgrimage sites, which include the Pool of Siloam.[43] Its water is like that of the Zamzam[44] well in Mecca; it comes from underneath the Dome of the Rock and flows in the valley to the south of the city. Also, the Church of the Ascension, from where it is said that the Messiah—peace be upon him—was raised up to heaven. There is as well the Church of Zion, where it is said that the table descended to Jesus son of Mary and his disciples.[45]

The Kidron Valley contains the tomb of Mary mother of Jesus—peace be upon them—to which one must descend thirty-six steps.[46] Beneath its dome are sturdy marble columns—sixteen of them, eight red and eight green. It has four gates, each of which has six sturdy marble columns. It contains a

---

40. Possibly the Pool of Bethesda where, according to John 5:1–15, Jesus healed an invalid man.

41. According to John 4:1–42, the story of the Samaritan woman took place in the Samaritan village of Sychar (i.e., Shechem, Nablus) near Jacob's well.

42. ❮*Have you heard of the litigants who jumped over the wall to his prayer niche?*❯ (Qur'an 38:21).

43. According to John 9:1–12, the Pool of Siloam is the site where Jesus healed a man who had been blind since birth. The Empress Eudocia (ca. 400–460) endowed the construction of a church at the site to commemorate this miracle.

44. According to the Islamic tradition, the Zamzam well in Mecca is the location where the angel Gabriel provided water to Hagar and her son, Ishmael (Isma'il). Its waters are said to have miraculous healing powers as well.

45. ❮*Jesus son of Mary said: "O God our Lord, send down upon us a table from heaven, and it shall be a feast-day for the first and the last among us, and a miracle from You, and grant us Your bounty—You are the best of providers." God said: "I shall send it down upon you. Whoso among you disbelieves hereafter, I shall torment him with a torment the like of which I shall torment no other human being."*❯ (Qur'an 5:112–115)

46. Al-Harawi used Wadi Jahannam here, which is a common mistake among some Muslim scholars. The name is derived from the biblical Valley of Gehenna or Gehennom. It is located south of Mount Zion. Mary's tomb is at the northern part of the Kidron Valley, between the city and the Mount of Olives.

1. Al-Harawi on Antioch, Tiberias, etc.

cloister that is now the shrine of Abraham the Friend[47]—peace be upon him. It also contains many artifacts, columns, and wondrous architecture.

On the Mount of Olives is the dwelling and tomb of Rabiʿa al-ʿAdawiyya. However, Rabiʿa al-ʿAdawiyya's tomb is actually in Basra, which we will mention in the Iraqi part of the journey.[48] This Rabiʿa who was buried on the Mount of Olives was the wife of Ahmad son of Abu al-Hawari.[49] The Mount of Olives also contains many blessed places and tombs of righteous people and Successors[50]—may God be pleased with them—but people (Muslims) cannot visit them because the Franks have taken possession of the country.

Beyond the eastern wall is the tomb of Shaddad son of Aws al-Khazraji[51] and Dhu al-Asabiʿ al-Tamimi.[52] It is said that Shaddad's tomb is elsewhere in Palestine. But God knows best.

As for the Christian community's pilgrimage sites, the noblest one is the Church of Refuse.[53] It is one of the aforementioned wonders. We will surely provide a description of its structure and all that it contains when we mention the ancient sites. They also have in it a tomb which they call "The Resurrection" because they believe that the Messiah's resurrection occurred there. The truth is that the site used to be called "Refuse" because it was the garbage dump of the city and it was located outside the town, where also the hands of the wicked were cut off and the thieves were crucified. This is mentioned in the Gospel. But God knows best. They allege that it also contains the rock[54] that when it split, Adam rose up from underneath it because it

---

47. In the Islamic tradition, Abraham is known as the Friend of God (*Khalil Allah*) or simply as the Friend (*al-Khalil*).
48. There is also a tomb dedicated to her in Damascus. Born in Basra, and renowned for her extreme virtue and piety, Rabiʿa al-ʿAdawiyya (ca. 718–801) is one of the most famous early ascetics and mystics in Islamic history. See Rkia Elaroui Cornell, *Rabiʿa from Narrative to Myth: The Many Faces of Islam's Most Famous Woman Saint, Rabiʿa al-ʿAdawiyya* (Oxford: Oneworld, 2019).
49. An early ascetic and mystic from Syria (d. 845 or 860).
50. The Successors (*tabiʿun*) belonged to the second generation of early Muslims, who did not receive their teachings about Islam from Muhammad directly, but from one of his Companions. On Companions (*sahaba*), see p. 29 (footnote 107).
51. A notable Companion of Muhammad. He died in 678.
52. He too was a Companion of Muhammad and died in Jerusalem.
53. Church of Refuse or *Kanisat al-Qumama* in Arabic is a pejorative pun on Church of the Resurrection (*Kanisat al-Qiyama*), which is the name by which Eastern Orthodox Christians refer to the Church of the Holy Sepulchre (the name used by Roman Catholics and Western Christians).
54. That is the rock of Golgotha or Calvary. The New Testament makes explicit comparisons between Jesus and Adam (Romans 5:12–21; 1 Corinthians 15:21–22), even referring to

was beneath the crucifix. They also have in Jerusalem the garden of Joseph the Righteous[55]—peace be upon him—that they visit. As for the descent of light, I resided in Jerusalem long enough during the Frankish period that I was able to determine how it was done.[56]

The route from Jerusalem to the city of Abraham the Friend[57]

The tomb of Rachel, the mother of Joseph the Righteous—peace be upon them—is on the right side of the road.

Bethlehem[58]

Bethlehem is the village, which is the birthplace of Jesus—peace be upon him. It is said that the tombs of David and Solomon—peace be upon them—are there as well. The Church of the Nativity contains artifacts and wondrous marble architecture made of gold inlay and columns. It was constructed more than 1,200 years ago; the date is inscribed in wood and has not changed until our time. Bethlehem is the location of the date palm mentioned in the Noble Qur'an, ❦*So shake towards you the trunk of the palm . . .*❧ (Qur'an 19:25).[59] It contains the prayer niche of 'Umar son of al-Khattab—may God be pleased with him. The Franks have not altered it to this day.

Jesus as the last Adam (I Corinthians 15:45–49). According to Christian tradition, Jesus was crucified over the place where Adam's skull was buried. Presently, in the Church of the Holy Sepulchre are two chapels atop Golgotha. To the right is the Catholic chapel of the Nailing to the Cross (the 11th Station of the Cross). To the left is the Orthodox chapel directly over the rock (the 12th Station). Underneath Golgotha is a small cave in which is the Chapel of Adam.

55. This is likely a reference to the chapel and tomb of St. Joseph of Arimathea, which are part of the Church of the Holy Sepulchre complex. According to the New Testament, Joseph of Arimathea took responsibility for the burial of Jesus (Matthew 27:57–61; Mark 15:42–47; Luke 23:50–56; John 19:38–42). Al-Harawi's sources apparently confused St. Joseph of Arimathea with Joseph the Righteous, the son of the biblical patriarch Jacob (Genesis 37–50; Qur'an 12:1–111).

56. This refers to the "Miracle of Holy Fire" that, according to Orthodox tradition, occurs each year on the day preceding Orthodox Pascha or Easter.

57. Al-Harawi, *Kitab al-isharat*, 77. As noted above (footnote 47), in the Islamic tradition, Abraham is known as the Friend of God (*Khalil Allah*) or simply as the Friend (*al-Khalil*). Hence, the town so closely associated with Abraham is known in Arabic as al-Khalil (Hebron in English). Abraham is also referred to as the friend of God in the Hebrew Bible (2 Chronicles 20:7; Isaiah 41:8) and the New Testament (James 2:23). The word Hebron is inter alia said to derive from the Hebrew word for friend (*haver*).

58. Al-Harawi, *Kitab al-isharat*, 77.

59. This verse ❦*So shake towards you the trunk of the palm and it will drop down on you dates soft and ripe*❧ is part of the Palm Tree story in Qur'an 19. See Suleiman A. Mourad, "From Hellenism to

1. Al-Harawi on Antioch, Tiberias, etc.

The city of Abraham the Friend—peace be upon him[60]

It contains a cave in which are the tombs of Abraham, Isaac, Jacob, and Sarah—peace be upon them. The tombs of Adam, Noah, and Shem are said to be in this cave as well. The cave is below the actual cave that is visited today.

In 570 (1175) in Alexandria, I studied a small book with the cleric and Hadith memorizer[61] Abu Tahir Ahmad son of Muhammad al-Silafi[62] that he attributed to a certain man, whose name escapes me—for in 588 (1192), the Franks had confiscated my books during the raid at Khuwaylifa by the English king (Richard the Lionheart).[63] He sent a messenger to me, promising to return what he took from me with compensation several times its value and requested a meeting with me, but I did not go to him.

As for the small book I mentioned, it recounts that that man came on pilgrimage to Hebron and befriended the Byzantine custodian of the cave. He bribed him with a gift and asked if he could go down into the cave. The custodian promised him so during the snow season when the pilgrims stop coming. When they stopped coming, he brought him to a stone and lifted it up. He brought a lamp, and they both descended a staircase of about 70 steps and reached a large breezy cave. There, on a slab, was laid Abraham the Friend—peace be upon him—covered in a green robe and the breeze

---

Christianity and Islam: The Origin of the Palm Tree Story concerning Mary and Jesus in the Gospel of Pseudo-Matthew and the Qur'an," *Oriens Christianus* 86 (2002): 206–216.

60. Al-Harawi, *Kitab al-isharat*, 79 and 81.

61. Hadith memorizer (*hafiz*); that is, a person who has memorized a great deal of hadiths and can recite them without the aid of books or memory prompts. It should be noted that Hadith scholarship was the principal field of Islamic scholarship open to women, some of whom achieved high standing and great renown—*hafiza* is the feminine form of *hafiz*. In modern times the honorific title *hafiz* has come to be applied to someone who has memorized the entire Qur'an whereas in the Crusader period memorization of the entire Qur'an was the foundation of all Islamic education. Hence, any Islamic scholar in any discipline would have memorized the entire Qur'an as part of his/her elementary education. On women Hadith scholars, see Asma Sayeed, *Women and the Transmission of Religious Knowledge in Islam* (Cambridge: Cambridge University Press, 2013).

62. Al-Silafi was a celebrated scholar of Hadith and a great transmitter of historical accounts and books. He was born in the Muslim East, and traveled westward until he reached Alexandria, where he spent the rest of his life and died there in 1180.

63. Khuwaylifa was a water stop in southern Palestine between Ramla and Ascalon, where Richard the Lionheart and his troops ambushed a Muslim reinforcement army that Saladin had requested from Egypt and looted everything they were carrying. On this ambush, which took place on 11 Jumada II 588 (24 June 1192), see Ibn Shaddad, *al-Nawadir al-sultaniyya*, 317–319; Ibn Shaddad, *The Rare and Excellent History of Saladin*, trans. D. S. Richards (Aldershot: Ashgate, 2002), 207–208.

was rustling his white hair. Next to him were Isaac and Jacob—peace be upon them. Then he brought him to a wall inside the cave and said to him: "Sarah is behind this wall." The man was curious to see what was behind the wall, but he suddenly heard a voice say: "Beware! She is a woman!" They returned whence they came.

I read in the Torah that in this village of Hebron is the cave that Abraham—peace be upon him—had purchased from 'Afrun son of Suhar al-Hitti for 400 silver coins, and he buried Sarah there. This is what the Torah says in the fifth section of the first book.[64] But God knows best. Also, in Hebron, there is the tomb of Joseph the Righteous; it is outside the cave. The truth, however, is what we mentioned earlier (i.e., that Joseph's tomb is in the village of Balata near Nablus).[65]

The author of this book, 'Ali son of Abu Bakr al-Harawi—may God pardon him and all the Muslims—says: In 569 (1173), I entered Jerusalem. I met there and in the city of Abraham the Friend—peace be upon him—with clerics who told me that in the time of King Baldwin[66] part of this cave had fallen in and a group of Franks entered it with the king's permission and found there Abraham, Isaac, and Jacob—peace be upon them—in their tattered burial shrouds. They were leaning against the wall with scarves over their heads and their faces were bare. The king renewed their shrouds and sealed the place in 513 (1119).

The knight Byron, who was living then in Bethlehem and was known among the Franks for his courage and old age, told me that he had entered this cave with his father and saw Abraham the Friend, Isaac, and Jacob and their faces were bare. I asked: "How old were you?" He replied: "Thirteen years." He then said to me: "The knight Godfrey son of George is one of those who the king had charged with renewing their shrouds and repairing the part of the cave that had fallen in. He is still alive." I inquired about him and was told that he had died only a few days ago. The author of this book (al-Harawi) says: "If that is true, then I have seen someone who had seen Abraham, Isaac, and Jacob—peace be upon them—while awake and not in his sleep.

---

64. Genesis 23:1–20, where Abraham purchased the Cave of Machpelah facing Mamre (Hebron) as a burial place for his wife, Sarah, from Ephron son of Zohar the Hittite for 400 shekels of silver.

65. Al-Harawi, *Kitab al-isharat*, 67, which corresponds closely to the account in Joshua 24:32, "The bones of Joseph, which the Children of Israel brought up out of Egypt, were buried in Shechem [Nablus] in a parcel of land that Jacob bought from the sons of Hamor, father of Shechem, for a hundred pieces of silver."

66. King Baldwin II (r. 1118–1131), Bardawil in Arabic.

1. Al-Harawi on Antioch, Tiberias etc.

The route from Jerusalem to Ascalon[67]

They say that Bayt Jibrin (Gibelin) is the town that almighty God mentioned in Surat al-Ma'ida (The Table) in the story of Moses.

> ❧*O people, enter the holy land which God has marked out for you, and do not go back to your old ways, only to end up as losers. They said: O Moses, in this land there are men of great might. We will not enter it until they leave it. When they leave, we will enter it.*❧ (Qur'an 5:21–22)

They say that the City of Giants,[68] about which these verses were revealed, is the city of Jericho. Others say that it is the city of 'Amman, which is more correct. Bayt Jibrin contains antiquities. On the road from it to Ascalon is the Valley of Ants[69] where they say that the ant spoke to Solomon son of David—peace be upon them.[70]

The frontier town of Ascalon is a noble site that few can rival with respect to its beauty and fortifications. Hadiths from the Messenger of God—may God bless him and grant him salvation—were transmitted about it and about garrisoning there for war. The well of Abraham the Friend—peace be upon him—is there. They say that he dug it with his own hands. God knows best. The shrine of the head of al-Husayn—may God be pleased with him—was once there. After the Franks took the city, the Muslims moved the head of al-Husayn to Old Cairo[71] in the year 549 (1154).[72]

---

67. Al-Harawi, *Kitab al-isharat*, 81 and 83.
68. *Madinat al-Jabbarin* in Arabic. Qur'an 5:21–22 is likely a reference to the biblical story of the Twelve Spies dispatched by Moses to scout out the land of Canaan where near Hebron they saw the giant sons of Anak "and to ourselves we seemed like grasshoppers, and so we seemed to them" (Numbers 13:1–13; Deuteronomy 1:22–40).
69. *Wadi al-Naml* in Arabic.
70. ❧*To Solomon We mustered his troops of jinn, humans, and birds, all held in strict order. Until, when they arrived at the Valley of Ants, an ant said: "O ants, enter your dwellings lest Solomon and his troops should crush you unawares." He smiled in amusement at its words and said: "My Lord, inspire me to offer thanks for the bounty You bestowed upon me and upon my parents, and to do a good deed of which you will approve, and admit me, through Your mercy, into the company of your virtuous servants"*❧ (Qur'an 27:17–19).
71. Technically speaking, Cairo (*al-Qahira* in Arabic) was built by the Fatimids in 969, adjacent to two major settlements: Heliopolis and Fustat. In order to distinguish between Fatimid Cairo and the entire cosmopolitan area comprised of the three cities, Muslim chronicles referred to them collectively as *Misr*, which is also what they used for Egypt. Hence, we refer to Fatimid Cairo as Old Cairo, and to the three cities as Cairo.
72. The head of al-Husayn, the grandson of the Prophet Muhammad who was killed at the Battle of Karbala in 680, was first taken to Damascus where it was buried in the Umayyad Mosque. Then the Fatimids in the tenth century moved it to Ascalon, and from there it was moved in 1154 to Old Cairo, where it was interred in the shrine-mosque named after him—*Masjid al-Husayn*—which exists there to this day and remains one of Egypt's holiest places.

Chapter 1: Travel Literature and Geographical Guides

The author of this book 'Ali son of Abu Bakr al-Harawi says: I entered the frontier town of Ascalon in 570 (1174) and resided at the shrine of Abraham—peace be upon him. I saw there on that very spot the Messenger of God in a vision and he was among a group of people. I greeted him, kissed his hand, and said: "O Messenger of God! How wonderful it would be if this frontier town was in Muslim hands." He replied: "It will be in Muslim hands and will also be a lesson for mankind." When I awoke, I inscribed what I saw on the southern wall of the shrine and dated it. Indeed, Jerusalem and Ascalon were conquered in 583 (1187). Many merchants and soldiers saw this inscription, dated 570 (1174). God knows best.[73] Many righteous people and Successors whose tombs are unknown are buried in Ascalon's cemetery. So, too, in Gaza, Acre, Tyre, Sidon, and all the towns along the coast.

Questions

1. In his *A Lonely Wayfarer's Guide to Pilgrimage*, on what kinds of information does al-Harawi focus in his descriptions of places he visited?
2. Why might this information be of interest to Muslim pilgrims?
3. How does al-Harawi depict places that were sacred to Jews, Christians, and Muslims—e.g., Jerusalem, Hebron, etc.?
4. What can we learn about the importance of visions and dreams from the accounts al-Harawi records?
5. How does al-Harawi depict the Franks and his interactions with them?
6. What did the Franks do to Muslim sacred places, especially the Dome of the Rock and the Aqsa Mosque, after they controlled them?

---

73. Here al-Harawi is invoking this expression to say that he was not certain if what he heard about merchants and soldiers seeing his handwriting was correct.

2. Ibn Jubayr on the Christians of Mount Lebanon and trade between Muslims and Franks[74]

Ibn Jubayr was born in 1145, in Valencia, Spain. He belonged to an Arab family of the tribe of Kinana. His family name comes from his ancestor 'Abd al-Salam son of Jubayr al-Kinani, who came to Spain during the Umayyad period in 740 with the army sent by the Umayyad Caliph Hisham son of 'Abd al-Malik (r. 724–743) to put down a Berber uprising. Ibn Jubayr was a judge and an administrator in Granada under the Almohads. His pilgrimage journey, which he recounts in his Travel Narrative, *lasted from 1183 to 1185. The book describes in detail his experiences and keen observations of daily life while on his journey from Granada to Mecca and back to Spain, much of it spent traveling on Genoese ships. The sections on Crusader territories in Palestine and Norman Sicily are rich with details about Crusader–Muslim encounters. He apparently did not rejoin government service when he returned to Spain. He also undertook two more journeys to the east, but he did not report on them. His second trip lasted from 1189 to 1191; he embarked on his third trip in 1217. He settled in the cosmopolitan city of Alexandria in Egypt, where there was a substantial community of Muslims from Spain and North Africa. While in Alexandria, he served as a teacher of Sufism (Islamic mysticism) and Hadith. He died in Alexandria in November 1217.*[75]

The Christians of Mount Lebanon

One of the marvelous things one hears was that the Christians who live around Mount Lebanon when they see there some Muslim hermits, they bring to them food and treat them well. They say: "These live as hermits for the sake of the great and glorious God. It is, therefore, an obligation to share things with them."

This mountain is one of the most fertile mountains of the world. It has many varieties of fruits, gushing water, and expansive shade. It is rarely empty of someone practicing a life of solitude and asceticism. If the

---

74. Ibn Jubayr, *Rihlat Ibn Jubayr* (Beirut: Dar Sadir, 1988), 259–261.
75. On Ibn Jubayr, see Yann Dejugnat, "Ibn Jubayr," *Encyclopaedia of Islam, Third Edition*; and "La Méditerranée comme frontière dans le récit de voyage (rihla) d'Ibn Jubayr: modalités et enjeux d'une perception," *Mélanges de la Casa de Velázquez* 38.2 (2008): 149–170. See also R. J. C. Broadhurst, trans., *The Travels of Ibn Jubayr*, with a new introduction by Robert Irwin (London: I. B. Tauris, 2020 [1952]).

Christians treat the opponents of their faith in this way, should not this be the way Muslims treat each other?

War and harmony between the Christians and Muslims

One of the marvelous things talked about was that the blazes of conflict flare up between the two factions—Muslims and Christians—and often the two camps meet and battle lines are drawn between them. Yet, Muslim and Christian companions go in between without any hindrance. At this time, that is the month of Jumada I 580 (August 1184), we witnessed an example of that when Saladin[76] marched with all the Muslim troops to attack the castle of Kerak, one of the most invincible of Christian castles.[77] It obstructs the road to Hijaz, hindering the Muslims' way overland. Between it and Jerusalem is a day's travel or a little more. It is located in the finest part of the land of Palestine. It has an imposing view over a vast region of numerous settlements; it is said they exceed 400 small towns. So, this sultan readied the attack against it, tightened the blockade around it, and laid siege to it for a long time.

Yet, the traffic of caravans between Egypt and Damascus via the Frankish dominions does not cease. Likewise, the traffic of Muslims between Damascus and Acre. And the Christian merchants, none of them is hindered or interfered with. The Christians levy in their countries a tax from the Muslims in return for specific protection. Christian merchants also pay a tax in Muslim lands on their merchandise. There is harmony between them and tolerance in all circumstances. The people of war are preoccupied in their war, the general public is in a state of well-being, and the world goes to the winner.

This is the conduct of the people of this land during war. Likewise, the unfolding conflict between the commanders[78] and monarchs of the Muslims. Neither citizens nor merchants are interfered with. Protection does not abandon them in any circumstances, whether during peacetime or war. The affairs of this land are too marvelous to be recounted here. May God, with His grace, exalt the word of Islam.

---

76. Saladin's full name was al-Nasir Salah al-Din Yusuf son of Ayyub, that is, Yusuf (Joseph) son of Ayyub (Job). Al-Nasir (Champion) and Salah al-Din (Righteousness of the Religion; Saladin) were his honorific titles. Because the authors of the texts in this anthology at times do not include his honorific, Saladin, for clarity we have added Saladin to his name each time his name appears without it.

77. See Yaqut's description of Kerak, p. 39.

78. *Amir* (pl. *umara'*) was a title used to designate a high-ranking military officer. We have translated *amir* as "commander" throughout.

3. Ibn Jubayr on the cities of Banyas,[79] Acre, Tyre, and the Muslims under Frankish rule[80]

The city of Banyas (Belinas)—may almighty God protect it

This city is the frontier of the Muslims' lands. It is small and has a fortress, surrounded by a river that meanders beneath the walls and leads to one of the city's gates, and then into a waterfall that operates a mill. It used to be in the hands of the Franks until it was recaptured by Nur al-Din—may God be merciful to him. Around it is a great deal of arable land extending over a wide plain. A Frankish castle called Hunin (Chastel Neuf) overlooks it; between it and Banyas is approximately three parasangs.[81] The farming of the plain is shared between the Franks and the Muslims. They have a stipulation between them known as the partnership stipulation: they share the crops equally. Their livestock are mixed and no harm occurs between them on account of that.

We departed from it on the eve of the aforementioned Saturday to a village known as al-Masiyya near the aforementioned Frankish castle, and we spent the night in it. We departed from it at dawn on Sunday, and crossed on our way between Hunin and Tibnin (Toron) alongside a valley, wooded mostly with sweet bay trees. It was so steep as if a bottomless abyss. Its edges come together and rise up toward the sky. It is known as al-Istil. If troops were to venture into it, they would disappear; there is no escape and no exit for anyone who dares to cross it. The descent to it and ascent from it are two insurmountable obstacles. We marveled at that place. We thus avoided it, and crossed alongside it, emerging next to a large Frankish castle known as Tibnin. It is the location where customs are levied on caravans. Its lady is a sow known as the Queen (Agnes of Courtenay). She is the mother of the pig king (Baldwin IV), lord of Acre—may God destroy it. We spent the night beneath that castle. The people paid a light customs fee; the tax being one Tyrian dinar and one qirat on each head.[82] Merchants, however, were not

---

79. Banyas (Belinas) is located to the north of Lake Tiberias, at the base of Mount Hermon. It is to be distinguished from the port city of Baniyas (Balanea), which is located on the northern Syrian coast.

80. Ibn Jubayr, *Rihlat*, 273–283.

81. A parasang was a unit of distance similar to the English league. There is no exact measuring for it, since it is based on the distance a person could cover on foot over a specific period of time. Medieval calculations range between 3 and 5 miles or 5–7 kilometers.

82. Dinar refers to the common gold coin at the time. A qirat is a silver coin generally worth one-twenty-fourth of a dinar. Qirat is also the word used for the unit of measure itself. The

interfered with because they were bound for the place of the cursed king, where they pay the tithe; the tax there was one qirat per dinar, and the dinar is comprised of 24 qirats.

Those on whom this customs fee was imposed were mostly North Africans. Muslims from other parts of the Muslim world were not interfered with. That was because the North Africans had done something that had angered the Franks; that is, an audacious group of them had joined Nur al-Din—may God be merciful to him—in a raid against one of the castles. They looted its riches, and it became well known. The Franks punished them with this customs tax imposed on them individually. Every North African has to pay the aforementioned dinar while crossing their country. The Franks said: "These North Africans used to traverse our land and we were peaceful toward them. We did not impose on them anything. But when they interfered in the war against us and allied themselves with their Muslim brothers, we were obliged to inflict on them this tax." The North Africans are thus praised for paying this customs fee on account of their provocation of the enemy, which makes it more tolerable and less distressful to them.

We departed from Tibnin—may God destroy it—at dawn on Monday, passing through numerous villages and organized communities. Their inhabitants were all Muslims living alongside the Franks in a state of comfort—may God protect us from temptation. That is because the Muslims hand over to them half of their crops at the time of harvest. They also pay a *jizya* tax on each head: 1 dinar and 5 qirats.[83] The Franks do not interfere with them otherwise. The Muslims also pay a light tax on the produce of trees. They own their houses, and all their affairs are left to them to administer. All the cities along the coast of Syria that are in the hands of the Franks are administered in this way: the rural areas, including villages and small towns, all belong to Muslims. Temptation has satiated the hearts of many of them, for they see that their Muslim brothers in the rural areas and provinces under Muslim control live in a contrary situation to theirs in terms of comfort and good care. This is one of the calamities that befell the Muslims,

---

English word carat is likely derived from qirat. Weights and measures often varied from region to region.

83. The *jizya* tax, according to Islamic law and historical practice, is imposed by Muslim rulers on members of revealed religions (e.g., Jews, Christians, Zoroastrians) and other religious communities in exchange for certain protections and limited freedoms and the acceptance of a range of disabilities imposed on them as inferior persons in the Islamic social order. It is interesting that Ibn Jubayr used the same term to indicate the tax the Franks imposed on the Muslims as *jizya*. See also p. 23 (footnote 91).

3. Ibn Jubayr on the cities of Banyas, Acre, etc.

namely that Muslims would complain about the injustice of their own kind who rule over them, and those under Frankish rule praise the conduct of their adversary and enemy, and feel comfortable under their justice. We complain to God about this situation. Our comfort and solace are what is revealed in the venerable Book: ❦*This is nothing but a trial from You; through it You lead astray whomsoever You will, and guide aright whomsoever You will*❦ (Qur'an 7:155).

On that aforementioned Monday, we lodged in one of the villages near Acre, around a parasang away. The village head was a Muslim, appointed by the Franks over the Muslims who reside there. He entertained all the members of the caravan with a generous feast. He gathered them, great and small, in one large room in his house, served them a variety of food, and overwhelmed them with his kindness. We were among those who attended this invitation.

We slept that night and then in the morning of Tuesday, the 10th of the aforementioned month (Jumada II 580), which corresponds to 18 September (1184),[84] we entered Acre—may God destroy it. We were taken to the Customs House, which is a caravanserai prepared to accommodate caravans. Outside its door were benches covered with cushions, on them sitting Christian scribes with inkwells made of ebony and ornamented with gold. They write in Arabic and they speak it too. Their boss was the Head of Customs who holds the lease to run it. He is known as lord,[85] which is an honorific title given to him on account of his position. They also apply it to every prominent appointee who is not a soldier. All levied dues go to the lease holder; the lease for this house is obtained by paying up front a huge sum of money. The merchants dropped their loads in the Customs House and lodged in the upper floor. The load of each one who did not have any merchandise was searched to make sure it did not include any hidden merchandise, and he was allowed to lodge anywhere he desired. All of this was done with good care and friendliness without any harshness or discrimination. We lodged in it in a house we rented from a Christian woman beside the sea. We asked almighty God for fast deliverance and to grant us safety.

---

84. Ibn Jubayr often used both lunar (Islamic) and solar (Christian) calendars for dating.
85. *Al-Sahib* in Arabic.

Chapter 1: Travel Literature and Geographical Guides

The city of Acre—may God destroy it and restore it [to the Muslims]

Acre is the base of the Frankish cities in Syria. It is the anchor of vessels sailing the sea like mountaintops.[86] It is the harbor for every ship, and comparable in greatness to Constantinople. It is the gathering place for ships and traveling companions, and where Muslim and Christian merchants from faraway places meet. Its streets and alleys are so crowded with traffic that one barely finds a place to walk. It beams with infidelity and injustice, and overflows with pigs and crosses. It is stinky and dirty; it is full of filth and excrement. The Franks took it over from the Muslims in the first decade of the sixth century (twelfth century); the world of Islam wept dearly over its loss and it became one of the distresses. Its mosques were transformed into churches, and its minarets into bell towers. Of its congregational mosque, God kept undefiled a part that remained in the hands of Muslims as a small place for prayer, where foreigners gather to fulfill the duty of prayer. In its prayer niche is located the tomb of the prophet Salih[87]—may God bless him and all prophets and grant them peace. May God guard this spot from the filth of infidels on account of the blessing of this sacred tomb.

In the east side of the city is the Spring of the Cattle from which God brought forth cattle for Adam[88]—may God bless him and grant him peace. The descent to this spring follows steep stairs. Over it is a mosque whose prayer niche is preserved. The Franks had installed a prayer niche for them on its eastern side. The Muslim and the infidel gather in it; each turns toward his prayer direction. It is under the control of the Christians; they venerate it and protect it. God saved a prayer spot in it for the Muslims.

We stayed in Acre two days, and then departed to Tyre overland on Thursday, the 12th of the aforementioned Jumada, which corresponds to the 20th of the aforementioned September. We passed on our way by a great castle known as al-Zab (Casal). It overlooks numerous small towns and communities, including a small walled town called Iskandaruna (Iscandelion). We were seeking in Tyre a boat that we were told was sailing toward Bijaya,[89] in the hope that we could embark on it. We arrived on the eve of

---

86. The pun is made here in reference to the verse: ❁*To Him belong running ships, galleons, ploughing the sea like mountain-tops*❁ (Qur'an 55:24).
87. See al-Harawi's description of this tomb, p. 5.
88. See al-Harawi's description of this spring, p. 4.
89. In modern-day Algeria. It is pronounced Bgayet in local Berber language, and Bougie in French.

3. Ibn Jubayr on the cities of Banyas, Acre, etc.

the aforementioned Thursday, because the distance between the two cities was around 30 miles.[90] We lodged in it in a caravanserai prepared for the lodging of Muslims.

The City of Tyre (*Sur*)—may God almighty destroy it

This is a city that is the epitome of invincibility. It does not submit or acquiesce to any conqueror. The Franks prepared it as a sanctuary for their emergencies, and made it a secure refuge. Its streets and alleys are cleaner than Acre. Its people are less inclined to infidelity, and more inclined, in character and intention, to be good to Muslim foreigners. Their manners are more pleasant, and their houses are larger and more spacious. The status of Muslims in it is nicer and more tranquil. For Acre is larger, more brutal, and inclined to infidelity.

As for its invincibility and fortification, it is something more marvelous than can be described. That is because of its two gates: one landward and the other seaward. The sea surrounds it except from one side. The landward gate is reached after going through three or four entryways, which are constructed into the walls around it. As for the seaward gate, it is an entrance between two constructed towers leading into a harbor. Nothing more marvelous is to be found in any coastal cities. It is surrounded from three sides by the city walls, and from the last side it is enclosed by a wall made of plaster. Ships come in under the walls and anchor inside. A huge chain stretches between the two aforementioned towers, preventing entry or exit when extended. There is no way for boats to come in unless the chain is removed. On that gate there are guards and agents who keep a close eye on everyone who enters or exits. This harbor is something to truly marvel at in terms of its location. Acre's has a similar location and description, but it cannot accommodate such large ships as that of Tyre, but rather they have to anchor outside and only small boats can enter. The harbor in Tyre is more perfect, more beautiful, and more spacious.

We stayed in Tyre 11 days; we entered it on Thursday and departed from it on Sunday, the 22nd of the aforementioned Jumada, which corresponds to the last day of September. That is because we found the boat in which we were hoping to sail too small and thought better not to sail in it.

---

90. This indicates the medieval Arab mile, which measured between 1.8 and 2 kilometers.

A Frankish wedding in Tyre

One spectacle of the vanities of the world that we saw while in Tyre was a bride's wedding, which took place on one of the days by the harbor. For that, all Christians—men and women—assembled and lined up on both sides of the betrothed bride's door. Horns were blowing, as well as reeds and other entertaining instruments. Then she came out swinging between two men, holding her from the right and left as if they were her brothers. She was beautifully outfitted and elegantly dressed, dragging a trail of golden silk strips in accordance with their customary dressing style. On her head there was a golden band decorated with a woven mesh made of gold. A similar one was arranged on her chest. She was swaggering in her jewelry and clothes, proceeding very slowly like a dove or a passing cloud. We ask protection from God against the temptation of such sights. In front of her were the city's most notable Christian men in their most splendid clothes, dragging behind them their robes. Following her were her peers and her kind of Christian women, swinging in the most precious dresses, and swaggering in the most boastful jewelry. The entertaining instruments were leading the way. The Muslim and other Christian spectators lined up on both sides of the street, gazing at them without any reproof. They paraded her until they brought her to the house of her groom, and spent that day feasting. Coincidence made us see this spectacle of vanity, from the temptation of which God is sought for protection.

The Muslims of Acre

We returned to Acre by sea, arriving on the morning of Monday, the 23rd of the aforementioned Jumada, which corresponds to the first day of October. We booked our fare on a large boat intending to sail to Messina, one of the towns of the island of Sicily. God almighty, by His majesty and power, is the guarantor to make it smooth and easy.

During our stay in Tyre, we lodged in a mosque that remained in the hands of the Muslims. They had other mosques in it, but one of the Muslim elders of Tyre told us that they were confiscated from them in the year 518 (1124). Acre was captured 12 years before Tyre after a long siege and because of the famine that befell the inhabitants. We were told that it brought them to a state from which we beseech God to save us. Pride drove them to initiate a plan, but God held them back from it. They decided to gather their spouses and children in the great mosque and kill them with the sword in order to protect them from being enslaved by the Christians. Then they were to march against their enemy in a resolute assault and fight them truly until they all died together and God's decree was realized. But their jurists and some God-fearing individuals among them stood in their way, and they all agreed to hand over the town and leave it peacefully. That was what ended up happening, and they dispersed in the Muslim lands. The love of the homeland lured some to return to live among the Franks after they guaranteed security of person and property, which was granted to them according to conditions they stipulated. ❮*God's decree will prevail*❯ (Qur'an 12:21)—glory be to Him. May His power reign and His will prevail on earth. There is no excuse before God to reside in one of the towns of the infidels except while crossing it, especially if one were to find an alternative in Muslim lands. That is because of the hardships and horrors that he will encounter in their lands, such as humiliation and submissive (*dhimmi*) status,[91] and such as hearing what causes pain in the hearts regarding the blasphemy of the Prophet Muhammad—whose mention God venerated and whose rank He exalted—especially from that wretched and base people of theirs. Also, there is the absence of cleanliness, the intermingling with pigs, and prohibitions all of which cannot be listed or enumerated. Beware, beware of entering their lands. God almighty is the one to be asked for proper absolution and forgiveness from this sin in which the foot slipped, and which one could not foresee until regret has set in. He—glory be to Him—is the Master of that; there is no Lord but He.

Muslim captives

Muslim captives are among the misfortunes that whoever travels to their lands witnesses. The Muslim men are shackled in chains and forced to do hard labor as if they were slaves. The Muslim women are treated likewise, with iron anklets on their legs. Hearts weep over them and pity benefits them not at all.

One of the benevolent things that almighty God has arranged for the North African captives in these Syrian lands under the Franks is that every Muslim in these and other parts of Syria designates a portion of his wealth specifically to liberate the North Africans on account of them being away

---

91. *Dhimmi*, according to Islamic law and historical practice, is the term used to designate the contract status by which members of other revealed religions (e.g., Jews, Christians, Zoroastrians), were afforded certain protections in exchange for paying an annual tax (*jizya*) and acquiescing to a range of disabilities imposed on them as inferior persons in the Islamic social order. Conversion to Islam changed one's status from *dhimmi* to Muslim and removed the obligation to pay the *jizya*. It is interesting that Ibn Jubayr used the same term to describe Muslims living under Frankish rule. See also p. 18 (footnote 83).

from their country and that they have no person to save them other than the great and glorious God. They are after all foreigners, separated from their lands. Thus, the Muslim monarchs of these parts, noble ladies, as well as affluent and wealthy people spend their money in this purpose. Nur al-Din—may God be merciful to him—made a vow during an illness that struck him to spend 12,000 dinars to ransom North African captives. When he was cured from his illness, he sent the money for their ransom. Among those dispatched in the deal were a group who were not from North Africa; they were from Hama, from the farmlands around it. He ordered them to be returned and replaced with North Africans. He said: "These should be liberated by their families and neighbors. The North Africans are foreigners and have no families." Behold the benevolence of almighty God toward this North African people![92]

God had also foreordained that they should have in Damascus two men who are among the most prosperous, noble, and rich merchants, who bask in wealth. One of them was named Nasr son of Qawwam[93] and the second one was Abu al-Durr Yaqut, the freed slave of al-'Attafi. All their trading is along this Frankish coast and no one else has a say there. They have honest partners, and caravans come and go carrying their merchandise. Their level of riches is immense, and their status before Muslim and Frankish princes is substantial. The great and glorious God has chosen them to liberate the North African captives with their money and the money given to them by those who make bequests. They are sought for this because of their well-known honesty, trustworthiness, and spending their own money in this cause. No North African is saved from captivity except at their hands. They have been doing this for a long time, expending their money and exerting their efforts to save the Muslim servants of God from the hands of the infidels, the enemies of God. God almighty ❮wastes not the reward of the virtuous❯ (Qur'an 12:90).

---

92. It was a common and praiseworthy practice at the time for wealthy Muslims to ransom Muslim captives from the Franks and vice versa.

93. We do not know much about him. But we know about his two sons: Nasir (1172–1238) and Muhammad (1181–1234) who, aside from their profession as merchants, were active in the circles of learning and Hadith scholarship. The family came to Damascus from the city of Rasafa in northern Syria: see al-Dhahabi, *Taʾrikh al-islam*, 46: 273–274 (Nasir) and 82–83 (Muhammad).

3. Ibn Jubayr on the cities of Banyas, Acre, etc.

An unhappy coincidence

Of the unhappy coincidences, from the evil of which we beseech God, was that we were accompanied on our way to Acre from Damascus by a North African man from Buna in the district of Bijaya. He was a captive and was saved at the hands of the aforementioned Abu al-Durr and became one of his young servants. He arrived with his caravan to Acre. While captive, he had befriended the Christians and picked up many of their habits. Satan kept enticing and tempting him until he renounced the religion of Islam. So, he became an infidel and converted to Christianity during our stay in Tyre. We left for Acre and were told about his affairs, that he had been baptized and had become abhorrent. He put on the girdle[94] and brought hell quickly upon himself. ❴*The verdict of torment will have come true*❵ (Quran 39:71) for him, ❴*an evil accounting*❵ (Qur'an 13:18) awaits him, and an abyss is the ❴*final destination*❵ (Qur'an 78:22). We implore the great and glorious God to confirm us in the firm confession in this world and the hereafter, to cause us not to deviate from the ❴*pristine faith*❵ (Qur'an 2:135),[95] and to let us die Muslims by His grace and mercy.

This pig, the lord of Acre, who is called by them king (Baldwin IV), is hidden from view. God has afflicted him with leprosy, hastening His vengeance upon him.[96] His affliction preoccupied him during his boyhood rather than the pleasures of his world. He suffers in it and ❴*the torment of the hereafter is more grievous and longer-lasting*❵ (Qur'an 20:127). His chamberlain and regent is his maternal uncle the count (Raymond III of Tripoli), who is the treasurer and the levied money is sent to him. He is also the most senior in terms of rank, prestige, and importance in the cursed Frankish dominions. The cursed count is the lord of Tripoli and Tiberias. He is a person of status and standing among the Franks. He is well qualified for kingship and the next candidate for it. He is also perceived as shrewd and cunning. He was the captive of Nur al-Din for almost 12 years or more, but then was able to free himself with a huge sum during the time of Saladin, at the beginning of his reign. He acknowledges to Saladin his servitude and emancipation.

---

94. Christians were often required to wear a girdle about their waist or some other distinctive apparel to publicly distinguish themselves as Christians. Similar rules applied to Jews as well. See al-Shayzari, *The Book of the Islamic Market Inspector: Nihayat al-rutba fi talab al-hisba (The Utmost Authority in the Pursuit of Hisba) by 'Abd al-Rahman b. Nasr al-Shayzari*, trans. R. P. Buckley (New York: Oxford University Press, 1999), 121–122. Al-Shayzari (d. ca. 1193) was a twelfth-century Syrian scholar.
95. As in ❴*the religion of Abraham, of pristine faith*❵.
96. As in ❴*God is Almighty, Vengeful*❵ (Qur'an 3:4).

Caravans from Damascus cross via the wilderness of Tiberias because of the accessibility of its road. But mule caravans pass through Tibnin because of its ruggedness, for its road is shorter. Lake Tiberias is famous; its water is sweet. Its width is approximately 3 or 4 parasangs, and its length is around 6 parasangs. But estimates about it vary, and what is said here is closer to the truth even though we did not see it. Its width varies in size in terms of wideness and narrowness. Near there are many of the prophets' tombs, God's blessings on them, such as Jethro (*Shu'ayb*), Solomon, Judah (*Yahuda*), Reuben (*Rubil*),[97] and Shu'ayb's daughter (Zipporah) the wife of Moses the Interlocutor of God, and others.[98] God's blessings and peace be upon them all. Mount Tabor is near to it.

Between Acre and Jerusalem is a distance of 3 days' march. Between Damascus and Jerusalem are around 8 days. It is to the southwest[99] of Acre in the direction of Alexandria.[100] May God—with His might and power—restore it to the Muslims' hands and purify it from the hands of the polytheists.[101]

Acre and Tyre

These two cities, Acre and Tyre, have no orchards directly around them. Instead, they are in a vast plain connected to the seacoast. Fruits are brought to them from nearby orchards. They control expansive districts and the mountains close to them are inhabited with villages from which fruits are brought to them. They are the most precious of cities. To the east of Acre, toward the edge of town, there is a creek with running water. Along the seacoast, it has a sandy beach the beauty of which is beyond compare, and its hippodrome is without equal. The lord of the city goes out to it every morning and evening, and the soldiers gather in it. May God destroy it.

As for Tyre, it has by its landward gate a gushing spring that one descends to via stairs. Wells and water sources are plentiful in it; every house has one.

---

97. Judah and Reuben, two of the sons of Jacob.

98. On the tombs of Solomon, Jethro, and Zippora, see al-Harawi on Tiberias, Hattin, and Kafar Manda, pp. 2–4.

99. Jerusalem is to the southeast of Acre. Very likely, this confusion on the part of Ibn Jubayr is the result of the fact that the route from Acre to Jerusalem followed the coast in the direction of the southwest, before it makes a turn past Jaffa to the east, heading up the hills to Jerusalem.

100. This would be correct from a traveler's standpoint. To go to Jerusalem from Acre, one would have to head southwest along the coast before turning east near Jaffa.

101. Ibn Jubayr was describing his visit to Acre in 1184. Jerusalem remained in Frankish hands for another 3 years, until Saladin conquered it in 1187.

3. Ibn Jubayr on the cities of Banyas, Acre, etc.

Almighty God—by His grace and benevolence—will surely restore to Tyre and its sister cities the word of Islam.

In the sailing boat

On Saturday, the 28th of the aforementioned Jumada, which corresponds to the 6th of October—by the grace of God on the Muslims—we embarked on the boat, which was one of the large ships, taking with us water and provisions. The Muslims secured their places away from the Franks. Also embarking were Christians, known as pilgrims; they were the pilgrims to Jerusalem, a countless crowd, probably more than 2,000 persons. May God—by His grace and benevolence—relieve us from their company, through speedy deliverance, anticipated ease, and graceful favor. There is no deity other than He. So, by the will of the great and glorious God, we stayed in the boat awaiting a favorable wind and the completion of loading.

Questions

1. How does Ibn Jubayr represent the Franks and his interactions with them?
2. What does he say about the living conditions of the Muslims who live under Frankish rule?
3. What types of relations do they have with Muslims from outside Frankish territories?
4. What rights and disabilities do they have?
5. How do the Franks treat them?
6. Do the Muslims have access to their religious spaces and sacred sites?
7. According to Ibn Jubayr, how do Muslims treat each other in the regions of Syria in which he traveled?
8. How does Ibn Jubayr depict the role of God in the events that unfold in Syria?

4. Yaqut al-Hamawi on Ascalon, Jaffa, Caesarea, Atlit, Acre, Tyre, Margat, Saône, and Kerak[102]

Yaqut al-Hamawi was a renowned traveler and scholar. He is sometimes referred to as Yaqut al-Rumi (the Byzantine—though to conceal his previous status as an enslaved person, he adopted the following genealogy: Shihab al-Din Abu 'Abd Allah Ya'qub son of 'Abd Allah al-Hamawi). Born somewhere in the Byzantine territories around 1179, Yaqut was enslaved as a very young child, and taken to Baghdad at around age six. His master provided him with an Islamic education so that he could be useful to him in his business. In fact, Yaqut made numerous business trips to Syria on behalf of his master. Around 1200, the two men had a falling out and his master manumitted and dismissed him but re-employed him several years later. During his frequent travels, Yaqut met many notable scholars and kept copious notes on the places he visited, which he later integrated into two major works: his geographical gazette The Dictionary of Countries *and his literary gazette* The Dictionary of Authors. *He stated, for instance, that he got the idea to write* The Dictionary of Countries *in 1218, during his studies in Merv, located near Mary in modern-day Turkmenistan. He completed the first draft in Aleppo in 1224, the final draft in 1228. Yaqut's* The Dictionary of Countries *is an extremely valuable compendium of geographical and toponymic information on cities, towns, and villages in the Islamic Near East. In addition to this type of information, he also includes some biographical details on important scholars who hailed from these places as well as information on literary and poetic subjects related to them.* The Dictionary of Authors *is equally valuable, especially for the scholars who flourished in the twelfth and early thirteenth centuries. He died in Aleppo in 1229.*[103]

---

102. Yaqut recorded his geographic notices alphabetically according to the Arabic alphabet. We have arranged them from south to north along the eastern Mediterranean coast and then conclude with Kerak in southern modern Jordan.

103. On Yaqut al-Hamawi, see Claude Gilliot, "Yakut al-Rumi," in P. Bearman, T. Bianquis, C. E. Bosworth, E. van Donzel, and W. P. Heinrichs, eds, *Encyclopaedia of Islam, Second Edition* (Leiden: Brill, 1954–2009).

4. Yaqut al-Hamawi on Ascalon, Jaffa, etc.

Ascalon ('Asqalan)[104]

With an "a" vowel above the *A*, no vowel above the soft *S*, then a *Q*, and an *N* at the end.[105] Ascalon is in the third zone. From the west its longitude is 55°; its latitude is 33°.[106] It is a foreign name as I was told. Some have mentioned that the word Ascalon means the front part of the head, which means that if it is indeed Arabic it indicates the nearest part of Syria.

Ascalon is a Syrian city in the province of Palestine on the Mediterranean coast between Gaza and Bayt Jibrin. It is called, by some, the Bride of Syria, but so too is Damascus. Many Companions[107] and Successors settled there, and a large group of scholars transmitted hadiths in it.

It flourished under Muslim rule until it was conquered by the Franks—may God curse them—on 27 Jumada II 548 (18 September 1153). It remained in their hands for 35 years until Saladin Yusuf son of Ayyub wrested it from them in 583 (1187). But then the Franks received reinforcements, recaptured Acre and set out for Ascalon. Fearing that what happened to Acre would happen to Ascalon, Saladin demolished the city's fortifications in Sha'ban 587 (September 1191).

. . .[108]

The Prophet—may God bless him and grant him salvation—said about Ascalon of Syria: "I present to you the two brides—Gaza and Ascalon." The first to conquer Ascalon was Mu'awiya son of Abu Sufyan during the caliphate of 'Umar son of al-Khattab—may God be pleased with him. Many reports and hadiths about Ascalon and its merits were transmitted by the Prophet Muhammad—may God bless him and grant him salvation—and by his Companions. Among them, 'Abd Allah son of 'Umar who said: "Each thing has its quintessence; the quintessence of Syria is Ascalon." To report more would take too long.

---

104. Yaqut al-Hamawi, *Mu'jam al-buldan* (Beirut: Dar Ihya' al-Turath al-'Arabi, 1979), 4: 122.

105. Following the style of Muslim lexicographers, Yaqut gave the spelling and the way a name is to be pronounced.

106. These and other coordinates recorded by Yaqut were calculated according to medieval conventions and do not correspond to modern coordinates.

107. The Companions (*sahaba*) were the early converts to Islam who knew Muhammad personally. Hence, they were considered the best generation of Muslims. The Companions played important roles in the preservation and transmission of Hadith, one of the foundations of Islamic thought and practice. On Successors (*tabi'un*), see p. 9, (footnote 50).

108. Yaqut's brief discussion of another Ascalon, a village near Balkh in Afghanistan, is omitted here.

Chapter 1: Travel Literature and Geographical Guides

Jaffa (*Yafa*)[109]

With an *F* and an elongated *A* at the end. It is a city on the Mediterranean coast in the third district of Palestine between Caesarea and Acre (*sic*).[110] From the west its longitude is 56°; its latitude is 33°.

In 442 (1050), Ibn Butlan[111] wrote in his treatise, "Jaffa is a barren town. Those born in it have a low survival rate. One even cannot find a teacher for boys there."

Saladin conquered the town when he captured the coast in 583 (1187). The Franks took it in 587 (1191). The Monarch[112] al-ʿAdil Abu Bakr son of Ayyub reclaimed it from them in 593 (1196) and laid waste to it.

Those from Jaffa are known as Yafuni, including Abu al-ʿAbbas Muhammad son of ʿAbd Allah son of Ibrahim son of ʿUmayr al-Yafuni. The Hadith memorizer Abu al-Qasim[113] said, "In Damascus, Abu al-ʿAbbas studied with Safwan son of Salih. In Palestine, he studied with Yazid son of Khalid son of Murashshal, ʿImran son of Harun al-Ramli, Yazid son of Khalid son of ʿAbd Allah son of Mawhab, Ismaʿil son of [Abu] Khalid al-Maqdisi, Abu ʿAbd Allah Muhammad son of Mikhlid al-Musabbahi, Abu Musa ʿIsa son of Yunus al-Fakhuri, Ismaʿil son of ʿAbbad al-Arsufi, and others. Sulayman son of Ahmad al-Tabarani and Abu Bakr Ahmad son of Abu Nasr [al-Qasim son of] Maʿruf son of Abban son of Ismaʿil al-Tamimi related hadiths on his authority. In Jaffa, he transmitted hadiths on the authority of ʿImran son of Harun al-Ramli, and Abu al-Qasim al-Tabarani transmitted from him hadiths he had studied with him in Jaffa as well. Also, from Jaffa was Abu Tahir ʿAbd al-Wahid son of ʿAbd al-Jabbar al-Yafuni, upon whose authority Abu Bakr Ahmad son of al-Qasim son of Maʿruf al-Tamimi al-Samiri—a resident of Damascus—related hadiths."

---

109. Yaqut, *Muʿjam al-buldan*, 5: 426.

110. *Acre* here should read *Ascalon*. Jaffa is located south of Caesarea and north of Ascalon. Acre is north of Caesarea.

111. Ibn Butlan (d. 1066) was an Arab Christian (Nestorian) physician who wrote a medical book on health, diet, and hygiene, titled *Taqwim al-sihha* (*The Maintenance of Health*).

112. The Arabic term here is *al-Malik*, one of the titles used for Ayyubid and Mamluk sovereigns. While the title *al-Malik* can be translated as "the King," we have translated it as "the Monarch" throughout in order to avoid the impression that the Ayyubid and Mamluk sovereigns were kings in the fashion of the European kings. When a ruler is referred to by both titles—*al-Sultan al-Malik*—we have translated them as "the Sultan and Monarch." For example, we have rendered *al-Sultan al-Malik al-Kamil* as "the Sultan and Monarch al-Kamil."

113. This is none other than Ibn ʿAsakir of Damascus, who included a biography for al-Yafuni in his *Taʾrikh*, 53: 323–325.

4. Yaqut al-Hamawi on Ascalon, Jaffa, etc.

Caesarea (*Qaysariyya*)[114]

With an "a" vowel atop the *Q*, a soft *S*, followed by an elongated *A*, an *R*, and a stressed *Y*. It is a town on the coast of Syria, located in the district of Palestine. The distance from it to Tiberias is 3 days' march. In the days of yore, it was one of the choicest cities, occupying a spacious area in a pleasant location; it was very rich and well populated. But now, it is not like that. It is closer to a small town than a city.

There is another Caesarea. It is a large and densely populated city in Anatolia, and it is the seat of the Seljuk sultans of Anatolia, who are the descendants of Qilij Arslan.[115]

In Caesarea, there is a place that people say was the prison of Muhammad son of al-Hanafiyya,[116] the son of ʿAli son of Abu Talib. There is also the mosque of Abu Muhammad al-Battal,[117] and the bathhouse which people say that the philosopher Apollonius (Balynias)[118] built to the Roman emperor and which can be heated with a single oil lamp.[119]

The ascription to Caesarea is *Qaysarani*, in deviation of the rule. In *Almagest*, Ptolemy said: "Its longitude is 67° and 20 minutes; its latitude is 41° and 5 minutes. It is at the edge of the fifth zone. Its night sky features at an angle of 12 degrees the Gemini (*al-Tawʾam*) constellation, as well as the entire constellations of Orion (*al-Jawzaʾ*), Virgo (*al-Sammak al-Aʿzal*), and Cassiopeia (*Dhat al-Kursi*). At 17 degrees, there is also Cancer (*al-Saratan*) on one side and Capricorn (*al-Jadi*) on the opposite side. In the easternmost sky where the sun rises, there is Aries (*al-Hamal*); and in the westernmost where it sets, there is Libra (*al-Mizan*)." The author of the *Astronomical Tables*

---

114. Yaqut, *Muʿjam al-Buldan*, 4: 421–422.
115. Qilij Arslan (r. 1092–1107) was the Seljuk Sultan of Anatolia.
116. The third son of ʿAli son of Abu Talib, but who was not a grandson of the Prophet Muhammad. That is, his mother was Khawla daughter of Jaʿfar of the Hanifa tribe; not Muhammad's daughter, Fatima, who was the mother of ʿAli's first two sons, al-Hasan (d. 669) and al-Husayn (d. 680), the second and third Shiʿi imams. He died in 700.
117. An Umayyad general who was famed for his courage and led several campaigns against the Byzantines. He died in battle sometime between 730 and 739.
118. Appolonius of Tyana (d. ca. 100). He was a Hellenic philosopher who lived for some time in Rome and was known for his miraculous visions.
119. Very likely this is a reference to Emperor Titus (r. 79–81), who visited Caesarea after his campaign as Roman general against Judea and his destruction of the Jewish temple in 70. This story of the bathhouse, however, is likely one of the many legends and miracles associated with Apollonius.

Chapter 1: Travel Literature and Geographical Guides

(al-Zij)[120] said: "Caesarea's longitude is 57° and 30 minutes; its latitude is 33° and 20 minutes."

In the *History of Damascus*,[121] there is an anecdote transmitted on the authority of Yazid son of Samura, who narrated: "We were told by al-Hakam son of 'Abd al-Rahman son of Abu al-'Asma' al-Khath'ami al-Fira'i, who had witnessed the Battle of Caesarea, that Mu'awiya laid siege to it for 7 years less 1 month. The Byzantine soldiers who were living in the city counted 100,000. There were as well 80,000 Samaritans and 100,000 Jews. A lunatic man, who had been a hostage in the city, showed the Muslims a gap in the city wall; an opening that was wide enough for a loaded camel to enter through it. The day was Sunday, and the people were in church; they had no idea about what was happening and were alarmed to hear 'God is Greater' announced at the door of the church. They were all ruined." Yazid son of Samura also said: "The leader of the fighting men from the Khath'am Tribe, 'Umar son of Tamim son of Warqa', was asked to announce the capture of the city, so he climbed atop the church tower and shouted: 'Let it be known that Caesarea is captured by force.'"[122]

Among those who came from Caesarea in Palestine, there were Ibrahim son of Abu Sufyan al-Qaysarani, who died in 278 (891), and 'Amr son of Thawr al-Qaysarani, who died in 279 (892). There was also Muhammad son of Muhammad son of 'Abd al-Rahim son of Muhammad son of Abu Rabi'a al-Qaysarani, who studied hadiths with Khaythama son of Sulayman in Tripoli (Lebanon), with Abu 'Ali 'Abd al-Wahid son of Ahmad son of Abu al-Khusayb in Tinnis (Egypt), with Abu Bakr al-Khara'iti and Abu al-Hasan Muhammad son of Ahmad son of 'Abd Allah son of Saffur in al-Massisa (Mopsuestia), and with others. He taught hadiths to a group of people, including Abu Bakr Muhammad son of Ahmad al-Wasiti[123] and Abu al-Hasan Jamil son of Muhammad al-Arsufi. There was as well Abu 'Isa Fudayq son of Salman or Sulayman son of 'Isa al-'Uqayli al-Qaysarani,

---

120. Very likely, this is a reference to *The Book of Astronomical Tables* (*Kitab al-Zij* in Arabic) of al-Battani (d. 929), known in Latin as Albategnius, who was one of the most celebrated Muslim astronomers and mathematicians. He corrected many of Ptolemy's calculations and observations.

121. Ibn 'Asakir, *Ta'rikh*, 15: 23–24.

122. The Arabic word used for "force" is *qasran*, which was meant as a pun on the name of the city.

123. The author of *Fada'il al-Bayt al-Muqaddas* (*Religious Merits of Jerusalem*), who died after 1019.

who transmitted hadiths on the authority of al-Awzaʿi,[124] Maslama son of ʿAli al-Khushani, and taught hadiths to al-ʿAbbas son of al-Walid son of Subayh al-Khallal, Ibrahim son of al-Walid son of Salama, and others. Fudayq was known for his great piety.

Atlit (*Athlith*)[125]

With an "a" vowel above the *A*, no vowel above the *Th*, an "i" vowel on the *L*, a silent *I*, and a *Th*. Atlit is the name of a fortress on the Mediterranean coast that is also known as the Red Fortress. The Monarch al-Nasir Yusuf son of Ayyub (Saladin) conquered it in the year 583 (1187).

Acre (*ʿAkka*)[126]

With an "a" vowel above the *A*, and stressing of the *K*. Abu Zayd[127] said: "The sandy desert that is overheated by the sun is called *al-ʿakka*." Al-Layth[128] said: "*Al-ʿAkka* comes from the heat, and it designates the excessive increase in heat during summer daytime when the wind is still." We have mentioned enough information about ʿAkk earlier.[129] The author of *Almagest* (Ptolemy) said: "Acre's longitude is 66°; its latitude is 31°." According to Ibn Abu ʿAwn,[130] however, its longitude is 58° 25 minutes; its latitude is 33° and 20 minutes. It is in the fourth zone.

Acre is the name of a city on the coast of Syria, in the district of Jordan (*al-Urdunn*). In our day, it is the best coastal town and the most populated. Abu ʿAbd Allah Muhammad son of Ahmad son of Abu Bakr al-Bannaʾ al-Bashshari said: "Acre is a fortified city with a large mosque that has its own olive orchard which supplies its requirements for lighting oil, and even more. The city was not well fortified until the arrival of Ibn Tulun.[131] He had seen Tyre and the walls that enclosed its port, and wanted to have something

---

124. A renowned early Muslim jurist and scholar of Hadith. He died in 774 and was buried in Beirut.

125. Yaqut, *Muʿjam al-Buldan*, 4: 85.

126. Yaqut, *Muʿjam al-Buldan*, 4: 143–144.

127. Saʿid son of Aws (d. ca. 830) was an Arab grammarian and lexicographer.

128. Al-Layth son of al-Muzaffar (d. 748) was a well-known early Arab philologist.

129. According to al-Harawi, "Acre is called Acre (ʿAkka) because it is where the tomb of ʿAkk is located. Some allege that he is a prophet." See p. 5.

130. Ibrahim son of Muhammad (d. 934) was an ʿAbbasid administrator and scholar, who wrote a geographical book titled *Kitab al-Nawahi wa-l-buldan* (*On Regions and Cities*).

131. Ruler of Egypt (r. 868–884), nominally for the ʿAbbasid caliphs, who extended his power to Syria.

similar for Acre. He assembled the architects from the neighboring areas and told them about his idea. They informed him that no one could construct such a thing in water in those days. But then, someone mentioned to him my grandfather the architect, Abu Bakr, and said: 'If any person knows how to build something like that, it would be him.' Ibn Tulun wrote to my grandfather and brought him from Jerusalem. He proposed to him the idea, and my grandfather replied that it was an easy thing to do. He requested large beams of sycamore wood, and when they were brought, he lined them up beside each other on top of the water and fastened them together following the contours of the land walls. He made an opening on the western side, as an access point. Using stones, he started building on top of these beams, and every time he finished five rows, he fastened them to massive pillars to strengthen the structure. Due to the weight, the beams gradually sank until they landed on the seafloor sand. At that point, he stopped the construction for a whole year in order for the foundation to firmly settle. He then came back and started from where he had stopped. When each side reached the adjacent land wall, he fused the two structures together. He also constructed atop the sea opening an arch, through which the boats accessed the inner harbor. There was as well a chain to close the access after the boats entered, similar to the way it is done in Tyre."[132]

Abu 'Abd Allah al-Bashshari also said: "Ibn Tulun paid my grandfather 100 dinars, not to mention the robes and horses. His name is still inscribed on the sea wall until today." He said as well: "Enemy pirates used to attack the boats in the inner harbor before the sea wall was constructed."

Acre was captured around the year 15 (636) by 'Amr son of al-'As[133] and Mu'awiya son of Abu Sufyan.[134] Mu'awiya in particular had a major role in its capture and the seizure of the entire coast. Moreover, when he attacked Cyprus, his fleet departed from there, and he decided to rebuild it and repopulate it. He did the same with Tyre. Afterward, Acre was destroyed, and it was reconstructed by Hisham son of 'Abd al-Malik.[135] Acre used to be the center of craftsmanship in the district of Jordan (*al-Urdunn*). But Hisham decided to move the craftsmen to Tyre, which remained the case until the

---

132. See Ibn Jubayr (pp. 20–21, 26–27) for a similar comparison between the two harbors.

133. One of the leading generals of the Muslim army that invaded Syria starting in 634, and then led the conquest of Egypt in 640–642.

134. One of the leading generals of the Muslim army that invaded Syria starting in 634. The caliph 'Umar son of al-Khattab promoted him to principal commander in Syria after the leading generals died from the Plague of Emmaus (638–639). He was the first Umayyad caliph (r. 661–680).

135. The tenth Umayyad caliph (r. 724–743).

caliphate of al-Muqtadir[136] when Tyre entered a phase of chaotic succession of governors. This chaos allowed Acre to grow again in a beautiful way and for the craftsmen to return to it, which remains the case in our time. Currently, it is in the hands of the Franks.

According to a prophetic hadith, it is said: "Blessed is the one who sees Acre." Al-Farra'[137] said: "This land is an ʿakkata or an ʿakkatun land—it cannot be rendered in the genitive case—and it means hot."[138]

Back in the day, Acre was in the hands of the Muslims until the Franks captured it. Their leader Baldwin, who was king of Jerusalem, seized it from its Egyptian governor Zahr al-Dawla (Radiance of the Realm) Bana' al-Juyushi, who was originally the slave of the army general Badr al-Jamali[139] or his son. The Franks attacked the town from land and sea in 497 (1104). The locals fought them until they ran out of supplies; the Egyptians sent them nothing. They surrendered the city to the Franks, who killed a large number of its people, enslaved another group and sold them beyond the sea. Zahr al-Dawla departed for Damascus, and from there he went to Cairo.

Acre remained in Frankish hands until Saladin Yusuf son of Ayyub conquered it from them in Jumada I of 583 (July 1187). He left there a large garrison and gave them good supplies. The Franks came back and attacked it, making trenches in front of the city walls. Saladin rushed from Damascus to help them and encamped there facing the Franks for 3 years, but the Franks were able to take the city from the Muslims by force on 7 Jumada II 587 (2 July 1191). They brought out the Muslim captives, who were around 3,000 persons, and slaughtered them all. The city remains in their hands until today.

Several scholars came from Acre, among them al-Hasan son of Ibrahim al-ʿAkki, who transmitted Hadith from al-Hasan son of Jarir al-Suri and taught Hadith to ʿAbd al-Samad son of al-Hakam.

---

136. The eighteenth ʿAbbasid caliph (r. 908–929).

137. Abu Zakariyya Yahya son of Ziyad al-Farra' (d. 822) was one of the most important early grammarians of Arabic.

138. That is, in Arabic, ʿAkka can only be rendered ʿakkata in the accusative case; and ʿakkatun in the nominative case, not ʿakkatin in the genitive case.

139. The famous Fatimid general and vizier of Armenian origin. On his son, al-Afdal, see Chapter 3, p. 63 (footnote 10).

Tyre (*Sur*)[140]

Spelled with a long "u" vowel and an *R* at the end. It is in the fourth zone. Tyre's longitude is 59° and 15 minutes; its latitude is 33° and 40 minutes. In Arabic *sur* means horn (*qarn*). According to the Qur'an commentators that is how *sur* is used in almighty God's word, ❧*A day shall come when the horns are blown*❧ (Qur'an 20:102). It is a famous city in which many ascetics and scholars lived, and some of its natives rose to prominence. It used to be one of the frontier towns of the Muslims. It overlooks the Mediterranean, jutting into the sea like an arm's fist. The sea surrounds it on three sides; the fourth is protected by its well-fortified gates and impenetrable towers. There is no way to conquer it except through treachery.

The Muslims conquered Tyre in the days of 'Umar son of al-Khattab—may God be pleased with him. It remained safely in their hands until 518 (1124) when the Franks attacked it. They laid siege to and harassed it until the city's residents began to run out of provisions. The ruler of Egypt, al-Amir,[141] tried to resupply them with provisions, but a storm stirred up the wind against the fleet and forced it to return to Egypt. Provisions were not able to reach it until 10 days after the people had surrendered the city; the Muslims capitulated on condition of safe passage, and thereafter departed. Only the destitute remained when the Franks took possession of it; they fortified it and reinforced its defenses. It remains in their hands until today. We seek refuge in God and assistance for every good thing, for He does what He wills.

Tyre is in the district of Jordan (*al-Urdunn*). The distance between it and Acre is 60 parasangs. It is east of Acre.[142] Many scholars are named al-Suri because they come from Tyre (Sur). Among them is the Hadith memorizer Abu 'Abd Allah Muhammad son of 'Ali son of 'Abd Allah al-Suri. He started the study of hadith at an older age and became an authority. He moved to Baghdad in the year 418 (1027), after he had traveled in Egypt and many places around Tyre, where he copied books on the authority of scholars, hadith masters, and poets. He transmitted hadiths on the authority of 'Abd al-Ghani son of Sa'id al-Misri, Abu al-Husayn son of Jami' [in Sidon], and Abu 'Abd Allah son of Abu Kamil [of Tripoli]. He was a great Hadith memorizer, meticulous, virtuous, pious, and fasted frequently. He

---

140. Yaqut, *Mu'jam al-Buldan*, 3: 433–434.
141. The tenth Fatimid Caliph, al-Amir bi-Ahkam Allah (r. 1101–1130).
142. While Tyre is north of Acre on the Mediterranean coast, its precise location is northeast of Acre.

only broke his fast for the two feasts and for the Days of Sun-drying.[143] His refined penmanship was exemplary; he could fit 70 or 80 lines on a Baghdad one-eighth-size paper.[144] The Hadith memorizer Abu Bakr al-Khatib,[145] the judge Abu 'Abd Allah al-Damaghani,[146] and others transmitted hadiths on his authority. Some scholars allege that when al-Suri died, al-Khatib al-Baghdadi purchased his books from one of al-Suri's daughters, and that the majority of what al-Khatib wrote, except the *History*, was taken from al-Suri's books. Some scholars said: "Al-Suri transmitted 200,000 hadiths." Ghayth said: "I heard many scholars say, 'We have never seen a more proficient Hadith memorizer than he.'" He died in Baghdad in Jumada II 441 (November 1049).

Margat (*al-Marqab*)[147]

With an "a" vowel on the *M*, a silent *R*, a *Q* and a *B*. It is the noun for a place used for spying. It is also a town and a well-fortified castle overlooking the Mediterranean coast near the city of Baniyas.[148] Abu Ghalib Hammam son of al-Muhadhdhab al-Ma'arri[149] said about its history: "In the year 454 (1062), the Muslims constructed the castle, which is known as al-Marqab, on the coast near Jabala. It is a castle that when anyone sees it for the first time, he says he has never seen anything like it. Once, the Muslims garrisoned there plotted against the Byzantines. They sold them the castle for a massive sum and sent an old man and his two children as hostages to Antioch

---

143. Yaqut did not need to name the two feasts as he was referring to the two most important feasts in the Islamic calendar: the Feast of Ramadan (*'Id al-Fitr*) at the end of the month of fasting (the 9th month in the Islamic calendar) and the Feast of Sacrifice (*'Id al-Adha*) at the end of the Pilgrimage (*Hajj*) to Mecca on the 10th of Dhu al-Hijja (the 12th month in the Islamic calendar). The Days of Sun-drying (*Ayyam al-tashriq*) are the 3 days of feasting that follow the Feast of Sacrifice; they are called so because of the pre-Islamic practice of sun-drying the meat of the sacrificed animals to preserve it.

144. *Al-thumn al-baghdadi* in Arabic. It was one of the best types of paper used at the time, and the one-eighth refers to its size; that is, each original sheet of paper was cut into eight parts.

145. Abu Bakr al-Khatib al-Baghdadi (1002–1071) was the eminent Hadith scholar and author of the *Ta'rikh Baghdad* (*History of Baghdad*). He visited Tyre several times.

146. Abu 'Abd Allah al-Damaghani (1007–1085) belonged to an eminent family of Hanafi jurists in Baghdad. He also served as the chief judge of Baghdad.

147. Yaqut, *Mu'jam al-buldan*, 5: 108–109.

148. Baniyas (Balanea) is the Syrian port city south of Antioch, between Latakiya and Tartus—not the Banyas north of Lake Tiberias described by Ibn Jubayr, p. 17.

149. A chronicler from northern Syria, who flourished in the eleventh century (died around 1096). His *Ta'rikh*, which he made on the basis of notes his father had collected and to which he added some of his own material, is lost.

to receive the money and agreed on handing them the castle. When the garrison received the money and 300 Byzantine soldiers came to claim the castle, they killed a few and captured the rest, who ransomed themselves with a large sum of money. The garrison ransomed the old man and his two children with a paltry sum; they kept the rest of the money and the castle."

Saône (*Sihyawn*)[150]

With an "i" vowel below the *S*, followed by a silent *H*, an "a" vowel above the *Y*, a silent *W*, and an *N* at the end. Al-Azhari[151] said that Abu 'Amr related: "*Sihyawn* (Zion) is Rome, and it is also said it is Jerusalem." Al-A'sha[152] said in his eulogy of Yazid and 'Abd al-Masih the sons of al-Dayyan—others said this was a eulogy for al-Sayyid and al-'Aqib the two bishops of Najran.

1- O two masters of Najran, I beg of you: / care for Najran after the calamity that struck it and struck you.

2- For you to do good and to pursue good / is not new for either of you.

3- Should you save Najran, it would demonstrate great leadership; / after all, your father was its master.

4- But if Sihyawn threatens you one day / the field of fierce battle is your domain.

I (Yaqut) say: *Sihyawn* is a well-known place in Jerusalem where the Church of Zion is located. *Sihyawn* is also a well-fortified castle on the coast of Syria in the district of Hims, but it is not near the sea. The castle is well fortified and well built on the edge of the mountain, surrounded by wide and deep ravines. It does not have a man-made moat except on one side; its length is around 60 cubits, dug into the bedrock. It has three concentric walls: two surrounding its courtyard, and one around its inner tower. It was in the hands of the Franks for a long time until the Monarch al-Nasir Saladin Yusuf son of Ayyub took it back from them in 584 (1188). Today, it remains in the hands of the Muslims.

---

150. Yaqut, *Mu'jam al-buldan*, 3: 436–437.
151. Abu Mansur Muhammad son of Ahmad al-Azhari (895–980) was a famous Arab lexicographer who flourished in Baghdad.
152. A famous pre-Islamic Arab poet who died in 625.

4. Yaqut al-Hamawi on Ascalon, Jaffa, etc.

Kerak (*Karak*)[153]

With an "a" vowel for both syllables and a *K* at the end. It is a foreign word: The name of a well-fortified castle in southern Syria in the al-Balqa'[154] mountains, midway between Eilat (*Ayala*) and the Red Sea in the south and Jerusalem in the northwest. It is on the edge of a steep mountain which is protected by ravines that surround it on all sides except from the northern hillside.

Kerak is also a large village near Baalbek in which there is a wide tomb that the people allege is the tomb of Noah—peace be upon him.

Questions

1. In his *The Dictionary of Countries*, on what kinds of information does Yaqut focus in his descriptions of the places he writes about?
2. Why would he focus on this kind of information specifically?
3. How does Yaqut react to the Franks' capture of Muslim towns and their presence there?
4. Al-Harawi, Ibn Jubayr, and Yaqut described some of the same sites in Syria and Palestine. How are their descriptions similar to and dissimilar to one another?
5. Taken together, what can we learn from these three Muslim travelers—al-Harawi, Ibn Jubayr, Yaqut—about Muslim perceptions of Syria and Palestine during the Crusader period?

---

153. Yaqut, *Muʃam al-buldan*, 4: 453.
154. The name of the region constituting most of Jordan today.

CHAPTER TWO
JIHAD BOOKS AND JURIDICAL DIRECTIVES

1. Ibn ʿAsakir on Jihad[1]

Ibn ʿAsakir was one of the most celebrated Sunni scholars of medieval Islam, both in his own time and in subsequent centuries. He was born in 1105 in Damascus to a scholarly family that adhered to the Shafiʿi[2] branch of Islamic law. His exceptional prowess in Hadith scholarship and his voluminous literary productivity were two important factors that contributed to his fame and made his family a household name in the Muslim world. Ibn ʿAsakir spent much of his early adulthood traveling in the eastern Islamic lands pursuing religious scholarship with as many notable scholars as he could meet.

Upon his return to Damascus, he took up a professorship of Hadith scholarship at the great Umayyad Mosque in the city. But it was his service to his political patron Nur al-Din—especially in shaping the sultan's religious agenda after he conquered Damascus in 1154—that cemented Ibn ʿAsakir's renowned position in Sunnism, in particular among Shafiʿi and Ashʿari[3] scholars. With Nur al-Din's encouragement and patronage, Ibn ʿAsakir completed his massive History of Damascus, *which he began in 1135. In the 1160s, Nur al-Din commissioned Ibn ʿAsakir to compose a short work on the virtues of jihad, which resulted in his* The Forty Hadiths for Inciting Jihad.

Nur al-Din also established the College of Hadith (Dar al-Hadith) *in Damascus and appointed Ibn ʿAsakir as its first professor, a position he held until his death. We do not know precisely how much Ibn ʿAsakir used the College of Hadith for teaching and propaganda as he continued to maintain his professorship at the Umayyad Mosque, and split his duties between both places. In any event, Nur al-Din's College of Hadith was an important center of Sunni scholarship well into the fourteenth century.*

---

1. Ibn ʿAsakir, *al-Arbaʿun fi al-hathth ʿala al-jihad*, in Suleiman A. Mourad and James E. Lindsay, ed. and trans., *The Intensification and Reorientation of Sunni Jihad Ideology in the Crusader Period* (Leiden: Brill, 2013), 132, 134, 136, 138, 140, 142, 150, 152, 154, 158, 168, and 182.
2. The Shafiʿi school is a Sunni branch of jurisprudence. It was powerful during the Crusader period as most of the rulers and scholars in Syria–Palestine and post-Fatimid Egypt belonged to it.
3. The Ashʿari school was one of the dominant theological schools in Sunni Islam.

Chapter 2: Jihad Books and Juridical Directives

Ibn ʿAsakir was also fond of poetry. His History of Damascus *includes many poems he heard from his teachers, and he had a habit of concluding all of his books with a relevant poem. He also composed a great deal of poetry himself, but his fellow Damascenes did not think highly of its quality; one of them quipped about Ibn ʿAsakir's poetic prowess: "This poetry is by one who has lost his demon." That is, every poet has a demon that inspires him/her. Apparently, Ibn ʿAsakir did not have one. He died in 1176. Saladin attended his funeral.*[4]

※

In the name of God, the Merciful, the Compassionate. May God bless our lord Muhammad and his family and grant them peace.

Thanks be to God, who lifted up the seven securely fixed heavens, spread the earth beneath them as a vast expanse, fastened it securely to the firm mountains and hills, and partitioned them into stable places like fixed poles. Far removed is He from having a female consort or progeny, or from seeking the aid of associates and peers. I thank Him for the countless gifts that He bestowed, and believe in Him like a true monotheist. I testify that there is no god but Him, the Creator of the beasts and things; I make this testimony as a provision for myself on the Day of Resurrection. I also testify that Muhammad is His servant and messenger, who guides to righteousness and opens the way of truth after being blocked and closed, the chosen one from the pure family and glorious masters—may God eternally bless him, his family, and his Companions until the Day of Assembly.[5]

Nur al-Din, the just monarch, the ascetic, the jihad fighter, and the garrisoned warrior—may God grant him success in that which is proper, assist him in fulfilling what is best for people, grant him favor against the recalcitrants, exalt him in victory with his army, and support him with aid—expressed his desire that I collect for him forty hadiths relating to jihad that have clear texts and uninterrupted sound chains of transmission so that they might stimulate the valiant jihad fighters, the ones with strong determination

---

4. On Ibn ʿAsakir and his work, see Suleiman A. Mourad, *Ibn ʿAsakir of Damascus: Champion of Sunni Islam in the Time of the Crusades* (Oxford: Oneworld, 2021), and Mourad and Lindsay, *Intensification*. For an example of Ibn ʿAsakir's poetry, see p. 89.

5. In an Islamic context, the Day of Judgment is referred to as the Day of Resurrection (*yawm al-qiyama*), that is, when the dead are resurrected for the final judgment, or as the Day of Assembly (*yawm al-hashr*), that is, after being resurrected, they will assemble for the final judgment.

and mighty arms, with sharp swords and piercing spears, and stir them up to truly perform when they meet the enemy in battle, as well as incite them to uproot the unbelievers and tyrants who, because of their unbelief, have terrorized the land and proliferated oppression and corruption—may God pour on them all types of torture, for He is all-watching. So I hastened to fulfill his desire and collected for him what is suitable for the people of learning and inquiry. I especially exerted a tremendous effort in collecting them in the hope that I should receive the reward [from God] for enlightening and guidance. God is the Guide to accuracy in what one initiates and completes, and the Director to right expression, be it thorough or succinct.

Hadith 1

Abu Hurayra said:

> The Messenger of God was asked: "Which aspect of belief is the best?" He replied: "Belief in God—glory and greatness belong to Him." He was then asked: "And what comes after that?" He replied: "Jihad in the path of God—glory and greatness belong to Him." He was asked again: "And what comes after that?" He replied: "An accepted pilgrimage."

Hadith 4

Al-Nu'man son of Bashir said:

> I was near the pulpit of the Messenger of God—may God bless him and grant him salvation—on a Friday when a man said: "I do not care if the only good deed I do after embracing Islam is to provide water for the pilgrims." Another man said: "I do not care if the only good deed I do after embracing Islam is to care for the Sacred Mosque." Yet, another man retorted: "Jihad in the path of almighty God is better than what you have said." This happened on a Friday. 'Umar son of al-Khattab reproached them, saying: "Do not argue loudly near the pulpit of the Messenger of God. When the Friday noon prayer is over, I will go to him and ask his opinion about the matter on which you have differed. Consequently, God—glory and greatness belong to Him—revealed: *Are you indeed equating provision of water to pilgrims and caring for the Sacred Mosque with one who believes in God and the Last Day, and wages jihad in the cause of*

Chapter 2: Jihad Books and Juridical Directives

God? They are not equal in the sight of God, and God guides not the evildoers
(Qur'an 9:20).[6]

Hadith 6

Al-Harith al-Ash'ari said:

> The Messenger of God—may God bless him and grant him salvation—said: "The almighty God commanded John son of Zachariah—peace be upon them—to abide by five words and to command the Israelites to abide by them too. Jesus son of Mary—peace be upon him—said to him: 'God has commanded us to abide by five words and to command the Israelites to abide by them too. So either you command them or I will.' John replied: 'If you do it before me I fear lest I be tortured or swallowed into the ground.' So John summoned the people to the Temple (*Bayt al-Maqdis*) until it was full and many sat on the terraces. He preached to them, saying: 'God has commanded me to abide by five words and to command you to abide by them too. First is that you worship God and do not associate with Him anyone, for the polytheist is like a man who bought a slave from his own wealth—gold or silver—and told him: "This is my house and this is my estate; work and bring the revenues to me." The slave started working but gave the revenues to someone other than his lord. Who among you is pleased if his slave does that? God has indeed created you and granted you sustenance so do not associate with Him anyone. I also command you to pray, and when you pray do not look around. I also command you to fast, for that is like a man who has a sack of frankincense and is followed by a gang who are eager to smell it. The person who fasts is worthier in God's sight than the pure smell of frankincense. I also command you to pay alms, for that is like a man who is taken captive by the enemy, who then tied his hand to his neck. He said to them: "Can I ransom myself from you?" He gave them everything so that he could be freed from them. I also command you to remember

---

6. Hadith 4 provides a brief commentary on Qur'an 9:20. Many in Ibn 'Asakir's audience were aware that Chapter 9 of the Qur'an (*Surat al-Tawba* or Repentance) was believed to have been revealed after Muhammad's conquest of Mecca in December 629 or January 630, toward the end of Muhammad's career, and hence it represented for them the last quranic pronouncement on jihad and warfare in the path of God. See Appendix B for the major quranic passages on war and peace.

God constantly, for that is like a man who is chased by the enemy, reaches an invulnerable fortress, and fortifies himself in it. Similar is the servant, for he is only fortified from Satan by the constant remembrance of God—glory and greatness belong to Him.' " The Messenger of God added: "I, too, command you to abide by five things which God has commanded me: membership in the community, hearing, obeying, making the migration, and waging jihad in the path of God—glory and greatness belong to Him. Whoever distances himself from the community, even for an arm's length, casts off the tie of Islam from his head unless he comes back, and whoever uses the supplication of the pre-Islamic Age of Ignorance is in the companies of hell." He was asked: "Even if he prays and fasts?" The prophet replied: "Even if he prays and fasts. Make sure you use God's supplication as a result of which God called the believing Muslims the worshipers of God."

Hadith 13

'Imran son of Husayn said:

> The Messenger of God—may God bless him and grant him salvation—said: "Lining up for a battle in the path of God is worthier than sixty years of worship."

Hadith 16

Anas son of Malik said:

> The Messenger of God—may God bless him and grant him salvation—said: "He who conducts a raid in the path of God—glory and greatness belong to Him—has rendered all his submission to God—glory and greatness belong to Him. ⟨*Whoso wishes, let him believe*⟩ in God's reward, and ⟨*whoso wishes, let him blaspheme. To the wicked We have prepared a Fire*⟩ (Qur'an 18:29)."[7] Anas asked:

---

7. Many in Ibn 'Asakir's audience were well aware of the subsequent verses of the quranic chapter *Surat al-Kahf* (The Cave) 18:29–31, which address themes of eternal rewards and punishments: ⟨*Say: 'The truth has come from your Lord. Whoso wishes, let him believe; Whoso wishes, let him blaspheme.' To the wicked We have prepared a Fire, with its wall surrounding it. When they cry out for help, they are helped to water resembling molten metal, scorching their faces. Wretched that drink and wretched that place of rest. As for those who believed and performed good deeds—We waste not the wage of one righteous in*

"O Messenger of God, now that we have heard this hadith from you, who would dare abandon jihad and stay behind?" The Messenger of God replied: "He whom God has cursed and is angry with, God has prepared for him a gruesome punishment. For at the end of days, there will appear a group of people who do not believe in jihad. God took an oath upon Himself that everyone who says that will be tortured like no other sinful human being."

Hadith 21

Fadala son of 'Ubayd said:

The Messenger of God—may God bless him and grant him salvation—said: "The deeds of the dead person are sealed, except those of the garrisoned warrior in the path of God whose deeds accumulate rewards until the Day of Resurrection; he will also be saved from the torment of the grave."

Hadith 29

'Abd Allah son of Zayd al-Azraq said:

When 'Uqba son of 'Amir would go out to shoot arrows, he used to bring with him a man. The man became annoyed with this, so 'Uqba said to him: "Should I tell you what I heard from the Messenger of God?" The man replied: "Yes." 'Uqba said: "I heard the Messenger of God say: 'God will admit into paradise three men for every arrow: the one who makes it and hopes it is used for something good, the one who donates it to be used in the path of God, and the person who shoots it in the path of God. You can shoot arrows or ride horses, but shooting arrows is better than riding horses. Every pastime that the believer pursues is devoid of virtue except for three: shooting his arrow from his bow, training his horse, and amusing himself with his wife and children, for they are virtuous.'" 'Uqba then died, leaving some sixty or seventy bows, each with a bag and arrows. He bequeathed them to be used in the

---

works. *To them belong the gardens of delight, beneath which rivers flow, and in which they shall be decked with bracelets of gold, and shall wear green raiment of silk and brocade, reclining therein on couches. Happy that reward and happy that place of rest.*

path of God. The Prophet—may God bless him and grant him salvation—said: "Whoever leaves the shooting of arrows after having mastered it rejects the gift he was given."

Hadith 40

'Utba son of 'Abd al-Salami, one of the Companions of the Prophet, said:

> The Messenger of God—may God bless him and grant him salvation—said: "The slain people are of three types. One is a believer who exerts his life and wealth waging jihad in the path of God—glory and greatness belong to Him—and when he meets the enemy in battle, he fights them until he is killed. He is a tested martyr whose abode will be the Tent of God, underneath His Throne; nothing separates him from prophets except their rank of prophethood. Another is a believer, having already committed transgressions and sins, who exerts his life and wealth waging jihad in the path of God, and when he meets the enemy in battle, he fights them until he is killed. His transgressions and sins are cleansed, for the sword purifies from sins. He will also be admitted to paradise from whichever gate he chooses, for paradise has eight gates, and hell has seven gates with some deeper than others. And a third is a hypocrite who exerts his life and wealth waging jihad in the path of God—glory and greatness belong to Him—and when he meets the enemy in battle, he fights them until he is killed. He is in hell, because the sword does not wipe out hypocrisy."

Questions

1. Why did Ibn 'Asakir compile his *The Forty Hadiths for Inciting Jihad*?
2. According to these hadiths, what is the importance of the religious duty of waging jihad?
3. What are the punishments for neglecting to fulfill the duty to wage jihad?
4. What are the rewards for the jihad fighters?
5. What are the prerequisites the jihad fighter is supposed to fulfill?

Chapter 2: Jihad Books and Juridical Directives

2. Al-'Izz son of 'Abd al-Salam on Jihad[8]

'Izz al-Din 'Abd al-'Aziz son of 'Abd al-Salam al-Dimashqi al-Shafi'i was born in Damascus in 1182 and died in Cairo in April 1261. His family came originally from North Africa. In Damascus, al-'Izz studied Hadith and jurisprudence with some of the leading Shafi'i and Ash'ari scholars of the city, including Fakhr al-Din Ibn 'Asakir (d. 1223) and the chief judge Jamal al-Din al-Harastani (d. 1217). As a fanatic theologian, he had a very confrontational and bullying personality toward those who differed with him on matters of religious observance and doctrine, especially the Hanbalis,[9] which got him in trouble with the rulers of the city. He was also a vocal voice against normalization of relations with the Franks, which was the main reason he was jailed and then fired from his prestigious post as preacher of the Umayyad Mosque.

He moved to Jerusalem and from there to Cairo, where Sultan al-Salih Ayyub appointed him as preacher and judge at the historically significant Mosque of 'Amr son of al-'As in the adjacent town of Fustat.[10] Al-'Izz's haughtiness toward commanders who were originally bought as slaves got him into trouble, which forced him to leave his official posts and restrict his activities to teaching at the Saladin College of Shafi'i law. His reputation as a notorious propagandist against the Franks, as reflected in his On the Laws of Jihad and Its Merits, *became the material of legends in later centuries.[11]*

In the name of God, the Merciful, the Compassionate. May God bless and grant salvation to our lord, Muhammad, and to his family.

The esteemed jurist, the leading and knowledgeable teacher, the perfect eminence, the one subsuming all virtues, the crusher of heresies, the supporter of the truth, 'Izz al-Din[12] Abu Muhammad 'Abd al-'Aziz son of 'Abd al-Salam son of Abu al-Qasim al-Sulami al-Shafi'i—may God always be on his side and prolong his life for our benefit—said:

The most important thing is to thank God whose power is manifest, whose word is dominant, whose mercy is widespread, and whose grace is

---

8. Al-'Izz Ibn 'Abd al-Salam, *Ahkam al-jihad wa-fada'iluh*, ed. N. Hammad (Jadda: Dar al-Wafa', 1986), 53.

9. The Hanbali school is a Sunni branch of jurisprudence.

10. On Fustat, see Chapter 1, p. 13 (footnote 71).

11. On al-'Izz son of 'Abd al-Salam, see E. Chaumont, "al-Sulami," *Encyclopaedia of Islam, Second Edition*.

12. The honorific 'Izz al-Din means "Glory of the Religion."

bounteous. The best of works, following the belief in God, is the waging of jihad in the path of God. For it provides the means to annihilate God's enemies and purify the earth from them, to save Muslim captives from their hands, to preserve the property, the wives, and the children of the Muslims, and—by God's permission—to benefit the Muslims with the exploitation of the lands and property of the unbelievers as well as the enslavement of their wives and children.

For that reason, God has greatly elevated the reward of the Muslims, irrespective of whether they attack or are attacked, defeat or are defeated, kill or are killed. He revivifies those killed while waging jihad after their death, and rewards them for the life they have dedicated to Him with an everlasting and eternal life, which no one can describe or even grasp.

Similarly, because they have forsaken their families and countries for His cause, God has lodged them in His proximity and made them enjoy His intimacy instead of the intimacy of their loved ones, whom they left behind because of Him. Blessed is he who has attained such a generous reward in the proximity of the venerated Lord. After all, this is only possible for the one who fights in the path of God in order to assure that God's word reigns supreme and that the unbelievers' word is crushed.

Questions

1. How does this introduction reflect al-'Izz's understanding of the duty of jihad?
2. Even though it is a brief excerpt, how does it compare to Ibn 'Asakir's understanding in his *The Forty Hadiths for Inciting Jihad*?

Chapter 2: Jihad Books and Juridical Directives

3. Al-Subki's account of al-'Izz son of 'Abd al-Salam's juridical directive banning the sale of arms to the Franks[13]

Taj al-Din (Crown of the Religion) Abu al-Nasr son of Takiy al-Din 'Ali was born in 1327 to a family of notable Shafi'i scholars who originated in the town of Subk al-Dahhak in the southwest Nile delta of Egypt; hence the name al-Subki. He studied in Cairo and Damascus and served as a professor and judge in Damascus as well as preacher at the Umayyad Mosque. He was a passionate advocate for Shafi'i jurisprudence and Ash'ari theology, which by his day was embraced by most Shafi'i scholars. His most notable work is The Great Generations of Shafi'i Scholars, *a biographical dictionary of Shafi'i scholars from the ninth century until his day. The biographies of Shafi'i scholars who lived during the Crusader period are rich with details about scholarly life, relations between rulers and scholars, as well as the influence these Shafi'i scholars had on some members of the general public and their pronouncements on different aspects of Muslim–Frankish relations, such as wars, alliances, truces, trade, etc. He died in 1368 of plague.*[14]

As for al-Salih Isma'il, he had seen the honorable and respectful treatment the cleric al-'Izz son of 'Abd al-Salam had received from the Monarch al-Ashraf, and also the treatment he had received from the Sultan and Monarch al-Kamil—may God be merciful to him. So, al-Salih Isma'il appointed him as the preacher of the Umayyad Mosque in Damascus, a post he held for some time.

Then, the Egyptians declared their allegiance to the Monarch al-Salih Najm al-Din Ayyub and wrote to him to confirm it. He moved there and became ruler of Egypt; his treatment of its people was commendable. Al-Salih Isma'il, however, was so apprehensive and fearful of the Monarch al-Salih Ayyub that he could not sleep, eat, or drink. Thus, he made a treaty with the Franks on condition that they assist him against the Monarch al-Salih Najm al-Din Ayyub. In return, he gave them Sidon, the castle of Beaufort (*al-Shaqif*), and other Muslim forts. The Franks even came to Damascus to purchase arms to use to fight the faithful servants of God.

---

13. Taj al-Din al-Subki, *Tabaqat al-shafi'iyya al-kubra*, ed. M. 'Ata (Beirut: Dar al-Kutub al-'Ilmiyya, 1999), 4: 377–379.

14. On al-Subki, see J. Schacht and C. E. Bosworth, "al-Subki," *Encyclopaedia of Islam, Second Edition*.

3. Al-Subki's account of al-'Izz son of 'Abd al-Salam's directive

The permission to sell arms to the Franks annoyed the cleric immensely; so, too, those God-fearing individuals who traded in arms. They asked the cleric for his legal opinion about selling arms to the Franks. He replied: "It is prohibited that you sell them arms because you are certain they will use them to fight your Muslim brethren." He also repeatedly recited a prayer from the pulpit at the end of his sermons, namely: "O God, decree for this community a matter that guides it, and which strengthens your sovereign and humiliates your enemies. If followed, it will assure obedience to you and avert disobedience. May the people raise their supplication for the safety of the Muslims and the victory against the unbelieving enemies of God."

The heinous people wrote to the sovereign[15] (al-Salih Isma'il) about this, distorting and exaggerating what the cleric had said. So, he issued an order to arrest the cleric, who remained in confinement for some time. Then, al-Salih Isma'il returned from travel, and following some discussions and interferences from local notables, he ordered the release of the cleric, who stayed in Damascus for a short while and subsequently left for Jerusalem. Al-Nasir Dawud, however, knew of his move and met him on the way. He took him to Nablus where he stayed for a short while, during which al-'Izz son of 'Abd al-Salam counseled al-Nasir Dawud on several occasions. He then moved to Jerusalem and stayed there for a while.

Meanwhile, al-Salih Isma'il, the Monarch al-Mansur (Ibrahim) of Hims, and the Frankish princes arrived with their armies and troops at Jerusalem, on their way to attack Egypt. Al-Salih Isma'il dispatched one of his servants, carrying his scarf, and instructed him: "Give my scarf to the cleric, be most courteous to him, plead with him and promise him that he will be reinstated in his positions in the most favorable way. If he says yes, bring him to me. If he says no, detain him in a tent next to my tent."

When the envoy met with the cleric, he spoke to him in a gentle and friendly way, and said to him: "What is necessary for you to return to your previous posts and situation, and even more prestige, is to apologize to the sovereign, kiss his hand, and nothing more." He replied to him: "By God, you miserable person! I refuse that he should kiss my hand, let alone that I should kiss his! You people are in one world and I in another. Thanks be to God who saved me from that which he inflicted upon you." The envoy said to him: "Al-Salih Isma'il instructed me that either you agree to what he is

---

15. An Ayyubid regional ruler was referred to as "sultan," but this is different from the sultan who was the head of the Ayyubid realm. In order to avoid confusion, in all cases where the term does not refer to the actual sultan, it has been translated as "sovereign."

requesting from you or I have to detain you." He replied: "Do as you wish." So, he took him and detained him in a tent adjacent to the sovereign's tent.

As the cleric sat reciting the Qur'an every day, the sovereign was listening. One day, he said to the Frankish princes: "Do you hear this cleric who is reading the Qur'an?" They answered: "We do." He said: "This is the most prominent of Muslim priests.[16] I have detained him because he condemned me for giving you the Muslim forts. I fired him from his post as preacher of Damascus and other positions and expelled him from Damascus, so he came to Jerusalem. I renewed his detainment and imprisonment for your sake." The Frankish princes replied to him: "If he was a priest of ours, we would have washed his feet and drank the water."

Afterward, the Egyptian armies arrived, and almighty God's victory was granted to the community of Muhammad.[17] They slaughtered the army of the Franks, and God—most high and exalted—saved the cleric, who moved to Egypt. The Sultan and Monarch al-Salih Ayyub—may God be merciful to him—welcomed him and appointed him to be preacher of Fustat and the city's chief judge. He also entrusted him with the task of renovating the deserted mosques in Old Cairo. During this time, many remarkable and marvelous things happened to him, after which he removed himself from the court. The sultan—may God be merciful to him—appealed to him to return, so he did for a while, but then removed himself again and appealed to the sultan to approve the removal, which the sultan did, but he kept all his deputy judges in their posts and confirmed their tenure. He also appointed the cleric as head professor in Saladin's College in the noble city of Cairo.

Questions

1. What can we learn from al-Subki's account about the relationship between the two sovereigns, al-Salih Isma'il and Sultan al-Salih Ayyub?

2. According to al-Subki, why did al-'Izz issue his juridical directive?

---

16. It is interesting here that al-Salih Isma'il is alleged to have used the Christian term for priest (Arabic: *akbar qusus al-muslimin*).

17. Meaning the Muslims in their entirety.

3. Al-Subki's account of al-'Izz son of 'Abd al-Salam's directive

3. What can al-Subki's depiction of the negotiations between the sovereign al-Salih Isma'il and the scholar al-'Izz teach us about the relationship between sovereigns and scholars in this period?

4. Is al-Subki's depiction of al-'Izz positive or negative? How so?

5. What might this positive or negative depiction tell us about al-Subki's opinion of al-'Izz and the juridical directive he issued?

Chapter 2: Jihad Books and Juridical Directives

4. Ibn Taymiyya's juridical directive against the Shi'is[18]

Taqiy al-Din Ahmad Ibn Taymiyya was born in 1263, to a family of notable Hanbali scholars in Harran in southeast modern Turkey just north of the Syrian border. However, when he was seven years old, he moved to Damascus with his family in the wake of the Mongol advances against Harran. It was in Damascus that Ibn Taymiyya made a name for himself. As a prominent Hanbali jurist and theologian, Ibn Taymiyya was one of the most notable and prolific representatives of mainstream Sunni Islam in his day, and has remained so ever since. Ibn Taymiyya's arguments and rhetoric in his Collected Juridical Directives *and other writings echo normative beliefs in his day that reflected what some among the Sunni religious establishment believed to be the true teachings of God in the Qur'an and the Sunna of His Prophet Muhammad. They clearly reflect his Sunni supremacism in that he argued vehemently that not only were the various Shi'i sects in his day not Muslims, they were collaborators with the enemies of Islam (Franks and Mongols). Ibn Taymiyya's anti-Shi'i animus even led him to participate in the 1305 jihad campaign of the governor of Damascus against the Druzes and Shi'is of the coastal region and mountain range of modern-day Lebanon. However, Ibn Taymiyya's passionate denunciation of errant Muslims was not limited to Shi'is, Franks, and Mongols. He occasionally directed it against the Sunni Mamluk sultans of Egypt, which resulted in his periodic imprisonment by the authorities in Damascus as well as in Cairo during his sojourns in Egypt. In fact, it was during his final imprisonment in the Citadel of Damascus in 1328 that Ibn Taymiyya took ill and died.*[19]

※

The Isma'ilis, Nusayris, and Druzes are not Muslims in the judgment of all the sects of Islam, that is, in the opinion of the scholars, rulers, and public of the Hanafis, Malikis, Shafi'is, Hanbalis, and others. Fighting them is therefore lawful. The scholars even specified that their genealogy is false and that their ancestor was 'Ubayd Allah son of Maymun al-Qaddah,[20] who

---

18. Ibn Taymiyya, *Majmu' al-fatawa*, ed. M. 'Ata (Beirut: Dar al-Kutub al-'Ilmiyya, 2000), 16 (part 28): 279–280.

19. For a broad treatment of Ibn Taymiyya and his work, see the studies in Yossef Rapoport and Shahab Ahmed, eds., *Ibn Taymiyya and His Times* (Karachi: Oxford University Press, 2010).

20. That is, 'Abd Allah al-Mahdi bi-Allah (r. 909–934), the founder and first caliph of the Fatimid dynasty in North Africa. The Isma'ili Fatimids traced his genealogy back to the Prophet Muhammad.

was not from the lineage of the Messenger of God. The scholars also wrote about them many a compilation, such as the testimonies of Abu al-Husayn al-Quduri, the imam of the Hanafis;[21] Abu Hamid al-Isfarayini, the imam of the Shafi'is;[22] the judge Abu Ya'la, the imam of the Hanbalis;[23] and Abu Muhammad son of Abu Zayd, the imam of the Malikis.[24] The judge Abu Bakr son of al-Tayyib authored a book about the secretive Qarmatis and named it *Exposing the Secrets and Unveiling the Hidden*. Those of them—the Isma'ilis, Nusayris, Druzes, and others like them—who live in Muslim lands have aided the Mongols in their war against the Muslims. Indeed, Hulegu's vizier, al-Nusayr al-Tusi,[25] was one of their imams. Those are the most notorious enemies of the Muslims and Muslim rulers.

The Shi'i rejectionists come next, for they ally themselves with whoever fights the Sunnis.[26] They allied with the Mongols, and with the Christians. Indeed, there was in the coastal areas a truce between the Shi'i rejectionists and the Franks. The Shi'i rejectionists would ship to Cyprus Muslim horses and armor, as well as captive soldiers of the sultan and other fighters and young warriors. If the Muslims defeat the Mongols, they mourn and are saddened, but when the Mongols defeat the Muslims, they celebrate and rejoice. They were the ones who advised the Mongols to kill the 'Abbasid caliph and massacre the people of Baghdad. Indeed, it was the Shi'i

---

21. Abu al-Husayn Ahmad son of Muhammad al-Quduri (d. 1037) was a notable jurist who was the leader of the Hanafis in Iraq, which was the most prestigious position in Hanafi circles: see M. Ben Cheneb, "al-Kuduri," *Encyclopaedia of Islam, Second Edition*.

22. Abu Hamid Ahmad son of Muhammad al-Isfarayini (d. 1016) was the most notable Shafi'i jurist of Baghdad, and left a great legacy especially in Iraq, Khurasan, and Syria: see Claude Gilliot, "al-Isfarayini, Abu Hamid," *Encyclopaedia of Islam, Third Edition*.

23. Abu Ya'la Muhammad son of Muhammad Ibn al-Farra' (d. 1165) was a highly regarded Hanbali jurist from Baghdad, who was also highly esteemed by Hanbalis elsewhere: see Henri Laoust, "Ibn al-Farra'," *Encyclopaedia of Islam, Second Edition*.

24. Abu Muhammad 'Abd Allah son of Abu Zayd (d. 999) was an extremely influential Maliki jurist in Qayrawan (now in Tunisia) and North Africa, who, for his expertise and fame, was nicknamed the small Malik (to compare him to the founder of the Maliki branch of Sunni jurisprudence, Malik son of Anas): see Miklos Muranyi, "Ibn Abi Zayd al-Qayrawani," *Encyclopaedia of Islam, Third Edition*.

25. Nasir al-Din al-Tusi (1201–1274) was a tremendously influential Shi'i philosopher, mathematician, and astronomer, who became a close advisor to Hulegu: see H. Daiber and F. J. Rageb, "al-Tusi, Nasir al-Din," *Encyclopaedia of Islam, Second Edition*.

26. The term Ibn Taymiyya used here, *al-Rafida*, is a collective plural of *Rafidi*, which means "rejectionist; defector; renegade; turncoat" (e.g., from the true faith). It is a standard Sunni epithet for Shi'is. Hence, Ibn Taymiyya used it to refer to all Shi'is, whether Twelvers, Isma'ilis, Fatimids, or other Shi'i factions.

Chapter 2: Jihad Books and Juridical Directives

rejectionist vizier of Baghdad Ibn al-'Alqami[27] who, through deception and trickery, conspired against the Muslims and corresponded with the Mongols to incite them to conquer Iraq, and instruct people not to fight them.

Those knowledgeable about Islam know that the Shi'i rejectionists favor the enemies of religion. When they were the rulers of Cairo,[28] they once had a Jewish vizier,[29] and another time an Armenian Christian vizier.[30] The Christians became influential as a result of that Armenian Christian, and built numerous churches in Egypt during the reign of those hypocrite Shi'i rejectionists. The Christians would even dare to declare in the heart of Cairo that whoever curses or blasphemes against Islam is rewarded with a dinar and a measure of grain. Also, in their days, the Christians conquered the coastal region of Syria from the Muslims, until it was reconquered by Nur al-Din and Saladin. In their days too, the Crusaders attacked Bilbis (also spelled Bilbays) and defeated them. They are hypocrites, and the Christians are their advocates. God does not support the hypocrites who befriend the Christians. They pleaded with Nur al-Din to send them help, so he sent to them Asad al-Din Shirkuh and his nephew Saladin. When the conquering jihad fighters reached Egypt, the Shi'i rejectionists rose with the Christians to fight the Muslim jihad fighters, and then events unfolded, which people know, until Saladin killed their military leader Shawar. Then Islam and Sunnism reigned supreme, and the hadiths of the Messenger of God were read again in public, such as the collections of al-Bukhari, Muslim, and similar collections. Also, the traditions of the four imams were reestablished, and people would bless the rightly guided caliphs.[31] Before then, they were

---

27. Mu'ayyid al-Din Muhammad son of Muhammad Ibn al-'Alqami (d. 1259) was the Shi'i vizier of the last Sunni 'Abbasid Caliph al-Musta'sam (r. 1242–1258) in Baghdad. For another negative Sunni assessment of Ibn al-'Alqami where he is described as "the pig" (*al-khinzir*), see J. A. Boyle, "Ibn al-Alkami," *Encyclopaedia of Islam, Second Edition*.

28. Here he is using *al-Rafida* to refer specifically to the Fatimids.

29. This is a reference to Ibn Killis (d. 991), who was vizier under the Fatimid caliph al-'Aziz bi-Allah (r. 975–996). A convert from Judaism, Ibn Killis had a major role in the promotion of Isma'ili scholarship: see Paul E. Walker, "Ibn Killis," *Encyclopaedia of Islam, Third Edition*.

30. This is most likely a reference to Bahram (d. 1140), the Armenian Christian general who, during the reign of the Fatimid caliph al-Hafiz (r. 1130–1149), held the powerful office of "vizier of the sword" (1135–1137) and was honored with the honorific title "Sword of Islam" (*sayf al-islam*) even though he never converted. It could also be a reference to the influential vizier Badr al-Jamali (d. 1094), who was also originally Armenian but converted to Islam and served the Fatimid caliph al-Mustansir bi-Allah (r. 1036–1094). On Badr al-Jamali's son al-Afdal, see Chapter 3, p. 63 (footnote 10).

31. According to the Sunni tradition, the first four caliphs in Islam are referred to as the Rashidun or "Rightly Guided" caliphs. According to the Shi'i tradition, the first three caliphs were illegitimate usurpers of the fourth caliph 'Ali's rightful position as Muhammad's successor.

4. Ibn Taymiyya's juridical directive against the Shiʿis

the most evil of people. Among them were groups who worshipped the planets and practiced astronomy, and unbelievers who worshipped time and believed neither in the hereafter, heaven or hell, nor in the exigency of praying, paying alms, fasting, and making the pilgrimage. Best among them were the Shiʿi rejectionists, who are the worst people among those who follow the direction of prayer.

Questions

1. According to Ibn Taymiyya, why are Ismaʿilis, Nusayris, and Druzes not Muslims?
2. What examples of malfeasance does Ibn Taymiyya charge them and others like them with?
3. What are Ibn Taymiyya's complaints against the Shiʿi rejectionists in general and the Fatimids in particular?
4. Why would Ibn Taymiyya spend so much time denouncing the Fatimids in his juridical directive when they were defeated by Saladin in 1171, and had been out of power for more than a century prior to Ibn Taymiyya issuing the directive?

Chapter Three
Chronicles, Memoirs, and Poetry

1. Ibn al-Athir on the emergence of the Franks[1]

Ibn al-Athir (1160–1233) was born in Jazirat Ibn ʿUmar in northern Mesopotamia—Gizre in southeastern modern-day Turkey, just north of the border with eastern Syria. He hailed from a well-to-do scholarly family that rose to positions of influence with the Zangid rulers of Mosul, and later with their Ayyubid successors. In his early twenties, he settled in Mosul with his father, where he devoted himself to his studies, specifically the history of the Islamic tradition. Although he spent most of his adult life in Mosul, he visited Baghdad often. For a time, he traveled with Saladin's army in Syria and later spent time in Aleppo and Damascus. Ibn al-Athir's The Complete History *depicts the Crusades in Syria and Egypt as part of a much larger Frankish assault on Islam and Muslims that had started in Spain and Sicily and subsequently reached Islam's heartland. The Complete History and Ibn al-Athir's other historical work*—The Dazzling History of the Zangid State, *which is a history of the Zangid rulers of Mosul from 1084 to 1210—are among the most important sources for the Islamic world during the Crusader period.*[2]

The emergence of the kingdom of the Franks, consolidation of their strength, their march against the lands of Islam and their occupation of some of it began in 478 (1085), when they captured the city of Toledo and others in the land of Andalusia,[3] the description of which has been

---

1. Ibn al-Athir, *al-Kamil fi al-Taʾrikh*, ed. ʿU. Tadmuri (Beirut: Dar al-Kitab al-ʿArabi, 1997), 9: 13–15.
2. On Ibn al-Athir, see François Micheau, "Ibn al-Athir," in *Medieval Muslim Historians of the Franks in the Levant*, ed. A. Mallett (Leiden, 2014), 52–83.
3. Andalusia (*al-Andalus* in Arabic) is the name the Arabs gave to the Iberian Peninsula (today Spain and Portugal). Today, the name Andalusia is given to the southernmost province in Spain.

mentioned earlier. Then, in the year 484 (1091), they sought the island of Sicily and captured it, which I have mentioned too. Subsequently, they ventured into parts of North Africa[4] and captured some of it, which was taken back from them, and then they captured other parts as you shall see.

When the year 490 (1097) came, they attacked Syria. The reason for their attack was that their king, Baldwin, gathered a large crowd of the Franks—he was a kinsman of Roger the Frank who had captured Sicily. He sent to Roger saying to him: "I have gathered a large crowd and am on my way to you, and from your land I shall proceed to North Africa to conquer it and be your neighbor." Roger convened his companions and asked their council about the matter. They said: "By the truth of the Gospel, this is good for us and for them. The land shall become Christian land." He lifted his leg and produced a loud fart, and said: "By the truth of my religion, this fart is better than your council." They said: "How is that?" He replied: "If they were to come to me, I should incur a huge expense and need boats to haul them to North Africa, as well as troops of my own. If they were to conquer the land, it would be theirs, and their provisions would have to come from Sicily. Thus, all my revenues levied every year from the value of harvest would cease. If they were to fail, they would return to my land and I would be harmed by them. Tamim[5] would also say to me: 'You betrayed me and broke our treaty.' Contacts and travel between us would cease. The land of North Africa is there for us, we can take it when we have enough strength."

Roger summoned the envoy and said to him: "If you intend to wage jihad against the Muslims, the best way is to conquer Jerusalem and rescue it from their hands. You would then have glory. As for North Africa, there are oaths and treaties between me and its people."

Hence, they prepared and marched against Syria. It has been said that the Fatimid rulers of Egypt were terrified after they saw the strength and power of the Seljuks and their occupation of Syria all the way to Gaza, and that there remained no territory to bar them from Egypt. They were equally panicked when al-Aqsis[6] tried to attack Egypt and blockaded it. So,

---

4. *Ifriqiya* in Arabic. It is the name the Arabs gave to what is today Tunisia, northwest Libya, and northeast Algeria—the same region the ancient Romans referred to as Africa, from which the Arabic term *Ifriqiya* is derived. It is also the name for the continent of Africa in modern Arabic.

5. Sultan Tamim son of al-Mu'izz of Tunis (r. 1062 –1108).

6. Al-Aqsis was the popular name of the Seljuk commander Atsiz (d. 1079), who captured Jerusalem from the Fatimids in 1071, and proceeded unsuccessfully to attack Egypt. He subsequently returned to Jerusalem and committed a massacre there against its Muslim population.

1. Ibn al-Athir on the emergence of the Franks

they sent to the Franks, inviting them to march against Syria and capture it, and become a barrier between them and the Muslims. But God knows best.

When the Franks embarked toward Syria, they traveled to Constantinople in order to cross the strait to the lands of the Muslims and then travel by land because it was easier for them. When they arrived, the king of Byzantium barred them from crossing his lands. He said: "I will not let you cross to the lands of Islam unless you swear to me that you will hand over Antioch to me." His intention was to exhort them to march against the land of Islam, thinking that the Turkomans, seeing how fierce they were and their intent to capture the Muslim lands, would not spare a single one of them. The Franks consented to that and crossed the strait at Constantinople in the year 490 (1097).

Questions

1. How does Ibn al-Athir, writing a century after the fact, depict the beginning of the Crusader enterprise?
2. How does he depict Roger of Sicily's perception of the Crusader enterprise?
3. According to Ibn al-Athir, why was Roger concerned about his good relations with his Muslim neighbors?
4. How does he portray the reaction of the Byzantine emperor to the Franks' arrival in Constantinople?

Chapter 3: Chronicles, Memoirs, and Poetry

2. Ibn al-Qalanisi on the capture of Antioch, Maʿarrat al-Nuʿman, and Jerusalem, and the attack against Ascalon in 1098–1099[7]

Abu Yaʾla Hamza son of Asad al-Tamimi, known as Ibn al-Qalanisi (ca. 1073–1160), was a learned and cultured author and litterateur who belonged to a notable Damascene family, which had played important roles in the administration of Damascus. His A Short Survey of the History of Damascus (Dhayl taʾrikh Dimashq) *is one of the most important chronicles for the history of Damascus and Syria from 1048 down to the year of his own death in 1160. We do not know much about his life and specific activities, and very likely his book on Damascus, which many scholars mistook as a continuation of an earlier work titled* The History of Damascus, *is actually an independent work; the word "dhayl," which can mean "continuation," is also used to designate a short survey or treatise. Nevertheless, Ibn al-Qalanisi's* Short Survey *is one of the most important Arabic chronicles for the early Crusader period and his eyewitness accounts of events of his own lifetime, including the Second Crusade's siege of Damascus in 1148 and Nur al-Din's entry into the city in 1154. He is also a valuable source for his commentary on the character and behavior of the Franks as well as the Muslim ruling dynasties of his day (Fatimids, Burids, and Zangids).*[8]

The Year 491 (9 December 1097–28 November 1098)

At the end of Jumada I of this year (beginning of May 1098), word came that certain men of Antioch who were armorers for commander Yaghi Siyan conspired with the Franks to hand over to them the city. The reason was an offense that Yaghi Siyan had committed against them and his confiscation of their belongings. They found an opportunity to do so with a tower on the city wall adjacent to the mountain, which they betrayed to the Franks. At night, they allowed the Franks to enter the city through it, and at dawn, the Franks launched their attack. Yaghi Siyan fled with a large entourage, but not a single one of them survived. When Yaghi Siyan reached the

---

7. Ibn al-Qalanisi, *Taʾrikh Ibn al-Qalanisi*, ed. H. F. Amedroz (Beirut: Jesuit Press, 1908), 135–137.

8. On Ibn al-Qalanisi and his *Dhayl taʾrikh Dimashq*, see Niall Christie, "Ibn al-Qalanisi," in *Medieval Historians and the Franks in the Levant*, ed. A. Mallett (Leiden: Brill, 2014), 7–28. See also H. A. R. Gibb, *The Damascus Chronicle of the Crusades: Extracted and Translated from the Chronicle of Ibn Al-Qalanisi* (Mineola: Dover Publications, 2002 [1932]).

2. Ibn al-Qalanisi on the capture of Antioch, Ma'arrat al-Nu'man, and Jerusalem

town of Armanaz, which is a village near Ma'arrat Misrin,[9] he fell from his horse. One of his companions picked him up and put him back on the horse, but he could not balance himself and fell off again and died—may God be merciful to him.

As for Antioch, the number of men, women, and children who were killed, captured, or enslaved there is incalculable. Around 3,000 fled to the citadel and fortified themselves there. Only those whom God destined to live survived.

In Sha'ban of this year (July 1098), word came that al-Afdal,[10] commander of the Egyptian army, had departed with a massive force heading for Syria. He laid siege to Jerusalem, which was controlled by the commanders Suqman and Il-Ghazi, sons of Urtuq, as well as a retinue of their kinfolk, soldiers, and a large group of Turkomans. He wrote to them imploring them to cede to him Jerusalem without war or bloodshed. They refused to do so. He attacked the city with mangonels, which destroyed a part of its wall and allowed him to capture the city. Suqman handed over to him the Tower of David. When his control of the city was secured, he was kind and generous to them, and released them with their men. They arrived in Damascus sometime in the first 10 days of Shawwal (1–10 September 1098). Al-Afdal returned with his troops to Egypt.

In this year too, the Franks marched with all their numbers against Ma'arrat al-Nu'man. They laid siege to it on 29 Dhu al-Hijja (27 November 1098), attacking it with towers and scaling ladders.

The Franks captured the city of Antioch by means of a plot made with an Armenian armorer called Nayruz.[11] This happened on the eve of Friday, the first day of Rajab (Thursday, 3 June 1098).[12] News of what had occurred spread quickly. An incalculable number of troops from Syria gathered and headed to the area of Antioch in order to fight the Frankish army. They besieged the Franks there until their food supplies ran out and they were forced to eat carrion. Despite their extreme weakness, they made an assault against the armies of Islam, which had great strength and massive

---

9. Armanaz and Ma'arrat Misrin are towns today in the Idlib province in northwestern Syria, near the border with Turkey.

10. That is, al-Afdal son of Badr al-Jamali. His father, Badr al-Jamali, was appointed vizier (1073–1094) by the eighth Fatimid caliph, al-Mustansir bi-Allah (r. 1036–1094). He was a Christian Armenian who converted to Shi'i Islam. Al-Afdal succeeded his father as vizier in 1094, a position he held until he was assassinated in 1124.

11. In Ibn al-Athir, the name of the armorer is Ruzaba.

12. In the Islamic calendar, the day starts on what today is customarily considered the evening of the previous day. Hence, the eve of Friday is Thursday evening.

numbers. Yet they defeated the Muslims and dispersed their multitudes. Those on swift horses fled, whereas the volunteers and jihad fighters who were eager to wage jihad and protect the Muslims were slaughtered. This occurred on Tuesday, 6 of Rajab of this year (9 June 1098).[13]

The Year 492 (29 November 1098–17 November 1099)

In Muharram of this year (early December 1098), the Franks made an assault against the wall of Ma'arrat al-Nu'man from the east and the north. When they placed their wooden tower against the wall, it was so tall, it exposed the Muslims who were stationed there. The fighting for control of the wall continued until sunset on the 14th of Muharram (12 December 1098). It was then that they scaled the wall and the locals deserted it and fled. Envoys from the Franks came to them asking to settle things and to hand over the city in return for the security of the people's lives and property. They also promised to let in food supplies. This did not happen, however, because of the disagreement among the city's inhabitants and what almighty God had preordained and decreed. They captured the town following the evening prayer. On that day, a large crowd of people from both sides were killed. The townsfolk sought refuge in the houses of the city, and the Franks assured them of safety but then betrayed them. They raised the crosses over the rooftops, imposed on the townsfolk excessive fees, and did not honor any of their agreements. They looted everything they could find and forced people to hand over sums of money beyond their means. On Thursday, 17 Safar (13 January 1099), they left for Kafartab (Capharda).

Thereafter, at the end of Rajab of this year (mid-June 1099), the Franks marched toward Jerusalem, and the locals fled their villages in panic. First, they laid siege to Ramla and captured it during the time of harvest. Next, they moved against Jerusalem and fought its inhabitants and besieged them. They also set up their wooden tower against the wall. Word came to them that al-Afdal had departed Egypt with a massive army to fight them and save and protect the city from them. So, the Franks renewed their assault more vigorously and unceasingly until the end of the day. They pretended to retire as if their plan was to renew their attack the next morning. Thinking it would be so, the defenders left their positions on the wall at sunset. But the Franks resumed their attack, climbed their tower, and gained a foothold

---

13. It is likely that the date is wrong. Ibn al-Qalanisi could have meant 26 Rajab (29 June), which was a Tuesday; 6 Rajab (9 June) was a Wednesday. The battle according to Crusader chronicles took place on the 28th of June.

on the city's wall. The townsfolk fled, and the Franks stormed the city and captured it. Some inhabitants sought refuge in the Tower of David. Many people were killed. The Franks gathered the Jews in the synagogue and burned it down. The Tower was handed over to them on an assurance of safety for those inside on 22 Sha'ban of this year (15 July 1099). But they destroyed the shrines and the tomb of Abraham—peace be upon him.

When al-Afdal arrived with the Egyptian army it was too late. The soldiers who had been stationed on the coast joined him and he returned to camp outside Ascalon on the 14th of Ramadan (4 August 1099). There, he awaited the arrival of the Fatimid fleet by sea and the Bedouin soldiers. The army of the Franks, however, hurried and attacked him with a large force. The Egyptian army retreated to Ascalon, and al-Afdal took refuge in the city. The Franks slaughtered the Muslims, killing approximately 10,000 people—foot soldiers, volunteers, and townsfolk. They also looted the army camp. When al-Afdal withdrew with his retinue back to Egypt, the Franks again laid siege to Ascalon until both parties agreed that a payment of 20,000 dinars would be sent to them. As the sum was being collected from the inhabitants, a quarrel broke out among the Frankish leaders and they left without having collected any of the money. It was said that the number of civilians in Ascalon who were killed during this battle—visitors and inhabitants, merchants and youths—was 2,700 persons, not counting those from the villages around it.

Questions

1. How might the fact that Ibn al-Qalanisi is a contemporary of the events described in this section affect his description of events?
2. How does he depict the Turkoman commander, Yaghi Siyan?
3. How does he depict the Egyptian commander, al-Afdal?
4. How does he depict the Franks?
5. What role does God play in Ibn al-Qalanisi's description of events?
6. What role do oaths play in Ibn al-Qalanisi's description of events?
7. What did the Franks, according to Ibn al-Qalanisi, do to the inhabitants of the cities they occupied?

3. Ibn al-Athir on the capture of Jerusalem and the attack against Ascalon[14]

Ibn al-Athir included a lengthy poem by Abu al-Muzaffar Muhammad son of Ahmad al-Abiwardi in his account of the capture of Jerusalem. Al-Abiwardi (ca. 1064–1113) was a specialist in the genealogies of Arab tribes but is most renowned as a poet. He was born in the village of Kufan near Abiward in Khurasan, just north of the modern-day border between Afghanistan and Turkmenistan. He claimed descent from the Umayyads, but this was disputed. As a young man he moved to Baghdad, where he worked in the service of the Seljuk grand vizier, Nizam al-Mulk (r. 1063–1092), and gained favor at the court because of his skills as a poet. At some point he was appointed head of the library at the great Nizamiyya College there. He was subsequently appointed to the office of Protector of the Honorable Members of the Prophet Muhammad's Household (wali al-ashraf) in Isfahan, where one day in September 1113, he collapsed and died in front of the Seljuk Sultan Muhammad I (r. 1105–1118). He had been apparently poisoned, but no names of who might have poisoned him nor reasons why he should have been poisoned are given. Al-Abiwardi wrote several works on history, genealogy, and other subjects, which are now lost. All that has survived is a Diwan *of poetry which was collected after his death in 1113.*[15]

The Capture of Jerusalem by the Franks—may God curse them

Jerusalem had been under the control of Taj al-Dawla (Crown of the Realm) Tutush, who appointed the Turkoman commander Suqman son of Urtuq to administer it. When the Franks defeated the Turkomans at Antioch, killing many of them, the Turkomans weakened and dispersed. The Egyptians saw the weakness of the Turkomans and decided to march against Jerusalem. Their commander was al-Afdal son of Badr al-Jamali.[16] They laid siege to the city, and among those besieged were the commanders Suqman and Il-Ghazi, sons of Urtuq, their cousin Suwanj, and their nephew Yaquti.

---

14. Ibn al-Athir, *al-Kamil fi al-ta'rikh*, 8: 424–428. For biographical information on Ibn al-Athir, see p. 59.

15. On al-Abiwardi, see Geert Jan van Gelder, "al-Abiwardi," *Encyclopaedia of Islam, Third Edition*. Diwan is the Arabic term for a collection of poetry or prose. It is also used for a register of persons or accounts as well as for a state administrative office where correspondences and chancery documents are written or stored.

16. On al-Afdal, see Chapter 3, p. 63 (footnote 10).

3. Ibn al-Athir on the capture of Jerusalem and the attack against Ascalon

The Egyptians arrayed against the city more than forty mangonels, which destroyed several parts of its wall. The inhabitants fought them; the fighting and siege lasted more than forty days. Finally, in Shaʿban 489 (25 July–22 August 1096), the Egyptians were able to capture Jerusalem on the condition they grant safe conduct to the defenders of the city. Al-Afdal was generous toward Suqman and Il-Ghazi and those with them. He gave them generous gifts, and let them go on their way. They left for Damascus, and then proceeded to cross the Euphrates; Suqman decided to stay in Edessa whereas Il-Ghazi went back to Iraq.

The Egyptians appointed over Jerusalem a man called Iftikhar al-Dawla (Pride of the Realm). He stayed there until the Franks attacked it, following their failed siege against Acre. When they arrived outside Jerusalem, they laid siege to it for more than forty days. They set up two wooden towers against its wall, one from the direction of Mount Zion, which the Muslims were able to burn down, killing those inside. No sooner had it burnt down than a person arrived from the other side of the city pleading for help as it had been captured. Indeed, the Franks captured Jerusalem from the north on Friday morning, the 23rd of Shaʿban (15 July 1099).[17] The people were put to the sword; the Franks spent a whole week killing the Muslims in the city. A group of Muslims sought refuge in the Tower of David, closed themselves in it, and resisted for 3 days. After the Franks promised them safe conduct—which they honored—they handed it over and departed at night for Ascalon where they settled.

The Franks then attacked the Aqsa Sanctuary where they killed more than 70,000 persons, including a large number of prayer leaders and scholars, worshipers and ascetics, even those who had left their native homelands specifically to come to dwell on that noble spot.[18] The Franks confiscated from the Dome of the Rock more than forty silver lamps, each lamp weighing 3,600 dirhams. They also took 150 smaller hollow lamps and more than twenty golden lamps. The booty they looted from there is incalculable.

---

17. Since ancient times, attacks against Jerusalem usually came from the north and occasionally from the area of Mount Zion to the south. The valleys to the east, south, and west of the city made it difficult to amass a successful siege from those directions. See Eric H. Cline, *Jerusalem Besieged: From Ancient Canaan to Modern Israel* (Ann Arbor: University of Michigan Press, 2005).

18. Dwelling in mosques and sanctuaries was and remains a popular social and religious habit in the Muslim world (a common practice in other religious traditions as well). One can envision in the case of Jerusalem that in addition to pilgrims, many locals, especially elderly people, and mystics spent a large part of their day on the Haram. See pp. 120, 128.

Chapter 3: Chronicles, Memoirs, and Poetry

In the month of Ramadan (22 July–20 August 1099), a delegation from Damascus, led by the judge Abu Sa'id al-Harawi, arrived in Baghdad pleading for help. In the caliph's court, they recounted what had happened, causing eyes to weep and hearts to ache. On Friday, they went to the mosque and summoned people to rescue Jerusalem. They wept and brought everyone to tears as they described what had happened to the Muslims in the noble and revered city: the slaughter of men, the enslavement of women and children, the looting of wealth. They were so overcome with weeping that they broke their fast. The caliph ordered that the judge Abu Muhammad al-Damaghani, Abu Bakr al-Shashi, Abu al-Qasim al-Zanjani, Abu al-Wafa Ibn 'Aqil, Abu Sa'd al-Hulwani, and Abu al-Husayn Ibn Simmak depart for Syria. But when they reached Hulwan,[19] they were told about the assassination of Majd al-Mulk al-Balasani,[20] which will be narrated later, so they returned without having achieved their destination or fulfilled their mission.

The Muslim leaders were preoccupied with their internal quarrels, which allowed the Franks to capture the land. Abu al-Muzaffar al-Abiwardi composed a poem about that, which includes the following verses:

1- Such blood and weeping have we shed / that none is fit to show pity.[21]
2- For weeping is man's worst weapon / when the embers of war enflame swords.
3- O Sons of Islam, beyond you / battles unfold, and heads roll.
4- And you: resting in safety, delighting in life / placid as blossoming trees.
5- How can the eye slumber serenely / amidst disasters that awaken every sleeper?
6- Your brothers in Syria, their eyes only dim / on the backs of old mounts or in the bellies of hyenas.
7- The Romans[22] parade them in humiliation, while you / gallivant about in peace, carefree.
8- So much blood has been spilt, even that of beautiful women / who lift their hands to cover their faces.
9- The blades of white swords have turned red / the pointy brown tips of spears are stained with gore.

---

19. A town north of Baghdad.
20. Majd al-Mulk al-Balasani was a senior administrator in the Seljuk Empire, and became vizier (1097–1099) for the Seljuk Sultan Barkiyaruq (1092–1105). He was Twelver Shi'i.
21. The point here is that weeping had made them pitiful, thus unable to show pity.
22. The general term used to refer to both Byzantines and Europeans. In Arabic, it is *al-Rum*.

3. Ibn al-Athir on the capture of Jerusalem and the attack against Ascalon

10- Sight of the bludgeoned and the impaled / turn the boy's hair white.

11- Whosoever flees these wars / for safety will gnash his teeth in shame.

12- The unbelievers' swords are drawn / to be sheathed in necks and skulls.

13- Seeing such carnage, the one entombed in Medina[23] screams / from the top of his lungs: "O, family of Hashim!"[24]

14- I see my compatriots balk at raising / their lances; Islam has lost its pillars.

15- They fear death and flee the inferno of war / but they forget that shame is an indelible stain.

16- Why do Arab heroes accept such humiliation / and non-Arab stalwarts turn a blind eye to disgrace!

The poem also includes:

17- If they will not fight in defense / of religion, let them at least fight for the honor of women.

18- If they dismiss the eternal reward of such a battle / let them embrace the promise of plunder.

19- Should they be paraded by their nose rings / they would still sneeze only reluctantly.

20- We implore you, war hastens / to us, like circling vultures.

21- We seek a true Arab attack / that compels the Romans to regret their folly for ages to come.

22- If you still cannot be moved to act / then let us surrender our wives to our enemies.

The War between the Franks and the Egyptians

In Ramadan of this year (22 July–20 August 1099), a battle took place between the Egyptian army and the Franks. The reason for it was that when the Egyptians heard what happened to the people of Jerusalem, the commander of the army, al-Afdal, assembled a large force and marched to Ascalon. He sent an envoy to the Franks denouncing what they had done

---

23. That is, the Prophet Muhammad.
24. A reference to the 'Abbasid caliph. The 'Abbasid caliphs were descendants of the Prophet Muhammad's uncle al-'Abbas, and like the Prophet, belonged to the Hashim clan of Quraysh.

and threatened them. They sent the envoy back with their reply and then set out after him. They attacked the Egyptians shortly after the envoy had reached the camp. The Egyptians were shocked by the Franks' arrival. They were unaware of their movement and were unprepared to fight. They immediately called on their cavalry to mount up and to don their armor, but the Franks attacked them quickly and routed them. They killed many of them and looted what they found in the camp: money, weapons, etc. Al-Afdal fled to Ascalon, while a number of his troops fled and hid among the sycamore trees, which were abundant in that area. The Franks set fire to some of the trees, burning those hiding in them. They also killed those who tried to escape. Al-Afdal retreated with his retinue to Egypt; the Franks laid siege to Ascalon and pressed their advantage. The town's inhabitants paid them 12,000 dinars—some said 20,000—and they returned to Jerusalem.

Questions

1. How does Ibn al-Athir, writing a century after the fact, depict the conquest of Jerusalem and the war between the Franks and Egyptians at Ascalon?

2. How is his account similar to and dissimilar to the account of Ibn al-Qalanisi, who was a contemporary of these events?

3. What role does God play in Ibn al-Athir's description of events?

4. What role do oaths play in Ibn al-Athir's description of events?

5. Why would Ibn al-Athir include Abu al-Muzaffar al-Abiwardi's poem in his account?

6. What argument is al-Abiwardi making in his poem? And what examples does he use to make his case?

4. Al-ʿAzimi on the Battle of the Field of Blood (1119) and several events between 1108 and 1141

Abu ʿAbd Allah Muhammad son of ʿAli son of Muhammad al-Tanukhi al-ʿAzimi (ca. 1090–after 1161) was a poet, scholar, and schoolmaster in Aleppo. Around 1140, he joined the entourage of ʿImad al-Din Zangi (r. 1127–1146), the ruler of Aleppo and northern Mesopotamia. Zangi was al-ʿAzimi's patron until his death in 1146. Al-ʿAzimi wrote three works of history, but only one has survived, History of Aleppo, *a concise work that focuses on the history of the biblical prophets down to Muhammad as well as a short survey of Islamic history down to 1144, with a specific focus on the city of Aleppo and its surroundings. It is a valuable source of the period as many of the events that it describes are not mentioned in other works, especially for the final five decades covered in the book. Al-ʿAzimi was the earliest Muslim source to indicate that the justification of war* (casus belli) *for the Franks' incursions into northern Mesopotamia and Syria was because Christian pilgrims had been prevented from entering Jerusalem in the year 486 (1093–1094). He also attributed the Franks' success against the superior Muslim armies in Antioch to the Muslims' bad intentions.*[25]

Year 502 (August 1108–July 1109)[26]

The wife of the Monarch Ridwan[27] died. Jawuli[28] captured the cultivated lands around Balis. Following a siege of 7 years, the Franks captured Tripoli on 2 Dhu al-Hijja (3 July 1109). Aq-Sunqur al-Bursuqi[29] captured al-Rahba,[30]

---

25. On al-ʿAzimi, see Taef El-Azhari, "al-ʿAzimi," *Encyclopaedia of Islam, Third Edition*; and *Taʾrikh Halab*, ed. I. Zaʿrur (Damascus: n.p., 1984); "La chronique abrégée d'al-ʿAzimi," ed. C. Cahen, *Journal Asiatique* 230 (1938): 353–448.
26. Al-ʿAzimi, *Taʾrikh Halab*, 364.
27. Seljuk Sultan of Aleppo (1095–1113).
28. A commander in the army of the Seljuk Sultan Ghiyath al-Din (Rescuer of the Religion) Muhammad (r. 1105–1118), who was dispatched to fight the Franks.
29. A Turkoman commander in the Seljuk army, who became chief commander (*atabeg*) of Mosul (1113–1114 and 1124–1126). On *atabeg*, see note 31 below.
30. An important citadel town on the Euphrates, in eastern Syria today near the city of Dayr al-Zur.

and joined forces with the chief commander (*atabeg*)[31] of Damascus and they jointly defeated the Franks of Tripoli. Tancred[32] captured the fort of Balatunus[33] and entrusted it to the Mazawirs.[34] The Franks captured Jabala after guaranteeing the people's safety. They also took Latakia from the Byzantines under a similar agreement. Ibn 'Ammar[35] arrived in Damascus. Buri Khan[36] and 'Asab al-Dawla Abaq[37] died in Damascus.

Year 503 (July 1109–July 1110)[38]

The Franks captured Beirut by force. Tancred captured the fort of Bikisra'il (Bikisrail)[39] and attacked the inhabited lands around al-Atharib[40] whose castle was surrendered to him. A meteor with a short tail appeared in the northern skies, causing the death of every tailed creature, even the fish in the water. Mawdud[41] brought his sheep to graze in the farmlands around Edessa, so the Franks came out, attacked him and killed them. Ibn Sulayman[42] fled from the sultan's army but his cousin was killed. On 19 Rajab (3 February 1110), the Muslims were defeated in al-Lukamiyya.[43] The chief commander Tughtakin[44] took Baalbek from his officer Kumashtakin al-Taji[45] in Ramadan (24 March–21 April 1110).

---

31. Tughtakin, who ruled between 1104 and 1128. *Atabeg* was a title used by members of the Seljuk ruling dynasty and their senior commanders who were appointed to rule major districts. It literally means "fatherly master." We have translated *atabeg* as "chief commander" throughout to distinguish it from *amir*, which we have translated as "commander."
32. The Frankish regent of Antioch between 1100 and 1112.
33. A fort east of Latakia.
34. It is not known what specific group this term signifies.
35. The former ruler of Tripoli (1099–1109).
36. We could not find any information about this person.
37. A senior local commander. In al-'Azimi's text, the name appears as Urtuq, which is a scribal error. The honorific title 'Asab al-Dawla means "Spine of the Realm."
38. Al-'Azimi, *Ta'rikh Halab*, 364–365.
39. A fort in the mountains near Jabala in northwestern Syria.
40. A town between Antioch and Aleppo.
41. A Turkoman commander in the Seljuk army, who became chief commander of Mosul (1109–1113).
42. Malik Shah, who was the son of Qilij Arslan (r. 1092–1107) and was held prisoner by the Seljuk Sultan. He became Sultan of Anatolia (r. 1110–1116).
43. Probably a reference to the mountains overlooking Latakia.
44. See footnote 31.
45. Senior commander in the Seljuk army, who was appointed as ruler of several cities.

4. Al-ʿAzimi on the Battle of the Field of Blood (1119)

Year 513 (April 1119–March 1120)—"The Battle of the Field of Blood"[46]

Najm al-Din[47] and Ibn Husam al-Dawla[48] routed the Franks of Antioch at Tall ʿAfrin, and none of the Franks escaped. Al-ʿAzimi said: "I composed a poem encouraging Najm al-Din to take on the Franks; it includes these verses:

1- Declare to tyrants of polytheism that you will / exact our revenge and even more on them.

2- That no one will survive to recount / how your traps ensnared them from every direction.

By God, the event unfolded as I described, for poetry is a good omen."[49] Only ten wounded Franks escaped, but when they reached Antioch they died. The Muslims lost fewer than ten of their men. Najm al-Din took the castle al-Atharib, and after that he laid siege to the fort of Zardana[50] and captured it.

Another Frankish army came and fought Najm al-Din at Danith.[51] It was a marvelous battle, and most of the Franks were either injured or killed. In Muharram (April–May 1119), there was a solar eclipse. Large hail fell on the coastal areas. The Franks were defeated at the Orontes valley[52] and the man with a large beard[53] was captured and killed by the chief commander Tughtakin. The judge Ibn ʿAmmar[54] was arrested and punished, and his estate was confiscated. A flood hit Armenian Cilicia, destroying its

---

46. Al-ʿAzimi, *Taʾrikh Halab*, 369–370.
47. His name was Il-Ghazi. He was a Turkoman commander in the Seljuk army, who became lord of Mardin, which is in southeastern Turkey today. He, along with his brother Suqman, ruled Jerusalem and surrendered it in 1098 to the Fatimids. See Ibn al-Qalanisi, p. 63; and Ibn al-Athir, pp. 66–67.
48. Chief commander Tughtakin of Damascus. See p. 72 (footnote 31). Husam al-Dawla is an honorific title meaning "Sword of the Realm."
49. Literally: "Indeed, poetry does not lie." This was none other than the infamous Battle of the Field of Blood (*Ager Sanguinis*) on 28 June 1119. It was the first major Muslim victory over the Franks by local commanders.
50. To the west of Aleppo.
51. A site southwest of Aleppo, near the town of Sarmin.
52. The Battle of Hab, which took place on 14 August 1119, was not a Muslim victory as al-ʿAzimi alleged. The Muslim armies retreated and the Franks were able to reclaim several towns and fortresses.
53. Possibly a reference to Roger of Salerno, regent of Antioch (1112–1119), who was killed at the Battle of the Field of Blood, and whose head was allegedly taken to Baghdad after the battle.
54. Former ruler of Tripoli (1099–1109), see p. 72 (footnote 35).

countryside. A battle took place between Sanjar and his nephew Mahmud,[55] and the latter escaped to Isfahan, but later, he came back to his uncle Sanjar. He reconciled with him and married his daughter. Shams al-Din, son of the chief commander Kumashtakin, died. Yaman[56] led the Pilgrimage caravan to Mecca.

Year 535 (August 1140–August 1141)[57]

The army of Damascus and the Franks departed after their unification against Zangi.[58] Lightning struck the new bathhouse in Hims, burning it and killing a number of people. The ruler of Balis,[59] Sunqur al-Jakurmushi, who was a commander in the army of the chief commander Zangi, fled to Damascus. The chief commander reacted by seizing Sunqur's family and possessions.

On Saturday, 19 Rabi' I (2 November 1140), the chief commander entered Hims. The Lady Zumurrud[60] returned to Aleppo on the 20th of Rabi' I (3 November 1140). On 24 Jumada I (5 January 1141), the chief commander came to Aleppo; after that he marched east to fight Qufjaq[61] and annihilated him. In Shawwal (10 May–8 June 1141), Ibn al-Danishmand[62] seized the city of Mir'ish[63] and captured a castle there, enslaving its people. This was his answer to the Franks doing the same in his land.

In Aleppo, the inspector al-Makin son of Abu al-Fihm al-Harrani was arrested. Also, 300 soldiers were dispatched to the east for military service. The commander Sayf al-Din Suwar[64] defeated the Franks who were

---

55. Mahmud was the son of the Seljuk Sultan Muhammad (r. 1105–1118); Sanjar (r. 1118–1153) was the Sultan's brother and successor.

56. Possibly an officer in the court of the 'Abbasid caliph.

57. Al-'Azimi, *Ta'rikh Halab*, 395.

58. In 1140, Zangi tried to lay siege to Damascus but his military venture failed in the face of the alliance between Damascus and the Franks.

59. Barbalissos in Greek, Balis was a city near the Euphrates, not far from Aleppo, known for its fortified castle.

60. *Khatun*, which was an honorific title for wives and daughters of sultans and other local sovereigns of Turkoman and Kurdish origin. Zumurrud, who was given in marriage to Zangi, was the mother of Shihab al-Din Mahmud, the Burid ruler of Damascus (r. 1135–1139).

61. A Turkoman commander.

62. Muhammad son of Gumushtagin, who was the leader of an area in north-central Anatolia, whose capital was Sivas.

63. In southern Turkey today; presently known as Kahramanmaraş.

64. Turkoman commander who was then ruling Hama.

attacking Shayzar.⁶⁵ In Dhu al-Hijja (8 July–6 August 1141), two small earthquakes occurred. That same year, the Shafi'i cleric Ibn al-Shahrazuri⁶⁶ died in Damascus. Sultan Mas'ud⁶⁷ spent the winter in Harran.⁶⁸ The Byzantine king returned to Constantinople.⁶⁹ On 3 Sha'ban, which was the 14th of March, the sun entered the Aries constellation, ushering in the spring season.

Questions

Al-'Azimi's *History of Aleppo* reads a bit like a series of almanac entries of what he deems to be the important events of a given year.

1. What kinds of things does al-'Azimi deem to be important in his brief accounts of the years 502, 503, and 535?

2. How does he insert himself into the story in his much longer account of the year 513?

3. How does he represent the Franks' treatment of the local population following their capture of several cities and fortresses?

4. What type of alliances, and how many actors do we see in the accounts of al-'Azimi?

---

65. Shayzar was a famous town-castle at the time, held by the infamous Ibn Munqidh clan.
66. A renowned scholar and jurist, he came often to Damascus as ambassador.
67. He was the sultan of Anatolia (r. 1116–1156), and grandson of Qilij Arslan (r. 1092–1107).
68. In Turkey today, it was an important city not far from Edessa.
69. That year, the Byzantine emperor advanced in the hope of restoring some former Byzantine lands from the Muslims and Franks.

Chapter 3: Chronicles, Memoirs, and Poetry

5. Hamdan al-Atharibi on receiving a land tenure from the Frankish lord of al-Atharib[70]

Hamdan al-Atharibi was a notable local figure from the al-Jazr district in northern Syria—a contested frontier area between Frankish Antioch and Muslim Aleppo. Consequently, he served both Muslim and Frankish rulers from time to time. He represented the rulers of Aleppo on several diplomatic missions to Egypt, Damascus, and Baghdad, and frequently served as a point of contact between the rulers of Aleppo and the Franks. He wrote a history of Aleppo and its region, which is now lost, as well as a Diwan of poetry.[71]

Abu al-Fawaris Hamdan son of 'Abd al-Rahim son of Sa'id son of 'Abd al-Rahim said:

> My father 'Abd al-Rahim son of Sa'id told me: "My uncle the mayor Abu al-Fawaris Hamdan studied grammar, language, engineering, astronomy, and other topics with Abu al-Hasan son of Abu Jarada. One day, he went out to Ma'ratha al-Atharib, which he had owned but which was then under the control of the Franks. The lord of al-Atharib,[72] Sir Manuel, the nephew of the prince of Antioch, had taken ill. Hamdan went to Manuel and treated him with some medicine, which cured him. After Sir Samuel was restored to health, he sent someone to Hamdan to tell him: "Ask of me what you wish." Hamdan requested a village estate. Manuel gave him Ma'arbuniyya.[73] Hamdan stayed there for 30 years, building it up and making it his residence. The cleric Abu al-Hasan son

---

70. Ibn al-'Adim, *Bughyat al-talab fi ta'rikh Halab*, ed. S. Zakkar (Damascus: Dar al-Fikr, 1988), 6: 2928–2930. For biographical information on Ibn al-'Adim, in whose *The Pursued Desire on the History of Aleppo* (*Bughyat al-talab fi ta'rikh Halab*) this brief account about Hamdan appears, see Appendix C, p. 235.

71. On Hamdan al-Atharibi, see Paul M. Cobb, "Hamdan al-Atharibi's *History of the Franks* Revisited, Again," in *Syria in Crusader Times: Conflict and Coexistence*, ed. C. Hillenbrand (Edinburgh: Edinburgh University Press, 2020), 3–20.

72. Al-Atharib was an important town in the principality of Antioch, roughly 30 kilometers west of Aleppo.

73. Possibly called today Kafar Buni, in northwest Syria, near Idlib.

5. Hamdan al-Atharibi on receiving a land tenure from a Frankish lord

of Abu Jarada sent a word to him, reproaching and berating him for living under Frankish rule. Hamdan replied to him:

1- You blame me for cultivating my passion in a village / whose people are not noble.
2- You ask: "Why would you do that?" I reply to you: / "Fate planned this for me, and the plans of fate will be accomplished."
3- My trustworthy friends are stingy, and boon companions have deserted me; / the sincere care not, and the Muslim sovereign is tyrant.
4- So, here I live. After all, is the musk not found / in buckskin; does the pearl not dwell in shells?

This village of Maʿarbuniyya, which the lord of al-Atharib gave to Hamdan toward the end of year 521 (1127), was a ruin on a desolate hill. Hamdan lived there and brought his household to reside with him. He constructed there a mansion, brought farmers and workers to cultivate the hinterland and to grow produce. He made a good income from that.

Questions

1. What can we learn about Muslim–Frankish relations from this account of Hamdan al-Atharibi receiving a land tenure from the Frankish lord of al-Atharib?
2. What can we learn from the poem that Hamdan recited in his response to the cleric Abu al-Hasan son of Abu Jarada?

Chapter 3: Chronicles, Memoirs, and Poetry

6. Al-Qaysarani's poems about the Frankish and Greek women in Antioch

Abu 'Abd Allah Muhammad son of Nasr al-Qaysarani—sometimes called mistakenly Ibn al-Qaysarani—was born in Acre in 1085 and grew up in Caesarea—hence the nickname al-Qaysarani. He moved to Damascus when the Franks captured Caesarea in 1101. In Damascus, he was educated in literature, astronomy, and engineering, and became a court poet. He was also appointed by the Burid ruler Taj al-Muluk Buri (r. 1128–1132) as keeper of the sun clocks outside the Umayyad Mosque. After that, he moved to Aleppo where he became curator of its public library. His poetry represents a unique testimony on the early interactions between Muslims and Franks.[74]

In 550 (March 1155–February 1156), the Damascene cleric 'Abd al-Wahhab recounted while in Baghdad that al-Qaysarani went to Antioch in 540 (June 1145–June 1146) for urgent business, and while there he composed a flirtatious poem about Frankish women; it includes the following description of the piercing eyes of a Frankish woman:

1- I was seduced by a Frankish woman / the scent of her fragrance alluring.
2- A silken design adorns her dress; / her face, a bright moon.
3- Her piercing blue eyes are not a defect[75] / for the tip of the spear pierces.[76]

Al-Qaysarani wrote describing Antioch:

1- In the frontier lands, there is a town / as seductive as luscious lips.
2- There you see palaces as churches / radiant with tender icons.
3- Teeming with tall-lean women, / each with a smile like a moon.

---

74. On al-Qaysarani, see 'Imad al-Din al-Isfahani, *Kharidat al-qasr wa-jaridat al-'asr: Qism Shu'ara' al-Sham*, ed. Sh. Faysal (Damascus: al-Matba'a al-Hashimiyya, 1955–1968), 1: 96–160; and al-Dhahabi, *Siyar a'lam al-nubala'*, eds. Sh. al-Arna'ut et al. (Beirut: Mu'assasat al-Risala, 1996), 20: 224–225.

75. Having blue eyes in the medieval Islamic world was not considered a sign of beauty.

76. 'Imad al-Din al-Isfahani, *Kharidat al-qasr*, 1: 99. For biographical information on 'Imad al-Din al-Isfahani, see p. 94. Al-Qaysarani used the same word (*azraq*) that has two meanings: blue and piercing.

6. Al-Qaysarani's poems about Frankish and Greek women

4- Their faces exposed; when they spy me / they blush, demure with modesty.

5- Each face a moon / encompassed with locks as dark as the night.

6- Should swords attack / their tresses most surely victorious.

7- Do not criticize or scold me for ogling them / even the radiant sun, does it have locks like theirs?

8- Be my helper against these deceivers, / gentle hearts, but eyes aflame.

9- I departed, abandoning in their lands / a heart; would that I had left my eyes.

10- I envy the one who lives there / for he is near them, so too the captives.[77]

He also composed the following lines about a gorgeous Greek Christian woman:

1- How many a virgin lives in churches / like a wild gazelle, whose beauty is her shyness.

2- She prostrates herself before the icon / but truth be told, the icons should prostrate before her.

3- A saint, with a necklace long / and straps short.

4- The blush of modesty glows on her cheeks / a rose, its shoots nourished by mere glances.

5- Her eyebrows speak on her behalf; should / you address her, her eyes reply.

6- Her tresses caress her garment, / her moonlit face shines on her dark dress.[78]

Questions

1. What can we learn about al-Qaysarani specifically from his poems?

2. What can we learn about Muslim–Frankish relations more generally from al-Qaysarani's poems?

---

77. 'Imad al-Din al-Isfahani, *Kharidat al-qasr*, 1: 100.
78. 'Imad al-Din al-Isfahani, *Kharidat al-qasr*, 1: 120.

Chapter 3: Chronicles, Memoirs, and Poetry

7. Ibn al-Qalanisi on the siege of Damascus in 1148 [79]

In this year (542/1147), news came from Constantinople, the lands of the Franks, Byzantium, and nearby territories that the Franks emerged out of their territories, led by (King Conrad) the German,[80] Alphonse (Jordan of Toulouse),[81] and a group of their leaders, in countless numbers that cannot even be estimated. They had made the call to arms in all of their lands and strongholds to prepare and march against the lands of Islam, leaving no one behind to protect and guard their lands and territories. They brought with them countless amounts of money, wealth, and weapons, so much so that it was said their numbers amounted to one million foot soldiers and horsemen; some even said more than that. They overran the region of Constantinople, forcing its king to negotiate and make peace with them and accept their conditions. When the news about them spread and became known, the rulers of the territories and Islamic border regions close to them readied their defenses and waged jihad against them. They targeted the roads the Franks followed and crossing points that might block them from going through to the lands of Islam. They went on attacking their flanks, killing and destroying them; a great many of them perished. The Franks could not find food, fodder, or provision, and if any was found the prices were exorbitantly high. A great many of them died of hunger and disease as well. The news about their deaths and the diminishing of their numbers kept coming until the end of 542 (1148), bringing some relief to our hearts and confirming the collapse of their endeavors. As the news kept arriving, worry and fear faded away.

Then came the year 543, its first day being Friday, 21 May (1148). The sun was in the Gemini constellation. At its beginning, news came from all sides that boats of those Franks mentioned earlier arrived at the seacoast and spread themselves among those Franks already there along the coastal areas from Tyre to Acre. It is said that those who perished through war, disease, and hunger were approximately 100,000 men. They sought Jerusalem and performed their pilgrimage there. After that, many returned to their lands by sea; a large crowd of them perished by death or disease. Some of their

---

79. Ibn al-Qalanisi, *Dhayl Ta'rikh Dimashq*, 297–301. For biographical information on Ibn al-Qalanisi, see p. 62.

80. A reference to King Conrad III of the Hohenstaufen Dynasty, who was king of the Holy Roman Empire (r. 1138–1152).

81. A reference to Count Alphonse Jordan of Toulouse (d. 1148), son of Count Raymond of Toulouse, who was one of the major leaders of the First Crusade.

7. Ibn al-Qalanisi on the siege of Damascus in 1148

kings perished too. Only (Conrad) the king of the Germans, who was the most prestigious of their kings, along with a few of lower ranks, remained. They disagreed as to whom they should fight in the Muslim lands and Syrian territories. They finally agreed to attack the city of Damascus, hoping in their wicked minds to capture it. They even distributed among themselves its villages and districts. When news about this arrived, the city's general commander Muʿin al-Din Unur started preparation for war to repel their threat. He fortified the areas from where it was feared they might attack, stationed men in the roads and crossing points, disrupted water canals that led to where they would camp, buried the wells, and obliterated the traces of springs. The Franks set their hostility against Damascus with their hordes, wrath, and arms: a large crowd, which is said to have numbered 50,000 horsemen and foot soldiers. They brought with them a huge quantity of war equipment, camels, and cattle.

The Franks arrived near the city and sought to camp in the location known as the Soldiers' Camps. Finding that there was no water there, they proceeded to Mizza and camped there because of its proximity to water. They then attacked the city with their horsemen and foot soldiers. The Muslims took positions in front of them on Saturday, 6 Rabiʿ I of 543 (24 July 1148) and war broke out between the two camps. A large crowd of militia and Turkoman soldiers as well as youths, volunteers, and bandits rushed to fight them. Fighting intensified and the infidels gained the upper hand on account of their numbers and arms. They took control of water sources, spread across the orchards, and camped for the night there. They drew very close to the city, reaching a spot that no army in previous or recent times was capable of capturing. On this day, the jurist and imam Yusuf al-Findalawi al-Maliki achieved martyrdom—may God be merciful to him. He was killed near al-Rabwa, next to a water spring. He stood there in their face, insisting on fighting them, as per almighty God's command in His glorious Book.[82] The fate of the ascetic ʿAbd al-Rahman al-Halhuli—may God be merciful to him—was the same.

The local defenders spent the night cutting down trees to use as fortifications and demolishing bridges. They were worried on account of the horrors they had witnessed, their hearts were demoralized and chests heavy. Very early in the morning of the next day, which was Sunday, they came out

---

82. A reference to the quranic verse 9:111: ❴*God has purchased from the believers their souls and their wealth and, in exchange, the garden shall be theirs. They fight in the path of God, they kill and are killed—a true promise from Him in the Torah, the Gospel, and the Qur'an. Who is more truthful to his promise than God? So be of good cheer regarding that business deal you transact. That is the greatest of triumphs.*❵. See Ibn ʿAsakir's biography of al-Findalawi in Chapter 4, pp. 162–164.

and advanced against the Franks. Fighting resumed and the Muslims gained the upper hand, killing and injuring many of them. The commander Muʿin al-Din did well in the fight, showing bravery, steadfastness, and heroism that were not seen from any other person that day. He showed neither exhaustion in chasing them away nor satisfaction in fighting them. War went on between them, the infidels' cavalry restraining from their usual attack waiting for an opportunity, until the sun reached the twilight and the night ushered in. The souls sought rest and each group retired to their camp. The Muslim soldiers camped close to the Franks and the inhabitants of the city spent the night guarding the walls; on alert, watching their enemies not far from them.

Correspondences to rulers of other territories were sent seeking aid. Turkomans on horseback showed up in waves and foot soldiers from all territories came one after another. With high spirits and their fear gone, the Muslims attacked early and were steadfast against the Franks. They stormed them with arrows, causing injuries to foot soldiers, horsemen, horses, and camels.

On that day, many foot soldiers arrived from the district of Biqaʿ and elsewhere. They were archers. With them, the numbers increased, and readiness multiplied. Then each group retreated to their base that day. From very early on the next day, Tuesday, the Muslims stormed them like falcons diving into mountain gorges and gyrfalcons swooping on the partridges' field. They surrounded them in their camps and sleeping tents, forcing them to take shelter behind the trees in the orchards, causing their ruin by arrows and catapulted rocks. The Franks refrained from attacking out of fear of losing. None of them came out, and it was thought that they were preparing a scheme or a ploy. Only a very few of their horsemen or soldiers showed themselves, feigning an attack, for they feared a surprise attack against themselves. They were clearly seeking either an opportunity to attack or escape. Each one of them who drew near was shot dead by an arrow or impaled by a spear. A large host of Muslim foot soldiers who were youths or from neighboring territories went after them. They ambushed the escaping Franks on the roads, killed what they could catch, and brought back with them many Frankish heads to claim the promised rewards.

News came to the Franks that the Muslim armies were hastening to wage jihad against them and rushing to eradicate them, which made them realize their impending defeat, annihilation, and destruction. They took counsel among themselves but the only escape they found from the trap in which they found themselves and the abyss in which they threw themselves was to leave at dawn the next day, Wednesday. They ran away frightened, disheartened, utterly defeated. When the Muslims learned of this and noticed their departure, they rushed very early on that day behind them, chasing them with so many arrows that they killed in their rear files a large number of foot soldiers, horses, and mules. Their dead people and priceless dead horses were discovered buried in their camps and the roads they followed; a number so large that it cannot even be estimated. The stench from their corpses would even kill the birds in the sky. The night before, they set fire to al-Rabwa and the long Qubba neighborhood.

People rejoiced with this grace that God bestowed on them, profusely giving thanks to God almighty, for He answered the prayers they made during the days of this trial. Praise and thanks to God for that.

Following this act of benevolence, Muʿin al-Din met with Nur al-Din, ruler of Aleppo, when he drew near to Damascus on his way to help it at the end of the month of Rabiʿ II 543 (mid-September 1148). They joined forces together to attack the castle that was near Tripoli, known as al-ʿUrayma, where the son of the king Alphonse (Bertrand of Toulouse) was; Alphonse was one of the kings of the Franks mentioned earlier who died in the region of Acre. The son of Alphonse had with him his mother,[83] a large crowd of his retinue and brave men, the most prominent of his soldiers. Nur al-Din and Muʿin al-Din besieged him and attacked him just when a unit of approximately 1,000 horsemen from the army of Sayf al-Din Ghazi son of the chief commander Zangi[84] arrived to reinforce their armies. War broke out and most of those who were in the castle were killed or taken as captives. The son of the aforementioned monarch was arrested alongside his mother. All the gear, horses, and furniture that were in the castle were looted. The army of Sayf al-Din returned to his camp in Hims. Nur al-Din returned to Aleppo with the son of the king, his mother, and the other captives. Muʿin al-Din went back to Damascus.

The Noble Shams al-Din Nasih al-Islam Abu ʿAbd Allah Muhammad son of Muhammad son of ʿUbayd Allah al-Husayni, who is an honorable member of the prophetic household,[85] arrived in Damascus, after having met Sayf al-Din Ghazi, the son of the chief commander Zangi. Shams al-Din had been sent as envoy from the ʿAbbasid caliph's court to all the rulers and Turkoman warlords to enjoin them to rescue the Muslims and wage jihad against the infidels. That was the reason behind the Franks' fear

---

83. We do not know her name; she was not the legal wife of Count Alphonse, and her son Bertrand was considered illegitimate. Ibn al-Qalanisi refers to Count Alphonse with the Arabic term for king (*malik*).

84. Sayf al-Din Ghazi (d. 1149) was the elder brother of Nur al-Din and ruler of Mosul (r. 1146–1149).

85. The word used in Arabic is *Sharif*, which is an honorific indicating the person in question is a male descendant of the Prophet Muhammad.

that the Muslims would be receiving reinforcements to fight them, which caused them to leave as described earlier. This honorable member of the prophetic household is from a noble lineage known for virtue and manners. His brother Diya' al-Din[86] is the leader of the prophetic household in Mosul; he is famous for his learning, manners, and knowledge. His cousin is leader of the prophetic household in Baghdad. His other cousin is the leader of the prophetic household in Khurasan. He resided for some time in Damascus, showing commendable and praiseworthy conduct in all his involvements and dealings. On Wednesday, 11 Rajab 543 (24 November 1148), he returned to Baghdad with a message in reply to the caliph.

In Rajab of this year (November–December 1148), news came from Aleppo that its ruler, chief commander Nur al-Din, ordered the ban of "hasten to do good deeds" uttered at the end of the call for prayer and the cursing in public of the Companions of Muhammad—may God be pleased with them. He found these acts very offensive and prohibited them being done at all. He was counseled on this matter by the jurist imam Burhan al-Din Abu al-Hasan 'Ali al-Hanafi and a group of Sunni scholars in Aleppo. The Isma'ilis and followers of Shi'ism were outraged, and their chests were filled with anger. They rioted but then calmed down and restrained themselves out of fear of Nur al-Din's famed force and vehement unyielding authority.[87]

Questions

1. How does Ibn al-Qalanisi depict the Franks' preparations for the siege of Damascus?
2. How does he depict the Franks' performance in the siege itself?
3. How does he depict Mu'in al-Din's response to the siege?
4. Why was Shams al-Din selected to serve as an envoy from the 'Abbasid court in Baghdad?
5. How does Ibn al-Qalanisi depict Nur al-Din's role in his account?
6. How does he employ the word "jihad" and God's role in his narrative?

---

86. Diya' al-Din Zayd son of Muhammad al-Husayni (d. 1168). Diya' al-Din means "Brightness of the Religion."

87. Nur al-Din's prohibition of these Shi'i practices was a very public demonstration of his victory over the former Shi'i rulers in Aleppo and his restoration of Sunni supremacy. See Ibn 'Asakir's biography of Nur al-Din in Chapter 4, pp. 165–173.

8. Ibn al-Athir on the siege of Damascus[88]

The Franks' siege of Damascus and the reaction of Sayf al-Din Ghazi son of Zangi

In this year (543/1148), (Conrad), the king of the Germans, marched from his lands with a large crowd and massive numbers of Franks intending to attack the land of Islam. He had no doubt that, given his troops, wealth, and equipment, he would seize it easily. When he reached Syria, the local Franks went to meet him, placed themselves in his service, and followed his commands. He ordered them to join him in the march against Damascus, to lay siege to it and capture it as he claimed. They marched with him, reached it, and laid siege to it. Its ruler was Mujir al-Din Abaq son of Buri son of Tughtakin, who did not have any real power. The real power in the city was in the hands of Mu'in al-Din Unur, the slave of Abaq's grandfather Tughtakin, for he was the one who installed Mujir al-Din. Mu'in al-Din was smart, just, charitable, and of good conduct. He gathered soldiers to protect the city.

The Franks besieged Damascus, and then on 6 Rabi' I (24 July) they attacked with the horsemen and foot soldiers. The inhabitants of the city as well as the soldiers came out against them and withstood their assault. Among those who went out on that day to fight was jurist Hujjat al-Islam[89] Yusuf son of Dunas al-Findalawi al-Maghribi. He was an aged scholar and a learned jurist. When Mu'in al-Din saw him walking, he went toward him, greeted him, and said to him: "O aged cleric, you are exempt because of your age, so let the defense of the Muslims be on us." Unur asked him to return but al-Findalawi refused and replied to him: "I sold and He purchased from me. By God, I will not rescind or ask Him to rescind the sale." For he meant the saying of almighty God: ❴*God has purchased from the believers their souls and their wealth and, in exchange, the garden shall be theirs*❵ (Qur'an 9:111).[90] He proceeded and fought until he died in al-Nayrab, approximately half a parasang from Damascus.

---

88. Ibn al-Athir, *al-Kamil fi al-Ta'rikh*, 9: 158–161. For biographical information on Ibn al-Athir, see p. 59.

89. Hujjat al-Islam is an honorific that means "Proof of Islam." It was only conferred on very learned and pious scholars such as al-Findalawi. Ibn 'Asakir, in his biography of al-Findalawi, referred to him by the honorific Hujjat al-Din (Proof of the Religion). See Chapter 4, p. 163 (footnote 30).

90. See Appendix B for the major quranic passages on war and peace.

The Franks grew strong and the Muslims waned. So, the king of the Germans advanced until he reached the Green Field.[91] People were convinced that he would seize the city. Mu'in al-Din sent to Sayf al-Din Ghazi, son of the chief commander Zangi, asking him to help the Muslims and repel their enemy, and Sayf al-Din gathered his soldiers and marched to Syria, taking with him his brother Nur al-Din Mahmud from Aleppo. He camped in the city of Hims and sent to Mu'in al-Din saying to him: "I came and brought with me everyone in my land who can carry a weapon. I demand that my deputies be allowed in Damascus so that I can proceed to meet the Franks. Should I be defeated, I will enter the city with my soldiers and take shelter in it. Should I be victorious, the city is yours and I will not lay a claim to it."

He also sent to the Franks threatening them if they did not cease their attack against Damascus. The Franks halted the fighting out of fear of additional injuries, especially that they might have to fight Sayf al-Din. They spared their souls, which allowed the people of the city to protect it and rest from the demands of war. Mu'in al-Din sent to the foreign Franks: "The king of the orient has arrived. So either you leave or I will turn over the city to him, which you will regret." He also sent to the Syrian Franks saying: "By what logic do you assist these foreigners against us? You know well that if they were to capture Damascus, they would also seize the coastal lands that you control. As for me, if I weaken in defending the city, I will turn it over to Sayf al-Din. And you know well, if he were to capture Damascus, you will not keep a foothold in Syria with him." The Franks agreed with Unur to desert the king of the Germans, and in return Unur gave them the castle of Banyas.

The Franks of the coastal lands met with the king of the Germans and filled him with fear of Sayf al-Din, his numerous soldiers, and the frequent arrival of reinforcements to him. They convinced him that Sayf al-Din might capture Damascus and that he could not resist him. They kept pressing the king until he left the city and they were handed the fortress of Banyas. The Frankish Germans returned to their land beyond Constantinople and God saved the believers from their evil. The great Hadith memorizer Abu al-Qasim Ibn 'Asakir mentioned in the *History of Damascus* that one of the scholars told him that he saw al-Findalawi in a dream and asked him:

---

91. The Green Field (or *al-Midan al-akhdar* in the local Damascene dialect) was a large open space outside the western gate of Old Damascus. It was planned by Sultan Nur al-Din as a training ground for cavalries and horsemanship. Today it is called *al-Marji*, which means the same thing, made to distinguish it from another neighborhood called the Stony Field (*Midan al-hasa*) or simply the Field (*al-Midan*) outside the southern gate of Old Damascus. The word in Arabic should be properly pronounced *maydan*, and can also mean a large public square.

"What did God do to you and where are you?" He replied: "He pardoned me and I am ❮*in gardens of delight, on couches face to face*❯" (Qur'an 37:43–44).[92]

Sultan Nur al-Din Mahmud son of Zangi's capture of the castle of al-'Urayma

When the Franks departed from Damascus, Nur al-Din left to the castle of al-'Urayma, which was in the control of the Franks, and captured it. The reason for that is that when (Conrad) the king of the Germans marched against Syria, he brought with him (Bertrand) the son of Alphonse, who was one of the kings of the Franks. It was the son of Alphonse's grandfather, Raymond IV of Toulouse, who seized Tripoli of Syria[93] from the Muslims. The son of Alphonse attacked the castle of al-'Urayma and captured it and made it known that he was seeking to take Tripoli from the count. The count sent to Nur al-Din Mahmud, when he and Mu'in al-Din Unur were in Baalbek, asking him and Mu'in al-Din to head toward the castle of al-'Urayma and capture it from the son of Alphonse. They proceeded toward it with their soldiers in earnest. They also wrote to Sayf al-Din in Hims asking him for reinforcements. He reinforced them with a large army headed by the commander 'Izz al-Din Abu Bakr al-Dubaysi, who ruled over Jazirat Ibn 'Umar,[94] and others. They arrived and laid siege to the castle. The son of Alphonse was in it, so he arranged its defenses and fortified himself there. The Muslims attacked several times. Then the sappers came and dug underneath the walls, which forced the Franks in it to surrender. The Muslims captured it and took captive every horseman, foot soldier, boy, or woman there, including the son of Alphonse. They destroyed the castle and returned to Sayf al-Din. The fate of the son of Alphonse was as in the saying: "the ostrich went looking for two horns, it came back without ears."

Questions

1. How is Ibn al-Athir's account of the Franks' siege of Damascus similar to and dissimilar to Ibn al-Qalanisi's?

---

92. See Ibn 'Asakir's biography of al-Findalawi in Chapter 4, pp. 162–164.
93. To distinguish this city from Tripoli of North Africa, today the capital of modern Libya.
94. Gizre in southeastern modern-day Turkey, just north of the border with eastern Syria.

2. How does he describe the ruler of Damascus Unur, and the exchange between him and al-Findalawi?
3. What can we learn from Ibn al-Athir's account of Nur al-Din's capture of the castle of al-ʿUrayma?
4. What does his narrative tell us about Muslim–Crusader hostilities and alliances?

9. Ibn 'Asakir's poem about Nur al-Din in honor of his forces taking Egypt in 1169[95]

Ibn 'Asakir recited to me this poem, which he composed. The Monarch Nur al-Din—may God purify his soul—exempted the Damascenes from supplying him with lumber, which happened at the same time the news came that his forces had seized Egypt. Ibn 'Asakir wrote to him to congratulate him, and dictated it to me to convey to Nur al-Din on 22 Jumada I 564 (21 February 1169):

1- Because you exempted the Damascenes from the levy of wood / you were compensated with Egypt and its plentiful goods.

2- Should you endeavor to conquer Jerusalem, / your reward shall be great, a recompense beyond calculation.

3- For the reward of God is already set; / indeed, deeds that merit His reward are a better bet.

4- As for renown among people, you have earned it; / it is worthier than the purest silver and gold.

5- Yet, you shall receive no pardon should you forsake jihad, for / you now rule from Egypt to Aleppo.

6- Even the lord of Mosul complies / with your wishes, so hasten to issue the call to arms.

7- The most steadfast of people is he who toughens his resolve / that he may attain the loftiest of ranks.

8- Good fortune and determination are bound together; / tenacity with steadfast intention; achievement with pursuit.

9- So, cleanse the Aqsa Sanctuary and its environs / from impurity, polytheism, and crucifixes.

10- May you earn in this world honorable acclaim / and on the Day of Resurrection a splendid welcome.

---

95. 'Imad al-Din al-Isfahani, *Kharidat al-qasr*, 1: 276–277. For biographical information on 'Imad al-Din al-Isfahani, see p. 94. For biographical information on Ibn 'Asakir, see pp. 41–42.

Chapter 3: Chronicles, Memoirs, and Poetry

Questions

1. What can we learn about Ibn 'Asakir's relationship with his patron, Nur al-Din, from his poem?
2. What actions is he advocating with his poem?

10. Ibn al-Athir on the defeat of the Franks at Hattin in 1187[96]

On the morning of Saturday, 25 Rabi' II (4 July 1187), Saladin and the Muslim army mounted up and rode out to meet the Franks. The two groups drew close to each other. The Franks were suffering from thirst and fatigue. They fought a fierce battle, and each side stood its ground. Muslim archers shot so many arrows at them the sky seemed as though it were full of locusts, killing a great many Frankish horses.

The fighting continued. The Franks regrouped their foot soldiers and set off in the direction of Lake Tiberias, all the while fighting as they advanced in the hope of reaching its fresh water. When Saladin realized what they were doing, he moved his army to block their progress. He himself stood before the troops, inciting the Muslims to fight, giving them proper instructions, and enjoining them from taking unnecessary risks. The soldiers followed his commands and prohibitions. But one of his young slaves valiantly charged the Franks and fought them in a way that astonished everyone. The Franks rallied against him and killed him. Seeing this, the Muslims launched a formidable attack and rattled the unbelievers, killing a great many of them.

When the count[97] saw the precariousness of the situation, he realized that they were severely outmatched by the Muslims. He decided with his soldiers to charge those directly in front of them. The Muslim commander in that sector was Taqiy al-Din 'Umar, the nephew of Saladin. He realized that the Franks were making a desperate attack and that he could not repel them, so he ordered his soldiers to make an opening for the Franks to pass through. They did as he ordered. After the count and his soldiers fled, the Muslim soldiers regrouped and closed ranks.

Some of the Muslim volunteer fighters had started a fire on the ground, which ignited the abundant dry grass. The wind was blowing in the direction of the Frankish soldiers, so it blew the heat of the burning fire and the smoke toward them. Thirst, the pressure of the moment, the heat of the raging fire, the smoke, and the heat of battle all aligned against them. When the count fled, the remaining Franks realized their looming defeat and were about to surrender. They knew that nothing could save them from death except to pursue death itself. They made charge after charge against the

---

96. Ibn al-Athir, *al-Kamil fi al-Ta'rikh*, 10: 25–27. For biographical information on Ibn al-Athir, see p. 59.
97. Raymond III, count of Tripoli (r. 1152–1187).

Muslims. They would have defeated them despite the Muslims' large numbers, were it not for God's benevolence.

Every time the Franks attacked, they lost men, weakening them considerably. The Muslims surrounded them like a closed circle. The Franks regrouped atop a hill in Hattin where they hoped to set up their tents as shelter. The Muslims dashed their hopes as the fighting intensified against them from every direction. The only tent they were able to set up was that of their king.

The Muslims seized the Franks' majestic Cross, which they call the True Cross. They allege that it contains a relic of the wood of the Cross on which Jesus—may God bless him—was crucified. That is their belief. Its seizure was a great catastrophe for them, which portended their imminent death and destruction. In the meantime, the Muslims kept killing or capturing their horsemen and foot soldiers. Only their king remained atop the hill with around 150 well-known and courageous knights.

I was told by one who heard the Monarch al-Afdal, the son of Saladin, say: "I was standing beside my father on that day; it was the first battle I experienced. The king of the Franks and his soldiers who were on the hill made a formidable attack against those Muslims facing them, and forced them to retreat down the hill. I looked at my father and saw a grim look on his face and his complexion pale. He grabbed his beard, took a few steps forward and shouted: 'Satan is deceitful,' and the Muslims were able to push the Franks back atop the hill. When I saw the Franks retreating and the Muslims pursuing them, I shouted with joy: 'We have defeated them.' But the Franks attacked again as they had previously, and forced the Muslims down the hill. My father did as he had done before, and the Muslims encircled them and pushed them back atop the hill. I screamed again: 'We have defeated them.' My father looked at me and said: 'Shut up. We are not going to defeat them until that tent falls down.' As he was saying this to me, the tent collapsed. So, the sultan bowed down, prostrated himself, and gave thanks to almighty God. He was so happy he wept tears of joy."

The reason for the tent's collapse was that every time the Franks made one of those attacks, they became more and more thirsty. They hoped to open an escape route for themselves, but when they realized that was impossible, they dismounted their beasts, and sat on the ground. The Muslims went up to them, broke down the king's tent, and imprisoned them all, including the king, his brother, and prince Reynald, the lord of Kerak. He was the most hostile of the Franks toward the Muslims. They also imprisoned the lord of Byblos (Jubayl),[98]

---

98. Ugo III (d. 1196), also spelled Hugues or Hugh. He belonged to the Embriaco family of Genoa.

10. Ibn al-Athir on the defeat of the Franks at Hattin in 1187

the son of Humphrey,[99] and the Grand Master of the Templars, who was among the most prestigious of the Franks. They also captured a number of Templar and Hospitaller soldiers. Most of the Franks were either killed or imprisoned. Anyone who sees their dead would think that the Muslims took no prisoners; anyone who sees their prisoners would think that the Muslims killed no one. Since they came to this coast—that is in 491 (1098)—the Franks have not suffered a setback like this one.

When the Muslim soldiers finished sorting the Frankish captives, Saladin retired to his tent. He had the Frankish king and the prince, the lord of Kerak, brought to him. He invited the king to sit next to him—the king was very thirsty—and Saladin gave him water with ice. He drank and passed what remained in the cup to the prince, the lord of Kerak, who took it and drank. Saladin said: "This cursed man did not drink water with my permission, and so my guarantee of safety to you does not cover him." He then addressed the prince, rebuking him for his offenses and recounting the many times he was perfidious toward the Muslims. He walked toward him and smote his neck, saying: "Twice have I sworn an oath to kill him should I catch him: the first oath was when he planned to attack Mecca and Medina; the second when he treacherously raided the trade caravan." When he killed him and had the body dragged outside, the king was shaken with fear, but Saladin assured him of his safety.

As for the count, the lord of Tripoli, who as we mentioned earlier fled the field of battle, he first went to Tyre, and from there he proceeded to Tripoli. A few days later, he died from the distress and anger caused by what befell the Franks specifically and the religion of Christianity more broadly.

Questions

1. What can we learn about the Franks' and the Muslims' military tactics from Ibn al-Athir's account of the Battle of Hattin?

2. What can we learn about the etiquette between opposing battle commanders?

3. How does Ibn al-Athir treat the religious significance of the True Cross for the Crusaders and their conviction in winning the battle?

---

99. Humphrey IV (d. 1198). He was the grandson of Humphrey II (d. 1179), the lord of Toron (Tibnin).

Chapter 3: Chronicles, Memoirs, and Poetry

11. 'Imad al-Din al-Isfahani on the seizure of the Relic of the True Cross, the capture of Tiberias, and the execution of the Frankish prisoners[100]

'Imad al-Din al-Isfahani was born in Isfahan in Persia on 6 July 1125 and died in Damascus on 4 June 1201. Educated in Isfahan, Baghdad, Mosul, and elsewhere in the Islamic east, al-Isfahani was a very capable scholar and compiled a voluminous anthology of Arabic poetry from the twelfth century. After Nur al-Din's success against the Franks in Syria, al-Isfahani benefited from the patronage of Nur al-Din in Damascus where he served as his secretary (hence his nickname al-Katib al-Isfahani, or the secretary from Isfahan); he later served in the same capacity under Saladin. Among the most important of his works for our purposes are his The Eloquent Prologue on the Conquest of Jerusalem *and his* Syrian Lightning, *which present eloquent and somewhat florid accounts of Saladin's jihads against the Franks, especially his victories at Hattin and Jerusalem in 1187. In addition to his glowing prose and eyewitness testimony about his patrons, Nur al-Din and Saladin, al-Isfahani is a valuable source for his occasionally positive, but usually biting and caustic, commentary on the character and behavior of the Franks.*[101]

The capture of the majestic Cross on the day of the battle

At the same time the Frankish king was captured, the Muslims also seized the True Cross, killing the tyrants who were defending it. When this cross is raised, brought out, or carried on high, every Christian prostrates before it and kneels down. They allege it is from the same wood on which their object of worship was crucified. They worship it and prostrate before it. They encased it with red gold and adorned it with pearls and gemstones, keeping it ready for the appointed moment: the day of their annual festival (Easter Sunday). The priests would bring it out, the leaders would carry it, and the people would rush toward it and swarm around it. No one can afford to ignore it, nor do they even think they can do anything except walk in train behind it. For them, its seizure is more consequential than capturing their king. Indeed, it was the gravest blow they suffered during that encounter. For

---

100. 'Imad al-Din al-Isfahani, *al-Fath al-Qussi* (Cairo: Dar al-Manar, 2004), 52–53.

101. On 'Imad al-Din al-Isfahani and his *al-Fath al-qussi fi al-fath al-qudsi*, see Lutz Richter-Bernburg, "'Imad al-Din al-Isfahani," in *Medieval Historians and the Franks in the Levant*, ed. A. Mallett (Leiden: Brill, 2014), 29–51.

11. 'Imad al-Din al-Isfahani on the seizure of the Relic of the True Cross

the seized cross is irreplaceable, everything else is secondary to them. Their religious duty is to revere it: it is truly their god. In front of it their foreheads bow down to the ground, and their mouths sing its praise. They faint when it is not in view, and ogle their eyes to catch a glimpse of it. When it is brought out, they become enraptured and boast for having seen it. They feel alive when it is there, and offer their most precious things for it. They seek solace from it. They even made crosses in its form, which they worship. They place them in their homes, prostrate themselves before them, and venerate them.

When this majestic Cross was seized, their catastrophe worsened and their strength waned. Countless was the number of the defeated, and exalted was the sight of the victors. It was as though they knew that when the Cross was taken to Hattin, none of them could fail to show up for the dreadful battle. They all perished, either dead or imprisoned. Victory over them was fierce and terrible. Like a desert lion or a full moon, the sultan then moved his camp to the plain outside Tiberias.

The capture of Tiberias

Saladin dispatched a messenger to its citadel to receive it in return for the guarantee of safe passage, seeking to reintroduce to it true faith after a spell of unbelief. The noble woman,[102] who was the lady of Tiberias, had defended it, and brought to it all her possessions and property. Saladin gave her a guarantee of safe passage for herself, her possessions, as well as her soldiers. She left with the women, men, and luggage, and took them all to Tripoli, the city of her husband the count. Tiberias was once again repopulated by the people of faith. Saladin appointed Sarim al-Din Qaymaz al-Najmi as its governor; he was one of the senior commanders. Meanwhile, the Monarch al-Nasir (Saladin) was encamped outside Tiberias. He boosted the Muslims' spirits, and his army covered the entire plain.

The execution of the Templar and Hospitaller prisoners, which pleased many

On Monday morning, 27 Rabi' II (6 July 1187), two days after the victory, Saladin asked the Templars and Hospitaller prisoners to be brought to him. He said: "I shall cleanse the earth from this type of filth." He promised to give 50 dinars to each soldier who captured a prisoner. They brought 200 prisoners, and he ordered them to be executed. He chose to kill them

---

102. Eschiva of Bures, who was Princess of Galilee between 1158 and 1187, and who married Count Raymond of Tripoli in 1174.

instead of selling them as slaves. There was with him a number of scholars and Sufi mystics, as well as a group of devout ascetics. He asked each one of them to roll up his sleeve, unsheathe his sword, and kill a prisoner. As the sultan sat before them, his face was jubilant whereas the faces of unbelief were morose. The soldiers lined up in ranks, the commanders standing in front of them. Some of the scholars and mystics lifted their blades, struck firmly, and gave thanks; others refused, withdrew, and asked to be excused. Some, their weakness was laughable, so others stepped in for them.

I witnessed in this encounter a man who smiles but knows how to fight, a man who speaks and follows through. Saladin fulfilled many a promise, earned effusive praise, and received an eternal reward for the blood of the Franks he shed. Every neck that rose against him, he severed. He bloodied his sword in pursuit of victory. He wielded a lance to capture a lion, and concocted a cure for a sickening enemy. He conferred strength on his commanders, and unfurled his banners of protection. He slaughtered unbelief so that Islam could live, and destroyed polytheism to build up monotheism. He fulfilled his promise to the Muslim community, shattering the enemy to protect the precious believers.

The Frankish king, his brother, Humphrey, the lord of Byblos (Ugo III), the Great Master of the Templars, and their senior commanders were taken in chains to Damascus, where they were imprisoned; the disturbance they caused has been replaced with tranquility. The soldiers dispersed with the abundant booty they amassed. The embers of unbelief have died down and been extinguished.

Questions

1. According to 'Imad al-Din al-Isfahani, why was the capture of the True Cross such a devastating blow for the Franks?
2. How does he see its function in Christian belief and religious worship?
3. What can we learn about the etiquette for the treatment of prisoners of war from 'Imad al-Din al-Isfahani's account of the execution of the Templar and Hospitaller prisoners?
4. How does it differ from what we saw in Ibn al-Athir's narrative?
5. How does he compare Islam and Christianity?

12. Rashid al-Din al-Nabulusi's poem on Saladin's liberation of Jerusalem in 1187[103]

'Abd al-Rahman son of Muhammad Rashid al-Din al-Nabulusi was born in Nablus. He studied The Rhymed Prose (al-Maqamat) *of al-Hariri (d. 1122)[104] with one of the latter's students. Al-Hariri's* The Rhymed Prose *is a collection of poetry and tales about the adventures of an itinerant scholar, told in dazzlingly ornate prose and poetry, the purpose of which is to test the reader's erudition and taste by deploying all the grammatical and lexical subtleties of the Arabic language. It very quickly became the model of what Arabic artistic prose should be. Rashid al-Din al-Nabulusi traveled between many courts and composed odes for several dignitaries, including the 'Abbasid caliph al-Nasir li-Din Allah (r. 1180–1225), Saladin, his son al-Zahir, and al-Mu'azzam. He died in Damascus in 1222.*[105]

1- Woe to the Franks, nay woe to their nation; is there / nary a one capable of learning from misfortune!

2- How often you defeated them and dispersed their assembly / then assembled them again with your sword when they fled.

3- How often you made them drink the cup of humiliation; / their lewdness no wonder, for they are drunk.

4- Should they approach you by sea, without doubt it is caused by their ignorance / for only wild asses seek a lion in the jungle.

5- As they approach tigers, their rudeness will not protect them, / for it is your lions that roar at their heroes.

6- So, protect the sanctuary of the sacred house[106] without / fear; May God protect you from harm and trepidation.

---

103. Abu Shama, *Kitab al-Rawdatayn fi akhbar al-dawlatayn al-Nuriyya wa-l-Salahiyya*, ed. I. al-Zaybaq (Beirut: Mu'assasat al-Risala, 1997), 4: 289–290.

104. On al-Hariri, see Jaakko Hämeen-Anttila, "al-Hariri," *Encyclopaedia of Islam, Third Edition.*

105. On Rashid al-Din al-Nabulusi, see al-Dhahabi, *Ta'rikh al-islam*, 44: 449.

106. A reference to Jerusalem.

7- It is the noble house that called for you "O, Mu'tasim";[107] / worry no more for its glory anon.

8- Days will soon regret their error; / the wicked will reap what they have sown.

Questions

1. How does Rashid al-Din al-Nabulusi depict the Franks in his poem?
2. How does he depict Saladin?
3. How does he depict the city of Jerusalem?

---

107. "O, Mu'tasim" is in reference to the 'Abbasid caliph al-Mu'tasim (r. 833–842), who, according to the legend, was forced to mount a campaign to liberate the town of 'Ammuriyya (in central Anatolia) in 838 after it was reported to him that a Muslim woman there was captured by the Byzantines and cried for him, saying "O, Mu'tasim." The caliph was forced to react, for doing nothing would have been a public humiliation for him.

13. Ibn Shaddad on the expedition of the German emperor and the letter of the Armenian catholicos to Saladin in 1190[108]

Baha' al-Din Yusuf son of Rafi' Ibn Shaddad was born in Mosul in 1145. His father died while he was a young boy; he was subsequently raised by his maternal uncles, who belonged to the Shaddad family, whose name he adopted. In Mosul, his maternal uncles provided him with a traditional Islamic education in Qur'an, Hadith, and Shafi'i jurisprudence. He then moved to Baghdad where he continued his studies at the famous Nizamiyya College. Around 1173, he returned to Mosul and took a teaching position there. It was in Mosul that he drew Saladin's attention. After Ibn Shaddad completed the pilgrimage to Mecca in 1188, Saladin summoned him to his court in Damascus, where he became Saladin's close friend, trusted advisor, and chief judge of the army. Consequently, Ibn Shaddad was an eyewitness to Saladin's campaigns against Acre, Arsuf, and elsewhere during the Third Crusade. Ibn Shaddad's sympathetic biography of Saladin, Sultanic Marvels and Josephian[109] Charms, *reflects this close relationship between the sultan and his friend and advisor. After Saladin's death, Ibn Shaddad served Saladin's son al-Zahir and grandson al-'Aziz in Aleppo, where he died in 1234.*[110]

The king of the Germans

Reports came continually of the arrival of (Frederick I), the king of the Germans,[111] to the land of Qilij Arslan,[112] and that a massive crowd of Turkomans rallied against him in order to impede his crossing the river.[113] However, they were unable to do so because of the large number of his troops and because the Turkomans lacked a leader to unify them. Qilij

---

108. Ibn Shaddad, *al-Nawadir al-sultaniyya wa-l-mahasin al-yusufiyya*, ed. J.-D. al-Shayyal (Cairo: Maktabat al-Khanji, 1994), 190–193.

109. Josephian in reference to Joseph, and its use in the title is a double entendre meant to invoke biblical Joseph and also refer to Saladin, whose first name was Joseph (Yusuf in Arabic). It is interesting to note as well that Ibn Shaddad's first name was also Yusuf.

110. On Baha' al-Din Ibn Shaddad and his *al-Nawadir al-sultaniyya*, see Ibn Shaddad, *Rare and Excellent*, 1–9. See also Anne-Marie Eddé, "Baha' al-Din Ibn Shaddad," *Encyclopaedia of Islam, Third Edition*.

111. Known as Frederick Barbarossa, he was Holy Roman emperor (r. 1155–1190).

112. See Chapter 1, p. 31 (footnote 115).

113. It is not clear which river this is. It could be the river today called Sakarya in western Anatolia, or Kizilirmak in central Anatolia.

Arslan tried to pretend he was against him, but in secret, he had made an agreement with him. Once the German king had crossed the river, Qilij Arslan revealed his true colors, gave him hostages from his own court[114] and promised as well to send guides to lead the king into the land of Leo's son.[115] Indeed, Qilij Arslan sent guides to accompany the German king. On the way, they suffered from famine, so much so that they discarded some of their luggage. We were told—and God knows best—that they assembled in a large pile chainmail vests, helmets, and weapons that they could no longer carry. They burned them to damage them so no one could use them; the iron pile is still there.

They proceeded in that state until they reached the region of Tarsus, where they camped by a river[116] and prepared to cross it. The king desired to swim in that river, and the water was very cold. On top of the fatigue, exhaustion, hardship, and fear, the swimming sickened him gravely; he continued to decline and died. While in the midst of this sickness, he passed the reign to his son, (Frederick VI),[117] who was accompanying him. When he died, they decided to boil his body in vinegar, collect his bones, put them in a bag and carry them to noble Jerusalem—may God protect it—to bury him there. His son assumed command, despite the disapproval of some commanders; for the eldest son, (Henry IV), had stayed behind in his country and those commanders favored him. Nevertheless, the present son was able to establish his command among the army commanders. When Leo's son saw the suffering that the Franks had experienced—the hunger, death, and weakness, and especially the death of their king—he decided to avoid them, for he was not sure how they would behave. For they were Franks and he was Armenian. He fortified himself in one of his impregnable castles away from them.

---

114. The practice of exchanging hostages was to assure honoring of the agreement. It was customary to send someone's son or a significant figure in the court. See also the account of Sibt Ibn al-Jawzi on the capture of Damietta, pp. 109–114.

115. Son of Leo (or Levon in Armenian) is a reference to Leo II, ruler of Cilicia (r. 1187–1219), in southern Turkey today. Muslim chroniclers referred to him as Leo's son, probably mistaking him as the son of Leo I (d. 1140).

116. The Saleph River, which is known today as Göksu.

117. He was Duke of Swabia, and died in Acre on 20 January 1191 at the age of twenty-three.

13. Ibn Shaddad on the expedition of the German emperor

The Letter of the Armenian catholicos

The sultan (Saladin) received a letter from the catholicos (Gregory IV); he is the leader of the Armenians[118] and the lord of the Roman Castle,[119] which sits on the banks of the Euphrates. This is the translation of the letter:

> This letter is from the so-called[120] catholicos, the loyal servant, to inform our master and monarch, the victorious sultan, the uniter of belief, the standard bearer of justice and benevolence, the rectifier of the world and religion, the sultan of Islam and Muslims—may God, through His might and majesty, prolong his presence, multiply his glory, protect his soul, and help him attain his aspirations.
>
> Concerning the affairs of the king of the Germans. When he left his country and conquered the land of the Hungarians by force, he compelled the king of the Hungarians to submit to him and become his vassal, and he also confiscated his money and men, as he wished. After that, he came to the land of the Byzantines and conquered it. He plundered it and stayed there, forcing the Byzantine emperor to obey him, and took the emperor's son, brother, and forty of his closest aids as hostages. He also took from him forty measures[121] of gold, fifty measures of silver, and satin clothes worth a huge sum. He also confiscated boats and used them to cross to this side, taking with him the hostages.
>
> He proceeded until he reached the territories of the Monarch Qilij Arslan, whence he sent back the hostages. He marched for three days and the Ivaj Turkomans[122] brought to him sheep, cattle, horses, and merchandise for sale. But the Turkomans became greedy and rallied their numbers from across the land, and war broke out between them and him. They harassed his troops for 33 days as they marched. Finally, when he approached Konya, Qutb al-Din, son of Qilij Arslan, assembled the army and headed

---

118. Catholicos is the title used for the patriarch of one of the autocephalous eastern Christian churches; for example, the Armenian Apostolic Church, the Syrian Orthodox Church, etc. The Armenian catholicos at this time was Catholicos Gregory IV (1174–1193).

119. Rumkale in modern Turkey. Located to the west of Edessa, it was the seat of the Armenian catholicos.

120. It was customary for Christian leaders in the Near East to use such terms next to their titles, as a sign of humility.

121. The word used is qintar, which was a measure of weight, and depending on region, it varied between 50 and 250 kilograms.

122. A type of Turkic people, who formed a large community in Qilij Arslan's state.

Chapter 3: Chronicles, Memoirs, and Poetry

toward the German king. The two met in a pitched battle, and the German king inflicted upon Qutb al-Din a resounding defeat and proceeded to Konya, where he was met by a large crowd of armed Muslims, but he repelled them. Then he attacked Konya, putting it to the sword and killing a large number of Muslims and Persians.[123] He stayed there for five days, and Qilij Arslan asked for terms of safety, which the king approved and the two reached a firm agreement. The German king took from him 20 hostages from among the highest-ranking members of Qilij Arslan's court, and the latter advised him to proceed to Tarsus and Mopsuestia (al-Massisa),[124] which he did.

Before his arrival to these lands, intentionally or compelled by the circumstances, we decided to dispatch the servant Hatim with a delegation of trusted ones to meet with the king and bring him what he asked for, as well as give him a response to the letter he had sent to us. Hatim was instructed to keep the king's march within the territory of Qilij Arslan if at all possible. When they met with the majestic king, they gave him the response and suggested to him the path he should take. His troops and followers gathered to him in massive numbers, and he camped next to a river. He ate dinner and slept. When he awoke, he desired to swim in the cold water, which he did. It was by God's decree that he was inflicted with a severe sickness because of cold water. He lived for a few days and died.

As for Leo's son, he was on his way to meet the king when this event happened. His envoys fled from the camp and came to him to tell him of the situation. He retreated to one of his castles and took refuge there.

As for the king's son, his father had designated him as his replacement since he had come to these lands; his succession was confirmed. He learned about the escape of the envoys of Leo's son, so he dispatched someone to plead with them to return. When they came, he said to them: "My father was an old man and he only desired to come to these lands to make the pilgrimage to Jerusalem. I have assumed real power and suffered on this journey, if anyone does not obey me, I will attack his land." He also sent to Leo's son, who thought meeting with the king was unavoidable, for he had a massive army; it was estimated that it was comprised of 42,000

---

123. This could mean Zoroastrians.
124. Called Tkish in Turkey today (Msis in Armenian).

13. Ibn Shaddad on the expedition of the German emperor

armored men, not to mention the countless footmen. It included all kinds of peoples, united in pursuit of the same goal and very disciplined. If one of them commits a crime, his punishment is to be slayed like a sheep. One of their leaders committed an offense against a servant of his, beating him excessively. The priests met and deliberated. They ruled that he should be slayed. A multitude pleaded with the king to save his life, but he ignored them and slayed him. They even prohibited themselves any pleasure, so much so that if they heard of one among them seeking carnal pleasure, they would abandon and rebuke him. All of this was because of their suffering for the loss of Jerusalem. We were told that some of them would refuse to wear clothes for long periods, even prohibit themselves things that are lawful, and they would only wear iron coats. Their leaders tried to dissuade them from that, but they insisted on this immense hardship, humiliation, and fatigue.

The humble servant is sending you this report, and will send you any further news in due course, if almighty God permits.

This is the letter of the catholicos, which means caliph.[125] His name is Saint Gregor son of Basil.[126]

Questions

1. The terminology that the Christian Armenian Catholicos Gregory IV uses to address the Muslim Sultan Saladin at the beginning of his letter is quite deferential and laden with Islamic vocabulary. Why do you think Gregory IV would use such language to address Saladin in his letter to him?
2. How is Ibn Shaddad's account of the German King Frederick I and his retinue similar to and dissimilar to the account in the Armenian catholicos' letter to Saladin?
3. How does the catholicos explain the Germans' religiosity and justice?
4. How does he see God's role in these events?

---

125. Ibn Shaddad used the term *al-khalifa*, which shows that he thought of the ʿAbbasid caliph at the time as a symbolic religious head of Islam and not much more than that.
126. Catholicos Gregory IV (1174–1193).

Chapter 3: Chronicles, Memoirs, and Poetry

14. Ibn al-Athir on the Franks' capture of Acre in 1191[127]

On Friday, 17 Jumada II (12 July 1191), the Franks—may God curse them—captured the city of Acre. The first sign of desperation in the city was when the commander Sayf al-Din ʿAli son of Ahmad al-Hakkari, known as al-Mashtub,[128] who held it and was assisted by subordinate and younger commanders, went out to meet (Guy of Lusignan), the king of the Franks. He promised him to surrender the city to him with everything in it on condition that he provide safe passage to the Muslims there so that they could join their sultan. The French king rejected his offer and ʿAli son of Ahmad returned to the city. Despairing and disheartened, the people of the city forsook their concern for its defenses and focused solely on their own personal safety. Realizing what al-Mashtub had done and that the Franks would not consent to give them safe passage, two of the commanders in Acre secretly sneaked out of the city in the middle of the night by a small boat. They took with them their soldiers, and fled to join the Muslim army. They were ʿIzz al-Din Arsal al-Asadi and Ibn ʿIzz al-Din Jawili, along with others. In the morning, when the people inside Acre awoke and saw what had happened, they became even more desperate and disheartened, and were convinced of their imminent demise.

The Franks sent to Saladin asking him to surrender the city. He accepted their request on condition that he would free as many Frankish prisoners in his hands as there were Muslims in the city, in return for the Franks allowing them safe passage. He also promised to return to them the relic of the Holy Cross. They refused. So, Saladin sent a message to the Muslims in the city that they should head out of Acre as one group, leave their belongings behind, proceed along the seaside under cover of darkness, and then attack the enemy as a united front. He promised them that he would bring his army and join them in the fight against the Franks. They started preparation, but each person so busied himself with packing his possessions that by the time they were ready, the morning had come and they could no longer proceed with the plan. They were unable to defend the city that day, as the Franks launched an all-out assault with all their troops and machines. The

---

127. Ibn al-Athir, *al-Kamil fi al-ta'rikh*, 10: 95–98. For biographical information on Ibn al-Athir, see p. 59.

128. Sayf al-Din ʿAli son of Ahmad was a powerful Kurdish commander in Saladin's army and achieved the highest rank of *Asfahsallar*, or leading general. Due to a war injury on his face, he was nicknamed *al-Mashtub*, or Scarface. See Chapter 6, p. 207 (footnote 5).

14. Ibn al-Athir on the Franks' capture of Acre in 1191

Muslims inside the city climbed the wall and unfurled their banners so that the Muslims in the camp would see them; this was the alarm that they were told to display in case of emergency. When the Muslims in the camp saw that, they started weeping and wailing. They attacked the Franks from several fronts, thinking that this would distract them from attacking those in the city. Saladin, who was the first one out, urged them on.

The Franks climbed out of their trenches and marched toward the city. The Muslims approached the trenches. Just as they were about to storm the trenches and kill the Franks who were still in them, the Franks sounded the alarm and part of the Frankish army returned and repelled the Muslims; they had left another group to fight those inside the city.

When al-Mashtub realized that Saladin could do nothing and was unable to defend them, he went out to the Franks and agreed to surrender the city on condition of safe passage for those inside along with their personal belongings. He promised them the payment of 200,000 dinars, the release of 500 of their notable prisoners, the return of the relic of the Holy Cross, and 14,000 dinars for the marquis of Tyre. They accepted his offer on condition that the terms for paying the money and releasing the prisoners be fulfilled within 2 months.

When they swore an oath in front of him, he handed over the city to them. They entered peacefully, but as soon as they were inside, they revoked their word and seized the Muslims and their possessions. They imprisoned them and said that they were doing so in order to make sure that what they were promised would be delivered to them. They dispatched a message to Saladin that he should send the money, the prisoners, and the relic of the Holy Cross before they would release the Muslims they held. He started to collect the money, but his treasury was empty as he was spending what revenue he collected as fast as it came in.

After having collected 100,000 dinars, he convened his commanders for counsel. They advised that he should not send the money until he could arrange for the Franks to take an oath to release his men. They also suggested that the Templars should guarantee the agreement because they are pious people and keep their word. Saladin wrote to the Templars about that, and they replied: "We cannot take an oath or guarantee such a thing because we do not trust our compatriots." The Frankish leaders then said: "If you hand us the money already collected, prisoners, and relic of the Holy Cross, we will subsequently decide which ones of the prisoners in our hand to release." Saladin realized then that they were intent on treachery and refused to hand them anything. He sent them a message: "We will give you the money we collected, prisoners, and relic of the Holy Cross, and mortgage the remaining sum, but you must release our men. The Templars can guarantee the mortgage and they will take an oath to honor it."

The Frankish leaders replied: "We will not take an oath. You must send us the 100,000 dinars that you already collected, the prisoners, and the relic of the Holy Cross. Only then will we release those of your men whom we wish and keep whom we wish until the rest of the money is delivered." People knew then that they were treacherous, and that they would only release the boys of the army, the poor, the Kurds, and those of no importance, and that they would continue to hold hostage the commanders and wealthy individuals and force them to pay ransom. The sultan rejected their offer.

On Tuesday, 27 Rajab (20 August 1191), the Franks came outside the city with their cavalry and footmen and the Muslims rode out to meet them and attacked them. The Franks were forced to retreat from their positions, and the Muslims discovered that the majority of the Muslim prisoners the Franks were holding had been put to the sword; they kept the commanders, captains, and those with money, but had killed everyone else—the commoners and those without money. When Saladin saw that, he spent the money on other issues, and ordered the Frankish prisoners and the relic of the Holy Cross taken back to Damascus.

Questions

1. How does Ibn al-Athir depict the Franks' capture of Acre in 1191?
2. How does he depict the Muslims' responses to the Franks' success?
3. How does he describe negotiations between Saladin and the Franks?
4. According to Ibn al-Athir, how are the Frankish and Muslim hostages used in these negotiations? How is money used?
5. What does he say about the moral and religious integrity of the Templars?
6. Do we see any discrepancy between the account of 'Imad al-Din al-Isfahani about Saladin's execution of the Templars following the Battle of Hattin and Ibn al-Athir's account here about the sultan's attitude toward them?

15. Sibt Ibn al-Jawzi on al-Muʿazzam's destruction of the wall of Jerusalem in 1219[129]

Shams al-Din Abu al-Muzaffar Yusuf son of Qizughlu, known as Sibt Ibn al-Jawzi (ca. 1185–1256), was a renowned preacher and historian. He was the son of a Turkoman freedman who had married the daughter of the famous Baghdadi preacher and historian Ibn al-Jawzi (d. 1201); hence, the nickname Sibt or grandson of Ibn al-Jawzi. He was tutored by his grandfather in Baghdad; after his grandfather's death in 1201, Sibt ibn al-Jawzi relocated to Damascus where he flourished in the service of the Ayyubid sovereign, al-Muʿazzam ʿIsa (r. 1201–1227), and his successors. He was especially renowned for his eloquence as a preacher in Damascus, moving both crowds and sovereigns to tears as he implored them to take up the cause of jihad against the Franks. He was especially upset by al-Kamil's negotiations with Frederick II to surrender parts of Jerusalem to him. His The Mirror of Time on the History of Notables *is a very valuable source on Ayyubid history.*[130]

Year 616 (19 March 1219–6 March 1220)

On the first day of Muharram (19 March 1219), al-Muʿazzam ordered the destruction of the wall of Jerusalem. He had gone to help his brother al-Kamil defend Damietta [during the attack of the Fifth Crusade], when he learned that a group of the Franks were planning to attack Jerusalem. The Muslim sovereigns agreed to destroy the wall of Jerusalem. Their rationale was that since Syria was devoid of soldiers, should the Franks take Jerusalem, they would rule over all of Syria. At the time, the governor of Jerusalem was the commander al-ʿAziz ʿUthman[131] along with his chamberlain ʿIzz al-Din Aybak. Al-Muʿazzam wrote them with orders to destroy the wall. They refused and replied: "We will protect the city." Al-Muʿazzam wrote to them again: "If they take the city, they will kill everyone there, and they will

---

129. Sibt Ibn al-Jawzi, *Mirʾat al-zaman fi taʾrikh al-aʿyan* (Hyderabad: Daʾirat al-Maʿarif al-ʿUthmaniyya, 1951), 8.2: 601–602.
130. On Sibt Ibn al-Jawzi and his *Mirʾat al-zaman*, see Alex Mallett, "Sibt Ibn al-Jawzi," in *Medieval Historians and the Franks in the Levant*, ed. A. Mallett (Leiden: Brill, 2014), 84–108.
131. Al-ʿAziz ʿUthman was the brother of al-Muʿazzam, and the half-brother of Sultan al-Kamil.

then capture Damascus and all of the Muslim lands. Necessity[132] requires that we destroy the wall." They started the destruction of the wall on the first of Muharram (19 March 1219). People panicked and started screaming in the city as if it was the Day of Resurrection. Veiled women and girls, clerics and the elderly, young men and boys, all hurried to the Dome of the Rock and the Aqsa Mosque. They so cut their hair and tore their clothes that the Dome of the Rock and the niche of the Aqsa Mosque were full of hair. Then, they fled the city, leaving behind their property and families as they were certain that the Franks were coming the next morning. The roads were crammed with these people, some fleeing toward Egypt, some toward Kerak, and some toward Damascus. Veiled young women tore their clothes and wrapped them around their feet as shoes. A large number died of hunger or thirst. Such a calamity never occurred before in Islamic history. Their properties in Jerusalem were looted and the price of 50 kilograms (one qintar) of olive oil reached 10 dirhams.[133] Most poets wrote verses cursing this calamity caused by al-Mu'azzam; one of them wrote deridingly:

1- In Rajab, he allowed wine / and in Muharram, he destroyed Jerusalem.

Questions

1. Why did al-Mu'azzam decide to destroy the walls of Jerusalem?

2. How did the Muslim residents of the city respond to al-Mu'azzam's decision?

3. How do Sibt Ibn al-Jawzi's words here compare to what he said in his biography of al-Mu'azzam in Chapter 4 (pp. 174–183)?

---

132. Necessity, or *darura* in Arabic, is a legal concept in Islamic jurisprudence that is typically invoked to legitimize certain acts, even if they violate clear statutes of Shari'a law. See p. 151 (footnote 222).

133. This is an absurdly cheap price for olive oil, which suggests that people were so desperate to sell that they essentially gave it away for a trivial price.

16. Sibt Ibn al-Jawzi on the Franks' capture of Damietta in 1219 and their defeat in 1221

Year 616 (19 March 1219–6 March 1220)[134]

In this year, in the month of Shaʿban (November 1219), the Franks seized Damietta. Al-Muʿazzam had dispatched al-Nahid Ibn al-Jarkhi[135] with a force of 500 men to defend it, but when they attacked the trenches, Ibn al-Jarkhi and those with him were killed. The Franks displayed the heads of the killed atop the trenches, after having buried them. The inhabitants of Damietta became desperate; they ate dead corpses. Disease and death spread among them; al-Kamil could not aid them. They sent a message to the Franks that they were ready to surrender the city to them on condition that they be allowed to leave with their families and possessions. The priests came and swore on that. The Franks boarded their ships, some came overland, and the people of Damietta opened to them the city gates. They entered and raised their standards on the walls. But they betrayed the people of Damietta, killing and imprisoning them. They spent the night raping women and violating girls in the mosque. They confiscated the pulpit, Qurʾan books, and the heads of the dead, which they sent to their islands. They also converted the mosque into a church.

Abu al-Hasan Ibn Qufl[136] was then in Damietta. The Franks asked about him, and they were told: "This Muslim cleric is a pious man, to whom the poor people come." So, they did not harm him. The loss of Damietta was a great calamity in Islam. Al-Kamil and al-Muʿazzam wept excessively. I had not arrived yet to witness what happened, but al-Muʿazzam told me about it later, saying: "If prayers were answered in our time, the prayers of the people of Damietta would have been heard. For almighty God told us in several places in His Book that He would answer our prayers, but the people of Damietta, when their sins increased and immorality spread, God sent those who exacted His revenge against them; as in ❧*If We desire to destroy a town . . .*❧"[137] (Qurʾan 17:16).

---

134. Sibt Ibn al-Jawzi, *Mirʾat al-zaman*, 8.2: 603–604. For biographical information on Sibt Ibn al-Jawzi, see p. 107.
135. A senior commander in al-Muʿazzam's army.
136. A Sufi mystic.
137. The verse reads fully: ❧*If We desire to destroy a town, We order its men of luxury, and they indulge in sin, so Our just decree comes to pass upon it, and We destroy it utterly.*❧

Feeling utterly helpless, al-Kamil told al-Muʿazzam: "It is too late to save those who died, and what was foreordained has come to pass. It is pointless for you to stay here. Return to Syria and try to distract the Franks there. Also, summon the soldiers from northern Mesopotamia."

The author (Sibt Ibn al-Jawzi)—may God be merciful to him—said: While I was still in Damascus, al-Muʿazzam wrote to me a letter in his own hand. It begins as follows:

> From lord ʿIsa, sibling of Sultan al-Kamil. Honorable brother, you must have heard about what happened in Damietta. I implore you to incite the people to jihad, tell them about what befell their brethren in Damietta at the hands of the obstinate unbelievers. I have tallied the estates of Syria and found that there are 2,000 villages; 1,600 of which are owned by their inhabitants, but 400 belong to the Ayyubid sultanate. Surely, many soldiers could be recruited from these 400 villages! I also implore the Damascenes—from the riffraff to the notables—to come out and defend their properties. Please bring them and let us all meet in Nablus on such and such a date.

I went to the Great Mosque of Damascus and read his letter to the people. They replied positively and obediently. They also said: "We shall heed his demand each according to his ability." They started preparing, but by the time al-Muʿazzam reached the coast of Palestine, the Damascenes refused to depart, for every situation has its people, and war requires a special kind of men. Their refusal was the reason al-Muʿazzam imposed on them the one-eighth and one-fifth taxes. He wrote to me again: "If they do not want to come out, leave them and come alone." I departed for the coast and found him encamped against Caesarea. We stayed there until he conquered it. We entered that frontier city and he ordered the destruction of its wall. He then returned to Damascus after causing mayhem in the Frankish territories.

Year 618 (February 1221–February 1222)[138]

In this year, al-Muʿazzam departed to meet his brother, al-Ashraf, and the two encamped against Harran. The lord of Mardin, Nasir al-Din,[139] wrote

---

138. Sibt Ibn al-Jawzi, *Mirʾat al-zaman*, 8.2: 618–621.
139. Nasir al-Din Urtuq (d. 1240) was a Turkoman commander and the great-grandson of Il-Ghazi who surrendered Jerusalem to the Fatimids (see Ibn al-Qalanisi, p. 63; and Ibn al-Athir, pp. 66–67). Mardin was a major city in northern Mesopotamia, today in southeastern Turkey.

16. Sibt Ibn al-Jawzi on the Franks' capture of Damietta

to al-Ashraf asking him to bring al-Muʿazzam to him. Al-Ashraf passed the message to al-Muʿazzam and he departed for Mardin. The lord of Mardin came out to meet al-Muʿazzam in Dunaysir,[140] took him to the citadel, and gave him a lavish welcome. He also presented him with gifts and jewelry. They made an alliance between themselves; al-Muʿazzam gave one of his daughters in marriage to Nasir al-Din, and a second daughter to Nasir al-Din's son. Nasir al-Din also gave presents to those accompanying al-Muʿazzam and distributed to them money. Afterward, al-Muʿazzam returned to Harran.

The news came that the Mongols (*al-Tatar*)[141] had reached Kermanshah,[142] not far from Baghdad. The caliph was frightened and instructed the people to invoke God intensely in their prayers. He also ordered that Baghdad be fortified and enlisted soldiers for its defense.

In Jumada II (July–August 1221), Damietta was recaptured. I will mention what led to that. Al-Muʿazzam was very keen to rescue Damietta from the invaders. At that time, his relationship with his brother al-Kamil was at its best, whereas al-Ashraf was not well disposed toward al-Kamil, conspiring against him in secret. After the armies had gathered near Harran, al-Muʿazzam marched with his army to cross the Euphrates, and al-Ashraf followed them with his army. Al-Muʿazzam camped in Hims, whereas al-Ashraf camped in Salamiyya.[143]

The author (Sibt Ibn al-Jawzi)—may God be merciful to him—said: I departed Damascus for Hims, seeking to join the war, for al-Muʿazzam and al-Ashraf were set to attack the county of Tripoli. I reached al-Muʿazzam in Hims in Rabiʿ II (June 1221). He said to me: "I dragged al-Ashraf to this place by force. He is not happy. Every day I goad him for his tardiness but he only frowns. I fear that the Franks might seize Egypt. Since he is your friend, I would love it if you would go speak to him; he frequently asks me about you." Al-Muʿazzam then wrote a letter with his own hand; around 80 lines. I took it and departed for Salamiyya. When al-Ashraf was informed about my arrival, he came out of his tent to meet me. He asked why I had not visited him earlier, and we conversed for some time. Then I told him: "The Muslims are in crisis. If the Franks seize Egypt, they will

---

140. A town to the southwest of Mardin.
141. *Al-Tatar* in Arabic. Technically speaking, the Tatars were Turkic–Mongol peoples from central Asia, Mongolia, and northwestern China, who joined ranks with the Mongols in the early thirteenth century and participated in the Mongol conquests. Muslim chroniclers used the term to apply to the Mongol army, without distinction of the different ethnic groups of which it was constituted.
142. Today in western Iran, near the Iraqi border.
143. A town at the edge of the Syrian desert, midway between Hims and Palmyra.

control all the way to Hadramaut.[144] Mecca and Medina will become ruins. You should not take this lightly. Get up at once and march." He said to his servants: "Pack up the tents and pavilions." I departed ahead of him for Hims. Al-Mu'azzam's spies were everywhere; when he was informed of my imminent arrival, he mounted his horse and rode to meet me. He said to me: "I did not sleep yesterday, and today I ate nothing." I replied to him: "Tomorrow, your brother will be here in Hims." In the morning, al-Ashraf's drummers arrived followed by his scouts. By God! I have never seen soldiers more beautiful, organized, or better equipped than they. Al-Mu'azzam was very pleased. They sat at night discussing their plans, and they agreed that at dawn they would attack the county of Tripoli in order to distract the Franks. Finally, they were on the same page.

God made al-Ashraf inadvertently say something. He said to al-Mu'azzam: "O lord, instead of us attacking the coast, weakening our horses and soldiers, and losing valuable time, let us depart for Damietta and be done with this!" Al-Mu'azzam replied: "You said that without thinking!" Al-Ashraf nodded: "Indeed." Al-Mu'azzam kissed his foot. When al-Ashraf retired for the night, al-Mu'azzam exited his tent roaring like a fierce lion: "Pack up, pack up. We are leaving for Damietta." He knew that al-Ashraf would not let that happen if he were to delay things for the morning. Al-Mu'azzam marched toward Damascus, and the armies followed him. Meanwhile, al-Ashraf was asleep in his tent. He awoke at noon, went to the washroom, and noticed that there was no one around his tent. He asked: "Where are the soldiers?" They told him what happened. He nodded and departed for Damascus. He arrived in Qusayr[145] on Tuesday, 4 Jumada I (26 June 1221), and stayed there until the end of the month. Then, al-Mu'azzam and al-Ashraf paraded their armies underneath the Citadel of Damascus as they reviewed them from the balcony above. They left for Egypt on the first day of Jumada II (23 July 1221).

As for the Franks, they manned their boats—horsemen and foot soldiers—and sailed down to a lagoon in the Nile River where they disembarked and made camp. The Nile had reached its crest at that time. The Muslims opened all the floodgates, flooding their camp. Al-Kamil's troops encircled them from every direction, cutting off their retreat to Damietta. Then the Muslim fleet arrived, captured their ships, blocked them from receiving supplies, and cut off their contact with Damietta. The Franks were

---

144. Eastern province of Yemen today. The point is that the heartland of Islam will become defenseless.

145. A town south of Hims on the way to Damascus.

16. Sibt Ibn al-Jawzi on the Franks' capture of Damietta

a massive force: 100 counts, 800 of their celebrated knights, the king of Acre,[146] the duke (Leopold VI) and the pope's legate (Cardinal Pelagius). As for foot soldiers, there was no way to tally them. When they realized they were doomed, they sent to al-Kamil a message seeking peace and the exchange of hostages. They also promised to surrender Damietta.

Al-Kamil was so eager to save Damietta that he accepted their offer. Had this lasted 2 more days, the Muslims would have killed them all. Al-Kamil sent to them as hostages his son al-Salih Ayyub and his nephew Shams al-Muluk. The Franks' hostages were the leaders identified above; when they arrived, al-Kamil received them with presents and assigned for them special tents.

It was at that moment—on 3 Rajab 618 (23 August 1221)—that al-Mu'azzam and al-Ashraf arrived in al-Mansura. Al-Kamil convened a majestic assembly in a huge, towering tent and ordered that a feast be laid out. He invited the Frankish leaders and sat surrounded by al-Mu'azzam and al-Ashraf. The poet al-Hilli[147] stood up and chanted:

1- O what delight! Good fortune is now eternal; / the Merciful has made this victory a pledge!
2- The God of all creation awarded us this conquest, / an evident benefaction, an everlasting glory.
3- The face of time jeered then cheered, / the face of unbelief darkened with tyranny.
4- When the great sea flooded with tyrannical people / and boats like foam atop it,
5- God raised for this religion a man who sharpened / its resolve like a sword sharpened for battle.
6- None survived but those with bloodstained bodies, / the rest dead or in chains.
7- The cosmos proclaimed throughout the earth, raising / its voice in the east and the west:
8- O worshippers of Jesus! Jesus and his party, / together with Moses, are here to serve Muhammad![148]

---

146. John of Brienne, who was actually king of Jerusalem (r. 1210–1225), but ruled from Acre because Jerusalem was under the control of the Ayyubids. He became later the Latin emperor of Constantinople (r. 1229–1237).
147. His name was Rajih son of Isma'il (d. 1230). He was a well-known poet at the time and regularly frequented the courts of the three Ayyubid sovereigns.
148. 'Isa (the name for Jesus in Arabic) and Musa (the name of Moses) are the names of al-Mu'azzam and al-Ashraf, respectively. Muhammad is the name of al-Kamil. The poet was punning on the three brothers' names as if they were the three prophets.

Chapter 3: Chronicles, Memoirs, and Poetry

With some remaining lines.

The peace was signed between al-Kamil and the Franks on Wednesday, 19 Rajab (8 September 1221). Some of the Franks departed overland, and some by sea to Acre. Al-Kamil took possession of Damietta. When the Mesopotamian and Syrian armies finally arrived, he had already recaptured Damietta.

Questions (Year 616)

1. How does Sibt Ibn al-Jawzi describe the Franks during the siege of Damietta?
2. How does he account for the loss of the city to the Franks? What explanation does he give for God not aiding the people of Damietta?
3. How does al-Muʿazzam enlist Sibt Ibn al-Jawzi to rally the Syrians to jihad?
4. What role do oaths play in this narrative? Why bother to demand that oaths be made if they were not honored?
5. Why did the Crusaders save the mystic Ibn al-Qufl? If they killed everyone in the city, who could have told them who he was?

Questions (Year 618)

1. How did al-Muʿazzam and Nasir al-Din seal their alliance?
2. What can we learn from Sibt Ibn al-Jawzi's account about the relationship between the three Ayyubid brothers and leaders—al-Kamil, al-Muʿazzam, and al-Ashraf?
3. How does al-Muʿazzam get his brother al-Ashraf to agree to join him on his way to help their brother, al-Kamil, in Egypt?
4. What can we learn from al-Hilli's poem composed for al-Kamil's banquet after the Franks surrendered Damietta?

17. Sibt Ibn al-Jawzi on the envoys of Frederick to al-Mu'azzam in 1226[149]

In this year (624/1227) al-Ashraf returned to his lands in northern Mesopotamia. The envoy of the emperor, following his meeting with al-Kamil, came to al-Mu'azzam to ask him to hand over some territory. Al-Mu'azzam spoke to him abrasively, saying: "Tell your master that I am not like others. The only thing he has from me is the sword."

. . .

Al-Ashraf advised al-Nasir Dawud: "Go to al-Kamil and fix your problem with him." Al-Nasir Dawud left to meet al-Kamil and upon arrival learned that his uncle had surrendered Jerusalem to the emperor. The news made him upset and he chastised al-Kamil, who replied: "It was your father al-Mu'azzam who forced my hand." What al-Kamil meant by this was that al-Mu'azzam had agreed to give the emperor all the land between the Jordan River and the Mediterranean Sea, the villages between Jerusalem and Jaffa, and others as well.

Questions

1. What do these two brief accounts tell us about al-Mu'azzam's willingness to negotiate with the envoy of Frederick II—5 years after the end of the Fifth Crusade?

2. How can we understand al-Mu'azzam's statement: "Tell your master . . . the only thing he has from me is the sword"? Is this a serious statement or mere posturing for effect?

3. Why did Sibt Ibn al-Jawzi in the first report only recount al-Mu'azzam's angry outburst, when he knew all along that al-Mu'azzam had actually agreed to negotiate and give the emperor control over a large part of Palestine?

---

149. Sibt Ibn al-Jawzi, *Mir'at al-zaman*, 8.2: 643, 654. For biographical information on Sibt Ibn al-Jawzi, see p. 107.

18. Ibn Wasil on Frederick arriving in Acre in September 1228[150]

Abu 'Abd Allah Jamal al-Din Muhammad son of Salim son of Nasr Allah son of Salim Ibn Wasil was born in Hama in 1208 to a family that played a prominent role in the civilian elite of the city throughout the thirteenth century. Ibn Wasil was given a traditional Islamic education and later moved to Jerusalem where he assisted his father, who was a professor at the Saladin College (1227–1229). He subsequently began to seek the patronage of local Syrian rulers to study and work on the rational sciences, especially logic and astronomy. During his studies he built up a network of relationships with Ayyubid military and political leaders in Hama, which led to him serving as part of a diplomatic mission to Baghdad in 1243–1244. He then moved to Cairo where he held a number of teaching and juridical positions for some two decades. Ibn Wasil accommodated himself to the transition from Ayyubid to Mamluk rule quite easily. In fact, from 1261 to 1262, he served as an envoy from the Mamluk Sultan Baybars (r. 1260–1277) to the Hohenstaufen king of Sicily, Manfred (r. 1258–1266). Ibn Wasil's scholarly work focused on history, metrics, and logic, including a treatise on logic that he wrote for Manfred, which is now lost. However, he is most famous for two chronicles: Dissipater of Anxieties on the Reports of the Ayyubids, *which covers the period from 1083 to 1261, and* The Upright History *(also known as* The History of the Reign of al-Salih Ayyub*),[151] which is a universal chronicle from creation to 1239, and was intended as a present to the Ayyubid Sultan al-Salih Ayyub (r. 1240–1249). Given his service as a judge and as a diplomat, Ibn Wasil's chronicles contain a wealth of historical information on the history of Syria–Palestine and Egypt during the thirteenth century. Upon returning from his mission on behalf of Baybars in 1262, Ibn Wasil returned to his hometown of Hama, where he became the chief judge of the city. He died in Hama in 1298.[152]*

---

150. Ibn Wasil, *Mufarrij al-kurub fi akhbar bani Ayyub*, eds. J.-D. al-Shayyal and H. Rabi' (Cairo: Dar al-Kutub wa-l-Watha'iq al-Qawmiyya, 1953–1977), 4: 233–235.

151. In Arabic, *salih* means morally upright; hence, the title is a pun on Sultan al-Salih Ayyub's name.

152. On Ibn Wasil and his works, see Konrad Hirschler, "Ibn Wasil: An Ayyubid Perspective on Frankish Lordships and Crusades," in *Medieval Historians of the Franks in the Levant*, ed. A. Mallett (Leiden: Brill, 2014), 136–160. See also Hirschler, *Medieval Arabic Historiography: Authors as Actors* (Abingdon: Routledge, 2006).

18. Ibn Wasil on Frederick arriving in Acre in September 1228

In this year (625/1228), the emperor arrived in Acre with a multitude of Germans and other Frankish groups. We have already mentioned the delegation of the commander Fakhr al-Din son of Shaykh al-Shuyukh to the emperor on behalf of the Sultan and Monarch al-Kamil; this was during the last days of the Monarch al-Mu'azzam. The Monarch al-Kamil's rationale for the agreement with the emperor and for inviting him to come was to disturb the Monarch al-Mu'azzam, and to foil the agreement that the Monarch al-Mu'azzam was arranging with Jalal al-Din Khwarazm Shah and the ruler of Irbil against him (al-Kamil) and the Monarch al-Ashraf. The emperor readied himself and arrived with his troops to the coast and disembarked in Acre. Ahead of him came a large group of Franks, but they refrained from any action out of fear of the Monarch al-Mu'azzam and because they were expecting the arrival of the emperor.

The meaning of this title—emperor—in the Frankish language is *king of kings*. His kingdom is the island of Sicily and the lands of Apulia and Lombardy. I have seen these lands and visited them when I visited as envoy of the triumphant (al-Zahir), pillar of the religion (Rukn al-Din), Sultan and Monarch Baybars—may God be merciful to him—to the son of the Emperor Frederick who is called Manfred.[153] Among the Frankish kings, he was the emperor, and he was gracious, loved wisdom, logic, and medicine. He was favorable toward the Muslims because his original base and upbringing were in Sicily; he, his father, and his grandfathers were the kings there. The people of this island were predominantly Muslims.

When the emperor reached Acre, the Monarch al-Kamil was stuck with him because his brother the Monarch al-Mu'azzam—who was the reason for which he had invited the emperor—had died and there was no need for the alliance with Frederick. But al-Kamil could not get rid of him or fight him on account of the agreement they had concluded, which would have spoiled the plans he had in mind at that time. So al-Kamil corresponded with Frederick and was courteous to him, and events occurred after that which we will mention later, if God wills.

---

153. From 1261 to 1262, Ibn Wasil served as an envoy from the Mamluk Sultan Baybars (r. 1260–1277) to the Hohenstaufen king of Sicily, Manfred (r. 1258–1266)—more than 30 years after Frederick II's arrival in Acre.

Chapter 3: Chronicles, Memoirs, and Poetry

Questions

1. What does Ibn Wasil's report tell us about the alliances between the different actors in the region at the time?
2. How does Ibn Wasil see Frederick's attitude toward the Muslims?
3. What does it mean when Ibn Wasil says that al-Kamil could not fight with Frederick because of the agreement they had reached? In other words, did some rulers feel they were bound by the terms of agreements? Did they think they could/should not violate them?

19. Sibt Ibn al-Jawzi on Frederick's visit to the Noble Sanctuary of Jerusalem in March 1229[154]

In this year (626/1229), the emperor entered Jerusalem while Damascus was under siege. He demonstrated some marvelous things while there. Among them: Once when he entered the Dome of the Rock, he saw a priest sitting near the footprint, collecting parchments from Frankish pilgrims. He drew near to him as if to ask for a prayer, but instead smacked him and threw him down on the floor, saying: "You pig, the sultan was gracious enough to allow us to visit this place and you do in it these things! If any one of you comes to this place in this way again, I will kill him."

The custodians of the Dome of the Rock reported what took place. They said that Frederick looked at the inscription around the Dome—*Saladin has purified this holy place from the polytheists*—and asked: "Who are the polytheists?" He then said to the custodian: "These screened windows above the doors, why are they there?" They replied: "In order to keep the birds out." He said: "God will come against you, haughty ones."

They said that when the noontime came, and the muezzin made the call to prayer, all of the emperor's assistants, slave boys, and even his teacher—who was from Sicily and taught him the books of logic—joined in the prayer, for they were all Muslims.

They said that the emperor was blond and had weak eyesight. Had he been a slave, he would not even fetch 200 dirhams. They also said that based on his conversation, it appeared that he was a materialist, and only pretended to be a Christian.

They said that al-Kamil had requested that the jurist Shams al-Din, chief judge of Nablus, instruct the muezzins as follows: "As long as the emperor is in Jerusalem, do not deliver a sermon from the pulpit or make the call to prayer in the Haram." The judge forgot to inform the muezzins. The emperor spent the night at Shams al-Din's house. During that night, the muezzin 'Abd al-Karim ascended the minaret before the time for the dawn prayer. He then recited the quranic verses that deal with the Christians, such as The Almighty saying, ❮*God did not take to Himself a son . . .*❯ (Qur'an 23:91), ❮*this is Jesus, son of Mary . . .*❯ (Qur'an 19:34), and similar verses.

---

154. Sibt Ibn al-Jawzi, *Mir'at al-zaman*, 8.2: 655–657. For biographical information on Sibt Ibn al-Jawzi, see p. 107. The Noble Sanctuary (*al-Haram al-Sharif* in Arabic) in Jerusalem refers to the entire esplanade where the Dome of the Rock and the Aqsa Mosque are located. In the Jewish and Christian traditions, the area is known as the Temple Mount. See al-Harawi's description of the area, Chapter 1, pp. 5–8.

When dawn came, the judge summoned 'Abd al-Karim and said to him: "What have you done? The sultan decreed such and such." 'Abd al-Karim replied: "You never told me. I won't do it again." The second night, 'Abd al-Karim refrained from ascending the minaret. When dawn came, the emperor summoned the judge, for he had come to Jerusalem to attend to the emperor's affairs; it was he who had turned Jerusalem over to him. The emperor said to him: "O judge, where is that man who yesterday ascended the minaret and recited those words?" The judge informed him what the sultan had instructed. The emperor said: "You did wrong. Do you, O judge, change your rituals, law, and religion because of me? Were you with me in my country would I have annulled the ringing of bells because of you! By God, by God, do not do this or you will diminish in our opinion." He then distributed money to the custodians, muezzins, and dwellers,[155] giving each person ten dinars. He only stayed in Jerusalem two nights and returned to Jaffa out of fear from the Templars who were seeking to kill him.

Questions

1. What might Sibt Ibn al-Jawzi be trying to convey with the expression: "In this year (626/1229), the emperor entered Jerusalem while Damascus was under siege"?

2. What does his description of the peculiar way Frederick II conducted himself in the Noble Sanctuary tell us about Frederick's perception of Islam and the Muslims?

3. What does it tell us about Sibt Ibn al-Jawzi's perception of Frederick?

---

155. See p. 67 (footnote 18).

20. Ibn Wasil on the negotiations between al-Kamil and Frederick, and the emperor's visit to the Haram of Jerusalem[156]

The handing over of Jerusalem to the Franks

After the Monarch al-Ashraf departed to Damascus, the Sultan and Monarch al-Kamil remained in Tall al-ʿUjul to finalize the terms of the truce with the Franks and to confirm in his heart their intentions. Envoys were exchanged between him and the emperor, king of the Franks, whose goal was to retain what he and the Monarch al-Kamil had previously agreed to when the Monarch al-Muʿazzam was still alive. The king of the Franks refused to return to his lands until the terms had been met; namely, that Jerusalem be turned over to him along with other territories conquered by Saladin. The Monarch al-Kamil refused to turn over all of that to him, but finally agreed to turn over Jerusalem to him on condition that its walls remain ruined and not be rebuilt; that the Franks not control any of the neighboring villages; that all the surrounding villages remain for the Muslims with their own ruler stationed in al-Bira, near Jerusalem to the north; that the Noble Sanctuary,[157] including the sacred Dome of the Rock and the Aqsa Mosque, remain in the control of the Muslims; that their symbols be publicly displayed; that the Franks not enter Jerusalem except for the purpose of pilgrimage; and that Jerusalem should be administered by the Muslims. As an exception to these terms, the Franks requested certain villages which lay on the way from Acre to Jerusalem, and that these villages should be under their administration out of fear that some Muslims might hurt them. The Monarch al-Kamil realized that if he were to break with the emperor and not give in to this request it might renew hostilities between him and the Franks and that his plans would be spoiled. He saw fit to please the Franks with the city of Jerusalem with its walls destroyed and to conclude a truce with them for some time, knowing that he could take Jerusalem back from them any time he wished.

The commander Fakhr al-Din son of al-Shaykh was the envoy who brought correspondences back and forth between the Monarch al-Kamil and the emperor. A variety of issues were raised during the negotiations. The emperor sent once to the Monarch al-Kamil a number of philosophical,

---

156. Ibn Wasil, *Mufarrij al-kurub*, 4: 241–251. For biographical information on Ibn Wasil, see p. 116.
157. See p. 119 (footnote 154).

geometrical, and mathematical questions in order to determine the level of the scholars in his court. The Monarch al-Kamil presented the mathematical questions to the scholar 'Alam al-Din Qaysar son of Abu al-Qasim who was the leading authority in this field. He showed the other questions to a group of learned men and they replied to each one of them.

The Sultan and Monarch al-Kamil and the emperor took an oath to honor what they had agreed. They concluded the truce for a fixed period of time and the matters between them were normalized. Each side trusted the other. I was informed that the emperor said to the commander Fakhr al-Din: "If I did not fear for my reputation among the Franks, I would not have bothered the sultan with anything. I do not have any need for Jerusalem or other than it. I only sought to preserve my rule in their midst."

When the truce was concluded, the sultan sent someone to Jerusalem to announce that the Muslims should leave and turn the city over to the Franks. My father—may God be merciful to him—told me that when this thing happened in Jerusalem, he had just arrived there from Mecca—may God protect it—where he had spent the previous year, whereas I had traveled to Jerusalem and spent the previous year there. He told me: "When it was announced in Jerusalem for the Muslims to leave and turn over the city to the Franks, the people of Jerusalem started to scream and wail. It was an immensely troubling thing for the Muslims; they were devastated that Jerusalem would no more be under their control. They disliked that the Monarch al-Kamil had done this, and found it repugnant. For the conquest and rescue of this noble city from the infidels was one of the most significant accomplishments of his uncle the victorious Monarch Saladin—may God purify his soul." But the Monarch al-Kamil—may God be merciful to him—had known that the Franks could not protect Jerusalem with its walls ruined, and that when his affairs were set and matters were settled for him, he could cleanse it from the Franks and expel them from it. Sultan al-Kamil once said: "We only gave them access to the churches and some ruined houses. As for the Haram and what is there, including the sacred Dome of the Rock and the other sites of pilgrimage, they remain in the control of the Muslims, the symbol of Islam is raised as it used to be, and the ruler of the Muslims is in control of the villages and farmlands around it."

When the truce was concluded, the emperor asked the permission of the sultan to visit Jerusalem, and he granted it to him. The sultan asked the judge Shams al-Din—may God be merciful to him—who was the chief judge of Nablus, revered in the Ayyubid state, and honored by the Ayyubid monarchs, to be at the service of the emperor during his entire visit to Jerusalem and until he returned to Acre. Shams al-Din—may God be merciful to him—told me: "When the emperor came to Jerusalem, I stayed with him as the Sultan and Monarch al-Kamil had instructed me. I went with him to the Noble Sanctuary and he saw the various sacred sites there; I then entered with him to the Aqsa Mosque. Its architecture and that of the sacred Dome of the Rock pleased him. When he reached the prayer niche in the Aqsa Mosque, he liked it and the pulpit; he climbed all the way to the top. He descended and took me by the hand and we exited the Aqsa where he saw a priest holding a Gospel, seeking to enter the Aqsa Mosque. He yelled at him in reproach and said: 'What brought you here? By God, if any of you enter here without my permission, I will pluck out his eyes. We are the servants of the Sultan and Monarch al-Kamil and his slaves. He was benevolent toward me and you with these churches out of his magnanimity. Let no one of you exceed his limits.' That priest left trembling in fear of him; the emperor went to the house that was assigned to him and lodged there."

Judge Shams al-Din also said: "I instructed the muezzins not to make the call for prayer that night out of respect for the emperor. When the morning came and I went to see him he said to me: 'O Judge, why did not the muezzins make the call for prayer on the minarets as per their custom?' I replied to him: 'I, your servant, asked them not to do that to honor the king and out of respect for him.' He said to me: 'You did wrong in that. By God, the primary purpose for me to spend the night in Jerusalem was to hear the muezzins' call for prayer and their Qur'an recitation during the night.' Then he left for Acre."

When the news reached Damascus that Jerusalem was turned over to the Franks, the Monarch al-Nasir (Dawud) ordered the denunciation of his uncle the Monarch al-Kamil. He asked the scholar and preacher Shams al-Din Yusuf—grandson of the scholar Jamal al-Din Ibn al-Jawzi and who was very well liked by the populace—to sit in the Grand Mosque of Damascus and preach about the religious merits of Jerusalem, what the histories and traditions say about it, and to cause people to grieve by reminding them how demeaning and humiliating to the Muslims is the act of turning the city of Jerusalem over to the infidels. The Monarch al-Nasir's intention was to alienate the people of Damascus from his uncle so that they would take his side in the fight against al-Kamil. Shams al-Din sat as he was instructed, and the people came to listen to his preaching. It was a remarkable day: the people's screams, sobbings, and lamentations were loud. I attended that event and heard him recite a poem that has a *t* ending, composed in a fashion similar to the poem of Di'bil son of 'Ali al-Khuza'i,[158] and which used one of its lines:

---

158. Di'bil son of 'Ali al-Khuza'i (d. 860) was a well-known poet in Baghdad who became famous for his satiric poetry. Shams al-Din Yusuf is Sibt ibn al-Jawzi. See p. 107.

1- No recitation is heard in the schools of the Qur'an / and empty courtyards in the houses and neighborhoods.

A line of his poem stuck in my head:

1- The Dome of the Ascension and the Rock which / boasts above all other rocks on Earth.

When the terms of the truce between the Sultan and Monarch al-Kamil and the emperor were finalized, the emperor sailed back to his country. He remained sincere and friendly toward the Monarch al-Kamil. The correspondence was continuous between them until the Monarch al-Kamil died and his son the Monarch al-'Adil Sayf al-Din became sultan. The emperor was sincere and friendly toward him too, and corresponded with him.

Following the arrest of the Monarch al-'Adil, his brother the Monarch al-Salih Najm al-Din Ayyub assumed the throne. The affairs continued as previously. The Monarch al-Salih sent to the emperor the scholar Siraj al-Din al-Urmawi, who is now chief judge of Konya in the land of the Byzantines.[159] Siraj al-Din stayed with him for some time and compiled for him a book on logic. The emperor was very charitable toward him, and Siraj al-Din retuned to the Monarch al-Salih with great honors.

When (Louis IX), the king of France, who was the most prestigious of the Frankish rulers, came against Egypt in 647 (1249), the emperor sought to discourage him, frighten him, and warn him of the consequences, but the king refused to heed the emperor's advice. Sarnard, the chancellor of Manfred son of the emperor, told me: "The emperor sent me in secret to the Monarch al-Salih Najm al-Din to let him know that the king of France was intending to attack Egypt, to warn him, and to advise him to prepare for the attack. The Monarch al-Salih did indeed make the preparations and I returned to the emperor. During my journey to and from Egypt I was disguised as a merchant. No one knew of my meeting with the Monarch al-Salih out of fear that the Franks might learn of the emperor's partiality toward the Muslims against them."

Following the Monarch al-Salih's death, the troops of the king of France were defeated and uprooted; the Monarch al-Mu'azzam Turanshah son of the Monarch al-Salih captured him. He was later rescued from captivity following the assassination of the Monarch al-Mu'azzam and he returned to his land. The emperor sent to him reminding him of his advice, of what had happened to him by going against it, and reprimanding him for not

---

159. The popular way in medieval Muslim scholarship to refer to Anatolia.

20. Ibn Wasil on the negotiations between al-Kamil and Frederick

heeding his advice. The emperor died in that year, which is 648 (1250), one year after the death of the Monarch al-Salih. After him came his son Conrad who died; his brother Manfred took over. They were all loathed by the pope, caliph of the Franks and ruler of Rome,[160] because of their partiality toward the Muslims. A war broke out between Manfred and the pope, which Manfred won.

I was dispatched to Manfred as envoy of the triumphant, pillar of the religion, Monarch Baybars—may God be merciful to him—during the month of Ramadan in 659 (July 1261). I was very well honored during my stay with him in one of the towns of Apulia, the long stretch of land that connects to Andalusia.[161] I met with him several times and found him to be a discerning man, a lover of the rational sciences. He knew by heart ten sections of Euclid's book on geometry (*The Elements*). Close to the town where I resided was a city called Lucera whose inhabitants were all Muslims from the island of Sicily. Friday prayer was convened and the sign of Islam publicly displayed. It has been like this since the days of his father the emperor. Manfred started to build a school there dedicated for the study of all types of speculative sciences.[162] I also found that most of his confidants who attend to his private affairs were Muslims. The call for prayer is declared in his army camp and the prayer is convened.

When I returned from that land, news arrived that the pope, ruler of Rome—which is at a distance of 5 days from where we were—and the brother of the king of France,[163] the one mentioned earlier, set out against Manfred. That was because the pope had excommunicated Manfred for his partiality toward the Muslims and breaking their laws. So, too, were his brother Conrad and the emperor; they all were excommunicated by the pope of Rome. For them, the pope of Rome was the successor of Christ and his deputy. It is up to him to prohibit, permit, and decide on all matters. He is the one who coronates their kings and instates them. Nothing in terms of their law can be settled without him. He should be a monk, and when he dies he is succeeded by another one who is also a monk.

---

160. It is interesting that Ibn Wasil employed Islamic terminology (*khalifa*) to refer to the pope, conveying his understanding that the pope was the religious leader of the Franks as well as the city of Rome. See also the use of the term by Ibn Shaddad to describe the Armenian catholicos, p. 103 (footnote 125).

161. Apulia is the region in southeastern Italy today whose main city is Bari. It includes the back part of the boot of Italy.

162. On Lucera, see Julie A. Taylor, *Muslims in Medieval Italy: The Colony at Lucera* (Lanham: Lexington Books, 2003).

163. A reference to Charles of Anjou (d. 1285), brother of King Louis IX (r. 1226–1270).

I was told a marvelous story about their country in which the office of emperor before Emperor Frederick, mentioned earlier, was occupied by his father. When he died, Frederick was a young boy. Several Frankish kings desired the post, each one hoping that the pope of Rome would give it to him. But Frederick—who was German, which is one of the Frankish ethnicities—was a crafty and conniving person. He met separately with each one of these kings who desired the post of emperor and told each one of them: "I do not seek this post because I am not fit for it. So when we meet before the pope, tell him 'this matter should be decided by the son of the previous emperor, and whoever he accepts to be appointed as emperor I accept.' If the pope grants me the say on who should be chosen, I will choose you and nobody else. My intention is to be in your service and seek your support." When Frederick said this to each one of the kings, they agreed and trusted him. They thought he was truthful. When they convened before the pope in the city of Rome, Frederick was with them. He had instructed a group of strong German horsemen who were in his service to be ready on their horses near the Great Church of Rome, where the meeting was convened. The pope addressed the kings in front of him: "What do you say about this post, and who in your opinion is worthy of it?" He placed the crown in front of them. Each one said: "I choose Frederick to decide on this matter. Whoever he chooses I accept and endorse, for he is the son of the emperor and the most suitable to be heard on this matter." Frederick stood up and said: "I am the son of the emperor and I am the most suitable for this post and crown and all the convened here are content and have chosen me." He placed the crown on his head, and they all bowed their heads. He left in haste with the crown on his head, mounted his horse in the company of the German horsemen—whom he told to wait for him near the church—and rushed back to his lands. After that he did things that, in accordance with their laws, necessitated that the pope excommunicate him, which the pope did.

I was told that when the emperor was in Acre, he said to the commander Fakhr al-Din son of al-Shaykh—may God be merciful to him: "Tell me about your caliph, what is his origin?" Fakhr al-Din replied: "He is the cousin of our Prophet Muhammad—may God bless him and grant him peace. He inherited the caliphate after his father, who inherited from his father. Thus, the caliphate continues exclusively within the household of the prophet." The emperor said: "How beautiful. These mindless people—he meant the Franks—select a man from the junkyard with no relation of any kind to Christ and who is an ignorant idiot and make him their caliph, acting as deputy to Christ, whereas your caliph is the cousin of your prophet and he is the most suitable for the post."

20. Ibn Wasil on the negotiations between al-Kamil and Frederick

When the pope and the brother of the king of France set out against Manfred, the son of the emperor, they fought him, defeated his army, and took him captive. The pope ordered that he be executed, and so he was. The land which belonged to the emperor's son was given to the brother of the king of France; he took control of it in 663 (1265), if I remember well.[164]

Questions

1. What were the central issues in the negotiations between al-Kamil and Frederick II regarding Jerusalem?
2. Do we sense any confusion in the way Ibn Wasil reported about the status of Jerusalem?
3. How does Frederick's purported rebuke of the monk exhibit the emperor's understanding of who actually controlled Jerusalem?
4. How is this report similar to or different from the one narrated by Sibt Ibn al-Jawzi?
5. What do we know from Ibn Wasil about the Muslims' knowledge of the affairs in Europe? What channels of communication existed between them?

---

164. Ibn Wasil was actually off by one year: Manfred was killed in battle on 26 February 1266, which corresponds to 19 Jumada I, 664.

21. Ibn Wasil on the handing over of Jerusalem to the Franks in 1243[165]

On the agreement between the Monarch al-Salih Isma'il of Damascus, the Monarch al-Mansur (Ibrahim) of Hims, and the Monarch al-Nasir Dawud with the Franks and the handing over of Jerusalem, Tiberias, and Ascalon to them

When they learned of the Monarch al-Salih Najm al-Din Ayyub's correspondence with the Khwarazmians and that the latter would surely come and ally with his Egyptian forces against them, which they knew they could not withstand, they joined ranks to make war against Sultan al-Salih Ayyub and oppose him. They made a truce with the Franks and agreed with them to hand over to them Jerusalem, and to give them control of the Noble Sanctuary and all the sacred sites on it. They also promised to hand over to them Tiberias, Ascalon, and Belvoir (Kawkab).[166] So they handed each of these to the Franks, who started rebuilding the fortifications of Tiberias and Ascalon.

The Hospitallers took possession of Belvoir and started rebuilding its fortifications. The Franks also entered Jerusalem and took control of the sacred Dome of the Rock, the Aqsa Mosque, and all the sacred sites on the Noble Sanctuary. The above-mentioned monarchs also assured the Franks, as it was rumored, that if they were to capture Egypt, they would give them a share there. The Franks rallied their cavalries and footmen for war.

The Monarch al-Salih Isma'il dispatched some of his men to Gaza where they camped, and they were set to advance to Egypt. The Monarch al-Mansur advanced to Acre, where he met with the Franks to confirm that they would indeed join him in fighting the Monarch al-Salih Ayyub. They agreed.

At the end of this year (640/Spring 1243), I decided to travel to Egypt, and stopped on my way in Jerusalem. I saw the monks and priests over the sacred Dome of the Rock, and wine jars on it intended for the Holy Communion. I went as well to the Aqsa Mosque and saw there a suspended bell. The call for prayer and dwelling in the Noble Sanctuary were abolished, and infidelity was proclaimed there.

---

165. Ibn Wasil, *Mufarrij al-kurub*, 5: 332–334. For biographical information on Ibn Wasil, see p. 116.
166. Kawkab, which the Franks called Belvoir, was a fortress near Tiberias, with a dominant view of the town and the Jordan River.

21. Ibn Wasil on the handing over of Jerusalem to the Franks in 1243

The Monarch al-Nasir Dawud arrived in Jerusalem on the same day I was visiting it; he camped on the western side of the city. I refrained from meeting with him out of fear that he might prevent me from proceeding to Egypt.

When I arrived in Gaza, I saw some of the troops of the Monarch al-Salih Isma'il already camping there. When I reached al-'Abbasa,[167] I found there some troops of the Egyptian army. Each side was set for war against the other. I also came upon the tent of the Sultan and Monarch al-Salih Najm al-Din Ayyub erected next to the al-Jubb pond, and the troops preparing to march toward Syria.

In the month of Muharram of this year (641/June–July 1243), I arrived in Cairo. I met with the commander Husam al-Din son of Abu 'Ali; the sultan had arranged for him to reside in the hall known as Government Hall, which is located on the banks of the Nile in Old Cairo. It is a massive hall that belonged to the Fatimid caliphs of Egypt. He wanted the commander to be close to him, for the sultan was residing in one of the halls in the citadel, which he had built on the island in the Nile. The sultan held the commander in high esteem, and ordered daily supplies to be delivered to him. The commander welcomed me nicely and asked that I reside in his house in Cairo, which is a beautiful residence in the Daylam neighborhood. He—may God be merciful to him—was very generous and charitable to me.

Questions

1. What is the nature of the alliance between some Muslim monarchs and the Franks?
2. How is this deal different from the one concluded between Sultan al-Kamil and Emperor Frederick II in 1229?
3. Why was al-Nasir Dawud so eager this time to give Jerusalem to the Crusaders, when in 1229 he orchestrated the rebuke of his uncle al-Kamil in Damascus for agreeing to share Jerusalem with Frederick? How can we explain both of al-Nasir's actions?

---

167. Al-'Abbasa was the first town one reached in mainland Egypt after crossing from Sinai. It was established and named after the daughter of Ahmad Ibn Tulun (d. 884), the founder of the Tulunid State that ruled Egypt and parts of Syria and Palestine between 868 and 905.

22. Al-Yunini on a local Christian ransoming a Muslim captive from a Frank[168]

Musa son of Muhammad al-Yunini (1242–1325) was a notable Hanbali scholar in Syria during the early Mamluk period, and a leading figure in the city of Baalbek. His father was a notable Hanbali scholar in Baalbek during the Ayyubid period. His family claimed descent from the sixth Shi'i imam, Ja'far al-Sadiq (d. 765), and are hence also known as al-Husaynis. Among his students were notable Damascene scholars: al-Dhahabi (1274–1348) and 'Alam al-Din al-Birzali (d. 1339), who between 1324 and 1339 occupied the chair of the College of Hadith in Damascus established by Nur al-Din. Hence, al-Yunini played an important role in the transmission of Sunni scholarship in Damascus. Al-Yunini's The Continuation of the Mirror of Time *is a continuation of Sibt Ibn al-Jawzi's* Mirror of Time, *and covers the period between 1256 and 1311.*[169]

The above mentioned one (Abu Talib al-Yunini) recounted to me something that can be summed up in what follows. The Christian 'Abd Allah son of Ilyas, from the village of al-Ra's, told him: "I came to Tripoli, and a Frankish knight said to me: 'I have a hostage from your area, would you ransom him?' I accompanied him to his house and found the hostage, named Sahl, who was from the village of Ra'ban. When he saw me, he took hold of me and said: 'I beg of you. Do not leave me here; ransom me. I will give you back the money when I reach Ra'ban.' I ransomed him for 60 Tyrian dinars, and brought him to Ra'ban. When we arrived at his house, I noticed that he had no food for himself and his children. I regretted having paid for his ransom and was unsure what to do. One of the people of the village said to me: 'It is the harvest season, and we will collect the sum you paid for him and send it to you.' I was distressed.

"It happened that I came to Yunin and saw shaykh 'Isa who had just finished doing the ablution for prayer. I had not met him before. When he saw me, he said: 'Aren't you the one who paid for the ransom of Sahl?' I said yes. He started conversing with me and asking me about the situation, while we were walking toward his cloister. When he reached the outer fence of the cloister, he summoned a mystic from inside and told him: 'Go look for

---

168. Al-Yunini, *Dhayl Mir'at al-zaman*, 1: 29–30.
169. On al-Yunini and his *Dhayl*, see Li Guo, *Early Mamluk Syrian Historiography: al-Yunini's* Dhayl Mir'at al-zaman (Leiden: Brill, 1998), vol. 1.

22. Al-Yunini on a local Christian ransoming a Muslim captive from a Frank

a folded paper inside the cloister under my bedcover and bring it to me.'"
The Christian continued: "I thought it was a letter he wrote to me to show it to the administrator of the religious fund for freeing the hostages so that he could pay me back, or something like that. The disciple brought the folded paper and handed it to the shaykh, and he passed it to me. I found it heavy. He said: 'Take it.' I stepped back and unwrapped the paper. I found inside the same exact 60 dinars that I had paid to free the hostage. I was stunned. I took them and left."

I asked Abu Talib: "Why did not he convert to Islam?" He replied: "God did not will it."

Questions

1. What does this story tell us about the local Christians in the Islamic Near East?
2. Is there something we learn from this report about the understanding of sainthood and "supernatural" powers of mystics that Muslims and Christians shared at the time?

23. Jamal al-Din Ibn Matruh's poem on the defeat of King Louis IX near Damietta in 1250[170]

Jamal al-Din Yahya son of 'Isa Ibn Matruh was born in Asyut[171] in 1196, where he studied Hadith and poetry. He soon became a great poet. In 1228, he entered the service of the Monarch al-Salih Ayyub when the latter was still governor of Egypt for his father Sultan al-Kamil, and accompanied him on several military campaigns. When al-Salih became sultan (r. 1240–1249), Ibn Matruh was promoted and attained the rank of commander, occupying such important posts as head of the treasury in Cairo and after that governor of Damascus (1245–1248). Later on, he fell out of favor, but remained in the service of al-Salih Ayyub until the sultan's death. Ibn Matruh died in Cairo in October 1251.[172]

1- Give the Frenchman[173] when you see him / a true word from an eloquent observer.

2- May God reward you for your deeds / you slayer of the followers of Jesus Christ.

3- You, fool, came to Egypt seeking its conquest / thinking the army's brass band was mere wind.

4- But your hesitation drove you to disaster / whence your eyes see no escape.

5- Your companions, with your fine planning, / you delivered to the grave.

6- Fifty thousand, either / dead or prisoners, wounded.

7- May God lead you to more folly / may Jesus finally be rid of you all.

---

170. Ibn Wasil, *Mufarrij al-kurub*, vol. 6, ed. 'U. 'A.-S. Tadmuri (Beirut: al-Maktaba al-'Asriyya, 2004), 125–126; and al-Yunini, *Dhayl Mir'at al-zaman* (Cairo: Dar al-Kitab al-Islami, 1992), 2: 212–213. The last line is missing in al-Yunini.

171. A city on the west bank of the Nile in upper Egypt approximately 400 miles south of Cairo. According to Yaqut al-Hamawi, in his day, Asyut was a city with many Christians and seventy-five churches. Yaqut, *Mu'jam al-Buldan*, 1: 193.

172. On Ibn Matruh, see al-Dhahabi, *Ta'rikh al-islam*, 47: 433–435.

173. The Frenchman (*al-Faransis*) is a reference to King Louis IX.

8- If your pope is pleased with your actions / then ignore me; for much counsel is truly deceit.
9- Tell them: Should they return / seeking revenge or another purpose.
10- The house of Ibn Luqman[174] stands ready / so, too, the chain and the eunuch Sabih.[175]

Questions

1. How does Ibn Matruh see the military expedition of King Louis IX?
2. Do you sense any ridicule in these lines?
3. Why does he invoke Jesus in this poem?

---

174. The house (*dar*) of Ibn Luqman is the house of Fakhr al-Din Ibn Luqman, secretary of the Ayyubid court, where Louis IX was held hostage until he was ransomed.
175. The eunuch Sabih was the officer who put the chains on Louis.

Chapter 3: Chronicles, Memoirs, and Poetry

24. Abu Shama on the Mongols' capture of Damascus in 1260[176]

Abu Shama Shihab al-Din 'Abd al-Rahman al-Maqdisi was born in Damascus in 1203. His family hailed originally from Jerusalem (hence the family name, al-Maqdisi), settling in Damascus in the wake of the Crusader conquest of Jerusalem. One of his distant ancestors, a certain Muhammad son of Ahmad al-Tusi, served as the imam of the Dome of the Rock and was killed in the conquest of the city in 1099. Abu Shama received a traditional education in Shafi'i jurisprudence and was known as an influential and outspoken critic of the city's civilian administration. Abu Shama is most known for two historical works. The Two Gardens Concerning the Kingdoms of Nur al-Din and Saladin *covers the Zangid and Ayyubid dynasties down to 1201. In it, he presents a rather idealized picture of Nur al-Din and Saladin. Because Abu Shama lifted his material from earlier sources available to him, his* Two Gardens *is more a commentary on past events than an original chronicle. Nevertheless, it is an important compilation of excerpts from many sources otherwise lost. Abu Shama's second work,* The Continuation of the Two Gardens *(also known as* Biographies of the People of the Sixth and Seventh Islamic Centuries*), covers notable persons who lived in Syria, Palestine, and Egypt in the twelfth and thirteenth centuries. As such, it includes valuable eyewitness accounts of events in Damascus during Abu Shama's lifetime. Apart from making the pilgrimage twice, and brief sojourns in his ancestral hometown (Jerusalem) and Egypt, Abu Shama lived his entire life in Damascus. He died in 1268.*[177]

Year 658

The year 658 commenced on a Thursday. On Sunday, 18 Muharram (4 January 1260), I had a son born in the afternoon. I called him Isma'il after my father, and also gave him the honorific Abu al-'Arab. May God bless him and make him a blessing. He was born in the month of January, in the worst month of winter. Those days were very turbulent and frightening due to the Mongols[178]—may God curse them.

---

176. Abu Shama, *Tarajim rijal al-qarnayn al-sadis wa-l-sabi'—Dhayl 'ala al-Rawdatayn*, ed. 'I. al-'Attar (Cairo: Dar al-Kutub al-Malikiyya, 1947), 203–204.

177. On Abu Shama, see Zayde Antrim, "Abu Shama Shihab al-Din al-Maqdisi," *Encyclopaedia of Islam, Third Edition*.

178. As in the case of Sibt Ibn al-Jawzi and Ibn Wasil, Abu Shama too referred to the Mongols as Tatars. See p. 111 (footnote 141).

24. Abu Shama on the Mongols' capture of Damascus in 1260

On 15 Safar (31 January), news reached Damascus that the Mongols captured Aleppo by force. Its former ruler,[179] who was inappropriate for the job and who was hiding in Damascus, fled with the commanders who were with him. His rule over Aleppo came to an end. The Mongols laid siege to Aleppo on 2 Safar (18 January) and captured it after 7 days on 9 Safar (25 January). They gave its people a guarantee of safety, but then broke their word and killed them.

The Mongol envoys arrived outside Damascus. They stayed in the village of Harasta, and on the eve of Monday, 17 Safar (2 February), they entered Damascus. On Monday at noon, following the prayer, the decree of their king, which they brought with them, was read publicly in the Great Mosque. It included a guarantee of safety for the people of Damascus and its surrounding countryside. The notables of the city started endearing themselves to the Mongols. The same day when the decree was read in the Great Mosque, the people performed the ritual prayer over the deceased al-Sharif Ibn 'Asrun.[180]

On 17 Rabi' I (1 March), the deputies of Hulegu arrived in Damascus. The notables of the city, very well dressed for the occasion, went out to welcome them. The Mongols brought with them a decree, which included a guarantee of safety, and it was publicly read in the Green Field.[181] The Mongol army soon arrived after them, proceeding from the northeastern side around the eastern Ghuta to the Kiswa on the south of Damascus. They destroyed on their way a group of local volunteers who had rallied to fight them, which included a number of people from the village of Hazrama, the muezzin Abu Hirmas Shuja', Salih, Qasim, and others.

On the 26th of Rabi' I (11 March), an order from Hulegu, king of the Mongols, came to judge Kamal al-Din 'Umar son of Bandar al-Tiflisi[182] appointing him as chief judge of Syria, Mosul, Mardin, Mayyafariqin,[183] the lands of the Kurds, and other places; he was first appointed chief judge

---

179. The Monarch al-Nasir Yusuf, who was a great-grandson of Saladin, and the last Ayyubid ruler of Aleppo. The Mongols captured him in Palestine and later executed him following their defeat at 'Ayn Jalut in September 1260.

180. Correctly, Sharaf al-Din Ibn Abu 'Asrun (1185–1260) was a notable Damascene personality and a public figure known for his generosity.

181. See p. 86 (footnote 91).

182. Al-Tiflisi was born in Tiflis (today Tbilisi, the capital of Georgia) around 1205. He became a well-known and well-respected scholar of Shafi'i law in Syria. He moved later in his life to Cairo to teach and died there in September 1273. Kamal al-Din means "Perfection of the Religion."

183. Mardin and Mayyafariqin (Silvan) are cities in northern Mesopotamia, today in southeastern Turkey.

of Aleppo on the 15th of Rabi' I (29 February). The decree was read publicly in the Green Field, and it included that all religious endowments should be under the chief judge's management, especially the Great Mosque of Damascus—may God protect it. Before him, the chief judge of Damascus was Ahmad Ibn al-Saniy, a position he held from 643 (summer of 1245) until this day, roughly 2 months shy of a full 15 years. The aforementioned Kamal al-Din al-Tiflisi was his deputy. God does with his creation what He wills.

Questions

1. What does Abu Shama tell us about the Mongols' capture of Damascus?
2. How did the local population react to it?
3. Why were the Mongols, who were not Muslims at the time, so keen to appoint a Muslim chief judge to administer their lands in Syria and northern Mesopotamia?
4. Could this report tell us something about the reaction of some Muslims to the Crusaders?

25. Ibn Wasil on the battle of 'Ayn Jalut in 1260 and related events[184]

The execution of the captain of the Citadel of Damascus and its governor

On the 15th of Sha'ban of this year (26 July 1260), the Mongols[185] took the captain of the Citadel of Damascus and its governor to Darayya[186] and beheaded them there; they had been detained since the Citadel surrendered to the Mongols. The Mongols marched to the coastal lands and took with them as forced conscripts many local men from the neighborhoods and markets. Then, word spread among the Damascenes that the Muslim army from Egypt was coming to fight the Mongols.

Retaliation against the Christians of Damascus

On the 27th of Ramadan (5 September), the Muslims of the city attacked the local Christians. They destroyed the Church of Mary,[187] which was a massive church located near the St. Thomas Gate (Bab Tuma) and the Eastern Gate (Bab Sharqi).

Capture of Damascus during the period of the Rashidun caliphs

When the Muslims captured Damascus during the caliphate of the Commander of the Faithful 'Umar son of al-Khattab (r. 634–644)—may God be pleased with him—Khalid son of al-Walid[188] entered the city by force

---

184. Ibn Wasil, *Mufarrij al-kurub*, 6: 288–293. For biographical information on Ibn Wasil, see p. 116.
185. As in the case of Abu Shama and Sibt Ibn al-Jawzi, Ibn Wasil too referred to the Mongols as Tatars. See p. 111 (footnote 141).
186. A town on the southwestern edge of Damascus.
187. The Cathedral of St. Mary has been the most important Christian Orthodox church in Damascus since the eighth century when it was restored to the Christians by the Umayyad Caliph 'Umar son of 'Abd al-'Aziz as compensation for the confiscation of the Basilica of St. John the Baptist by the Umayyad Caliph al-Walid. Located in the Christian quarter in Old Damascus, it became the seat of the Orthodox Patriarch of Antioch in the fifteenth century and remains so until today. See p. 138.
188. A Companion of the Prophet Muhammad and leading general in the conquering Muslim army. He died in the city of Hims in 642, and his mausoleum became the city's most significant mosque, which was named after him. On the renovation of his mausoleum, see inscription 9 in Chapter 6, p. 210.

from the Eastern Gate, whereas Abu ʿUbayda[189]—may God be pleased with him—entered it from the Jabiya Gate by means of a peace agreement.[190] The Church of Mary was in the part of the city that had been taken by force, whereas the main church was in the part that had been taken peaceably. Consequently, Abu ʿUbayda allowed the Christians to retain their church, which formed part of the Great Mosque, but not the Church of Mary because it was in the part of the city that had been taken by force.

When al-Walid son of ʿAbd al-Malik (r. 705–715)[191] became caliph, he destroyed the church[192] that was part of the Great Mosque and incorporated its location into the Great Mosque. The church's bell tower remains to this day.[193] When ʿUmar son of ʿAbd al-ʿAziz (r. 717–720)[194]—may God be pleased with him—became caliph, he restored to them the Church of Mary[195] as compensation for the confiscation of the other church.

However, on this day (27th of Ramadan/5 September) the Muslims destroyed the church. They were enraged because under the Mongols the Christians had gained the upper hand over the Muslims, and took it upon themselves to ring the church bells; they even brought wine[196] into the Great Umayyad Mosque. The Muslims not only destroyed the church, they also

---

189. The commanding general of the conquering Muslim army in Syria, and one of the most significant Companions of Muhammad. He died in 639 during the Plague of Emmaus.

190. The gate that opens to the south.

191. The sixth Umayyad caliph. In addition to establishing the Great Mosque in Damascus, al-Walid is known for commissioning the expansion of Muhammad's mosque in Medina and the construction of the Aqsa Mosque in Jerusalem. Some sources indicate that it was his father, ʿAbd al-Malik, who initiated the construction of the Aqsa Mosque and that al-Walid completed it.

192. The Basilica of St. John the Baptist established in 391 by the Byzantine emperor Theodosius I. Previously, the site had been a temple to Jupiter erected during the reign of Caesar Augustus (r. 27 B.C.–14 A.D.). Prior to the Roman conquest of Syria, the site had been the location of an Aramaean temple to the local god Hadad.

193. This is known as the Eastern minaret (al-Manara al-Sharqiyya). It is located on the southeastern side of the Umayyad Mosque and local legends speak of Jesus descending on it to usher in the Day of Judgment.

194. The eighth Umayyad caliph. He served as governor of Medina during the caliphate of his cousin, al-Walid, who commissioned him to undertake the expansion of Muhammad's mosque there. In the Islamic tradition, he is remembered as the most pious and devout of the Umayyad caliphs.

195. On the Cathedral of St. Mary, see p. 137 (footnote 187).

196. Because alcoholic beverages are prohibited according to Islamic law, bringing wine into the Great Umayyad Mosque was considered a terrible sacrilege. However, because wine is a necessary component of the Eucharist (Holy Communion), it is likely that this may have been part of an effort by Christians in Damascus to reestablish Christian worship in the former Basilica of St. John the Baptist during the brief period of Mongol control over the city.

plundered and destroyed the homes of the Christians. Many Muslims did not take the Christians' possessions; rather, they left them on the ground. They even killed some Christians.

The next day, they plundered the Jews, demolishing their shops and houses. Had it not been for the Muslim soldiers, they would have even destroyed the synagogue. The local Christians hid; not a soul dared to come out in public. A number of Muslims were likewise killed because they were allied with and in the service of the Mongols. The Damascenes also killed some Mongolian[197] and Persian residents of the city and its outskirts, because they were supporters of the Mongols.

It was rumored that as a result of the Mongol invasion, the Christians intended to destroy the mosques and commit atrocities against the Muslims. But God protected the Muslims from their evil and made the wheel of fortune turn against them.

The victory of the Muslims against the Mongols at 'Ayn Jalut

When the Muslim troops in Egypt rallied together, almighty God inspired the victorious Sultan and Monarch Sayf al-Din (Sword of the Religion) Qutuz the former slave of 'Izz al-Din Aybak[198]—may God be merciful to him—to march with the Muslim army to fight the Mongols. The people's hearts had lost hope of defeating them when they saw their massive numbers, their swift conquest of most of the Muslim lands, that every place they attacked they captured, and that every army they fought they defeated. In the eastern lands, only Egypt, the Hijaz, and Yemen remained outside their grasp. A group of North Africans fled from Egypt to the west; others fled to Yemen and the Hijaz. Those who remained were greatly terrified and panicked as they awaited the imminent arrival of the Mongol enemy and the capture of the land.

The first meeting between the author (Ibn Wasil) and the Monarch al-Mansur

I frequently visited and served in the court of our master the sovereign, the martyr Monarch al-Mansur (Muhammad II), lord of Hama—may God be merciful to him. When I was in the service of the victorious Sultan and

---

197. Here Ibn Wasil used the term *Moghul*.
198. The third Mamluk Sultan (r. 1259–1260). After the Battle of 'Ayn Jalut, Qutuz was ambushed and assassinated by one of his commanders, Baybars, on their return journey to Egypt: see D. P. Little, "Kutuz," *Encyclopaedia of Islam, Second Edition*.

Monarch Qutuz, I had not yet been introduced to the Monarch al-Mansur. At that time, he was still very young—only nine years old—and I had already departed Hama when his father fell ill. When the Monarch al-Mansur came to Egypt, he stayed in his residence on Shams al-Dawla street. My brother, who was in his service and of whom the Monarch al-Mansur was quite fond, introduced me to him. Since my brother had often spoken to him about me, he asked to meet me. When I finally visited him in Cairo, he was very pleased to meet me—may God be merciful to him. During my residence with him in Cairo, I once said to him: "O lord, God willing you shall return to the seat of your rule, my brother shall remain in your service, and I shall live under your protection." He marveled at what I said and replied: "Praise be to God! That someone as intelligent and as knowledgeable as you would say something like this and have such a hope! When could this ever happen or even be possible?" I said: "Praise be to God! He can bring this to pass, for nothing such as this is beyond His power."

The victorious Monarch Qutuz determined in his mind to fight the Mongols. He marched from Cairo with the Syrian and Egyptian troops in Ramadan of this year (August). In his company was the sovereign Monarch al-Mansur—may God be merciful to him. I accompanied the Monarch al-Mansur as far as al-Salihiyya.[199] I broke my fast with him, bade him farewell, and recited to him these two verses:

1- Seeking you is my true intention, but what / you see is the way fate moves me.
2- When I draw near you, fate pulls me back; / I orbit like the orbiting of the planets.

I think these verses were composed by the judge al-Arrajani.[200] Their meaning is very pleasant. According to the astronomers, the seven planets follow their own individual orbits from west to east. But the universe pulls them back toward the west, thus subjecting them to a gravitational force opposite to that of their orbits. Al-Arrajani used that to analogize the person he was praising; that is, every time he tried to draw near to that person, fate pulled him in the opposite direction, just as the universe pulls the seven planets from the direction of their orbits.

---

199. A town on the eastern edge of the Delta, northeast of Cairo, on the route to Syria.
200. Al-Arrajani (d. 1149) was the judge of the city of Tustar (Shooshtar today in western Iran), and was a well-known poet. The poetry here is indeed by him.

25. Ibn Wasil on the battle of ʿAyn Jalut in 1260 and related events

The victorious Monarch Qutuz had with him the chief commander Faris al-Din Aqtay al-Mustaʿrib,[201] the most senior of the commanders who were once the slaves of Sultan al-Salih Ayyub. As we mentioned earlier, he became chief commander of the army for the victorious Monarch ʿAli son of the venerable monarch (Aybak)[202] following the arrest of commander ʿAlam al-Din Sanjar al-Halabi.[203] Moreover, when the victorious Monarch Qutuz ordered the arrest of the victorious monarch (ʿAli), the son of his master, the chief commander remained in his post and was entrusted with all the affairs of the state. He sent orders to our sovereign, the Monarch al-Mansur, while we were in al-Salihiyya: "Do not hold a feast for the breaking of the fast; rather, simply instruct each in your company to break his fast with the piece of meat in his sack."[204]

The victorious Monarch Qutuz departed with the large army from Salihiyya and arrived in Gaza. People's hearts were anxious and fearful for the Muslims. Kutbugha rallied all the Mongols in Syria and marched to fight the Muslims. In Kutbugha's company was the Monarch al-Saʿid son of the Monarch al-ʿAziz son of the Monarch al-ʿAdil.[205]

Death of the Mongol general Kutbugha

The victorious Monarch Qutuz departed from Gaza and reached the Jordan River valley, where the Mongols were amassing. The fighting broke out between the two groups on Friday, 25 Ramadan of this year (3 September), and the Mongols were utterly defeated. The Muslims' swords slaughtered them. Their general Kutbugha was killed, and his son was captured. Those who survived ran to the hills, and the Muslims pursued them, killing most of them. The rest fled in defeat toward the east. The commander Rukn

---

201. A leading commander in the early Mamluk sultanate, and general of the army under Sultans Qutuz and Baybars. He died in 1273. Faris al-Din means "Knight of the Religion."
202. ʿAli was the son of the first Mamluk Sultan ʿIzz al-Din Aybak (r. 1250–1257), and became sultan himself between 1257 and 1259. He was deposed by the victorious Sultan Qutuz.
203. A leading commander in the Mamluk state, and once the chief of the army. He later became governor of Damascus. ʿAlam al-Din means "Banner of the Religion."
204. The point of Sultan Qutuz's order here is that as an observant Muslim sovereign, he most certainly wanted his troops to fulfill their religious obligation to break their Ramadan fast properly. However, because he was eager for them to hasten to engage the Mongols in battle, he ordered them to do so quickly with the minimum requirement of eating a piece of meat in their sacks, rather than with a customary, festive, and time-consuming feast.
205. A grandson of the Ayyubid Sultan al-ʿAdil, and grandnephew of Saladin. His honorific title, al-Malik al-Saʿid, literally means "The Happy Monarch."

al-Din al-Bunduqdari[206] along with a group of brave soldiers chased them to the boundaries of Syria. As for the Monarch al-Sa'id son of the Monarch al-'Aziz, who had joined the Mongols, he was captured and brought before the victorious Monarch Qutuz who ordered his execution, and so he was beheaded.

Questions

1. How is this account by Ibn Wasil different from the one by Abu Shama, especially in the way it conveys the internal dynamics in Damascus as a result of the Mongol capture of the city, and which led to sectarian tensions and bloodshed?
2. How can you describe the general mood of the Muslims at the time?
3. Were there Muslims fighting alongside the Mongols? If so, should we be careful in reading Ibn Wasil's words about the Muslims' reaction to the Mongols as only applicable to some but not all (especially given what Abu Shama said about the local Damascenes welcoming the Mongols)?

---

206. The future Mamluk Sultan and Monarch al-Zahir Rukn al-Din Baybars al-Bunduqdari (r. 1260–1277).

26. Ibn Wasil on a Muslim embassy to Emperor Manfred in 1262[207]

In the month of Shaʿban of this year, meaning 660 (June–July 1262), the commander Sayf al-Din al-Kurdi and judge Asil al-Din Khawaja came back. They were sent as envoys to the emperor, king of the Franks, with a present from the sultan (Baybars), which included a giraffe. They also carried a letter from the sultan. They reported that the emperor took exceptional care of them and was enormously courteous to them. When the present was offered to Manfred, he immensely liked the giraffe. Amazement filled his eyes when he saw the other gifts. The sultan's letter was read to him eleven times; he asked for it to be reread so he could understand it. He was very benevolent toward the envoys, and ordered an envoy of his own to be readied to return along with a present that included innumerable items.

When the envoys of the triumphant sultan (Baybars)—may God be merciful to him—arrived, they had with them two mamluk companions who misbehaved during the trip. When he saw them, he ordered they be punished, for he was told of what they did. He then dispatched them to the Citadel on the island to work there in chains. This was a disciplinary punishment and fine statesmanship to hinder such offenses, guard the laws of the sultanate, and protect its esteem.

Questions

1. What does this report tell us about diplomacy between the early Mamluks and Emperor Manfred?
2. Does this continue the diplomatic relations that were instated between Sultan al-Kamil and Emperor Frederick II?

---

207. Ibn Wasil, *Mufarrij al-kurub*, 6: 329–330. For biographical information on Ibn Wasil, see p. 116.

27. Baybars al-Mansuri on the capture of Crac des Chevaliers (1271); the death of the Sultan Baybars (1278); and the capture of Tyre, Sidon, Atlit, Beirut, and Haifa (1291)

Rukn al-Din Baybars al-Dawadar al-Mansuri al-Khataʾi (d. 1325) was a slave (mamluk) *in the service of the Mamluk Sultan Qalawun (r. 1279–1290). He was purchased from the prince of Mosul around 1260 and participated in several of Qalawun's campaigns during the reign of Sultan Baybars (r. 1260–1277). As was customary, he likely would have been manumitted once in the service of his master. In 1286, he was appointed governor of Kerak, a post which he held until Qalawun's death in 1290, after which he was removed by Sultan al-Ashraf Khalil (r. 1290–1293) and appointed chief of the chancery. He was commander of the pilgrimage to Mecca in 1302. Baybars al-Mansuri's historical works are especially notable for the material that he included that does not appear anywhere else. His* The Finest Contemplation on Islamic History *is a universal chronicle that ends just prior to his death. His* Regal Treasure on the Turkic-Mamluk State *is based on his universal chronicle and covers only the early Mamluk period, 1249–1312 and 1321–1322; his* Anthology of Noteworthy Events *accounts for the Ayyubid and Mamluk periods up to the year 1303.*[208]

The capture of Crac des Chevaliers in Shaʿban 669 (April 1271)[209]

On 9 Rajab 669 (21 February 1271), the sultan (Baybars) encamped against Crac des Chevaliers (*Husn al-Akrad*). He laid siege to it and fought against it, and was determined to uproot its valiant soldiers and defenders. On the 20th of Shaʿban (3 April), Crac des Chevaliers' outer citadel was captured, and the army proceeded to the inner citadel and took control of it. The Franks retreated to the tower and asked for safe passage; the sultan granted it to them. They came out and were dispatched to their lands (County of Tripoli) on the 24th of the month (7 April). The sultan received the fortress

---

208. On Baybars al-Mansuri, see Linda Northrup, *From Slave to Sultan: The Career of Al-Mansur Qalawun and the Consolidation of Mamluk Rule in Egypt and Syria (678–689 A.H./1279–1290 A.D.)* (Stuttgart: Franz Steiner, 1998), 38–40. See also Li Guo, "Baybars al-Mansuri," *Encyclopaedia of Islam, Third Edition*.

209. Baybars al-Mansuri, *Zubdat al-fikra fi taʾrikh al-hijra*, ed. D. S. Richards (Beirut: German Orient Institute, 1998), 127–128.

27. Baybars al-Mansuri on the capture of Crac des Chevaliers (1271)

and wrote a letter to the Grand Master of the Hospitallers, under whose command Crac des Chevaliers fell. Here is the text:

> This letter is to Friar Hugues—may God make him one of those who do not object to His decree nor oppose the One who facilitated the victory and conquest for His army. He should not think that the prudent can escape God's judgment or that the one hiding behind fortified walls can protect himself from Him. You know that God has facilitated the capture of Crac des Chevaliers, which you have built, fortified, and made into a shelter. You would have been better advised to desert it instead of leaving it to the care of your brothers, who rendered you no benefit. You confounded them by asking them to stay there; they abandoned it, causing you confusion. When my soldiers lay siege to a castle, it has no chance to endure against them; the happy one they serve, they shall never let him suffer.

In this year, too, the Commander of Antartus (Tortosa)[210] and the Grand Master of the Hospitallers sued for peace; the sultan approved their request. The truce involved Antartus and Marqab[211] only, not Safita and its land. In return, the sultan took from them Belda[212] and its land, as well as the areas they captured during the time of Sultan al-Nasir (Saladin). He also imposed on them the condition that they should abandon all their rights and joint interests in the areas under Muslim control, that the revenues from the land of Marqab should be split in half between the sultan and the Hospitallers, and that the Marqab castle should not be renovated. He swore an oath to them about that and they withdrew from the Tower of Qarafis, burning what they could not carry with them.

Year 676 (June 1277–May 1278)—The death of the Sultan and Monarch al-Zahir Baybars—may God be merciful to him[213]

In this year, the triumphant monarch (Baybars) died in Damascus—may God protect it. He arrived at the White Palace in the Midan area[214] on the

---

210. Coastal town, known today as Tartus in northwestern Syria, to the south of Latakia.
211. Known to the Crusaders as Margat near the town of Baniyas, it featured a very strategic castle that controlled the coastal route in northwestern Syria. See Yaqut's description of Margat (*al-Marqab*), Chapter 1, pp. 37–38.
212. A town near Jabala known today as 'Arab al-Mulk. The Franks also called it Beaude.
213. Baybars al-Mansuri, *Zubdat al-fikra*, 160–161.
214. A neighborhood on the southern edge of the old city of Damascus.

5th of Muharram of this year (8 June 1277). He thought that he controlled all things and that fate served him to achieve his goals. However, his vitality fled and his good health waned like the daylight when night falls. God's decree had come to him, and there was no stratagem that could be employed.

The narrator (Baybars al-Mansuri) says: The moon was in full eclipse, and the night was very dark. Some seers interpreted this as a sign of the death of an honorable man of high esteem. It was mentioned that when the sultan heard of this, he feared he might be the one, so he tried to interpret it to mean someone other than he, hoping this might save him. At that time, there was a man in Damascus, a descendant of one of the Ayyubid sovereigns, whose honorific title was the Monarch al-Zahir. As it was said, Baybars sought to kill him. So, he invited him to have a drink with him. This man was the son of the Monarch al-Nasir Dawud, lived in the desert, and had married a Bedouin woman. He resided among the Bedouins, behaved like them, and joined them in their raids. He came to Damascus after having finished a raid, and Baybars ordered the server to give him a small glass which contained poison and wine. The server gave him that glass to drink. The man started to take ill; he left the place feeling the pangs of death. The server became so agitated by the sight of the man that he inadvertently filled the same glass and gave it to the sultan, who drank it. In short order, Baybars felt an intense burning in his guts, but dared not say anything to his doctors, not even to his friends. He spent a few days suffering day and night from the intense burning pain, and finally when the pain became unbearable, he was forced to inform his doctor hoping for a cure from him. But the treatment was unhelpful, and the knowledge of his crime did not help improve his mood. He died on Thursday, 27 Muharram (30 June); God's decree came at the end of the day.

His deputy, the commander Badr al-Din Baylik al-Khazindar, who was also in charge of the treasury, kept his death a secret from the army. He made it seem as though Baybars were still sick; he even arranged for the doctors to come and concoct remedies and cures as if everything were normal. He moved the corpse to the Citadel of Damascus. It remained there embalmed until his well-known mausoleum in Damascus was built;[215] he was interred there. In the meantime, the commander Badr al-Din al-Khazindar departed with the victorious army and the guarded and loaded treasury. The drummers were lined in their proper places, and the sultan's sedan was carried as though he were sick inside it. No one dared to say anything about his death, but rumors started to circulate about his fate; people disagreed as

---

215. This is the infamous Zahiriyya mausoleum, which became a major library in Damascus.

to whether he had died or whether he was alive and merely ill. They continued to travel, stopping to rest and resuming the next day, until they reached Cairo—may God protect it. The treasury, their camping equipment, horses, and gear were brought to the Citadel. Only then was Baybars's death proclaimed and made public. His son al-Sa'id sat to receive condolences, and the news spread far and near. His reign was 17 years, 2 months, and 10 days. He left behind several children, including the Monarch al-Sa'id Nasr al-Din Baraka Khan, Najm al-Din Amir Khidr, Badr al-Din Salamish, and three daughters.

The capture of the strongholds that God has made wonders to behold[216]

They are Tyre, Sidon, Atlit, Beirut, and Haifa. In the month of the aforementioned Jumada II (June), God blessed these strongholds and eased their suffering. There was never any doubt about Him doing that, for when the Sultan al-Ashraf Khalil captured Acre and ordered its destruction, it was reduced to rubble. It had been a flourishing kingdom but became a ruin. This terrified the Franks, and God spread His anger throughout the coastal lands. Those living there feared the sultan's might and were concerned about his vengeance. They agreed to submit to him, asked for safe passage, and surrendered the towns to the Muslims. They left them reluctantly, though eagerly for their own safety. Sultan al-Ashraf Khalil received them without any effort or fighting and raised his flags over them without any trickery. This blessed endeavor and well-earned bliss rewarded him for the exhaustion of his troops and their bearing of swords. He became like his namesake.[217] Indeed, how similar they are to each other. He even exceeded Saladin, by achieving through swift action and bravery what the latter achieved gradually over many years throughout his reign. He ordered that the cities be destroyed, and so they were.

It was said that an occurrence happened at the same time as these towns were being destroyed. On the aforementioned Friday, a church outside Siwas[218] collapsed, which the Christians allege had remained in their hands since the days of Jesus—may God bless him. Its ceiling and walls fell down, even though they had no cracks. It suddenly collapsed, revealing a secret

---

216. Baybars al-Mansuri, *Zubdat al-fikra*, 282–283.
217. Sultan al-Ashraf Khalil (r. 1290–1293), whose honorific title was Salah al-Din (Righteousness of the Religion; Saladin). Thus, the pun of Baybars al-Mansuri to compare him with Saladin.
218. In central Anatolia, known today as Sivas. Its Byzantine Greek name was Sivasteia.

in its foundation and the predestined divine will about its eminent collapse and end.

Questions

1. What do we learn from this report about diplomacy as a way to resolve conflicts between Muslims and Franks? What do we learn about the role of oaths?

2. What information does this account by Baybars al-Mansuri give about the moral character of his patron Sultan Baybars?

3. How does he present the accomplishments of Sultan al-Ashraf Khalil?

4. In his treatment of Saladin, do we sense an aggrandizement of the sultan's achievements? (It is true that Saladin captured many Crusader strongholds, but he was sometimes forced to and other times through the process of negotiations agreed to give most of them back.)

5. From this report, and other reports included in this anthology, how did people explain and interpret unusual incidents that occurred at the same time as major battles?

28. Al-Nuwayri al-Iskandarani on Peter of Cyprus's sack of Alexandria in 1365[219]

Muhammad son of al-Qasim al-Nuwayri al-Iskandarani hailed from Alexandria in Egypt; hence the name, al-Iskandarani. We do not know the year of his birth nor the precise year of his death, though it was sometime after 1374. We do not know much about him other than that he was a historian. He is most remembered for his The Informative Book on the Ordained Calamities that Befell Alexandria, *which chronicles the history of his hometown, Alexandria, with a special focus on his eyewitness account of the sack of the city in October 1365 at the hands of King Peter of Cyprus.*[220]

We return to the discussion of the Cypriot king's attack on Alexandria and his capture of the city. On Wednesday, 20 Muharram of the year 767 (7 October 1365), ships appeared on the sea, from east and west; the people of Alexandria thought they were Venetian merchants, whom they expected to arrive with their merchandise as was their annual custom. Muslim merchants had brought spices from Yemen to trade for the merchandise the Venetians would bring with them. But when they did not drop anchor in the inner harbor, the people became very apprehensive. On Thursday morning, the multitude of these ships approached the peninsula to the west of the harbor with their sails billowing like white castles. People started spreading rumors and panicking. As the ships neared, they filled the entire horizon. They churned up the sea like an earthquake and lowered their sails in the Chain Harbor.[221] The Chain Harbor is adjacent to the Green Gate, which was blocked by plastered stone because of this raid. It was later reopened with three new smaller gates in 767 (late fall 1365) during the Alexandrian governorate of the commander Sayf al-Din al-Akuzz, which, if God permits, will be mentioned later along with his achievements.

---

219. Al-Nuwayri al-Iskandarani, *Kitab al-Ilmam bi-l-iʿlam fima jarat bih al-ahkam wa-l-umur al-maqdiyya fi waqʿat al-Iskandariyya*, ed. A. S. Atiya (Hyderabad: Matbaʿat Majlis Daʾirat al-Maʿarif al-ʿUthmaniyya, 1968–1976), 2: 136–152.

220. On al-Nuwayri al-Iskandarani, see Aziz S. Atiya, *A Fourteenth Century Encyclopedist from Alexandria: A Critical and Analytical Study of al-Nuwairy al-Iskandarani's "Kitab al-Ilmam"* (Salt Lake City: Middle East Center at the University of Utah, 1977).

221. Alexandria's open harbor.

Returning to the prior discussion: when the armed ships dropped anchor in the Chain Harbor facing the coast, the Alexandrians readied for a siege, war, and combat. The towers facing the sea and the peninsula were manned with countless archers and people atop the wall, many of whom operated trebuchets. A boat tried to approach the inner harbor, but the Muslim archers shot arrows at it, forcing it to retreat toward the other boats.

After sunset, lamps were lit along the wall, making it glow with light, while the Muslims kept watch, holding the wall. The enemy, however, was calm and remained where they were anchored, lined up side by side like a small raft in a giant ocean. The Muslims thought they could easily repel it, assuming such a force could never capture a walled city, well fortified with strong towers. At sunrise on Friday, a large crowd of Muslims gathered along the peninsula, some with swords and shields, some with bows and arrows, and some with spears and daggers. Some came only wearing their clothes, some wore their coats of mail, and some came naked from the waist up.

The street vendors also came out during the previous night with their tables, trays, and kettles full of food to sell to those gathering on the peninsula. They hurled curses on every monk and priest they saw. They were unfazed by the presence of the ships in the sea, which had arrived on Wednesday, nor were they frightened by the Frankish fleet that assembled on Thursday. They were cursing the Cypriot king as though he were Satan. Their principal concern was selling to the groups mentioned earlier, so much so that a vendor would become enraged if a customer took one or two extra pieces, but would be pleased if he outsmarted him. The vendors were as the poet said:

1- Do not enrage the vendor; / you can please him with most trivial thing.
2- Taking a cent from his hand / is like extracting a tooth from his mouth.

The people continued to buy from the vendor and eat as they always had. None concerned themselves with nor were they afraid of the Frankish fleet. The rabble and commoners continued to curse the Cypriot king openly, calling him every despicable name. When the Cypriot king heard them from his ship, he remained calm. Neither did his aides say anything.

It was said that at night, the Cypriot king sent his spies dressed like Muslims to the tip of the peninsula. Those demons spoke Arabic and mingled among the Muslims to get information. They realized that the Muslims were not dressed for war. It is said that they even bought food and brought it back to the king of Cyprus who was with the fleet. They informed him that

28. Al-Nuwayri al-Iskandarani on Peter of Cyprus's sack of Alexandria in 1365

the entire gathering on the peninsula did not include a single warrior nor was anyone dressed for war. They were there to eat and drink; some even dug holes in the sand in which to sleep.

Before sunrise on Friday, the Bedouins arrived from every corner, dressed in their everyday attire. Local women were eyeing the Frankish ships from the surrounding dunes, behind the wall that overlooks the cemetery. When the Bedouins arrived, the women made trilling sounds, singing: "Here come the fearless to kill the worshippers of the cross." The Bedouins raced their horses in front of the dunes, letting them gallop freely as they harkened to the trilling. The Bedouins were so numerous as they streamed from the Green Gate that they spread along the peninsula like a swarm of locusts. They were not attired for war; each carried only his scabby sword and spear, seeking to kill the king of Cyprus or maim him.

One of the North Africans, among others, said to the commander Jangara [deputy of Sayf al-Din al-Akuzz]: "This is a well-armed enemy, and the townsfolk have come out of the city unprepared and useless for battle and war. Exigency (*al-maslaha*)[222] requires that they be returned to the city's protection behind its fortified wall. If they fight from behind the wall, the enemy will think he is fighting fearless lions as they hurl projectiles against them until help arrives from Cairo." But those who owned cottages on the peninsula and had spent large sums building them among the graves as night lodges for the riffraff objected, saying: "We shall not let the feet of those filthy Franks tread on the tombs in the cemetery." They said this out of fear that the Franks might destroy their cottages should their multitudes disembark on the peninsula. The North African merchant ʿAbd Allah said to Jangara: "It is more proper that the Muslims return to the city." The owners of the cottages replied: "You North Africans destroyed your city, Tripoli, when the Franks attacked it. Now you want to destroy our cottages by asking us to go inside the city. You are neither men of war, nor are you men of honor. We will not allow them to disembark from their ships, and we will make them taste torture with our arrows."

Two years after the attack of the Cypriot king, Sultan al-Ashraf Shaʿban[223] ordered the destruction of all the cottages and halls built on the peninsula. He did so in order to deprive the enemy use of them as shelters should they

---

222. As with the concept of necessity (*darura*), exigency (*maslaha*) is a legal concept in Islamic law that allows certain things to be done even if they do not agree with the statutes of Shariʿa law: see p. 108 (footnote 132).

223. The Mamluk Sultan al-Ashraf Shaʿban ruled between 1363 and 1377.

attack and benefit from the water cisterns, which are filled by rainfall. Thus, the cottages and halls were destroyed.

Had the Muslims left the peninsula to the Cypriot king and fortified themselves behind the wall and fought the filthy unbelievers from there, they would have saved themselves from slaughter, looting, and imprisonment. Instead of fearing the Franks' destruction of their cottages, they should have concerned themselves with protecting Alexandria from the Christians' predations. Those who worried about the fate of their cottages had their homes inside the city destroyed and looted. Their errant opinion led them to disaster. For when God's decree comes, there is nothing that stands athwart it; when God wills something, it is done. A poet said:

1- The decree of the Hegemon is inevitable; / when it comes, who can stop it?

Another poet said:

1- When God ordains His decree / no human can escape it.

We return to commander Jangara, his agreeing with the owners of the cottages, and not heeding what the North African merchant 'Abd Allah had said to him. His reply to the aforementioned merchant 'Abd Allah was: "I will not allow a single Frankish soldier to reach the coast, even if it leads to the cutting of my jugular veins and I die fighting." If God were to be merciful toward His servant, He would inspire him to manage things well, but if He were to desert him, He would confuse him.

In the meantime, the Franks evaluated the people's condition from their ships. Since they saw them mostly naked from the waist up, they were eager to fight them. A galley led the charge, which was met by a group of North African fighters who rowed toward it. They fought those in the galley and were able to prevent it from advancing. They called upon the naphta slingers to bring fire to burn it, but alas, no one brought a spark because they were lazy, negligent laggards. The naphta slingers launched a volley at the boat, but the fireball fell in the water and was extinguished. A sword fight ensued between the North Africans and those in the galley; it ended with the slaughter of the North Africans. Then, the galley landed on the beach and another, shooting arrows, came after it. Once they controlled the coast, other galleys followed from different directions. The Franks disembarked promptly—foot soldiers and cavalries—throughout the forenoon of Friday. The cavalries attacked the Muslims with arrows, while foot soldiers, carrying shields and swords, advanced ahead of them.

28. Al-Nuwayri al-Iskandarani on Peter of Cyprus's sack of Alexandria in 1365

When the food vendors—who used to quarrel with buyers over a scrap or two—saw that, they dropped their merchandise and fled barefoot. Some escaped the wrath of the unbelievers; others tripped and fell. The Franks wore shields and coats of mail, with bright helmets on their heads. They carried sharp swords and well-tuned bows, and hoisted large flags with crosses on them. They discharged their arrows against the believers and the Bedouins, which so panicked their horses that the Bedouins sought protection inside the city wall. The Muslim troops were exposed due to the Bedouins' retreat and abandoned the fight against the bastard Franks. They had become like hanging meat, so they ran for shelter behind the city gates. For how can flesh defeat iron; and how can the naked man fight the ironclad? The Muslims retreated, escaping from the unbelievers. A poet said about that:

1- Lo, the Muslims escaped when / well-armed fighters blitzed.
2- For how can they but escape them? / The poor ones are flesh; the others steel.

When the Alexandrians saw what they had neither experienced nor witnessed in their history, their hearts trembled. The sight of bashed skulls and dead horses drove them mad. They ran to the city gates, trampling each other. Dead corpses were everywhere. A few groups stood their ground and fought valiantly, killing whatever Franks they could before achieving martyrdom. It is said that the butcher Muhammad al-Sharif ran toward the Franks with his meat cleaver. He broke the bones of a few of them as he shouted: "God is Great, He kills the unbelievers." But a large enemy crowd gathered against him on the peninsula where he achieved martyrdom. Also, a schoolmaster known as Muhammad son of al-Taffal was seen rushing against the Franks with his sword. Someone asked him: "Are you seeking to die, O master Muhammad?" He replied: "That would be my joy, for I will be the neighbor of the Prophet Muhammad. There is no better death than that achieved fighting jihad in the path of God, which would usher me to paradise." He charged and exchanged blows with them until he achieved martyrdom and God granted him everlasting joy.

It was told that ʿAmr son of al-Jamuh, who suffered from a bad limp in his foot, had four sons like lions who fought in many battles alongside the Messenger of God—may God bless him and grant him salvation. On the day of the Battle of Uhud,[224] they insisted that he stay at home and not fight,

---

224. The Battle of Uhud took place mid-March 625 between Muhammad and his followers, and the army of Quraysh. It was the Muslims' first significant military defeat.

saying to him: "God has excused you as His verse says: ❧*No blame attaches to the blind; no blame attaches to the lame*❧" (Qur'an 24:61). When the Messenger of God came—may God bless him and grant him salvation—he said to him: "O Messenger of God, my sons want to prevent me from fighting and joining you in war. By God, I desire to limp into heaven with my withered foot." The Messenger of God—may God bless him and grant him salvation—replied to him: "Yes, God has granted you an excuse, so you are not obliged to wage jihad." He then turned to 'Amr's sons and said: "Why are you denying him this chance, for God might grant him martyrdom." So, he joined the Prophet Muhammad and was killed—may God be merciful to him.

We now return to the discussion of those Muslims who fought on the peninsula against the unbelieving Franks. A group of volunteer archers who were positioned in the cemetery were surrounded inside the Sufi hospice. The pious cleric Abu 'Abd Allah Muhammad Ibn Sallam had built it on the peninsula outside the Sea Gate as a lodging, and as a prayer and ritual space for his Sufi followers. It was built a little more than a year before the raid; he spent 300 dinars on its construction. When large numbers of Franks surrounded the hospice, the Muslim archers started shooting arrows at them from the roof, killing a few of them. When they ran out of arrows, they started dislodging stones and hurling them down on the Franks until they ran out of stones. The Franks broke the windows of the hospice and attacked them. When they were face to face with the Franks, they cried: "O Muhammad," then, they fell silent. 'Abd Allah son of the cleric Abu Bakr—who was the attendant of al-Qushambari Mosque and who was hiding in the cistern of the hospice—told their story. The Franks slaughtered them all with daggers, their blood flowing in the gutters of the hospice like rain. It is said that the Muslims who were slaughtered on the rooftop of the hospice numbered more than 30. Blessings on them for being granted martyrdom and everlasting joy.

When those Alexandrians who fled the city through the Desert Gate during the Frankish attack, as will be described later, returned, they saw the dead lying everywhere inside the city and outside it on the peninsula. They went to the aforementioned hospice of Ibn Sallam and found a large pool of congealed blood underneath the gutter spouts. They climbed to its rooftop and found the slaughtered archers, who are the truly happy and triumphant ones. They dug a large grave outside the hospice and buried them in it. May God be merciful to them. They became, as God has described: ❧*Who fought or were killed, I shall wipe away their misdeeds, and I shall admit them into gardens beneath which rivers flow: A reward from God. With God is the best of rewards*❧ (Qur'an 3:195).

28. Al-Nuwayri al-Iskandarani on Peter of Cyprus's sack of Alexandria in 1365

The author[225]—may God pardon him, his parents, and all of the Muslims—said: I was told by the pious cleric Ahmad son of al-Nashsha'i, who was the Sufi master of those archers in the cemetery in Alexandria, that the tailor Muhammad had said to him following his return from captivity in Cyprus alongside the other Alexandrian captives: "I was in the company of the Muslim archers on the rooftop of the hospice of Ibn Sallam when the Franks stormed us. They slaughtered the archers, and I trembled with fear. They did not kill me because of my young age. As for the vendor Husayn, when they were about to slay him, he smiled at them, which made the Franks laugh at him and say: 'Do not kill him, he smiled when he should have cried.' So, the two of us were taken captives. But later Husayn regretted what he had done and started crying. When we returned in the company of the Alexandrian captives and he saw the city from the sea, he stood to his feet, made a loud cry, and dropped down. We checked on him, but he was dead. He thus received the joy of escaping the land of the unbelievers and seeing again the land of the Muslims. With God's magnanimity, he joined the happy people of paradise."

Questions

1. According to al-Nuwayri al-Iskandarani, what was the reaction of the people of Alexandria to the attack of the king of Cyprus?
2. What was the Franks' strategy?
3. What was his depiction of the Muslim Bedouins and their fighting capability?
4. What point is al-Nuwayri al-Iskandarani trying to make by telling the story about the Battle of Uhud?
5. Toward the end of his account, al-Nuwayri al-Iskandarani informed us that all the archers atop the Sufi lodging were massacred by the Franks. Yet a few lines after that, he admitted that at least two were taken prisoner. Does this tell us something about the exaggeration of chroniclers in reporting about events?

---

225. This refers to al-Nuwayri al-Iskandarani. Muslim chroniclers would occasionally add such notes in order to specify personal marginalia.

CHAPTER FOUR
BIOGRAPHIES

We have included these remarks on Ibn 'Asakir's biography of Jesus here because we believe it is important for the reader to have an understanding of Jesus's importance to the Islamic conception of history—especially sacred history in the Holy Land—but also the important role that he plays in the Islamic conception of the End of Days, which many in Ibn 'Asakir's day thought may well be approaching.

The biography of Jesus in Ibn 'Asakir's History of Damascus *reflects the Islamic view of Jesus. Some aspects of it were by the time of Ibn 'Asakir well established and commonly accepted, other aspects were contested. For instance, Jesus is portrayed as a Muslim prophet, who enjoined the reading of the Qur'an. We also see an eagerness to dissociate Jesus (and his Disciples) from his historical followers (i.e., the Christians). And most importantly, the biography focuses on Jesus as an ascetic, which is the paramount representation of Jesus in medieval Islamic literature.[1] Among the contested aspects of this biography are the inclusion of the name of Jesus in the Islamic Shahada (the foundational Islamic credo), and the identification of Jesus with the End-of-Days Guide (the figure of Islamic eschatology); but Jesus's return before the end of time is an uncontested Islamic dogma.*

With respect to the prophecy, which is attributed to a Companion of Muhammad named 'Abd Allah son of 'Amr son of al-'As (d. 684), it speaks directly to the troubling circumstances of Ibn 'Asakir's time. Together with other traditions about the End of Days, it highlights Jesus as waging jihad in the path of God. The themes that are peculiar to the Frankish presence in the Near East are especially interesting, as they reflect some editing done on the part of Ibn 'Asakir (or one of his direct sources) to adapt it to the challenges posed by the Crusaders, with their two most notorious bases: Acre and Tyre. There is also the information about the common ways major Crusader campaigns arrived in the Near East: simultaneously by land and by sea. Moreover, the Frankish challenge exacerbated the divisions among Muslims, especially in Syria and Egypt, which created some sort of an eschatological hope for a Muslim leader to reunite the Muslims and defeat the Christians. Jesus's role in Islamic eschatology is that he will return (first appearing in Damascus) to

---

1. Tarif Khalidi, *The Muslim Jesus: Sayings and Stories in Islamic Literature* (Cambridge: Harvard University Press, 2001).

kill the Antichrist (at the Jaffa Gate in Jerusalem), break the crosses, slaughter the pigs, end the jizya tax on non-Muslims, making warfare against People of the Book (e.g., Jews, Christians, Zoroastrians) and others licit, and thus usher in the Day of Judgment. But it is the Muslims' responsibility to prepare the conditions for his return. Hence, in Ibn 'Asakir's opinion, it was incumbent upon the Muslims to unite, obviously under the leadership of Ibn 'Asakir's patron Nur al-Din. In this respect, the identification of caliph Mu'awiya son of Abu Sufyan as the Muslim sovereign who will lead the prayer when Jesus returns might have been inserted to give the prophecy certain historical validity and show that it was an ancient one.

This eschatological expectation is reminiscent of the version of Pope Urban II's sermon at Clermont in 1095, recorded by Guibert of Nogent (d. 1125), which raises similar eschatological hopes regarding the need to liberate Jerusalem (Mother of Churches) in order to prepare the way for the return of Christ and his battle with the Antichrist. According to Guibert's account, because the Antichrist is to do battle with Christians in Jerusalem, "if Antichrist finds there no Christians (just as at present when scarcely any dwell there), no one will be there to oppose him."² Of course, one should not assume a connection between Guibert and Ibn 'Asakir or any concrete influence of one on the other, for there was none. However, highlighting the similarities illustrates how common these issues were in Christian and Muslim apocalyptic and eschatological religious literature and expectations at the time of the Crusades.³

1. Ibn 'Asakir on Jesus⁴

Once the Prophet Muhammad—may God bless him and grant him peace—recited this verse: ❴And We gave them to retire to a high place (rabwa), with level ground and a fountain❵ (Qur'an 23:50). He asked: "Do you know where it is?" They replied: "God and His messenger know better." He said: "It is in

---

2. Edward Peters, *The First Crusade: The Chronicle of Fulcher of Chartres and Other Source Materials* (Philadelphia: University of Pennsylvania Press, 1998), 35. For the full text of Guibert of Nogent's account of Urban II's sermon at Clermont, see Peters, *First Crusade*, 33–37.

3. The similarity in apocalyptic language and imagery in Christian and Islamic religious literature is not limited to the period of the Crusades, and also extends to Jewish religious literature. On Muslim apocalyptic literature, see David Cook, *Studies in Muslim Apocalyptic* (Princeton: Darwin Press, 2002).

4. The entire biography of Jesus from Ibn 'Asakir's *Ta'rikh* can be found in *Sirat al-Sayyid al-Masih li-Ibn 'Asakir al-Dimashqi*, ed. S. A. Mourad (Amman: Dar al-Shuruq, 1996). For biographical information on Ibn 'Asakir, see pp. 41–42.

1. Ibn ʿAsakir on Jesus

Syria, in a place called Ghuta in a city called Damascus, which is the best of Syrian towns."[5]

The Prophet—may God bless him and grant him peace—said: "Whoever testifies that there is no god but God, alone with no partner, and that Muhammad is His servant and messenger, and that Jesus is His servant and messenger, the son of His servant, His word which He gave to Mary, and a spirit from Him, God will admit him to paradise for saying that."[6]

A woman said to Jesus son of Mary: "Blessed is the womb that bore you and the breast that suckled you." Jesus replied: "No, but blessed is he who reads the Qur'an and follows what is in it."[7]

The followers of Jesus split into three sects. One sect said: "God was among us as long as He wished, then He ascended to heaven." Those were the Jacobites. Another sect said: "The son of God was among us for as long as He wished, then He made him ascend to Him." Those were the Nestorians. Yet another sect said: "He was the servant of God and His messenger for as long as He wished, then God made him ascend to Him." Those were the Muslims.[8] The two infidel sects gained ascendancy over the Muslim sect and destroyed it. Thus, Islam remained in eclipse until God sent Muhammad—may God bless him and grant him peace.[9]

God says: ❮*They killed him not, nor did they crucify him, but so it was made to appear to them. Those who disputed concerning him are in doubt over the matter; they have no knowledge thereof but only follow conjecture. Assuredly they killed him not, but God raised him up to Him, and God is Almighty, All-Wise*❯ (Qur'an 4:157). The Jews and the Nazarenes[10] said that they killed him. But the Disciples knew that he was not killed, and they rejected the assertion of the Nazarenes and the Jews.[11]

---

5. Ibn ʿAsakir, *Taʾrikh*, 1: 203. The exact location has been known in Islamic history as al-Rabwa, and remains to this day. It is not clear whether it was called so because of this quranic verse or the association was made much later. See pp. 81, 83, and 163 for mentions of al-Rabwa.

6. Ibn ʿAsakir, *Sirat al-sayyid al-Masih*, 73 (no. 63); idem, *Taʾrikh*, 47: 378. This hadith includes a variant form of the Muslim *shahada* (attestation of faith). On the development of the *shahada* in early Islam, see Suleiman A. Mourad, "The Shahada and the Creation of an Islamic Identity," in *Geneses: Comparative Study of the Historiographies of the Rise of Christianity, Rabbinic Judaism and Islam*, ed. John Tolan (London: Routledge, 2019), 216–237.

7. Ibn ʿAsakir, *Sirat al-sayyid al-Masih*, 152 (no. 161); idem, *Taʾrikh*, 47: 434.

8. That is, the true followers of Jesus.

9. Ibn ʿAsakir, *Sirat al-sayyid al-Masih*, 213–214 (no. 261); idem, *Taʾrikh*, 47: 475.

10. Nazarene (*Nasara*) is the word the Qur'an uses for Christians. It is derived from Nazareth (*al-Nasira*). See al-Harawi on Nazareth, p. 4.

11. Ibn ʿAsakir, *Sirat al-sayyid al-Masih*, 214 (no. 262); idem, *Taʾrikh*, 47: 476.

Chapter 4: Biographies

The Messenger of God—may God bless him and grant him peace—said: "The matter is only growing dire, the world is vanishing, people are becoming more covetous, and the Hour of Judgment will be held for the wicked, and there is no End-of-Days Guide[12] other than Jesus son of Mary."[13]

'A'isha[14] said: "I asked the Messenger of God: 'If I were to outlive you, would you permit me to be buried beside you?' He said: 'Alas no. In that place there is only room for my grave, for Abu Bakr's grave, for 'Umar's grave, and for the grave of Jesus son of Mary—may God bless him and grant him peace."[15]

The Messenger of God—may God bless him and grant him peace—said: "The biblical prophets are siblings of the same lineage. I and Jesus too are siblings because he prophesied me and there are no prophets between me and him."[16]

Jesus son of Mary used to eat barley. He traveled by foot and did not ride on beasts. He did not live in houses, nor did he use a lamp for light. He neither dressed in cotton, touched women, nor used perfume. He never mixed his drink with anything or cooled it. He never greased or washed his hair or beard. He never had anything between his skin and the ground except his garment. He had no concern for lunch or supper, and coveted nothing of the desires of the world. He used to consort with the weak, the chronically sick, and the poor. Whenever food was offered to him on something, he would place it on the ground, and he never ate meat. Of food, he would eat little and say: "This is too much for one who has to die and be judged for it."[17]

---

12. According to Muslim beliefs, the End-of-Days Guide (*Mahdi* in Arabic) will appear before the Day of Judgment to rule the world and reestablish justice. Ibn 'Asakir's depiction of Jesus as the Guide is a minority opinion, as the general Muslim consensus was that the Guide would come from Muhammad's house. On the debate and identity of the End-of-Days Guide in medieval Islamic scholarship, see Sandra Campbell, "Millennial Messiah or Religious Restorer: Reflections on the Early Islamic Understanding of the Term *Mahdi*," *Jusur: The UCLA Journal of Middle Eastern Studies* 11 (1995): 1–11.

13. Ibn 'Asakir, *Sirat al-sayyid al-Masih*, 272–273 (no. 346); idem, *Ta'rikh*, 47: 515–516.

14. One of Muhammad's wives and his most beloved. 'A'isha (d. 678) was an important transmitter of many hadiths. See Denise A. Spellberg, *Politics, Gender, and the Islamic Past: The Legacy of 'A'isha bint Abi Bakr* (New York: Columbia University Press, 1996).

15. Ibn 'Asakir, *Sirat al-sayyid al-Masih*, 282 (no. 361); idem, *Ta'rikh*, 47: 522–523.

16. Ibn 'Asakir, *Sirat al-sayyid al-Masih*, 61–62 (no. 50); idem, *Ta'rikh*, 47: 372. This is a reference to Qur'an 61:6: ❴*When Jesus son of Mary said: "O children of Israel, I am the messenger of God to you, confirming what came before me of the Torah, and bringing good news of a messenger to come after me, whose name is Ahmad." When he came to them with clear signs they said: "This is obvious magic."*❵

17. Ibn 'Asakir, *Sirat al-sayyid al-Masih*, 129 (no. 113); idem, *Ta'rikh*, 47: 417–418.

1. Ibn 'Asakir on Jesus

Son of the sheep-bearing, a Byzantine, one of whose parents is a demon, is about to come out against the Muslims leading 500,000 soldiers by land and another 500,000 by sea and disembarking between Acre and Tyre. Then he will say: "People of the ships, come out from them," and he will order the ships to be burnt. The Muslims will seek each other's help. Then they will fight them for a month, and the victorious Muslims will find no people to stand between them and Constantinople and Rome. While the Muslims are advancing, news will reach them that the Antichrist (*al-Dajjal*) has taken over among their families. They will drop what is in their hands and rush back. A famine will fall upon the people, and while they are in this situation, they will hear a voice from heaven saying: "Rejoice, help is coming to you." They will say: "Jesus son of Mary has descended." They will rejoice in him, and he will rejoice in them, and they will say to him: "Lead us in prayer, O Spirit of God," and he will say to them: "God has honored this Muslim community; therefore, no one should lead their prayers except one of them." So, the commander of the faithful—that is, Mu'awiya son of Abu Sufyan—will lead the people in prayer, and Jesus will pray behind him. After Jesus finishes his prayer, he will take his lance, go toward the Antichrist and kill him. Then Jesus will die and the Muslims will wash him and bury him.[18]

Questions

1. How does Ibn 'Asakir depict Jesus as a Muslim prophet?
2. How does he depict him as the model Muslim ascetic?
3. What, according to Ibn 'Asakir, is Jesus's role in the End of Days?
4. Why might he focus on these depictions of Jesus in the context of the Crusader period?
5. What is the implication of the Prophet Muhammad instructing his followers to utter an attestation of faith (*shahada*) that includes the affirmation that Jesus is the prophet of God?

---

18. Excerpted from Ibn 'Asakir, *Sirat al-sayyid al-Masih*, 257–261. For a discussion of this prophecy, see Suleiman A. Mourad, "Jesus According to Ibn 'Asakir," in *Ibn 'Asakir and Early Islamic History*, ed. J. E. Lindsay (Princeton: Darwin Press, 2001), 31–32.

2. Ibn 'Asakir on al-Findalawi[19]

Yusuf son of Dunas son of 'Isa, Abu al-Hajjaj al-Maghribi al-Findalawi, the Maliki jurist. He came to Syria on his pilgrimage to Mecca. He resided at Banyas for a time where he was a mosque preacher. He then moved to settle in Damascus where he taught jurisprudence according to the branch (*madhhab*) of Malik. He also transmitted *al-Muwatta*'[20] and Abu al-Hasan al-Qabisi's *Kitab al-Talkhis*.[21] Many hadiths were transmitted on his authority. He was a good-humored and pleasantly sociable scholar, exceedingly zealous for Sunnism, generous of spirit, unpretentious, and stouthearted.

I heard Abu Turab son of Qays son of Husayn al-Ba'labakki[22] recount that he used to adhere to the doctrine of physical anthropomorphism[23] and strongly hated Yusuf al-Findalawi because he used to refute and ridicule them. Once, when al-Ba'labakki departed for the Hijaz, he was taken prisoner along the way, and thrown into a pit that was sealed with a stone on top. He remained there for a time, eating what might be thrown to him. One night, he sensed something. He called out: "Who are you?" A person replied: "Give me your hand." So he did, and that person pulled him from the pit. When he got out he saw that it was none other than al-Findalawi, who said: "Repent from what you used to believe in." He repented and became one of his dearest friends.

Once, on the Night of Completion[24] in the month of Ramadan a preacher was preaching in his section in the Great Mosque and making the supplication following the completion of the Qur'an. There was also the

---

19. Ibn 'Asakir, *Ta'rikh*, 74: 234–236. For biographical information on Ibn 'Asakir, see pp. 41–42.
20. Malik ibn Anas, *Kitab al-Muwatta'*, ed. M. F. 'Abd al-Baqi (Beirut: al-Maktaba al-Thaqafiyya, 1988). *Kitab al-Muwatta'* is the major work of jurisprudence of the Maliki school, compiled by Malik's students. It comprises traditions attributed to the Prophet Muhammad and several of his Companions.
21. Abu al-Hasan al-Qabisi, *Mulakhkhas li-ma fi al-Muwatta' min al-hadith al-musnad*, ed. M. 'A. al-Maliki (Abu Dhabi: al-Majma' al-Thaqafi, 2004). Al-Qabisi was also a Maliki jurist and his book is an abridgment of Malik's *Muwatta'* that only includes the traditions attributed to the Prophet Muhammad.
22. Al-Ba'labakki is a reference to the city of Baalbek.
23. The *Hashwiyya* in Arabic, which was a pejorative label used against a group of Sunnis who believed in physical anthropomorphism, namely that God has a physical body like humans: see Jon Hoover, "Hashwiyya," *Encyclopaedia of Islam, Third Edition*.
24. Night of Completion (Arabic, *Laylat al-Khatm*) indicates the night when the customary reading of the entire Qur'an, which starts at the beginning of Ramadan, is completed. It is always scheduled on the 28th of Ramadan because, depending on the sighting of the Moon, it is not known whether the last day of fasting is the 29th or 30th of Ramadan.

2. Ibn ʿAsakir on al-Findalawi

scholar Abu al-Hasan ʿAli son of al-Musallam.[25] Someone from outside the section threw a stone at them, but no one could identify who did it because there were too many people there. Al-Findalawi said: "O God, cut his hand off." A little time after, Khudayr al-Rikabi, who was sitting in the Hanbali section, was taken into custody. In his box were found many keys that he had made to open doors of houses and steal from them. So Shams al-Muluk[26] ordered that his hand be cut off; he died from this.

Al-Findalawi—may God be merciful to him—was killed on Saturday, 6 Rabiʿ I 543 (24 July 1148) at Nayrab below al-Rabwa. He had gone out as a jihad fighter against the Franks—may God abandon them—on the day they attacked Damascus—may God protect it.[27] They departed early on Wednesday morning 4 days after they attacked. They attacked from the direction of Qayniya.[28] But they departed due to the scarcity of fodder and fearing the successive waves of troops coming from Mosul and Aleppo to reinforce the people of Damascus. He was buried on the road, below al-Rabwa, but was then moved and interred in the Small Gate cemetery. He came out against them on foot.

I was informed that the commander Unur, who was in command to fight them that day, encountered al-Findalawi prior to the combat; the cleric was exhausted from walking. Unur said to him: "O honorable cleric, go back; you are exempt because of your old age." Al-Findalawi replied: "I will not go back. We have sold and He has purchased from us." He meant the saying of the great and glorious God: ❴*God has purchased from the believers their souls and their wealth and, in exchange, the garden shall be theirs*❵ (Qurʾan 9:111).[29] Before the day was over, it happened as he had wished; namely, to achieve martyrdom that would lead him to the happiness he so desired.

Ahmad son of Muhammad al-Qayrawani said: "I saw in a dream the honorable teacher Hujjat al-Din[30] sitting where he used to teach in the

---

25. ʿAli son of al-Musallam son of Muhammad son of ʿAli, Abu al-Hasan al-Sulami (d. 1139) was a notable jurist of the Shafiʿi branch in Damascus and teacher of Ibn ʿAsakir.
26. Shams al-Muluk Ismaʿil son of Buri (d. 1135) was the Burid ruler of Damascus: see Daniella Talmon-Heller, "Burids," *Encyclopaedia of Islam, Third Edition*.
27. For the attack of the Second Crusade against Damascus, see pp. 80–87.
28. Qayniya was a village near the Small Gate (Bab al-Saghir) on the southwestern side of Damascus.
29. See Appendix B for the major quranic passages on war and peace.
30. Hujjat al-Din or "Proof of the Religion" is an honorific used to describe al-Findalawi because of his piety and scholarship. Ibn al-Athir, in his account of the siege of Damascus, referred to him by the honorific Hujjat al-Islam (Proof of Islam). See Chapter 3, p. 85 (footnote 89).

Great Mosque. I approached him and kissed his hand. He kissed my head. I said to him: 'O my honorable master; by God, I shall never forget you. You are to me as one once said:

1- When I speak, you are the first thing I utter, / and when I am silent, you are in my innermost thoughts.'

He said to me: 'May God bless you.' I inquired from him: 'O my honorable master and teacher, where are you now?' He replied: '❨*in the gardens of delight, on couches face to face*❩'" (Qur'an 37:43–44).

Questions

1. According to Ibn 'Asakir's biography of al-Findalawi, where was he from?
2. How did al-Findalawi end up in Damascus?
3. How does Ibn 'Asakir depict al-Findalawi's moral qualities?
4. What can we learn about the ideology of jihad from Ibn 'Asakir's depiction of al-Findalawi's martyrdom during the Second Crusade?
5. What can we learn about the importance of visions and dreams from Ibn 'Asakir's account of al-Findalawi's appearance in Ahmad son of Muhammad al-Qayrawani's dream after al-Findalawi's martyrdom?

3. Ibn 'Asakir on Nur al-Din[31]

Abu al-Qasim Mahmud son of Abu Sa'id Qasim al-Dawla (Beauty of the Realm) Zangi son of Aq-Sunqur al-Turki, the just Monarch Nur al-Din and helper of the commander of the faithful.

Nur al-Din's grandfather Aq-Sunqur was appointed by Sultan Abu al-Fath Malik Shah[32] son of Alp Arslan over Aleppo and other parts of Syria. His father Qasim al-Dawla was brought up in Iraq and, under the advice of Caliph and Commander of the Faithful al-Mustarshid bi-Allah,[33] was delegated to govern the region of Mosul by Sultan Mahmud[34] son of Muhammad son of Malik Shah son of Alp Arslan following the assassination of Aq-Sunqur al-Bursuqi and the death of his son Mas'ud.[35] Nur al-Din's grandfather displayed his prowess and bravery in fighting the enemy—may God abandon them. He also displayed his steadfastness when the ruler of Byzantium showed up to siege Shayzar but had to return to his country disappointed.

Nur al-Din's father Qasim al-Dawla besieged Damascus twice, but could not capture it; he did capture Edessa, Ma'arrat [al-Nu'man], Kafartab, and other Syrian castles and rescued them from the control of the infidels. When he died—may God be merciful to him—his son Nur al-Din—may God honor his service to Islam—took his place in caring for Islam.

Nur al-Din's birth, as I was informed by his secretary Abu al-Yusur Shakir son of 'Abd Allah al-Tanukhi al-Ma'arri, was at sunrise on Sunday 17 Shawwal in 511 (11 February 1118). When he reached adulthood, he entered in the service of his father until his time on earth came to an end on the eve of Sunday,[36] 6 Rabi' II in 541 (15 September 1146) outside the fortress of Ja'bar while he was besieging it. His coffin was transported to the cemetery of Raqqa and was buried there.

On Sunday morning, when Nur al-Din sent to Mosul the Monarch Alp Arslan son of Sultan Mahmud son of Muhammad and a group of senior officials from his father's court, he said to them: "If my brother Sayf al-Din

---

31. Ibn 'Asakir, *Ta'rikh*, 57: 118–124. For biographical information on Ibn 'Asakir, see pp. 41–42.
32. The sultan of the Seljuk Empire (r. 1072–1092).
33. The twenty-ninth 'Abbasid caliph (r. 1118–1135).
34. The sultan of the Seljuk Empire (r. 1118–1131).
35. Aq-Sunqur al-Bursuqi (d. 1126) and his son Mas'ud (d. 1127) were commanders in the Seljuk army who became rulers of Mosul.
36. The Islamic practice considers the beginning of the day to take place on the eve of the previous night. So Sunday night starts after sunset at the end of day on Saturday.

Ghazi arrives in Mosul, then it is his and you should be in his service. But if he is late to arrive, I will arrange the affairs in Syria and come to you."

Nur al-Din then went to Aleppo and entered the invincible citadel with tremendous ease and immense grace on Monday, 7 Rabi' II (16 September 1146). He appointed deputies in the castle and the city and was generous to the commanders and gave them robes of honor. In the meantime, the son of Joscelin[37] had been seeking to take back Edessa and he managed to sneak into the city. But Nur al-Din sent to it the commanders from his court to take it back and he (Joscelin II) left it and ran away.

When the matters of succession were secured, Nur al-Din showed the eagerness to fulfill the duty of jihad, subjugate the unbelievers and the tyrants, and attend to the business of the citizens. So he went out to raid in the region of Tall Bashir where he conquered many fortresses: the fortress of Apamea, the fortress of A'zaz, Tall Bashir, Duluk, Mar'ash, the fortress of 'Ayntab, Nahr al-Jawz and others, the castle of al-Bara, the fortress of al-Rawandan, the fortress of Khalid, the castle of Kafar Latha, and the castle of Basarfut in the Mountain of Banu 'Ulaym. He also raided the castle of Innib, but the Prince (Raymond of Poitiers), who ruled Antioch and who was among the heroes of the enemy and one of their devils, came out so Nur al-Din raised the siege and fought him in a nearby place where the Sultan broke him and killed him along with 3,000 Franks with him.[38] Raymond's young son (Bohemond III)[39] stayed behind with his mother (Constance of Hauteville)[40] in Antioch, and she married another prince (Reynald of Châtillon).[41] Nur al-Din in another raid captured the second prince, so Antioch reverted back to the son of the first prince, who was named Bohemond who also fell captive to Nur al-Din during the attack against Harim and Nur al-Din sold him for a large sum that he used in jihad.

Nur al-Din reintroduced in Aleppo the Sunna and reestablished true religion, corrected the heresy that they used to follow in the call for prayer, and crushed in it the heretical Shi'is. He revivified the four Sunni branches of jurisprudence, relieved its inhabitants from all hardships, and barred them

---

37. That is Joscelin II (d. 1159) of Edessa son of Joscelin I (d. 1131).

38. This is a reference to the Battle of Innib in 1149, where Nur al-Din defeated the army of Frankish Antioch and killed Raymond; he was beheaded by Shirkuh, Saladin's uncle.

39. Prince of Antioch between 1163 and 1201.

40. Born in 1128, she became princess of Antioch in 1130 following the death of her father Bohemond II (d. 1130). She married Raymond in 1136 and died in 1163.

41. The infamous Frankish ruler of Transjordan who was killed by Saladin following the Battle of Hattin in 1187. See pp. 91–96.

from involvement in civil disturbances. He built in Aleppo schools, set up endowments, and showed justice and evenhandedness.

Nur al-Din made a truce with al-Muʿin Unur of Damascus and married his daughter ('Ismat al-Din),[42] and thus they united and Nur al-Din helped him against the enemy. He laid siege to Damascus twice but could not capture it. Then he marched against it a third time and was able to conclude a truce; its inhabitants turned it over to him because of the soaring prices and out of fear of being overwhelmed by the infidels. Nur al-Din fixed its affairs, fortified its walls, built in it schools and mosques, and increased the benefits for its inhabitants. He also fixed its roads and enlarged its markets, and because of his blessed ways, God made the businesses of his subjects prosper. He put an end to mishaps and lifted the burdens placed on them. He banned the fees that were imposed to trade in the markets of watermelons and vegetables, on water assignments and measurements, in the sheep market and other similar injustices. He also ordered a ban on levying taxes on the sale of wine,[43] prohibited its drinking and ordered the legal penalty and imprisonment be imposed on those Muslims who consumed it. He also rescued from the enemy—may God abandon them—the frontier city of Baniyas (Balanea)[44] and other fortified places such as al-Munaytra and others when everyone despaired of that.

I was informed that in war Nur al-Din is calm, steadfast, very focused, and good with shooting arrows. He hits firmly with the sword in tight spots, lets his companions roll during attack and protects them when they retreat, risking his own martyrdom which we all seek in order to achieve everlasting bliss.

A man who served Nur al-Din for some time and assisted him in doing charitable deeds heard him once imploring God to cause him to meet his end inside the bellies of lions and vultures. May God protect his life from the worst and reward him with victory against all enemies, for he is kind and generous to the scholars, brings the religiously devout people close to him

---

42. Nur al-Din married the daughter of Unur, the general who called the shots in Damascus under the Burid ruler Abaq. Al-Khatun (Lady) ʿIsmat al-Din (Chastity of the Religion), who died in 1186, endowed several buildings in Damascus, including a mausoleum for her father and a school known as al-Khatuniyya College. On Unur, see pp. 81–83.

43. Muslim rulers often collected taxes on the sale of wine, to which some jurists and scholars objected because they believed Shariʿa law bans alcohol and everything associated with it (sale, consumption, production, etc.), which is not a matter of agreement among Muslim jurists, and definitely not among Muslims in general.

44. Baniyas is the Syrian port city south of Antioch, between Latakiya and Tartus—not the Banyas north of Lake Tiberias described by Ibn Jubayr, p. 17.

and shows them respect, seeks justice in judgments and adjudicated cases, spreads his protection, and shows mercy toward the subjects. He built in most parts of his dominion houses for justice and appointed in them judges and jurists to adjudicate matters. Seeking fairness and virtue, and eager to establish justice, he would often attend in person to hear the cases and testimonies of those with grievances.

For those with no support and the orphans, Nur al-Din instituted charities and took the responsibility to care for people with disabilities who regularly attend prayers, so much so that he would visit the physically and mentally ill and assign to them physicians and people to treat them. So, too, with the blind, teachers of calligraphy and Qur'an, and those who reside in the two sanctuaries[45] who spend their time in the two mosques. He also handsomely rewarded al-Husayni,[46] the ruler of Medina, was generous to him and assigned to him a nice lodging when he came to visit, sent with him troops to protect Medina, and prepared them with what they might need in terms of provisions. For the commander of Mecca, he granted a land with splendid revenues. Essentially, he gave them both what they could consume with ease and joy.

For the pilgrims, Nur al-Din lifted the tax that was imposed on them, and granted to the Bedouin commanders lands with splendid revenues so that they would not intimidate the pilgrims. He ordered the walls of the Medina of the Prophet[47] be completed, and the spring in Uhud be dug again after it was buried by floods. Special invocations were made for him in the two sanctuaries and his fame spread to east and west.

Nur al-Din built Sufi retreats and lodges, hospitals, bridges over the roads, and caravanserais. For the Muslim orphans, he appointed a group of teachers to teach them, set up their teachers' salaries, and a budget for the orphans' expenditures. He did the same when he took control of Sinjar, Harran, Edessa, Raqqa, Manbij, Shayzar, Hama, Hims, Baalbek, Sarkhad, and Palmyra. In every one of these cities he did memorable things and every one of its inhabitants regarded him very highly.

Nur al-Din purchased a large quantity of books on many topics and placed them in an endowment for the benefit of those seeking knowledge. He paid for their scribes, people to study them, and their authors. He also renewed many roads and with his effort guided many to virtue.

---

45. Meaning Mecca and Medina.

46. Qasim son of al-Muhanna al-Husayni al-'Alawi, the ruler of Medina, whose lineage traces back to 'Ali and the Prophet Muhammad.

47. The full name of Medina.

3. Ibn ʿAsakir on Nur al-Din

Nur al-Din exerted himself waging jihad against the enemies of God and fighting them. He took captive a number of the commanders of the Franks—may God abandon them—such as Joscelin and his son (Joscelin II), Alphonse's son,[48] the count of Tripoli, and others of their rank.

The Byzantine king marched out of Constantinople seeking Syria and desiring to take over Antioch. Nur al-Din distracted him from his purpose with correspondences until his brother Qutb al-Din[49] arrived with his troops from Mosul. Thus, he readied for him the armies and troops, spending lots of money and fortunes. The Byzantine despaired from ever attaining what he intended, so he sought to conclude peace with Nur al-Din hoping to escape unharmed. He turned back to his land disappointed, back to where he left, not having achieved anything in Syria despite his large army. His horse did not even eat a single wheat shaft from the farms around Harim. He did not achieve his purpose, and his efforts were in vain. Nur al-Din brought back to the Muslim treasury loads of valuable items.

Nur al-Din's brother Qutb al-Din, his troops from Mosul, and other jihadists joined him. He defeated the Franks, Byzantines, and Armenians and made them taste the cup of death with sharp cutting swords. He wreaked such devastation upon them that of the initial 30,000 horsemen and foot soldiers only a few bewildered ones were saved. He laid siege to the fortress of Harim and captured it for the second time and retained it, occupying the largest town in the area of Antioch and enslaving its inhabitants. Before that, he defeated them outside Baniyas, killed a number of their heroes, and enslaved many of their horsemen and foot soldiers. Shawar al-Saʿdi, the leading general of the Egyptian armies, came to Nur al-Din seeking help when he was about to be deposed. Nur al-Din was hospitable to him and honored him, showing him generosity and respect. He sent with Shawar a large army to reinstate him in his post. They killed Shawar's opponent, but Shawar did not fulfill what he had promised and instead sought help from the army of the enemy to keep his eminent rank. Nur al-Din sent another army to him, but Shawar insisted on his evasiveness and showed arrogance, sending to the enemy for assistance—may God abandon them. They sent Shawar assistance and support, and he promised them an enormous sum of money. The army of the Muslims withdrew to Syria. (Amalric I), the king

---

48. A reference to Bertrand, the son of Alphonse Jordan of Toulouse (d. 1148). See pp. 83, 87.
49. Qutb al-Din was Nur al-Din's younger brother. After their father, Zangi, died in 1146, Nur al-Din and his elder brother, Sayf al-Din, split their father's holdings. Nur al-Din took Aleppo and northern Syria; Sayf al-Din took Mosul and northern Mesopotamia. After Sayf al-Din died in 1149, Qutb al-Din succeeded him and recognized Nur al-Din as overlord of Mosul, thus uniting Mosul and Aleppo. Qutb al-Din means "Pole of the Religion."

of the Franks, thought he could rule Egypt, and after two years he marched against it hoping to benefit from the opportunity. He occupied Bilbis and camped there waiting for a chance to move against Cairo.

When Nur al-Din heard of this, he exerted his effort to rush an army there fearing the enemy of religion might capture it. When the enemy—may God abandon them—heard that Nur al-Din's army was heading their way, they retreated in disappointment. Nur al-Din's supporters gained the upper hand in Cairo, and the people were relieved at the sight of his army in their midst; their fear was gone. He was informed about Shawar's scheme and that he had corresponded with the enemy hoping for gain and asked them to send troops to repel the army of the Muslims. When Nur al-Din recognized Shawar's evilness and deceitfulness, and realized his treachery and disloyalty, the matter became evident. The lion pretended to be sick to catch the snake.[50] So when Shawar came to visit Asad al-Din Shirkuh as it was his custom, Nur al-Din's slaves Jurdik and Buzghush jumped on Shawar and killed him. They relieved the people and the land of his evil. Nur al-Din was the only person who succeeded in arresting Shawar and sullying his honorable hand with his blood. The situation was normalized for Asad al-Din and he was declared ruler. Robes of honor were placed on him, he settled in, and his supporters took over Egypt. His affairs were successful, and he showed praiseworthy behavior and good traits. The infidel shall learn who inherits the land.

The word of the people of the Sunna triumphed in the land of Egypt and the sermons were read there in the name of the 'Abbasid caliph after complete despair.[51] God had relieved those who were there from disaster and ended their suffering. Therefore, God is deserving of thanks for His graces, and for the success of conquests.

On top of all these glorious traits—only a few notable ones have I mentioned in detail—Nur al-Din has a handsome and firm handwriting. He is eager for knowledge with diligence and discernment, and studies and copies a lot of it. He is also keen to acquire the collections of authentic Hadith and Sunna irrespective of cost or expense. He regularly reads the religious sciences, seeking the prophetic traditions. He is keen to perform the prayers properly with the community and according to their precise schedule, and

---

50. Asad is Arabic for lion. This is a pun on Asad al-Din Shirkuh's name as he (the lion) pretended to be ill in order that Shawar would come visit him in his illness, at which point Asad al-Din's slaves killed him. Asad al-Din means "Lion of the Religion."

51. That is, because the names of the Isma'ili Fatimid caliphs had been invoked in the Friday sermons since 969, the year the Fatimids conquered Egypt.

following exact requirements and directions; if he were to miss one prayer, he would make a big deal of it. He devotes time each day to recite the Qur'an and is keen to do good deeds such as giving charity and fasting. He often invokes and glorifies God; he seeks to perform the end of night prayers during Ramadan. He does not eat anything forbidden or seek sexual affairs. He is economical with personal expenditures and cash, selective in his food, drink, and dress. He is not interested in haughtiness, posturing, or competition; he is free of pomposity and arrogance. He has no concern for astrology and fortune-telling. God had blessed him with a solid intellect, firm and upright judgment, eagerness to model his life after that of previous ancestors, and to imitate scholars and virtuous people by following their conduct and good manners, and imitating the way they preserved themselves and their time on earth.

Nur al-Din even transmits the Hadith of the Chosen One—may God bless him and grant him peace—and teaches it. He had received a license from those he read and studied with, for he is so eager to spread the Sunna and transmit Hadith in hope of being one of those who preserve forty hadiths for the Muslim community, as the prophetic hadith stipulated.[52] Whoever sees him is captivated by the aura of statehood and kingship that he exhibits, and when speaking to him is bewildered by his gentleness and humility.

One who is usually in his company when in town or on travel said that he never heard Nur al-Din utter a vile word in happiness or boredom. The best thing to him is receiving advice for him to heed or guiding him to a prophetic practice to follow.

Nur al-Din loves the virtuous and associates with them, thinks highly of them and visits their houses. When his slaves reach adulthood, he frees them and arranges for the males to marry the females and gives them a stipend. If someone complains to him about the conduct of one of his officials, he orders the harm to be stopped, and those who ignore him he demotes or sacks. Because God arranged for him all these noble characteristics, he achieves his objectives with ease, and it is simple for him to conquer castles and fortresses, and control lands and territories, so much so that he captured the castle of Shayzar and the fortress of Dawsar, which are among the most fortified strongholds and castles. He acquired what was in them

---

52. As per the prophetic Hadith: "He who preserves forty hadiths that are beneficial for the religious needs of my community will be resurrected on the Day of Resurrection as a scholar. The scholar is ranked seventy ranks above the worshiper; only God knows what is between each two ranks." Mourad and Lindsay, *Intensification*, 135.

of well-protected wealth without a single drop of blood and not a single Muslim was killed for them. Most of the territories he seized, he took over from their inhabitants by means of truces, and he honored his promises and pledges, and left them in peace.

If one of his soldiers is martyred, Nur al-Din protects his family and children and grants them stipends. He would appoint those who were fit to certain positions. Each time God allows him to conquer a place and add a region to his many holdings, he eliminates some taxes and increases his care for them. Injustices and taxes gradually disappeared, and in all his regions fees and disasters decreased. His subjects' businesses are flourishing and their sales soaring. On account of his good fortune, accord between them has thrived, and rivalry and animosity disappeared. Some cursed ones would commit deplorable acts knowing how lenient and gentle he is. But if he were to combine his might and gentleness, even the lion in his den would fear him.

Through Nur al-Din God protects Muslims from killing each other, pacifies for him the populace, prolongs his graces, and makes his glory reach the heavens. He lets good deeds unravel at Nur al-Din's hands and makes him a shelter. God entrusted to him our current tragedy and gave him the knowledge of our needs. His achievements are significant, and his merits are manifold. I have only mentioned a few of his many good qualities; his merits are legion. A group of poets composed many eulogies for him, but they fell far short in describing his blessings. He does not like poetry, another indication of his humility. May God prolong his shadow over the people, spread his leniency and justice among them, make him reach his intention in this world and the next, and seal with happiness and success his affairs, for He is the One who hears and is capable of everything. God knows best.

Questions

1. According to Ibn ʿAsakir's biography of Nur al-Din, what was the primary focus of Nur al-Din's achievements and accomplishments?

2. How does Ibn ʿAsakir represent Nur al-Din's relations with fellow Muslim sovereigns?

3. How does he represent Nur al-Din's relations with Frankish sovereigns?

4. Why might Ibn 'Asakir be interested in Nur al-Din's support for Sunnism?
5. Can we detect any particular biases for or against Nur al-Din on the part of Ibn 'Asakir?

Chapter 4: Biographies

4. Sibt Ibn al-Jawzi on al-Mu'azzam[53]

In this year (624/1227) died the Monarch al-Mu'azzam 'Isa son of al-'Adil Abu Bakr son of Ayyub—the learned jurist, benefactor, jihad warrior in the path of God, conqueror, grammarian, and lexicographer.

Some of his affairs

Al-Mu'azzam was born in Cairo in the year 576 (1180) and grew up in Syria. He read the Qur'an and studied jurisprudence according to the branch of Abu Hanifa with Fakhr al-Din al-Hasiri.[54] He memorized *al-Mas'udi*,[55] and specialized in *The Great Legal Compendium (al-Jami' al-Kabir)*.[56] He also read literature with Taj al-Din al-Kindi,[57] learning from him the *Book (al-Kitab)* of Sibawayh,[58] its *Commentary (Sharh)* by al-Sirafi,[59] *The Authority on the Seven Readings of the Qur'an (al-Hujja fi al-qira'at)* by Abu 'Ali al-Farisi,[60] and *al-Hamasa*.[61] He also recited to him the *Book of Clarifications on Arabic Syntax (Kitab al-Idah)* also by Abu 'Ali from memory and studied the *Musnad* of Ahmad Ibn

---

53. Sibt Ibn al-Jawzi, *Mir'at al-zaman*, 8 (part 2): 644–652. For biographical information on Sibt Ibn al-Jawzi, see p. 107.

54. Mahmud son of Ahmad al-Hasiri (d. 1238) was a renowned Hanafi jurist and specialist in Hadith scholarship in Damascus.

55. An important legal source on Hanafi law authored by Abu Muhammad al-Nasihi (d. 1055), the famous chief judge for the Ghaznavids. The book is titled *al-Mas'udi* after Sultan Mas'ud, the son of the notorious Mahmud of Ghazna.

56. *Al-Jami' al-Kabir* is a major early Hanafi legal encyclopedia by al-Shaybani (d. 805), who was the student of Abu Hanifa.

57. Taj al-Din al-Kindi (1126–1217) was a Hanbali scholar from Baghdad who became an authority on Arabic grammar. He later moved to Damascus and adopted the Hanafi branch.

58. The *Book (Kitab)* of Sibawayh (d. ca. 796) was one of the foundational books on Arabic grammar.

59. Al-Sirafi (d. 979) was a celebrated grammarian, and his *Commentary* was a very authoritative source for understanding Sibawayh's *Book*; often the latter was read by using the former: see Geneviève Humbert, "al-Sirafi," *Encyclopaedia of Islam, Second Edition*.

60. An important source on the variant readings of same words in the Qur'an by Abu 'Ali al-Farisi (d. 987), who was a noted grammarian who also authored *Kitab al-Idah (Book of Clarifications on Arabic Syntax)*: see Reinhard Weipert, "al-Farisi, Abu 'Ali," *Encyclopaedia of Islam, Third Edition*.

61. A renowned anthology of poetry by the early 'Abbasid poet Abu Tammam (d. 845). He arranged it according to themes, which made it an indispensable resource of Arabic verse composed on various topics in pre-Islamic and early Islamic times: see Beatrice Gruendler, "Abu Tammam," *Encyclopaedia of Islam, Third Edition*.

4. Sibt Ibn al-Jawzi on al-Mu'azzam

Hanbal.[62] Al-Mu'azzam learned these in Damascus. In Egypt, he studied with Ibn Tabarzad[63] some of his licensed Hadith transmissions, and with Ibn al-Mahalli he studied the *Life of Muhammad (Sira)* by Ibn Hisham[64] and other works.

Al-Mu'azzam composed several expositions on books such as *The Great Legal Compendium*, *Refutation of al-Khatib al-Baghdadi (al-Radd 'ala al-Khatib)*,[65] and *On the Metric System of Poetry (al-'Arud)*.[66] He also authored a collection of poems and a book on prosody, but sometimes he failed to compose in correct meter. I used to tell him: "This shows that you have a trace of prophethood, for God said about Muhammad: ❮*We did not teach him poetry* . . .❯" (Qur'an 36:69).

He was courageous and daring, very shy and humble, with a beautiful face, humorous, jealous, magnanimous, and of good company who preserved friendship and amity.

There used to be a man in al-Balqa'[67] from the clan of Mahdi named Nudar, who composed poetry in the old style of the Bedouins. He composed a panegyric poem for al-Mu'azzam, saying:

1- Of the many deceptions of time, he is distinguished; / honorable when fate is unkind to him.

He always marveled at the expression *unkind to him*.

When al-Mu'azzam went to see his brother al-Kamil in the year 607 (1210) or 609 (1212) when al-Kamil was in Alexandria, he rode the same horse all the way, and crossed the distance from Damascus to Alexandria in 8 days. Al-Kamil came out to greet him. They dismounted and hugged each other.

---

62. The *Musnad (The Hadiths Arranged According to the Companion Transmitters)* was one of the authoritative collections of Hadith in Sunni Islam, and the most important for the Hanbali branch.

63. Ibn Tabarzad (1123–1210) was a famous Hadith scholar.

64. The *Sira* of Ibn Hisham (d. after 828) was one of the authoritative biographies of the Prophet Muhammad.

65. This is likely a critical response to al-Khatib al-Baghdadi (d. 1071), a famous Sunni Hadith scholar and author of the *History of Baghdad*, for his disparaging biography of Abu Hanifa.

66. *Kitab al-'Arud* was the earliest and most important book written on the metric system of Arabic poetry by al-Khalil son of Ahmad al-Farahidi (d. after 776).

67. Today, it is the central part of Jordan where the capital city Amman is located.

Chapter 4: Biographies

During al-Muʿazzam's rule over Damascus, al-Baha' Ibn al-Bayni[68] was in charge of the Zakat agency. The poet al-Badr Ibn al-Musajjif[69] came back from the East with a large quantity of textile. Ibn al-Bayni overtaxed him, so Ibn al-Musajjif wrote to al-Muʿazzam complaining:

1- O Monarch, who ferociously annihilated many an enemy / and revivified every outstanding trait and virtue.
2- Like the Messiah[70] in name and deed; / confronting life with firm resolve.
3- Al-Baha' imposed on me the payment of Zakat / which is unlawful and not permitted.
4- So please hurry your grace, because I consider / your duty to collect Zakat nobler than needing the money of one like me.

Al-Muʿazzam accordingly decreed that at the beginning of the year only the one-tenth tax should be levied from Ibn al-Musajjif.[71]

When al-Muʿazzam marched against an invader he would sleep while riding; his pillow was his shield. He would not cease reading the Qur'an, *The Great Legal Compendium*, and *The Book of Sibawayh*. He was continuously on his mount, so much so that if he dismounted, they served the meal right away. When everyone was done eating, he would attend to their requests until noon.

During the days of war with the Franks, al-Muʿazzam would arrange fire signals over the mountains, from the gate of Nablus to Acre. Acre had a nearby mountain called al-Karmil[72] on which fire-attendants were stationed. They had signals and spies between them; he had in Acre several news gatherers, most of them were wives of knights. They had windows

---

68. Shams al-Din al-Bayni was a scholar and local administrator in Damascus, who also, between 1202 and 1207, was in charge of the religious endowments of the Great Mosque in Damascus.

69. Badr al-Din ʿAbd al-Rahman son of Abu al-Qasim, known as al-Badr Ibn al-Musajjif, was a Damascene poet and merchant. He died in 1238. *Al-Musajjif* means "curtain maker," and must refer to one of his ancestors who started the business.

70. One of Jesus's titles in the Islamic tradition is Messiah (*al-masih*). The Arabic version of the name Jesus is ʿIsa, which is al-Muʿazzam's first name.

71. This refers to the usual zakat tax, which Sunni Muslims are expected to pay at the beginning of a given year on the profit they generated during the previous year. Shiʿis are expected to pay one fifth. The Ayyubids introduced alongside the zakat tax several other taxes on a variety of commodities.

72. The Mount Carmel that appears in the story of Elijah and the prophets of Baal (1 Kings 18:20–40).

4. Sibt Ibn al-Jawzi on al-Muʿazzam

facing al-Karmil. When the Franks were preparing to embark on a raid, a woman would open her window. If the raiding party was 100, she would light one candle, if they were 200, two candles. If they were seeking Hawran or the direction of Damascus, she signaled in the direction of that area, and likewise to Nablus. Accordingly, he would ambush the Franks on the roads. He rewarded the women and the spies for every incident with great sums.

I once asked al-Muʿazzam: "Don't you think it is too much to spend all of this from the public treasury?" He replied: "Let me tell you why I do, then you can give me your opinion. When the emperor (Frederick II) decided to march against Syria, he thought of landing in Acre suddenly and then proceeding to the gate of Damascus. He sent ahead of him a powerful knight and told him: 'Keep the news of our arrival secret so that we can make a surprise attack.' There was a socialite woman in Acre who wrote to me to inform me. I sent to her colored robes, amber jewelry, and silk veils. One day she wore them and met with the knight, and he was surprised and asked her: 'From where did you get this?' She replied: 'A Muslim friend sent them to me.' He asked: 'Who is he?' She replied: 'The little Kurd.'[73] He made on his face the sign of the cross and stood up and left her house. That woman kept endearing herself to the knight and sweet-talking to him so much so that when the sealed correspondences from the emperor came to him, he would send them to her and tell her to write to al-Muʿazzam whatever she wanted. So tell me: Shouldn't I preemptively care for the Muslims? Would it be better if the emperor were to come and harass the people of Syria and take from their cattle and wealth what cannot be counted? After all I am only sacrificing a little sum for the well-being of the Muslims, and thus saving the significant by using the insignificant (i.e., money)."

Al-Muʿazzam ordered the jurists to distill for him the thought of Abu Hanifa without the opinions of Abu Hanifa's two disciples.[74] The jurists compiled it in ten volumes, which he called *The Reminder (al-Tadhkira)*. He would not part ways with it, whether while traveling or in town. He read it constantly. He even wrote on the back of each volume: *ʿIsa son of Abu Bakr son of Ayyub memorized it all*. I asked him: "This might be held against you. The biggest teacher in Syria could barely memorize al-Quduri's

---

73. *Al-Kuraydi* in Arabic, which indicates the ethnic background of al-Muʿazzam. As for the use of "little," it could be to distinguish him from his uncle Saladin.
74. These were Abu Yusuf (d. 798) and al-Shaybani (d. 805). It was they who preserved and elucidated the legal thought of their teacher, transforming it into the Hanafi branch of Sunni jurisprudence.

(*Mukhtasar*)[75] even though he had plenty of time. You, however, have a kingdom to administer, and yet you write with your hand on ten volumes saying that you memorized them?" He replied: "The consideration is not about word-for-word memorization, but about the import. By the name of God, ask me about all the issues the book discusses. If I fail to answer, you would be correct. Otherwise, accept what I wrote."

Sa'd al-Din Mas'ud, who was in charge of the dining hall, once told me: "I used to be the governor of Shawbak, and there was a solitary monk there living in solitude in one of the mountains. One day I received a letter from al-Mu'azzam asking me to exile him. So I exiled him. He went away for a year and returned with a letter from al-Mu'azzam stating: "Send him back to his old place and take care of him." I researched his story and found out that al-Mu'azzam had sent him overseas to seek for him the whereabouts of the emperor. Al-Mu'azzam had ordered him to be exiled so that the monk would not be suspected. He later granted him a piece of land to cultivate and gave him 100 dinars."

Al-Mu'azzam loved the jurists and encouraged them to devote themselves to learning. He used to say: "Whoever memorizes the text of the *Great Legal Compendium* by al-Shaybani I will give him 100 dinars. Whoever memorizes the *Book of Clarifications on Arabic Syntax* by Abu 'Ali, I will give him 200 dinars." A group of scholars memorized both books, and al-Mu'azzam honored his pledge.

His death

Al-Mu'azzam prepared soldiers to march to Tripoli, fearing the agreement between the emperor and al-Kamil. However, he fell ill on the 15th of Shawwal (28 September 1227), when the envoys of the Khwarazmian[76] were in his court. Najm al-Din Ibn Sallam[77] told me: "In a period of 9 months, he levied from the Khwarazmians 900,000 dirhams." His illness worsened; he was inflicted with a severe diarrhea that evacuated a piece of his liver and intestine. Rumors spread that he was given poison and a group of individuals were accused of that. But the Lord knows what is the truth (e.g., Qur'an 6:17–18). The last time I saw him was on the night

---

75. Abu al-Husayn al-Quduri (d. 1037) lived in Baghdad and was the most senior Hanafi jurist in his time.

76. This is a reference to the Seljuk Sultan Jalal al-Din (r. 1220–1231). Jalal al-Din means "Splendor of the Religion."

77. Al-Hasan son of Salim (d. 1245), known as Najm al-Din Ibn Sallam, was the secretary of al-Mu'azzam, very influential in the political life of Damascus: al-Dhahabi, *Ta'rikh al-islam*, 47: 115–116. Najm al-Din means "Star of the Religion."

4. Sibt Ibn al-Jawzi on al-Mu'azzam

of Friday, 29 Dhu al-Qa'da (9 November 1227). I visited him at the end of the day and found with him his son the Monarch al-Nasir Dawud, Karim al-Din al-Khilati,[78] and Ya'qub the physician.[79] He was on a bed, looking old, his appearance deteriorating. Death could be seen in his once handsome face. I cried. He said: "Far be it from you, far be it from you to do this." He was lying on a thin mattress covered with a Venetian cloth as well as a pillow and a quilt of similar make. He had a scarf on his head and a copper tray full of sand in front of him. I asked Karim al-Din: "What is this?" He replied: "For him to perform the ablution before each prayer."[80] Al-Mu'azzam used to say: "By God, I never missed a prayer." Karim al-Din told me: "He insisted on staying awake the entire night preceding his death. His eyes drifted at dawn, but he opened them just as the sun was about to rise. He could not perform the ablution, so he prayed by gesturing as best he could." Al-Mu'azzam used to say: "I do not think a monarch is admitted to paradise." He also used to say: "Death is better than life and needing people." He also said: "The prophet—may God bless him and grant him peace—said, a true hadith: 'Dust from waging jihad in the path of God and the smoke of hell can never join together in the nose of a servant.' My nose is filled with dust from waging jihad in the path of God."

Al-Mu'azzam died in the third hour of Friday, the first day of Dhu al-Hijja (12 November 1227). He was washed by al-Najm Khalil,[81] and Karim al-Din poured water on his body. His will was that he not be buried in the citadel, but rather that he should be taken to the square in Qasyun and buried in front of his mother's grave, under the tree. But his will was ignored, and he was buried in the citadel. After some time when al-Ashraf took over Damascus in an objectionable manner, al-Mu'azzam's body was disinterred. He was holding in his hands half a candle, and was accompanied by al-Gharz Khalil.[82] I was informed that the porters asked for a rope to tighten his body on the bier but one of them was told: "Tighten him with your turban." Al-Mu'azzam was buried next to his mother in the grave by the door, where his brother al-Mughith had been buried.

---

78. Al-Khilati (d. 1234) was one of the commanders in the Ayyubid sultanate: Sibt Ibn al-Jawzi, *Mir'at al-zaman*, 8.2: 692. Karim al-Din means "Benefactor of the Religion."

79. On physician Ya'qub son of Siqlab (d. 1229) see Chapter 4, pp. 186–190.

80. When clean water is not available or practical, sand is a suitable substitute for performing one's ablutions prior to prayer.

81. Al-Najm Khalil (d. 1243) was a close confidant of al-Mu'azzam and judge of his army: al-Dhahabi, *Ta'rikh al-islam*, 47: 76.

82. Al-Gharz Khalil (d. 1236) was the governor of Damascus under al-Mu'azzam: Sibt Ibn al-Jawzi, *Mir'at al-zaman*, 8.2: 609; and al-Dhahabi, *Ta'rikh al-islam*, 46: 145–146.

We held the mourning assembly for al-Muʿazzam in the Great Mosque of Damascus over the course of 3 days. The citizens grieved over him immensely, something not seen before when one of the monarchs died. I saw ladies from well-reputed households, who had never ventured unveiled in public. At the beginning of the night they arrived at the foot of the citadel, having torn their robes and untied their hair. They were accompanied by mourners who were beating themselves. They beat their chests then they walked in the markets and continued to beat themselves until the morning. They did this for an entire month. Likewise, throughout the day in major squares.

When I delivered a speech on the first day of his mourning, I was overwhelmed by weeping, for he was benevolent to his subjects, protective of their women, and gentle toward them. He knew them all, the humble ones and the notables. He used to attend my classes in the Mosque of Damascus and Jerusalem. He used to come very early to the Mosque of Damascus and sit among the common people near the pulpit at the entrance of the Shrine of Husayn.[83] When he returned from the Pilgrimage to Mecca in 621 (1225), he attended my class in the Mosque of Damascus and chanted a poem by my grandfather—may God be merciful to him:[84]

1- Greeting to the House which we rarely visit / for this heart of ours is its captive.

He chanted several other lines as well. When he finished the poem, he wept profusely. I feared that he might be ridiculed by people. I said to him: "May God never forget your endeavors done to please Him and your passing the nights waging jihad against His enemies."

Schools built by him and other projects

Al-Muʿazzam built a school in Qasyun and buried his mother there, and then his brother al-Mughith. He also built a school in Jerusalem and a lodge for pilgrims.[85] He took care of the Hijaz and the route to it. He built two baths in Amman, one for men and one for women. He set up lodging stations on the way to and from Mecca. He let people use the baths for free. He planted trees along the road to the Hijaz, from the Jabiya Gate in Damascus

---

83. For some reason, the Damascenes referred to this place as the Shrine of ʿAli.
84. Sibt's maternal grandfather was the famous Hanbali scholar Ibn al-Jawzi.
85. Al-Muʿazzam also endowed a gate to the shrine in Hebron housing the cenotaphs of Isaac and Rebecca. See inscription 5 in Chapter 6, pp. 207–208.

to Mecca. He ordered the construction of pools and water reservoirs, and allocated for the pilgrims and schools the revenues of villages from the coastal areas. Had he lived longer, people would have been able to travel to Mecca without a guide. He went on pilgrimage in 611 (1214) by way of Tabuk and al-Muʿalla. He constructed the things we mentioned along that road. Al-Muʿalla used to belong to the clan of Ibn Sakhr. It was a single parcel. He purchased it from them, and appointed a group to take care of it. He built mosques such as the one near the shrine of Jaʿfar al-Tayyar,[86] and set up the lodging stations for pilgrims. He also renovated the walls of Damascus, the cabin by the Iron Gate, the pavilion by the Postern Gate (*Bab al-Sirr*) that overlooks al-Muʿazzam's old house, the caravanserai by the Jabiya Gate, as well as the new residency, the bridge, the palace, the roofed market, and other buildings.

Praise for him from caliphs and monarchs

When my maternal uncle[87] came in the year 623 (1226), he said to me: "I was instructed by the caliph's court that I should not address al-Muʿazzam except as *Shahrayar* of Syria," which means king. When I met the Monarch al-Zahir[88] in the year 612 (1215), he said to me: "By God, al-Muʿazzam is the centerpiece of the chain and the jewel of the necklace. If it was not for al-Muʿazzam's efforts and being constantly involved in waging jihad against the enemies, I would not have been left in peace to rule Aleppo." Al-Kamil used to say: "Only the Monarch al-Muʿazzam made hair grow on our heads."

Al-Kamil once told me while in Egypt: "Who other than al-Muʿazzam protected the lands and saved me from near death?"—he meant the plot of Ibn al-Mashtub.[89] Al-Ashraf also used to say: "God curse the year in which

---

86. Jaʿfar son of Abu Talib was a cousin of Muhammad, killed during a raid on the town of Muʾta in southern Jordan in 629. He was known as al-Tayyar for the legendary tale that wings grew on his body to replace his hands that were cut during the battle.
87. Muhyi al-Din Ibn al-Jawzi was the maternal uncle of Sibt Ibn al-Jawzi. He was a vizier in the ʿAbbasid court, and often came to Syria and Egypt with letters from the ʿAbbasid caliphs to confirm the Ayyubid sultans and governors in their posts. He was killed by Hulegu in 1258.
88. Al-Zahir was the son of Saladin, who, of all of his father's empire, was left with Aleppo.
89. ʿImad al-Din Ibn al-Mashtub (d. 1220) was a very influential commander who plotted to assassinate Sultan al-Kamil and replace him with his brother al-Faʾiz. The plot was supposed to be executed when al-Kamil was near Damietta in 1219 to face the challenge of the Fifth Crusade. Only the arrival of al-Muʿazzam in the nick of time saved al-Kamil's life, and led to Ibn al-Mashtub's exile to northern Mesopotamia and his eventual death there in prison: al-Dhahabi, *Taʾrikh al-islam*, 44: 27. On his father, al-Mashtub, see pp. 104–105.

I was born." The meaning of this is that al-Ashraf was born a month or a day before al-Mu'azzam, and so he had a higher rank than al-Mu'azzam in the service of their father al-'Adil, because of their custom regarding seniority of age.

Some examples about his courage

We have mentioned that he met the Franks in Qaymun[90] and killed 100 of their horsemen, and took hostage another 100. He brought them to Jerusalem with their standards broken. He defeated the Franks more than once, and demolished Caesarea, al-Naqar, Da'uq, and many other castles along the coast.

In the Dead Sea valley, there was a bandit called Qandil, who had with him 100 men. He used to lay ambushes along the road from Beit Shean (*Baysan*) to Jericho. Al-Mu'azzam once recounted: "I was informed that the Franks were intent on taking Jerusalem, so I marched from Damascus in the afternoon with only the horse attendant and an armed slave. I informed my troops to follow me. Along the way, I spent part of the night in Tawq. I then left while it was still dark, reached Beit Shean in the morning, and had breakfast there; the governor of Beit Shean joined me. I had forgotten all about Qandil. As I started my journey toward Jericho, and while I was still in the hills above Beit Shean, Qandil arrived with his 100 men. I barely had ten horsemen. Nevertheless, I stopped and screamed at him: 'Woe to you, are you Qandil?' He replied: 'Yes.' He was holding in his hand a bow; if he were to shoot an arrow with his bow against a mountain, it would pierce through it. I ordered one of the slaves: 'Dismount and tie him up with the string of his bow.' He tied him up, and Qandil's party ran away. I took the string in my hand and proceeded to Qarawa, all the while he was silent. When the notables of Qarawa came out to meet me, they were frightened. I disembarked and told them: 'The fear of this man is in your heads. I only know about him from what you told me in Jerusalem.' I spent the night in Qarawa; at dawn I mounted and came to Jerusalem." Al-Mu'azzam's habit was to spend only one night and part of a night between Damascus and Jerusalem.

"In the morning, they came and brought Qandil along. I ordered them to go out and hang him; he was a handsome and courageous young man. He pleaded with me: 'O master, instead of hanging me, keep me to protect your land and wage jihad in your service against the heretics.' My heart felt

---

90. A village near Ramla where a battle between al-Mu'azzam and the Franks took place in August 1218.

compassion for him. I granted him a robe, took an oath from him, and let him go. He went down to the Dead Sea valley and resided in al-Haqwa. The roads became safe and the possessions were protected. When the Franks came to Mount Tabor, he waged a great jihad against them and protected the gate. When he perceived victory, he went out, killed a number of their soldiers, and achieved martyrdom—may God be merciful to him."

His children

Al-Mu'azzam had three sons: The Monarch al-Nasir Dawud, 'Abd al-'Aziz who was nicknamed al-Mughith (Succorer), and 'Abd al-Malik who was nicknamed al-Qahir (Vanquisher). As for daughters he had seventeen, and it was also said nineteen.

This completes his biography. God knows best.

Chapter 4: Biographies

5. Al-Dhahabi on al-Muʿazzam[91]

Shams al-Din Abu ʿAbd Allah Muhammad al-Dhahabi was of Turkman descent. He was born in 1274 in Mayyafariqin in northern Mesopotamia (known today as Silvan, northeast of Diyar Bakr in eastern Turkey). His family relocated to Damascus where his father was a goldsmith (hence, his nickname, al-Dhahabi, or the Golden One). His father married the daughter of a wealthy merchant from Iraq, which afforded al-Dhahabi the opportunity to receive the best Islamic education available in Damascus. He also was able to study with some of the most notable scholars in Mamluk Syria and Egypt, including in Baalbek, Cairo, Alexandria, Mecca, Aleppo, and Nablus. Consequently, al-Dhahabi became one of the most respected Shafiʿi Hadith scholars, biographers, and historians in Damascus. Because of his expertise in Hadith scholarship, he was known by the honorific "traditionist of his age" (muhaddith al-ʿasr). *He is most known for his historical and biographical works, especially his* History of Islam, *which is one of the most important histories composed during the early Mamluk period. It covers the period from the Prophet Muhammad until 1301, and draws on a wide variety of sources, some of which are no longer extant. It is important not only for the historiography of the Crusader period, but even more so for understanding how later historians remembered and commented on the Crusader period. As a contemporary of Ibn Taymiyya, it is not surprising that there was personal, theological, and professional friction between the Shafiʿi scholar al-Dhahabi and the eminent and controversial Hanbali scholar Ibn Taymiyya. Near the end of his life, al-Dhahabi lost his eyesight. He died in Damascus in 1348.*[92]

... I copied from the notes written in the hand of al-Diya',[93] who said: "Al-Muʿazzam was courageous and learned. He used to drink alcohol and encourage its drinking. He would even give a lot of money to one who does not drink just to get him to drink. He caused a lot of injustice in Syria, and ordered the destruction of the walls of Jerusalem and other castles." ...

---

91. Al-Dhahabi, *Taʾrikh al-islam*, 45: 205.
92. On al-Dhahabi, see Catarina Bori, "al-Dhahabi," *Encyclopaedia of Islam, Third Edition*.
93. Diya' al-Din al-Hanbali.

5. Al-Dhahabi on al-Muʿazzam

Questions

1. How does Sibt Ibn al-Jawzi represent the career of his patron, al-Muʿazzam?
2. Why might he place such a great emphasis on al-Muʿazzam being a learned scholar?
3. According to Sibt Ibn al-Jawzi's biography of al-Muʿazzam, what was the primary focus of al-Muʿazzam's achievements and accomplishments?
4. Can we detect a bias on the part of Sibt Ibn al-Jawzi?
5. Why might al-Dhahabi have been interested in al-Muʿazzam's fondness for drink and why did Sibt Ibn al-Jawzi not mention it?

Chapter 4: Biographies

6. Ibn Abu Usaybi'a on the Christian physician Ya'qub son of Siqlab[94]

Muwaffaq al-Din Abu al-'Abbas Ahmad son of al-Qasim son of Khalifa son of Yunus al-Shi'ri al-Khazraji was a Damascene physician who hailed from a family of physicians who had served at the courts of various Ayyubid sultans and sovereigns, including Saladin. We do not know where he got his nickname, Ibn Abu Usaybi'a (the son of the man with a little finger). He studied medicine in Damascus and in Cairo with some of the most influential physicians of his day and practiced at the Nur al-Din Hospital in Damascus. Ibn Abu Usaybi'a is most well known for his Best Accounts on the Generations of Physicians, *which is the earliest biographical dictionary of its kind in Arabic. It contains notices for some 440 physicians spanning from the ancient Greeks down to the thirteenth century. True to its name, Ibn Abu Usaybi'a's book carefully cites the sources from which its author garnered his information. It also includes material on practical medicine in his day. As such, it is a valuable and detailed source for the history of science and medicine in medieval Islam. Ibn Abu Usaybi'a died in 1270.*[95]

Muwaffaq al-Din Ya'qub son of Siqlab

A Christian who was the most knowledgeable man of his time about the books of Galen,[96] be that in studying them, understanding their language, or preserving them. His dedication to the craft of medicine, his constant reading and study of Galen's books, his fine intuition and extreme intelligence made it so that he could recite by heart all the books of Galen and his statements therein. Indeed, everything Ya'qub said about the science of medicine, its many areas, diverse categories, and many subcategories, he took from Galen. Whenever he was asked a medical question concerning unresolvable or uncurable matters or other issues, he would always say: "Galen said," and follow that with a quote from Galen. It was truly some-

---

94. Ibn Abi Usaybi'a, *'Uyun al-anba' fi tabaqat al-atibba'*, 697–699.
95. On Ibn Abu Usaybi'a, see Ibn Abi Usaybi'ah, *A Literary History of Medicine: The 'Uyun al-anba' fi tabaqat al-atibba' of Ibn Abi Usaybi'ah*, ed. and trans. E. Savage-Smith et al. (Leiden: Brill, 2020).
96. Galen (129–ca. 200) was the most celebrated physician of antiquity. His books were translated into Arabic by the famous Arab Christian (Nestorian) scholar Hunayn son of Ishaq (808–873) and formed one of the bases for the study of medicine and medical practice during the medieval Islamic period. On Hunayn son of Ishaq, see G. Strohmaier, "Hunayn b. Ishaq," *Encyclopaedia of Islam, Third Edition.*

6. Ibn Abu Usaybiʿa on the Christian physician Yaʿqub son of Siqlab

thing for which many admired him. Due to his frequent study and familiarity with Galen's books, he would quote in some cases something written by Galen and say: "This is what Galen said on such-and-such page of such-and-such section of his book," and he would specify the book's title; he meant obviously the copy he had in his possession.

I witnessed these habits of his when we were together in the army camp of al-Muʿazzam. It was at the start of my study of medicine when my father was in the service of the Monarch al-Muʿazzam—may God be merciful to him—that I read with Yaʿqub some parts of Hippocrates's discourse on medicine,[97] to memorize it and know how to explain it. I noticed his meticulous explanations and extensive examination of the language so that he would rephrase things in such an eloquent, concise, and comprehensive manner that no one would dare attempt to equal it, let alone surpass it. He would then conclude with a summary of what he taught and discussed. He left nothing in Hippocrates without an explanation so exhaustive that no one could improve upon it. He would follow that with Galen's commentary on that section from Hippocrates, one section after the other until the end of the book. I would check Galen's commentary and, to my surprise, find that all that Yaʿqub had said matched what Galen wrote, often word for word, nothing more and nothing less. He was indeed unrivaled in this in his time.

During his residence in Damascus, he frequently met with the cleric Muhadhdhab al-Din ʿAbd al-Rahim son of ʿAli[98] in the gallery where physicians congregated outside the sovereign's palace. They would converse about medical questions; the cleric Muhadhdhab al-Din was more eloquent in his expressions and better skilled with his erudite knowledge; whereas the physician[99] Yaʿqub exhibited better composure and precision in his words and his ability to cite extensively from the ancient sources, for he was a translator and had memorized everything Galen wrote in his books on medicine.

The treatments of physician Yaʿqub were superb in their quality and effectiveness. He would first seek to understand the disease thoroughly, then

---

97. Hippocrates (ca. 460–370 BCE) was a Hellenic physician whose works were collected in the *Corpus Hippocraticum*; the Hippocratic Oath is named after him.
98. Muhadhdhab al-Din ʿAbd al-Rahim son of ʿAli (d. 1230) was a famous Damascene physician during the Ayyubid period who also specialized in several scientific fields. He endowed a college to train physicians in Damascus. Muhadhdhab al-Din means "Refinement of the Religion."
99. The Arabic term—*hakim*—was used to refer to polymath scholars who were knowledgeable in several fields, including medicine, science, mathematics, religion, philosophy, language, and so on. We have translated *hakim* as "physician" here because it was for his medical expertise that Yaʿqub was most well known, though he would have been well trained in the whole range of sciences and humanities as well.

start treating it according to the directions mentioned by Galen, with some improvisations according to the methods of his time. He was exhaustive in his examination and diagnosis, so much so that if he examined a patient, he would ask him about all the symptoms and pain caused by the illness, without missing a thing, in order to diagnose the disease. This made his treatments unmatched in their superb quality.

The Monarch al-Muʿazzam valued this disposition of Yaʿqub and praised him for it. He would say: "Even if one were to say that physician Yaʿqub's only merit is his diagnoses of diseases in order to treat them properly and avoid confusion, he would still be the best physician."

Physician Yaʿqub was also fluent in Greek and knew well the Greek language and how to translate it into Arabic. He owned some of Galen's books in Greek, such as *The Method of Healing*, *On Causes and Symptoms*, and others, which he repeatedly read and studied.

He was born in Jerusalem and lived there for many years. There, too, he spent time with a virtuous man, a philosopher and monk, who lived in the monastery of al-Siq.[100] This monk was a master of natural sciences, expert in geometry and arithmetic, and skilled in astronomy and astronomical observation. He made exact predictions and amazing warnings. Physician Yaʿqub told me a great deal about the monk's knowledge of philosophy, good insight, and intelligence. In Jerusalem, too, physician Yaʿqub met the Christian cleric and physician Abu Mansur, studied medicine with him, started his practice of medicine under his supervision, and learned from him a great deal.

Physician Yaʿqub was one of the most intelligent persons, with sound judgment and unwavering composure. When he entered into the service of the Monarch al-Muʿazzam ʿIsa son of Abu Bakr son of Ayyub, and became one of his companions, al-Muʿazzam held him in high esteem and sought his advice on many medical questions as well as other issues. Al-Muʿazzam always found them useful and beneficial. The Monarch al-Muʿazzam even thought of appointing him to administer and run his state, but Yaʿqub declined the offer, opting instead to devote his time entirely to the medical profession.

---

100. One of the important Christian Orthodox monasteries near Jerusalem, known as Monastery of Mar Saba (or Holy Lavra of St. Sabbas). It is located in the southeastern hills overlooking the Kidron Valley from one side and the Valley of Jericho from the other side. The Arabic word *al-Siq* means the narrow lane or path, and is a translation of the Greek word *laura* (or lavra) which designates a monastery consisting of rooms and caves built along a narrow lane.

6. Ibn Abu Usaybi'a on the Christian physician Ya'qub son of Siqlab

Physician Ya'qub suffered from gout in both feet; when it flared up it caused him pain and made it difficult to walk. The Monarch al-Mu'azzam often brought him along in his travels, and had Ya'qub carried in a sedan. Al-Mu'azzam frequently attended to him and honored him. He also awarded him a yearly salary and many favors. One day, al-Mu'azzam said to him: "O physician, how come you cannot cure this ailment in your feet?" He replied: "O master, when wood rots, there is no cure for it."

He remained in the service of the Monarch al-Mu'azzam until the latter's death—may God be merciful to him—which occurred in Damascus at the third hour of Friday, the last day of Dhu al-Qa'da of the year 624 (11 November 1227).[101] Al-Mu'azzam was succeeded by his son the Monarch al-Nasir Dawud. Physician Ya'qub came to him, praised him and reminded him of his long companionship and service to his father and that he had reached old age, decay, and weakness. He also recited to al-Nasir Dawud the following, which was originally composed by Ibn Munqidh[102]—may God be merciful to him:

1- I came to you when the shirts of my boyhood were new; / how could I leave now that they have become rags?
2- I deserve the honor you show to the guest and to the old neighbor / for I came to you when the aged today were then but boys.

The Monarch al-Nasir was very generous toward him and gave him some money and a robe. He ordered as well that Ya'qub should continue to receive all that the Monarch al-Mu'azzam had allocated for him and that he should not be burdened with service in the court. Ya'qub lived for a short period after that and died in Damascus on Easter Day of the Christians, in the month of Rabi' II 625 (2 April 1228).

---

101. In the Islamic calendar, the day starts on what today is customarily considered the evening of the previous day. Hence, this would have been Thursday night.
102. The famous Usama Ibn Munqidh.

Chapter 4: Biographies

7. Al-Dhahabi on the Christian physician Ya'qub son of Siqlab[103]

Al-Muwaffaq, the Christian physician Ya'qub son of Siqlab al-Qudsi. He lived in Jerusalem for a while, where he accompanied a philosopher monk who was skilled in astronomy and astrology as well. He had his training in medicine under the Christian physician Abu Mansur.

The accursed Ya'qub was clever, composed, and calm. He was fluent in Greek, and knew how to translate it into Arabic. He was one of the most learned of his time in Galen's books, so much so that he could recite them all by heart.

Al-Muwaffaq Ibn Abu Usaybi'a studied with him, and others as well. He was skilled in curing illnesses. The Monarch al-Mu'azzam used to praise his medicine and recommend it.

The wise Ya'qub became afflicted with gout. They used to carry him in a sedan to accompany the Monarch al-Mu'azzam on his travels. He once said to him: "O wise one, how come you cannot cure your own illness?" He replied: "My lord, when wood rots, there is no trick that can fix it." He died in Rabi' II 625 (late March or early April 1228).

Questions

1. In what ways are Ibn Abu Usaybi'a's and al-Dhahabi's depictions of Ya'qub son of Siqlab's career as a physician similar to and dissimilar to each other?

2. Why does al-Dhahabi refer to Ya'qub as "the accursed"?

3. Based on these two accounts, what can we learn about the role of Christian physicians at Muslim courts during this period?

---

103. Al-Dhahabi, *Ta'rikh al-islam*, 45: 240. For biographical information on al-Dhahabi, see p. 184.

CHAPTER FIVE
CORRESPONDENCES, TREATIES, AND TRUCES

1. Al-Qalqashandi's account of Saladin's letter of condolence to King Baldwin IV in 1174[1]

Shihab al-Din al-Qalqashandi (1355–1418) was a Shafi'i legal scholar and secretary in the chancery of the Mamluk court in Cairo. As such, his The Guiding-Light for the Dim-Sighted in the Profession of Chancery *is a massive encyclopedia of chancery records. It preserves a few correspondences and records from the Crusader period found nowhere else, including the correspondence herein.*[2]

The second type of correspondence issued by the sovereigns of Egypt to the Franks

I have seen one example of this type of correspondence. They start with the formulaic "now"[3] and the acknowledgment of the sovereignty of the addressed person, and conclude with supplication for the well-being of the addressed. It was written by al-Qadi al-Fadil[4] at the request of Sultan Saladin Yusuf son of Ayyub to Baldwin—one of the kings of the Franks,[5] who then controlled Jerusalem and its surrounding areas—to express condolence

---

1. Al-Qalqashandi, *Subh al-a'sha fi sina'at al-insha*, 14 vols. (Cairo: Dar al-Kutub al-Misriyya, 1913–1919), 7: 115–116.

2. On al-Qalqashandi, see C. E. Bosworth, "al-Kalkashandi," in *Encyclopaedia of Islam, Second Edition*. Shihab al-Din means "Shooting Star of the Religion."

3. *Amma ba'd* in Arabic, which is a transition statement to indicate the actual start of the message.

4. Al-Qadi al-Fadil (1135–1200)—literally the judge al-Fadil—was the head of Saladin's chancellery and his vizier as well as an accomplished poet. He was famous for his elevated prose style and composition skills.

5. Al-Qalqashandi meant all of the Franks, including those in Europe, and not only in coastal Syria.

191

to him upon the death of his father King Amalric and to congratulate him on inheriting the throne. The form of the letter is as follows:

> Now, God has allocated for the esteemed king, the guardian of Jerusalem, a brilliant destiny and good fortune; He has provided him special care and guidance. May He make joyful his kingship over his people, which He arranged for him to inherit. May He guide him successfully through what time will bring and initiate for him.
>
> Our letter is being sent to the new king upon receipt of the news that made the hearts of friends ache: the announcement of death—we hoped that the one who delivered it was a liar—the passing away of the just and dear King Amalric. May God arrange for him a better reception than that of his peers. May He preserve his good name on earth in the same way He made him king. We extend condolences, hoping it will be a solace to you; we regret his loss, which is a great disaster. But God—praise to Him—diminished the weight of the incident by making his son the heir; He alleviated the harm by preserving the proper order of things. He granted the new king the two graces: kingship and youth. May he enjoy what he earned, for that will be a comfort for his deceased father who deserves such sacrifice, if such a thing were permissible.
>
> Our envoy, the chief diplomat Mukhtar al-Din[6]—may God protect him—will deliver on our behalf the verbal message of condolence, and express our state of shock at losing such a friend and the emptiness we feel. Pray tell! How can the neighbor not mourn the passing of his neighbor?
>
> We are sending the new king our letter and greetings, for it pleases us that he is the heir of his father. May he reciprocate our gesture and respond well so that it is known he is a man of goodness. Let him know that he has from us what his father had: a true friendship, a sincere bond, an affection that endured in life and in death, and a loyal heart despite our differences in religion. So, may he trust us confidently and feel he can depend on us like the son depends on his father. May God preserve his land, guard his rule,

---

6. An officer in Saladin's court. Mukhtar al-Din means "Favorite of the Religion."

1. Al-Qalqashandi's account of Saladin's letter of condolence to King Baldwin IV

ordain that he remain on the path of success, and inspire him to find confidence in his friends.

Questions

1. Al-Qalqashandi includes this letter in his *Guiding-Light* as an example of a specific type of correspondence. According to al-Qalqashandi, what type of correspondence does this letter conform to?
2. Who composed this letter, and what was the occasion?
3. What can we learn from this letter about the relationship between Ayyubid and Frankish sovereigns?
4. What might account for Saladin's respectful tone when writing to Baldwin IV and Ibn Jubayr's reference to him as "the pig king, lord of Acre" (pp. 17, 25)?
5. Does this letter confirm or contradict the general stereotype of Muslim–Frankish relations?

Chapter 5: Correspondences, Treaties, and Truces

2. Ibn Shaddad on Saladin's negotiations with Richard the Lionheart in 1191 and the latter's proposal that al-'Adil marry Richard's sister Joan[7]

The message that the Monarch al-'Adil gave to me and a group of commanders to deliver to the Sultan

On the 29th of Ramadan (20 October 1191), the Monarch al-'Adil summoned me to his court and he invited as well a group of commanders: 'Alam al-Din (Banner of the Religion) Sulayman, Sabiq al-Din (Trailblazer of the Religion), 'Izz al-Din (Glory of the Religion) son of al-Muqaddam, and Husam al-Din (Sword of the Religion) Bishara. He explained to us that his envoy to the English king came back with a letter along with a verbal message saying that he wished for the Monarch al-'Adil to marry the king's sister, whom he brought from Sicily. She was married to the king of Sicily but upon his death, Richard asked her to accompany him as he stopped there on his way. The proposal stipulated that Jerusalem would be the seat of her realm, and that her brother would give her the entire coastland that he currently controls from Acre to Jaffa and Ascalon, as well as other possessions, and that he would make her queen of the coastal lands. Similarly, Saladin should make al-'Adil Monarch of the coastal lands in addition to the lands al-'Adil currently controls and possesses. The sultan should also give the king the relic of the Holy Cross. The villages would remain in the hands of the Templars and Hospitallers, but the castles would be under the control of the married couple. They would release our prisoners and we would release their prisoners. These would be the bases of the peace. Then the king would set sail for his country and everything would be resolved. This was what al-'Adil's envoy conveyed from the king.

When al-'Adil first heard the message, he thought to summon us and ask us to relay the message to Sultan Saladin. He asked me to deliver it in the presence of the other commanders, to discuss it with the sultan, and to see his reaction. If he liked it and found it beneficial for the Muslims, we were to be the witnesses that the sultan gave his permission and approved this matter. If he rejected it, we were to be the witnesses that the peace negotiations had produced this proposal and that the sultan decided to put an end to them.

When we arrived in the sultan's court, I presented the matter to him and relayed the message in the presence of the aforementioned group. He swiftly

---

7. Ibn Shaddad, *al-Nawadir al-sultaniyya*, 292–293. For biographical information on Ibn Shaddad, see p. 99.

2. Ibn Shaddad on Saladin's negotiations with Richard the Lionheart in 1191

approved the terms, believing that the English king was only bluffing and mocking, and that he would not truly agree to them. I asked him three times if he was really approving the matter, and each time he said yes, with a smile on his face and averring that it would be binding on him. When we established that, we returned to the Monarch al-'Adil and informed him about what the sultan had said. The group also attested to him that I repeated the message in order to assure that the approval would be binding. The sultan was adamant in his approval to go ahead with the agreement; the terms were approved accordingly.

The return of the envoy to the English king with the reply to his message

On the 2nd of Shawwal (23 October 1191), Ibn al-Nahhal left as an envoy from Sultan Saladin and the Monarch al-'Adil. When he reached the enemy camp and asked someone to inform the king of his arrival, he was told that when the marriage proposal had been suggested to the queen by her brother, she fainted and was outraged. She rejected the idea completely, swore by her faith and made a binding oath that she would never accept it nor allow a Muslim to sleep with her. The king suggested to the envoy: "If the Monarch al-'Adil converts to Christianity, I will resolve the matter." He left the door open for negotiations.

Questions

1. What can we learn from Ibn Shaddad's account of the negotiations between Richard the Lionheart and Saladin about the relationship between the two sovereigns, and the role of al-'Adil as a go-between?
2. According to Ibn Shaddad, what was Richard's proposal, and what was Saladin's response?
3. How does Richard's sister, Joan, respond to the proposal?
4. How does Richard propose to resolve the impasse in the negotiations?

Chapter 5: Correspondences, Treaties, and Truces

3. Ibn Nazif al-Hamawi's account of Frederick's letter to the commander Fakhr al-Din son of Shaykh al-Shuyukh[8]

Abu al-Fada'il Muhammad son of 'Ali son of 'Abd al-'Aziz, known as Ibn Nazif al-Hamawi, was a thirteenth-century Muslim chronicler and historian of the Ayyubid era. We do not know the year of his birth or his death. He belonged to the influential Nazif family of Hama (hence his name) and served in the administration of the Ayyubid ruler, the Monarch al-Hafiz son of al-'Adil (d. 1240) in Qal'at Ja'bar on the Euphrates in northern Syria. He was imprisoned in 1230, after a falling-out with al-Hafiz. He was eventually released as a result of the intervention of the Monarch al-Ashraf, the Ayyubid ruler of northern Mesopotamia. After his release, he moved to the Euphrates fortress town of al-Rahba and received the patronage of its commander, al-Mansur Ibrahim. When al-Mansur succeeded his father as ruler of Hims, Ibn Nazif went with him, where he received a pension from al-Mansur. It was in Hims that Ibn Nazif wrote his history, dedicated to his patron, and called it The Victorious History; *the term victorious in the title is a double entendre, meant as an homage to his patron al-Mansur, which in Arabic means "the victorious."*[9]

Year 627 (November 1229–November 1230)

Sultan al-Kamil was in northern Mesopotamia. The Khwarazmian (Seljuk) sultan was in Khilat,[10] and al-Ashraf was laying siege to Baalbek.

In this year too, the envoy of the Emperor Frederick II to al-Kamil arrived while he was in Harran, with letters for Fakhr al-Din son of Shaykh al-Shuyukh.[11] One letter reads as follows:

> In the name of God, the Merciful, the Compassionate. Then the title of the Addressee—Fakhr al-Din.

---

8. Ibn Nazif al-Hamawi, *al-Ta'rikh al-mansuri: talkhis al-Kashf wa-l-bayan fi hawadith al-zaman*, ed. A.-'I. Dudu (Damascus: Matba'at al-Hijaz, 1981), 189–193.

9. On Ibn Nazif al-Hamawi, see Alex Mallet, "Ibn Nazif al-Hamawi," in *Christian–Muslim Relations, 600–1500*, ed. D. Thomas (Leiden: Brill, 2010), 4: 245.

10. A significant city at the time on the western shores of Lake Van, today called Ahlat in eastern Turkey.

11. On Fakhr al-Din, see pp. 119, 121–126. Fakhr al-Din means "Glory of the Religion."

3. Ibn Nazif al-Hamawi's account of Frederick's letter to Fakhr al-Din

From the august Caesar, the Roman Emperor Frederick son of Emperor Henry son of Emperor Frederick, who is victorious by God's support, invested by His power, and exalted by His magnificence. king of Germany, Lombardy, Tuscany, Italy, Longobardy, Calabria, Sicily, and the Syrian kingdom of Jerusalem. Aid of the pope[12] of Rome and champion of the Christian religion.

Praise to God, the Merciful, the Compassionate. Poetry:

1- When we set sail our heart remained; / it abandoned its body, its soul, its kin.
2- It chose to cling to your affection / forever; it obeys my will no more.

How can we even describe our great longing or the aching melancholy and desire for his esteemed and majestic[13] company—may God prolong his days, make his years never end, fortify his post in leadership, protect the affection and honor he enjoys, grant him success in his endeavors, guide his actions and words, heap on him generous graces, and renew his success every day and every night. Though this exordium may sound inelegant and excessive, yet it expresses the anguish of our loneliness after that time of felicity and companionship; the pain of separation after those days of happiness and delight. We now realize that comfort is no more, patience is severed, composure is splintered, and fortitude is shattered.

1- Were I required to choose between a life without you / or death, I would have cried: "Let my demise come quickly!"[14]

If he—may God honor him—grew bored with us, replaced us with other friends, was indifferent to our departure, or forgot our love, we would then console ourselves with the words of Abu al-Tayyib:[15]

---

12. The word used for pope is *imam*.
13. The word used here is *al-fakhri*, bringing to mind the honorific title of the addressed: Fakhr al-Din.
14. The poet cannot be determined, but a similar line appears in a poem by the Andalusian poet Muhammad al-Tutili (fl. twelfth century).
15. The famous poet al-Mutanabbi. He originally recited this line, as part of a poem, to his Hamdanid patron Sayf al-Dawla of Aleppo (r. 945–967). Sayf al-Dawla means "Sword of the Realm."

Chapter 5: Correspondences, Treaties, and Truces

1- When you take your leave from friends who could have / compelled you to stay, it is they who truly left.

Now, we know that he likes to hear of our news, affairs, and noble deeds, so we are apprising him, following on what we explained to him in Sidon, that the pope—written with a P for perfidy and pretense—seized one of our castles, which is called Montecassino. Its cursed abbot handed it over to him, and he is seeking even more from our subjects and refuses to wait for our successful return. The pope is spreading a false rumor that we have died; he made the cardinals swear to its veracity and that we would never return. They sought to deceive the people with such falsehoods, and pretended that after us there would be no one who could protect our dominion or safeguard it in our young son's name other than the pope. Because of their faith in these people, who are the leaders of religion and heirs of the disciples,[16] a group of criminals and crooks were drawn to them. Upon our arrival at the port of Brindisi—may it be protected—we discovered that King John[17] and the Lombards had started a rebellion against us. They received the news of our arrival incredulously, for the cardinals had sworn to them that we were dead.

Upon our arrival, we dispatched our letters and envoys to announce our safe return. Our enemies were alarmed, and were overcome with panic and fear. They fled in retreat, a 2-day march. Our obedient subjects returned under our protection. So, too, did the Lombards. Although they had been the majority of the rebels' army, upon learning of our enemies' deception they ceased their rebellion and oath breaking; they returned to their land. As for the aforementioned King John and his soldiers, they were ashamed and frightened, and withdrew to a remote canyon, afraid to leave it or come out. Since the entire dominion had returned to our hand and obedience, it was impossible for them to do anything.

Meanwhile, we assembled a large army of Germans who had been with us in Syria and had sailed back to our shores, as well as other trusted officers and commanders of our empire. We have begun preparations to march against the territory of our enemies.

---

16. Disciples of Jesus, *al-Hawariyyun* in Arabic.

17. John of Brienne, who was once king of Jerusalem (r. 1210–1225) but lost the title to Emperor Frederick II. He later became the Latin king of Constantinople (r. 1229–1237).

3. Ibn Nazif al-Hamawi's account of Frederick's letter to Fakhr al-Din

We beseech his eminence to keep writing to us, informing us about his happy state, his undertakings, and his affairs; and to extend our salutations to the leaders of his army, servants, slaves, and courtiers. Peace to him, and God's blessing and mercy. Written in Barletta—may it be protected—on 23 August of the second Indiction[18] (1229).

Questions

1. What can we learn from al-Hamawi's account of the letter from Frederick II to the commander Fakhr al-Din about the relations between the Frankish sovereign and the Muslim commander?

2. Frederick begins his letter with the standard Islamic invocation, "In the name of God, the Merciful, the Compassionate." Why might a Christian sovereign employ an Islamic invocation in his correspondence?

3. Frederick also cites three examples of Arabic poetry. What might this tell us about his attitude toward Arabic culture and customs?

4. According to this letter, what were Frederick's concerns about religious and political affairs back in Europe?

5. Why might he raise these Christian European concerns with his Muslim interlocutor?

---

18. Indiction is a medieval term used to designate both (1) a cycle of 15 years and (2) each year in that cycle. Here it likely means the second year in the indiction, which started in 1228.

4. Al-Qalqashandi's account of the oaths of the truce between Sultan Qalawun and the Franks of Acre, Sidon, and Atlit[19]

This is the text of an oath document whose contents the victorious monarch, Sultan Qalawun, swore to honor: the truce between him and the Hospitaller rulers of the kingdom of Acre, Sidon, Atlit, and their territories. It was concluded in the month of Rabiʿ I 682 (June 1283), and written in the hand of his chancellor, the judge Fath al-Din son of ʿAbd al-Zahir,[20] and preserved by Ibn Mukarram[21] in his *Anthology* (*Tadhkira*). It reads:

> I swear, and my name is so-and-so, by God, by God, by God; by God, by God, by God; by God, by God, by God.[22] God is the great, the seeker, the conqueror, the punisher, the supporter, the vanquisher, the destructor, the knower of what is overt and covert, the omniscient of what is secret and manifest, the merciful, the compassionate. By the veracity of the Qurʾan, He who revealed it, and he upon whom it was revealed, that is, Muhammad son of ʿAbd Allah—may God bless him and grant him salvation—and what it says therein, chapter by chapter, verse by verse, and by the veracity of the month of Ramadan,[23] I swear to fulfill and uphold this blessed truce, which was established between myself and the kingdom of Acre and its leaders who rule over Acre, Atlit, Sidon, and their territories, which are the areas covered by this truce, and whose duration is 10 full years, 10 months, 10 days, and 10 hours, starting on Thursday, 5 Rabiʿ I of the year 682 of the Hijra

---

19. Al-Qalqashandi, *Subh al-aʿsha*, 13: 311–315. For biographical information on al-Qalqashandi, see p. 191.

20. Head of the Chancellery under Sultan Qalawun and Sultan al-Ashraf Khalil. His father was the famous early Mamluk historian and court secretary Muhyi al-Din Ibn ʿAbd al-Zahir (1223–1292). See Appendix C, pp. 231–32. Fath al-Din means "Triumph of the Religion;" Muhyi al-Din means "Revivifier of the Religion."

21. Ibn Mukarram is none other than the most famous medieval lexicographer Ibn Manzur (d. 1311). His *Tadhkira*, which was a literary anthology, does not seem to have survived until today.

22. It was customary to swear by repeating the same expression three times. Here we have three different forms of swearing by God—*wa-Allah*, *bi-Allah*, and *ta-Allah*, all of which mean "I swear by God"—each repeated three times.

23. The month of Ramadan has a special holiness in that it is the month of fasting and also the month in which it is believed that the Prophet Muhammad received his first revelations. In fact, there is a tradition that Abraham, Moses, and David received their revelations during the month of Ramadan as well.

4. Al-Qalqashandi's account of the oaths of a truce

(3 June 1283). I will uphold it from its beginning to its end, protect it, adhere to all of its terms explained herein, and abide by its conditions until it expires. I will not seek to reinterpret it or any terms in it, nor will I seek a juridical opinion to revoke it as long as the rulers of the cities of Acre, Atlit, and Sidon—who are: the current regent of the kingdom of Acre, the current grand master of the Templars, the current grand master of the Hospitallers and his deputy, and whoever takes their places either as regent or grand master in this aforementioned kingdom—fulfill their oaths which they swore to honor.

It will also remain in effect in the time of my son the righteous monarch[24] and his children; they will follow it and honor its terms explained herein until it expires. If I do violate this oath, I will be obliged to make a pilgrimage to the Sacred House of God in Mecca thirty times, while barefoot and shirtless. I will be obligated as well to fast my entire life except for the forbidden days.

He then listed the remaining terms of the oath, and concluded with: God is witness to what we say.

And here is the text of the oath document whose contents the Franks—with whom the truce was concluded—swore to honor on the same date mentioned earlier, as preserved by Ibn Mukarram as well. It reads:

By God, by God, by God; by God, by God, by God; by God, by God, by God; by the veracity of the Messiah, by the veracity of the Messiah; by the veracity of the Cross, by the veracity of the Cross; by the veracity of the Trinity which comes from the same substance and signifies the Father, the Son, and the Holy Spirit forming one God; by the divinity[25] that dwelled in the human body; by the veracity of the pure Gospel and what it contains; by the veracity of the four Gospels which were written by Matthew, Mark, Luke, and John, their prayers and benedictions; by the veracity of the twelve disciples, the seventy-two church fathers, and the 318 Nicaean fathers. By the veracity of the voice that came down from heaven over the Jordan River and ordered its waters to back up;[26]

---

24. Sultan al-Ashraf Khalil (r. 1290–1293), see Chapter 3, p. 147 (footnote 217).
25. In the Arabic text, the term for divinity is *al-salib*, meaning the cross. It must be a scribal error because the exact sentence is repeated later on in this oath.
26. A reference to the Israelites crossing from the east side of the Jordan into Canaan. "So when those who bore the ark had come to the Jordan, and the feet of the priests bearing the

by the veracity of God who revealed the Gospel to His Spirit and Word, Jesus son of Mary; by the veracity of the Lady Saint Mary the mother of light, John the Baptist, Saint Martha, and Saint Mary Magdalen. By the veracity of the great Lent; by the veracity of my religion, the divinity I worship, my Christian faith, and the catechism that I received from the consecrated fathers and priests who baptized me. From this moment and hour, I devote my intention and set my conscience before the victorious Sultan Qalawun, his son the Monarch al-Salih, and their children; to honor all the terms contained in this blessed truce, which is the basis of the peace that was concluded, and which covers the kingdom of Acre, Sidon, Atlit, and their territories as stipulated in this truce and named herein. Its duration is 10 full years, 10 months, 10 days, and 10 hours, starting on Thursday, 3 June 1594 of the year of Alexander son of Philip, the Greek.[27] I will honor its conditions, one by one, and comply with each article of this declared truce until its expiration. By God, by God; by the veracity of the Messiah, by the veracity of the Cross, by the veracity of my religion, I will not harm the lands of the sultan and his son, its people who now live there or might do so in the future, or those who might visit the territories included in this truce, with respect to their persons or possessions. By God, by the veracity of my religion and the one I worship, I will pursue the treaty, the truce, the concord, the sincerity, and the protection of Muslim subjects—those who dwell in the lands of the sultan and those who enter or exit them—in the manner of truthful and faithful people who commit to not harming and to avoiding aggression against persons and possessions. I commit to fulfill all the terms of this truce until its expiration, and as long as the victorious monarch (Qalawun) fulfills the oath he has sworn with respect to this truce. I will not revoke the oath I make or any terms of the truce, nor will I make any exceptions to its terms in order to revoke it. If I do violate it or revoke it, I shall become a castaway from my religion, faith, and the one I worship. I shall become an outcast of the Church, and must undergo thirty pilgrimages to noble Jerusalem barefoot

---

ark were dipped in the edge of the water, the waters flowing from above stood still, rising up in a single heap. . . . Then the people crossed over opposite Jericho" (Joshua 3:15–16).

27. In the Near East at the time, Christians used what is known as the Seleucid or the Greek calendar (*anno Graecorum*). People referred to it as the "year of Alexander," even though it started in 311 B.C., long after the death of Alexander the Great. It would require subtracting 311 to get to the Gregorian year.

4. Al-Qalqashandi's account of the oaths of a truce

and shirtless. I shall be compelled to ransom 1,000 Muslim prisoners who are held by the Franks and release them. I shall be denied the blessing of the divinity that dwelled in the human body. This oath is made by myself, and my name is so-and-so. This intension, which I am making to the victorious monarch (Qalawun) and his son the righteous monarch (al-Ashraf Khalil), I swear by the sacred Gospel to honor it. I have no other intention than this one. God and the Messiah are witnesses to what I say.

Likewise, were the two texts of the oaths made between the Sultan and triumphant Monarch Baybars and the Hospitaller lords of Beirut, Crac des Chevaliers, and Marqab, in the month of Ramadan of 665 (June 1267).

Questions

1. Al-Qalqashandi includes this text in his *Guiding-Light* as an example of formal oaths of truce sworn between combatants. Who are the parties to these oaths of truce?
2. What can we learn from these oaths of truce about the importance that Muslim and Frankish sovereigns placed on oaths?
3. What can we learn from the respective Islamic and Christian sacred language and symbols invoked to guarantee oaths?
4. What can we learn from the onerous penalties the parties swore themselves to, should they fail to keep their word, especially as the army of Qalawun's son al-Ashraf Khalil drove the Franks from the region in 1291, 8 years after the 10-year truce was concluded (1283)?

Chapter Six
Inscriptions

1. Fatimid inscription on a tower fortification in Ascalon (1150)[1]

In the name of God, the Merciful, the Compassionate. Support from God and speedy victory to God's servant and vicegerent, our lord and master, Isma'il Abu Mansur, the Imam al-Zafir bi-Amr Allah,[2] commander of the faithful—God's blessing upon him, his pure ancestors, and his noble descendants. The sublime master Abu al-Hasan 'Ali al-Zafiri, the just, the commander of the armies, the glory of Islam, the helper of the Imam, the protector of the judges of the Muslims, and the guide of the missionaries of the believers, the slave of our lord the caliph—God's blessings upon him—ordered the construction of this blessed tower—may God support the religion through him and benefit the commander of the faithful by prolonging his life, extending his power, and elevating his authority. His slave the commander Abu Mansur Yaqut al-Zafiri al-'Adili, the leader, the victorious, the splendor of the caliphate and its support, the possessor of perfect and most charming traits, the succor of the Muslims, the protector of the state and its sword, the pride of the country and its crown, the virtuous, the right arm of the commander of the faithful, accomplished this work—may God sustain His support for him and his power, make him victorious, and grant him the best of aid. The project was realized under the supervision of the venerable judge Abu al-Majd 'Ali son of al-Hasan son of al-Hasan son of Ahmad al-'Asqalani, the honorable, the blissful, the trustworthy, the content, the revered, the splendor of the religion, the trustee of the caliphs, the confidence of the Imam, the crown of judgments, the glory of missions, the splendor of those gifted, the possessor of the two majesties, the vicegerent of the commander of the faithful in Dhu al-Qa'dah of the year 544 (March 1150).

---

1. Moshe Sharon, *Corpus Inscriptionum Arabicarum Palaestinae* (Leiden: Brill, 1997–2016), 1: 165–166; henceforth, *CIAP*. This inscription follows the inflated—even pompous—protocol of Fatimid inscriptions even though the actual situation of the Muslims in Ascalon at the time was quite precarious.
2. The Twelfth Fatimid caliph (r. 1149–1154).

Chapter 6: Inscriptions

2. Inscription on the pulpit that Nur al-Din commissioned for the Aqsa Mosque in Jerusalem (1168–1169)[3]

In the name of God, the Merciful, the Compassionate. The construction of this pulpit was ordered by the slave, the one in need of His mercy, the one thankful for His grace, the jihad fighter in His path, the frontier warrior against the enemies of His religion, the just Monarch Nur al-Din, the pillar of Islam and the Muslims, the helper of those oppressed by the oppressors, Abu al-Qasim Mahmud son of Zangi son of Aq-Sunqur, the helper of the commander of the faithful. May God empower his supporters and preserve his power; may He raise his signs and spread his standards and emblems to the ends of the earth; may He strengthen the commanders of his state and humiliate those ungrateful for his favor; may He grant him unrestricted success, allow him to achieve conquest, and delight his eyes with victory and closeness to Him. By Your mercy O Lord of the Worlds. This was done in the months of the year 564 (October 1168–September 1169).

3. Inscription panel marking the foundation of a trench around the fortification wall of the old city of Jerusalem during the reign of Saladin (1191)[4]

In the name of God, the Merciful, the Compassionate; His blessings upon the Prophet Muhammad and his household. Our master Abu al-Muzaffar Yusuf son of Ayyub (Saladin), the victorious monarch, the rescuer of the world and of religion, sultan of Islam and the Muslims, servant of the two sanctuaries and this holy Jerusalem, reviver of the state of the commander of the faithful—may God extend his days and make his war standards victorious—ordered the construction and excavation of this trench in the days of the great commander and leading general Sayf al-Din 'Ali son of

---

3. *Répertoire Chronologique d'Épigraphie Arabe* (Cairo: Institut français d'archéologie orientale, 1931–1991), 9: 56, inscription no. 3281; henceforth, *RCEA*. See also Yasser Tabbaa, "Monuments with a Message: Propagation of Jihad under Nur al-Din," in V. P. Goss and Christine Verzar Bornstein, eds., *The Meeting of Two Worlds: Cultural Exchange between East and West during the Period of the Crusades* (Kalamazoo: Medieval Institute Publications, 1986), 233. This inscription was eventually moved to Jerusalem after Saladin's conquest of the city in 1187.

4. http://islamicart.museumwnf.org/database_item.php?id=object;ISL;pa;Mus01;2;ar#. Currently displayed on the Haram al-Sharif in Jerusalem.

Ahmad[5]—may God strengthen him—in the year 587 of the Hijra (January 1191–January 1192).

4. Inscription above the entrance to St. Anne's Church in Jerusalem,[6] transformed into a college of Shafi'i law and named after Saladin—al-Madrasa al-Salihiyya (1192)[7]

In the name of God, the Merciful, the Compassionate. ❧*Every grace you receive comes from God*❧ (Quran 16:53). This blessed college was endowed by our master, the victorious monarch, the rescuer of the world and of religion, sultan of Islam and the Muslims, Abu al-Muzaffar Yusuf (Saladin) son of Ayyub son of Shadi, reviver of the state of the commander of the faithful—may God empower his supporters and rally them around him for the good of this world and the hereafter. This college was endowed for the jurists of the branch of Imam Abu 'Abd Allah Muhammad son of Idris al-Shafi'i—may God be pleased with him—in the year 588 (1192).

5. Inscription above the main entrance gate to the shrine in Hebron housing the cenotaphs of Isaac and Rebecca (1215)[8]

In the name of God, the Merciful, the Compassionate. The construction of this gate was ordered by our master, the sovereign monarch, honor of the world and religion, the fearless warrior al-Mu'azzam 'Isa son of our master

---

5. Sayf al-Din 'Ali son of Ahmad was a powerful Kurdish commander in Saladin's army and achieved the highest rank of *Asfahsallar* or leading general. Due to a war injury on his face, he was nicknamed *al-Mashtub* or Scarface. Saladin later appointed him as governor of Acre, but he lost the city to the Franks in 1191. See Chapter 3, pp. 104–106.

6. St. Anne's Church was built during the reign of Queen Melisende (d. 1161), who was queen-regent between 1131 and 1161, on behalf of her son King Baldwin III (r. 1143–1163). Located near the Pool of Bethesda where, according to John 5:1–15, Jesus healed an invalid man.

7. http://islamicart.museumwnf.org/database_item.php?id=monument;ISL;pa;Mon01;33;ar&pageD=N

8. *CIAP*, 5: 40.

Monarch al-ʿAdil Sayf al-Din Abu Bakr son of Ayyub, the friend of the commander of the faithful—may God prolong their rule and elevate their authority. This is in addition to what he has endowed, consecrated, and bequeathed for the sacred shrine which contains the tombs of the prophets—peace be upon them—namely all the revenues from the two villages known as Dura and Kafar Burayk, and everything within their boundaries—they are all described in the endowment document—to be used for the repair of the mentioned shrine, wages of its attendants, provisions for their visitors, as well as clothing and heating costs. It is a perpetual endowment, an inviolable bequest ❮until God inherits the earth and everyone upon it❯ (Qurʾan 19:40), for ❮He is the best of inheritors❯ (Qurʾan 21:89). May God accept this from al-Muʿazzam and be merciful to him, his parents, and all the Muslims. May God bless Muhammad, the seal of the prophets. The first day of Muharram 612 (2 May 1215).

6. Foundation inscription on the wall of the Fortress of Subayba (Nimrod's Fortress) on the hills overlooking Banyas (1228)[9]

In the name of God, the Merciful, the Compassionate. The construction of this blessed fortress was ordered by our master, the sovereign monarch, the mighty pillar of religion, the sword of Islam, the crown of kings, the sun of sultans, Abu al-Fath ʿUthman son of the Monarch al-ʿAdil, helper of the commander of the faithful, as an offering to God—may He be praised—in the year 625 (1228).

---

9. *CIAP*, 2: 64–65. ʿUthman established the Fortress of Subayba in 1228 and expanded it in 1230 (see p. 209, inscription 7). The Mongols captured the fortress in early 1260 and held it briefly. After the Mamluks defeated the Mongols at the Battle of ʿAyn Jalut on 3 September 1260, Baybars restored the fortress and added several towers (see pp. 211–12, inscription 12).

7. Inscription above the arch of the gate to the northwest tower of the Fortress of Subayba (1230)[10]

In the name of God, the Merciful, the Compassionate. The construction of this divinely protected outpost was ordered by the sinning, culpable servant, the one in need of his Lord's mercy, 'Uthman, the son of our master, the great Sultan and Monarch al-'Adil, the scholar, the doer of good deeds, the jihad fighter, the frontier warrior, the raider, the martyr, Abu Bakr son of Ayyub—may God protect his soul in His mercy. The construction of this auspicious outpost was begun in the month of (Rabi' I) 627 (January–February 1230) by the poor servant Abu Bakr son of Nasr Allah son of Abu Suraqah al-Hamdani al-'Azizi.

8. Inscription on a mosque in the village of Bayt Hanun (1239)[11]

In the name of God, the Merciful, the Compassionate. ❦*There shall frequent the mosques of God only he who believes in God and the Last Day, who performs the prayer and dispenses alms, fearing God alone*❦ (Qur'an 9:18). Shams al-Din Sunqur, the illustrious commander, the leading general, the raider, the jihad fighter, the combatant on the frontiers, the former chief of protocol (*mehmandar*)[12] in the courts of the Monarch al-Kamil and the Monarch al-'Adil, ordered the construction of this blessed mosque after the defeat of the Franks—may God deny them His help—at Bayt Hanun on Sunday in 15 Rabi' II 637 (14 November 1239). He named it the Victory Mosque and buried next to it his companions who died in that battle. He built it out of a desire to please God. May God's mercy be upon whoever reads the inscription and asks mercy and forgiveness for Sunqur and for all Muslims, and for the inscriber, the one in need of God's mercy, Muhammad son of Hamdan son of 'Uqayl al-Ansari.

---

10. *CIAP*, 2: 69. There are several similar inscriptions with minor variations commemorating 'Uthman's construction of this fortress, *CIAP*, 2: 63–74. See also Reuven Amitai, "Notes on the Ayyubid Inscriptions at al-Subayba (Qal'at Nimrod)," *Dumbarton Oaks Papers* (1989), 43: 113–119.

11. *CIAP*, 2: 99. Bayt Hanun is a village situated between Gaza and Ascalon in southwest Palestine.

12. A *mehmandar* was an officer who was responsible for receiving envoys and official guests who came to visit the sultan.

9. Inscription on the mausoleum of Khalid son of al-Walid in Hims (1266)[13]

In the name of God, the Merciful, the Compassionate. On the sanctuary of the sword of God and the companion of the Messenger of God, Khalid son of al-Walid—may God be pleased with him—our master, the sultan, the victorious monarch, the pillar of the world and religion, the sultan of Islam and the Muslims, the slayer of infidels and polytheists, the defeater of errant Muslims and apostates, the reviver of justice in the world, the possessor of the two seas, the lord of the two qiblas,[14] the servant of the two noble sanctuaries, the heir of the kingdom, the sultan of the Arabs, the Persians, and the Turkomans, the Alexander of the age on whose side are celestial fortunes, Baybars, the former slave of al-Salih Ayyub, the partner of the commander of the faithful—may God strengthen his dominion—on the occasion of his passing through Hims to fight in the land of Armenia. It was done in the month of Dhu al-Hijja in the year 664 (September 1266).

10. Inscription on the shrine of Salman al-Farisi in Ashdod (1269)[15]

In the name of God, the Merciful, the Compassionate. ❮There shall frequent the mosques of God only he who believes in God and the Last Day❯ (Qur'an 9:18).

---

13. *RCEA*, 12: 104, inscription no. 4556. See also Carole Hillenbrand, *The Crusades: Islamic Perspectives* (Edinburgh: Edinburgh University Press, 1999), 230. Khalid son of al-Walid (d. 642) was a Companion of Muhammad and one of the most famous early Arab–Muslim commanders.

14. The two qiblas are Jerusalem and Mecca. Jerusalem was the original direction of prayer during Muhammad's early career in Mecca. The direction of prayer was changed from Jerusalem to Mecca in 624, after Muhammad had established himself in Medina. The honorific title "lord of the two qiblas" indicates that Baybars was sovereign over both Jerusalem and Mecca, also known as the two noble sanctuaries.

15. *CIAP*, 1: 126–127. Salman al-Farisi (d. ca. 652) was a Companion of Muhammad, believed to have been of Persian origin (hence al-Farisi). He was also an early hero of Islam and contributed to the early conquests. His tomb near Mada'in in Iraq had become a place of pilgrimage by the tenth century. As was the case with some other sacred figures from the early Islamic period, Salman also had a shrine in Palestine. In addition, there was a shrine to him on the Mount of Olives and another east of Lydda. Some legends hold that he lived to the age of 250 and was a contemporary of Jesus.

12. Inscription commemorating Baybars's renovations of the Fortress of Subayba (1275)

The slave who is in need of his Lord and who hopes for His mercy, Balaban son of ʿAbd Allah the freedman of the great commander ʿAlam al-Din Sanjar al-Turkistani, ordered the construction of this blessed mosque over this blessed shrine of Salman al-Farisi in the day of our master the exalted sultan, the victorious monarch, the pillar of the world and religion, Baybars, the former slave of al-Salih Ayyub—may God perpetuate his rule. He also built the well and made the land as an endowment for it. May God reward him for this work. Cursed be anyone who changes or effaces this inscription. It was done in Rajab of the year 667 (March 1269).

11. Inscription commemorating Baybars's renovations of Crac des Chevaliers (1271)[16]

In the name of God, the Merciful, the Compassionate. This blessed fortress was renovated through the benefaction of our master the sultan, the vanquishing monarch, the scholar, the just, the jihad fighter, the frontier warrior, the heavenly confirmed, the triumphant, the victorious, the cornerstone of the world and the religion, Abu al-Fath Baybars, the former slave of al-Salih Ayyub, the partner of the commander of the faithful. This was dedicated on Tuesday, 25 Shaʿban 669 (8 April 1271).

12. Inscription commemorating Baybars's renovations of the Fortress of Subayba (1275)[17]

In the name of God, the Merciful, the Compassionate. This blessed tower was renovated through the benefaction of our master the sultan, the vanquishing monarch, the most majestic lord, the scholar, the just, the jihad fighter, the frontier warrior, the heavenly confirmed, the victorious, the

---

16. *RCEA*, 12: 148, inscription no. 4623. There are several inscriptions with nearly identical language. Baybars conquered Crac des Chevaliers in 1271. See pp. 144–145.

17. *CIAP*, 2: 77–78. Baybars's renovation and reinforcement of Subayba was part of his strategy to strengthen his defensive measures in Syria against the Mongols to the east and the Franks in the west.

cornerstone of the world and religion, sultan of Islam and the Muslims, slayer of the errant rebellious Muslims, restorer of justice in the world, Abu al-Fath Baybars, the former slave of al-Salih Ayyub, the partner of the commander of the faithful. Its construction was ordered by our master, the honorable lord, the confirmed, the magnanimous, the obedient, the princely, the glorious, the felicitous, the exulted, the well-served, the radiant, the moon of the world and religion, the glory of Islam and the Muslims, the leader of the armies of the monotheists, the monarch of the commanders in the world, Bilik, the slave of the triumphant sultan (Baybars) and his son al-Sa'id—may God perpetuate his life. The task was supervised by the great commander Badr al-Din Baktut and the great commander 'Alam al-Din Sanjar, the former slave of the Monarch al-Mujahid.[18] The construction was directed by the master architect 'Abd al-Rahman, and executed by the master builder 'Abd al-Wahhab. Made on the 22nd of Muharram 674 (18 July 1275). Inscribed by Yusuf.

13. Inscription on a hospice in Hebron for visitors to the shrine of Abraham (1280)[19]

In the name of God, the Merciful, the Compassionate. Praise to God whose grace encompasses everything, and may God bless our lord Muhammad and his family. Our master, the sultan, the victorious monarch, the venerable, the sword of the world and religion, Qalawun, the former slave of the monarch al-Salih Ayyub, ordered the construction of this blessed hospice and endowed it for the poor visitors of Abraham the Friend[20]—peace be upon him. May God perpetuate Sultan Qalawun's life and accept this from him. In the year 679 (May 1280–April 1281). May God bless our master Muhammad and his household.

---

18. The Monarch al-Mujahid was the grandson of Asad al-Din Shirkuh (Saladin's uncle). He ruled Hims for a long time and died in 1240.

19. *CIAP*, 5: 54.

20. In the Islamic tradition Abraham is known as the Friend of God (*Khalil Allah*) or simply as the Friend (*al-Khalil*). See Chapter 1, p. 10 (footnote 57).

14. Inscription on a hospice for pilgrims in Jerusalem (1282)[21]

In the name of God, the Merciful, the Compassionate. Praise to God whose grace encompasses everything, and may God bless our lord Muhammad and his household. Our master the sultan, the victorious monarch, the venerable, the sword of the world and religion, the former slave of the monarch al-Salih Ayyub, ordered the construction of this blessed hospice and endowed it for the poor pilgrims of the noble Jerusalem—may God prolong his life, and accept this from him. In the year 681 (April 1282–March 1283).

15. Inscriptions on the top and the bottom of the two doors of the gate that leads to the shrine housing the cenotaphs of Abraham and Sarah (1286)[22]

Upper Inscription:

❦Who is more excellent in religion than he who surrenders his face wholly to God, and acts charitably? Who follows the religion of Abraham, of pristine faith? For God had taken Abraham for a friend. To God belongs what is in the heavens and what is on earth.❧ (Qur'an 4:125–126)

Lower Inscription:

Our master the Sultan and the victorious Monarch Qalawun, the former slave of al-Salih Ayyub, the partner of the commander of the faithful, ordered the construction of this door at the tomb of our father Abraham the Friend—may the most excellent blessing and peace be upon him—on the first day of Rajab I, in the year 685 (23 August 1286). May his victory be glorified.

---

21. *CIAP*, 5: 56. The inscription on the hospice in Hebron (inscription 13) clearly served as the model for the inscription on this hospice in Jerusalem.
22. *CIAP*, 5: 71.

Chapter 6: Inscriptions

Questions

Inscription 1 is an Ismaʻili Fatimid inscription; inscription 2 is a Sunni Zangid inscription; inscriptions 3–8 are Sunni Ayyubid inscriptions; inscriptions 9–15 are Sunni Mamluk inscriptions.

1. For what kinds of structures were these inscriptions commissioned?
2. What do they have in common?
3. Is there anything that makes them distinctly different from each other?
4. Is there a difference in the language employed based on the kind of structure it was commissioned for?
5. Is there a difference in the language employed based on the dynasty that commissioned it?
6. What can we learn about Fatimid, Zangid, Ayyubid, and Mamluk conceptions of royal authority from the language used in these inscriptions?

APPENDIX A
ISLAMIC CALENDAR

The Islamic calendar is known as the *hijri* calendar because it begins with the year in which the Prophet Muhammad (ca. 570–632) made his hijra or migration from Mecca to Medina (622). According to Islamic tradition, the *hijri* calendar was instituted in 638, by the second Caliph, 'Umar son of al-Khattab (r. 634–644). Under this system, the first day of the first year of the *hijri* calendar (1 Muharram 1) corresponds to 16 July 622 of the Gregorian Christian calendar. Most Western scholars employ the abbreviation A.H., *Anno Hejirae*, to distinguish the Islamic *hijri* calendar from the Gregorian Christian calendar (A.D., *Anno Domini*; or C.E., Christian Era/Common Era, which has become more common in American academic circles in the past few decades).

The Islamic calendar, like many other calendars, is based on a lunar year of 12 months totaling approximately 354 days, or about 11 days fewer than a solar year's 365.25 days. The order of the 12 Islamic months is as follows:

1. Muharram
2. Safar
3. Rabi' al-Awwal (Rabi' I)
4. Rabi' al-Thani (Rabi' II)
5. Jumada al-Ula (Jumada I)
6. Jumada al-Akhira (Jumada II)
7. Rajab
8. Sha'ban
9. Ramadan
10. Shawwal
11. Dhu al-Qa'da
12. Dhu al-Hijja

In order to align the lunar months with the four seasons, most lunar calendars periodically add an extra or "leap" month. For example, the Jewish tradition follows a lunar calendar; however, because many Jewish holy days and festivals have their origins in the agricultural practices of ancient Israel, they are tied to the seasons of the year as well as a specific Jewish month. Hence, a leap month—called Second Adar—is periodically added after the sixth Jewish month (Adar). Thus, a holiday such as Passover, which begins on the fifteenth day of the seventh Jewish month (Nisan), will always occur in the spring, typically in March or April of the Gregorian calendar.

In seventh-century Arabia, it was customary to insert a leap month periodically to ensure that the sacred months (in which pilgrimages to shrines took place, fighting was forbidden, and trade flourished) occurred roughly at the same time each year. According to Islamic tradition, near the end of his career Muhammad received a revelation forbidding the practice of inserting an extra month.

> *God ordained twelve months when He created the heavens and the earth. Of these, four are sacred. This is the correct religious practice. So do yourselves no wrong therein. Fight the polytheist all of them, as they fight you all; and know that God is with the pious. To postpone the sacred month is to increase unbelief. The unbelievers err in this. They allow it one year and forbid it the next, so that they may make up for the months which God has sanctified, thus making lawful what God has forbidden. What they do seems fair to them. God guides not the unbelievers.* (Qur'an 9:36–37)

Some scholars have argued that this passage is speaking against the practice of the Quraysh leaders of Mecca manipulating the sacred months of the year for their own economic and political advantage; how this was done remains a mystery. Others have argued that another reason for this may have been related to the fact that the annual pilgrimage in and around Mecca had been held during the spring season. That is, forbidding the practice of adding a leap month may have been done specifically to ensure that the new Islamic pilgrimage would no longer coincide with the Jewish Passover and Christian Easter holidays, which also occurred in the spring season. In any case, one of the results of this prohibition is that none of the Islamic religious holidays—including the Ramadan fast and the annual pilgrimage—correspond in any way to the seasons.

Reasons for this prohibition aside, there is no easy way to make the Islamic lunar calendar match up with the Gregorian Christian solar calendar. Subtracting 622 from the Gregorian year can provide a rough approximation of the Islamic year in which an event occurred, especially for the first decades of Islamic history. However, by the time we reach the Crusader period, it is more complicated. The Franks conquered Jerusalem in the summer of A.D.

Appendix A: Islamic Calendar

1099 or A.H. 492 (1099 − 622 = 477 not 492); Saladin re-conquered Jerusalem in the summer of A.D. 1187 or A.H. 583 (1187 − 622 = 565 not 583). Not to worry; all is not lost. All Islamic dates in this anthology are followed by their Gregorian equivalents: for example, 492 (1099). For an easy-to-use Islamic–Gregorian conversion calculator as well as several other calendar conversion calculators see https://calcuworld.com/calendar-calculators/islamic-calendar-converter/.

Appendix B
Quranic Verses on War and Peace

The Qur'an discusses war and fighting in different chapters, and this material has historically represented an important element in legal discussions of war as well as in jihad manuals and propaganda. Alongside Hadith, the opinions of the Companions of Muhammad and those of major jurists, as well as the historical experience of Muslims, the Qur'an is one of the sources of Islamic law of war. More correctly, certain verses in the Qur'an were the go-to material on matters of war—its target, its justification, and its conduct—that scholars, jurists, and propagandists often used in order to substantiate and promote warfare. There are as well a number of verses that were often invoked to explain and sanction peace initiatives in times of war. Muslims generally deployed these verses according to need and circumstances. Although some scholars were careful in the way they handled these verses, especially if they were to be read together, one cannot dismiss the fact that others, as a result of dogmatic persuasions, were convinced that only specific verses represented divine orders on war that must be obeyed by the believers, irrespective of time and context.

Moreover, the historical context of these verses was generally ignored, and many scholars applied them universally, in that the original target—mainly the polytheists of Arabia—was substituted by groups with whom the Muslims engaged in warfare in later centuries: Byzantine Christians, Franks, Hindus, Turkic people, and so on.

The quranic passages below represent some of the most common verses that we encounter in the various types of Crusader-era literature that address jihad and Muslim–Crusader encounters.

Quranic verses on war

The two chapters *al-Anfal* (Spoils; 8:1–75) and *al-Tawba* (Repentance; 9:1–129) provide the principal quranic material that many religious scholars and chroniclers invoked when stressing the duty of jihad and extoling its virtues. Chapter (*Surat*, in Arabic) *al-Anfal* was supposedly revealed in 624 shortly

Appendix B: Quranic Verses on War and Peace

after Muhammad's victory against the army of Quraysh at Badr. It explicitly asserts that Muhammad's first major military victory was due to divine aid. Chapter *al-Tawba* is dated to the end of Muhammad's career, after his capture of Mecca in December of 629 or January of 630.

One quranic passage that is regularly encountered in the literature of the period under discussion is the following. It articulates the covenant between God and the believer in the context of sacred warfare:

> ❦*God has purchased from the believers their souls and their wealth and, in exchange, the garden shall be theirs. They fight in the path of God, they kill and are killed—a true promise from Him in the Torah, the Gospel and the Qur'an. Who is more truthful to his promise than God? So be of good cheer regarding that business deal you transact. That is the greatest of triumphs.*❦ (Qur'an 9:111)

As we saw in Chapters 3 and 4, the scholar al-Findalawi invoked this passage when he went out from Damascus to fight against the Franks during the attack of the Second Crusade in 1148.[1]

Other verses that were commonly repeated include the following:

> ❦*Fighting has been prescribed for you, although it is a matter hateful to you. Yet, for all you know, you may hate something and it is good for you. For all you know, you may love something and it is harmful to you. God knows, and you do not know.*❦ (Qur'an 2:216)

> ❦*Do not imagine those killed in the path of God to be dead. Rather, they are alive with their Lord, enjoying His bounty, jubilant at what God has granted them from His grace, eagerly expecting those who have not yet followed, to come after them. In truth, no fear shall fall upon them, nor shall they grieve.*❦ (Qur'an 3:169–170)

> ❦*As for those who emigrated, and were driven away from their homelands, who suffered harm for My sake, who fought or were killed, I shall wipe away their misdeeds, and I shall admit them into gardens beneath which rivers flow: A reward from God. With God is the best of rewards.*❦ (Qur'an 3:195)

> ❦*So fight in the path of God—you can only impose it on yourself—and encourage the believers to do so as well; perhaps God will repel the might of the unbelievers. For God is more mighty and more grievous in torment.*❦ (Qur'an 4:84)

---

1. See Chapter 3, p. 85; Chapter 4, p. 163.

Appendix B: Quranic Verses on War and Peace

❧*Let those, who sell the present life for the next, fight in the path of God. Whoso fights in the path of God—is killed or is victorious—We shall bestow upon him a magnificent recompense.*❧ (Qur'an 4:74)

❧*Among the believers, those who stay behind, unless disabled, are not equal to those who wage jihad in the path of God with their wealth and their souls. God has given those who wage jihad with their wealth and their soul a higher rank over those who stay behind. God has promised each group a happy ending. But God has a glorious recompense for those who wage jihad over those who stay behind: closer proximity to Him, forgiveness and mercy. God is All-forgiving, compassionate.*❧ (Qur'an 4:95–96)

❧*Remember when God revealed to the angels: 'I am with you, so grant the believers resolve. I shall cast terror into the hearts of the unbelievers.' So strike above the necks, and strike their every finger.*❧ (Qur'an 8:12)

❧*O believers, when you meet the unbelievers in combat, turn not your backs to them. Whoso turns his back upon them that day, except to retreat and re-attack, or to join another troop, suffers the burden of God's anger and his refuge is hell—a wretched fate indeed. You did not slay them; it was God who slayed them. It was not you who threw when you threw, but God it was Who threw, in order to bestow upon the believers, from His grace, a fine achievement. God is All-hearing, Omniscient. That is so, and God shall subvert the cunning of the unbelievers.*❧ (Qur'an 8:15–18)

❧*O believers, when you meet a fighting party, stand firm and mention God often—perhaps you will prevail.*❧ (Qur'an 8:45)

❧*Prepare against them whatever force and war cavalry you can gather to frighten therewith the enemy of God and your enemy, and others besides them whom you do not know but God does. Whatever you expend in the path of God will be returned in full to you, and you shall not be wronged.*❧ (Qur'an 8:60)

❧*Once the sacred months are shorn, kill the polytheists wherever you find them, arrest them, imprison them, besiege them, and lie in wait for them at every site of ambush. If they repent, perform the prayer and pay the alms, let them go on their way: God is All-forgiving, Compassionate.*❧ (Qur'an 9:5)

❧*Are you indeed equating provision of water to pilgrims and caring for the Sacred Mosque with one who believes in God and the Last Day, and waged jihad in the cause of God? They are not equal in the sight of God, and God guides not the evildoers.*❧ (Qur'an 9:20)

❦*Fight those who do not believe in God or the Last Day, who do not hold illicit what God and His Messenger hold illicit, and who do not follow the religion of truth from among those given the Book, until they offer up the* jizya *tax, by hand, in humble mien.*❧ (Qur'an 9:29)

❦*If you do not march forth, God will punish you most painfully and will substitute another community in your stead, nor will you harm Him one whit, for God is Omnipotent.*❧ (Qur'an 9:39)

❦*March forth, then, whether light or heavy in armor. Labor hard in the path of God, with your wealth and souls; this is best for you, if only you knew.*❧ (Qur'an 9:41)

❦*But the Messenger and the believers with him have waged jihad with their wealth and souls. These—to them belong the finest rewards. These shall truly gain success. God has readied for them gardens beneath which rivers flow, abiding therein forever. This is the greatest of triumphs.*❧ (Qur'an 9:88)

❦*When you encounter the unbelievers, blows to necks it shall be until, once you have routed them, you are to tighten their fetters. Thereafter, it is either gracious bestowal of freedom or holding them to ransom, until war has laid down its burdens. Yet, had God willed, He could Himself have vanquished them, but it was so in order that he might test some of you through others. And those who were killed in the path of God, He shall not cause their works to founder.*❧ (Qur'an 47:4)

Quranic verses on peace

One specific quranic verse was regularly invoked as justification for seeking peace and truces with Frankish rulers:

❦*Should they incline to peace, incline to it also, and put your trust in God. He is indeed All-hearing, Omniscient.*❧ (Qur'an 8:61)

There was as well another verse that encouraged a positive disposition toward the People of the Book (principally, Jews and Christians):

❦*Among the People of the Book are some who believe in God, and in what was revealed to you and what was revealed to them, bowing in piety before God, and bartering not the signs of God for a paltry price. These shall have their reward with their Lord, and God is swift in reckoning.*❧ (Qur'an 3:199)

Appendix B: Quranic Verses on War and Peace

Finally, it is important to note that early Qur'an commentators developed a variety of methodologies for dealing with contradictory passages in the Qur'an that are relevant to the quranic material on warfare and peace. The principal methodology that concerns us here is the doctrine of abrogation (*naskh*). In short, the doctrine of abrogation posits that verses that were revealed later in Muhammad's career abrogated or superseded verses that were revealed earlier in his career. As noted above, chapter *al-Tawba* was believed to have been revealed after Muhammad's conquest of Mecca in December 629 or January 630. Consequently, most commentators argued that the verses about warfare in this chapter abrogated verses about peace that were revealed earlier in his career (including the verses on peace noted above). In fact, some commentators stated that more than 120 verses had been abrogated by 9:5 and 9:29 (known as the "sword verse" and the "*jizya-*tax verse," respectively).[2]

---

2. For an extensive discussion of jihad in the Qur'an, see M. A. S. Abdel Haleem, "Qur'anic '*Jihad*': A Linguistic and Contextual Analysis," *Journal of Qur'anic Studies* 12 (2010): 147–166. The significance of Abdel Haleem's contribution is that he analyzes the verses that call for waging jihad against Muhammad's and Islam's enemies in the context of the quranic suras where they occur, which makes them limited in scope and applicability. But he acknowledges, nevertheless, that traditional Muslim scholars never did this before. On jihad and the doctrine of abrogation, see Ella Landau-Tasseron, "*Jihad*," in *Encyclopaedia of the Qur'an*, ed. Jane Dammen McAuliffe (Leiden: Brill, 2001–2006), 3: 35–43. See also David Cook, *Understanding Jihad* (Berkeley: University of California Press, 2015), especially chapters 1–3. For a historical examination of war and peace in Islam, see Suleiman A. Mourad, "War and Peace in the Medieval Islamic World, 622–1453," in *The Cambridge History of International Law, Vol. 8*, ed. I. Rabb (Cambridge: Cambridge University Press, 2022).

Appendix C
Bibliographic Overview of the Major Muslim Sources of the Crusader Period

There are several advantages to studying the Muslim sources of the Crusader period. One is that they generally present the Muslims' reactions to the Franks in the broader context of Islamic history. The importance of such contextualization is that events unfolding elsewhere weighed on the region—directly or indirectly—and affected the strategies of the various Muslim and Frankish actors and relations between them. Another advantage is that they convey a range of reactions from individual to communal, from how things are to how things should be, from pragmatism to radicalism, from adulation of rulers to passive reporting. Hence, through studying these sources the historian can better grasp the interactions between Muslims and Franks in the broader context of other events occurring in a wider geography that also impacted dynamics among Muslim actors themselves.

The Muslim sources of the Crusader period comprise a wide array of literary genres and subgenres. We find universal and era-specific chronicles. There are also local histories about specific towns or regions, monarchs or dynasties. The sources include, as well, biographical dictionaries, literary anthologies, compendia of folktales, memoirs, personal correspondences, travel narratives, geographical dictionaries, religious and legal treatises, books on the religious merits of a city or a particular sacred site, poetry, and inscriptions on buildings. This rich archive provides many different perspectives, albeit perspectives that represent the views and reactions of scholarly elites—especially in greater Syria, northern Mesopotamia, and Egypt—which were shaped by the authors' historical, legal, and ideological agendas. Moreover, sometimes the same source encompasses multiple agendas. We have divided this wide array of sources into five categories.

While chronicles predominate, we should emphasize that not all chronicles are primary sources. Many are indeed secondary sources in that the author of a given chronicle plagiarized earlier books or related what he was told by others who were involved in the events. An example of this is the *Kitab al-Suluk li-ma'rifat duwal al-muluk* (*The Path to Knowing the History of Monarchs*) by al-Maqrizi, who lived in the fifteenth century, long after the main events of the Crusader period occurred. Hence, he lifted all of his material about the period from sources well before his time. One can also say that sources from the Crusader period itself can be both primary and secondary at the same time. An example of this is Ibn Wasil's *Mufarrij al-kurub fi akhbar bani Ayyub* (*Dissipater of Anxieties on the Reports of the Ayyubids*), where he gave accounts of events he witnessed himself, but for earlier periods, he quoted from other chronicles (such as those by Ibn al-Athir and Sibt Ibn al-Jawzi). Similarly, in *Kitab al-Rawdatayn fi akhbar al-dawlatayn al-Nuriyya wa-l-Salahiyya* (*The Two Gardens Concerning the Kingdoms of Nur al-Din and Saladin*) Abu Shama lifted his material from earlier sources available to him, especially the works of 'Imad al-Din al-Isfahani.

Biographical dictionaries, prosopographies, geographical dictionaries, and monumental inscriptions provide many details about intellectual life and scholarly networks during the period as well as information about rulers, notable commanders, scholars, and social figures, and how they employed monumental architecture to project political and religious legitimacy. One can glean from them a great deal of material about the movement and networks of scholars and their interests, their involvement in politics and military events, as well as politicians' involvement in religious and scholarly life. These types of sources also stand as testimonies to the way the past was remembered and redeployed as the biographies of each individual only offer a selective portrait of his/her life and career.

Literary anthologies that narrate history for entertainment are treasure troves of historical anecdotes, poetry, and folktales, and even though their main objective might be the demonstration of literary prowess and entertainment, they remain nonetheless indispensable for the historian of the Crusader period. There are additional benefits of literary anthologies. One, they include a great deal of poetry, which is a historical register that modern scholarship on the Crusades rarely uses.[1] Two, they paraphrase correspondences between different actors at the time and terms of treatises and truces concluded between Muslims and Franks. Such correspondences and treatises did not survive independently as documents, and it is therefore impossible to verify their accuracy. Nevertheless, while they are not chancery documents, this should not diminish the significance of what we can learn from them.

---

1. For an exception, see Osman Latiff, *The Cutting Edge of the Poet's Sword: Muslim Poetic Responses to the Crusades* (Leiden: Brill, 2018).

Appendix C: Bibliographic Overview of the Major Muslim Sources of the Crusader Period

Memoirs and travel narratives are rich sources of information on the Crusader period that have been systematically used by modern scholars. They give us access to aspects of daily life and interactions between Muslims and Franks that we do not find elsewhere. They also furnish "behind the scenes" details about negotiations and personal relations that often stand in contrast to the formal nature of chronicles and biographical dictionaries.

The final category of sources is composed of legal opinions on specific issues (e.g., sale of arms to the Franks), treatises on specific religious duties (e.g., jihad), and works on the religious merits of certain towns (e.g., Jerusalem). While they often do not furnish historical anecdotes or annalistic material as such about the Crusades, nevertheless, they tell us about the reactions of some Muslim scholars to particular events: reactions against the capture of certain cities, attempts to pressure rulers and motivate Muslims to defend or liberate them, reactions against truces, and so on. They also unveil the contribution of their authors, sometimes at the behest of a ruler, to what we generally call the "Counter-Crusade."

Below is a list of the most important Muslim sources we have on the Crusader period, divided according to the five categories.

Chronicles

- *Dhayl ta'rikh Dimashq* (*A Short Survey of the History of Damascus*) by Ibn al-Qalanisi (ca. 1073–1160): Abu Ya'la Hamza son of Asad al-Tamimi, known as Ibn al-Qalanisi, was a learned and cultured author and litterateur who belonged to a notable Damascene family, which had played important roles in the administration of Damascus. His *Short Survey*, which chronicles the history of Damascus and Syria from 1048 down to the year of his own death in 1160, provides very important accounts for the early Crusader period, including the siege of Damascus by the Second Crusade in 1148 and Nur al-Din's entry into the city in 1154.[2] The section of the *Short Survey* on the early Crusader period has been translated by H. A. R. Gibb.

- *Ta'rikh Halab* (*History of Aleppo*) by al-'Azimi (ca. 1090–after 1161): Abu 'Abd Allah Muhammad son of 'Ali al-'Azimi was a poet, scholar, and schoolmaster in Aleppo, who served 'Imad al-Din Zangi (r. 1127–1146). He wrote three works of history, but only one has survived, *History of Aleppo*, which gives concise narratives about

---

2. See also p. 62.

biblical history and Islamic history down to 1144, with a specific focus on the city of Aleppo and its surroundings. Al-ʿAzimi was the earliest Muslim source to indicate that the justification of war (*casus belli*) for the Franks' incursions into northern Mesopotamia and Syria was because Christian pilgrims had been prevented from entering Jerusalem in the year 486 (1093–1094).[3]

- *Al-Muntazam fi taʾrikh al-muluk wa-l-umam* (*The Organized History of Monarchs and Nations*) by Ibn al-Jawzi (1115–1201): *The Organized History* is a chronicle and biographical dictionary. It covers the period from creation to 1179. Each year includes biographical obituaries for the notables who died during that year. Ibn al-Jawzi was a celebrated Hanbali scholar from Baghdad who contributed many major works on Islamic religious thought as well, including a short book on the merits of Jerusalem. As such, his *Organized History* provides a valuable perspective for understanding the Crusader period in the broader context of Islamic history and dynamics among Muslims, especially that of people who were far away from the scene.

- *Al-Barq al-Shami* (*Syrian Lightning*) by ʿImad al-Din al-Isfahani (1125–1201): ʿImad al-Din al-Isfahani was born in Isfahan in Persia and died in Damascus on 4 June 1201. Educated in Isfahan, Baghdad, Mosul, and elsewhere in the Islamic east, al-Isfahani was a very capable scholar and compiled a voluminous anthology of Arabic poetry from the twelfth century. Al-Isfahani benefited from the patronage of Nur al-Din in Damascus where he served as his secretary; he later served in the same capacity under Saladin. *Syrian Lightning*, which is only partially extant, presents eloquent accounts of the careers of Nur al-Din and Saladin. In addition to his glowing prose and eyewitness testimony about his patrons, *Syrian Lightning* offers al-Isfahani's own reflections on his career and time.[4]

- *Al-Fath al-qussi fi al-fath al-qudsi* (*The Eloquent Prologue on the Conquest of Jerusalem*) by ʿImad al-Din al-Isfahani: *The Eloquent Prologue* focuses on Saladin's career and campaigns against the Franks, especially from the Battle of Hattin and the capture of Jerusalem in 1187 until 1193. It also features occasionally positive, but usually biting and caustic, commentary on the character and behavior of the Franks. A French translation was made by H. Massé.

---

3. See also p. 71.
4. See also p. 94.

Appendix C: Bibliographic Overview of the Major Muslim Sources of the Crusader Period

- *Al-Kamil fi al-ta'rikh* (*The Complete History*) by Ibn al-Athir (1160–1233): Ibn al-Athir was born in Jazirat Ibn 'Umar in northern Mesopotamia—Gizre in southeastern modern-day Turkey, just north of the border with eastern Syria. He hailed from a well-to-do scholarly family that rose to positions of influence with the Zangid rulers of Mosul, and later with their Ayyubid successors. Ibn al-Athir traveled with Saladin's army in Syria and later spent time in Aleppo and Damascus. His *Complete History* depicts the Crusades in Syria and Egypt as part of a much larger Frankish assault on Islam and Muslims that had started in Spain and Sicily and subsequently reached Islam's heartland. It covers the period from the beginning of creation and up to the year 1231. The volumes on the Crusader period have been translated by D. S. Richards.[5]

- *al-Ta'rikh al-bahir fi-l-dawla al-atabakiyya* (*The Dazzling History of the Zangid State*) by Ibn al-Athir: *The Dazzling History* chronicles the period of the Zangid rulers of Mosul from 1084 to 1210, and therefore gives us a valuable view from the perspective of Mosul.

- *Al-Nawadir al-sultaniyya wa-l-mahasin al-yusufiyya* (*Sultanic Marvels and Josephian*[6] *Charms*) by Baha' al-Din Ibn Shaddad (1145–1234): Baha' al-Din Yusuf son of Rafi' Ibn Shaddad was born in Mosul. He was educated there and later in Baghdad at the famous Nizamiyya College. In 1188, he was summoned by Saladin and made court advisor and chief judge of the army. Consequently, Ibn Shaddad was an eyewitness to Saladin's campaigns against Acre, Arsuf, and elsewhere during the period of the Third Crusade. Ibn Shaddad's sympathetic biography of Saladin, *Sultanic Marvels and Josephian Charms*, reflects this close relationship between the Sultan and his friend and advisor. After Saladin's death, Ibn Shaddad served Saladin's son al-Zahir and grandson al-'Aziz in Aleppo.[7] The *Sultanic Marvels* has been translated into English by D. S. Richards.

- *Mi'rat al-zaman fi ta'rikh al-a'yan* (*The Mirror of Time on the History of Notables*) by Sibt Ibn al-Jawzi (1186–1257): Shams al-Din Yusuf son of Qizughlu, famously known as Sibt Ibn al-Jawzi, was a renowned preacher and historian. He was the grandson of the famous Ibn

---

5. See also p. 59.

6. Josephian in reference to Joseph, and its use in the title is a double entendre meant to invoke biblical Joseph and also refer to Saladin, whose first name was Joseph (Yusuf in Arabic).

7. See also p. 99.

al-Jawzi (d. 1201) of Baghdad; hence, the name Sibt or grandson of Ibn al-Jawzi from his daughter. Sibt Ibn al-Jawzi relocated to Damascus after 1201 where he flourished in the service of the Ayyubid sovereign al-Muʿazzam (r. 1201–1227) and his successors. He was especially renowned for his eloquence as a preacher in Damascus. The *Mirror of Time* is one of the most valuable sources for Ayyubid history. It is largely a chronicle, with a section at the end of each year for biographical obituaries.[8]

- *Zubdat al-halab min taʾrikh Halab* (*The Crème de la Crème from the History of Aleppo*) by Ibn al-ʿAdim (1192–1262): Ibn al-ʿAdim was a well-known scholar from a notable family from Aleppo, and often led diplomatic missions on behalf of the Ayyubid rulers there, namely al-ʿAziz and his son al-Nasir Yusuf (r. 1236–1260). *The Crème de la Crème* is a survey of the history of Aleppo from the Islamic conquests to 1243. It furnishes a very important north Syrian perspective on the events of the time, which is especially valuable because he derived a large part of his material from local sources that do not exist any longer.[9]

- *Kitab al-Rawdatayn fi akhbar al-dawlatayn al-Nuriyya wa-l-Salahiyya* (*The Two Gardens Concerning the Kingdoms of Nur al-Din and Saladin*) by Abu Shama (1203–1267): Shihab al-Din ʿAbd al-Rahman al-Maqdisi, best known as Abu Shama, was born in Damascus. His family hailed originally from Jerusalem (hence the family name, al-Maqdisi). Abu Shama received a traditional education in Shafiʿi jurisprudence and was known as an influential and outspoken critic of the city's civilian administration. His *Two Gardens* covers the Zangid and Ayyubid dynasties down to 1201. In it, he presents a rather idealized picture of Nur al-Din and Saladin. Because Abu Shama lifted his material from earlier sources available to him, his *Two Gardens* is more a commentary on past events than an original chronicle. Nevertheless, it is an important compilation of excerpts from many sources otherwise lost.[10]

- *Dhayl ʿala al-Rawdatayn* (*Continuation of the Two Gardens*), also known as *Tarajim rijal al-qarnayn al-sadis wa-l-sabiʿ* (Biographies of the People of the Sixth and Seventh Islamic Centuries) by Abu Shama: The *Continuation of the Two Gardens* is a chronicle with biographical obituaries

---

8. See also p. 107.
9. See also p. 235.
10. See also p. 134.

Appendix C: Bibliographic Overview of the Major Muslim Sources of the Crusader Period

of notable persons who lived in Syria, Palestine, and Egypt in the twelfth and thirteenth centuries. As such, it includes valuable eye-witness accounts of events during Abu Shama's lifetime.

- *Al-Ta'rikh al-Mansuri (The Victorious History)* by Ibn Nazif al-Hamawi (fl. thirteenth century): Abu al-Fada'il Muhammad son of 'Ali, known as Ibn Nazif al-Hamawi, was a thirteenth-century Muslim chronicler and historian of the Ayyubid era. We do not know the year of his birth or his death. He belonged to the influential Nazif family of Hama (hence his name) and served in the administration of the Ayyubid ruler, the Monarch al-Hafiz son of al-'Adil (d. 1240) in Qal'at Ja'bar on the Euphrates in northern Syria. He later moved to al-Rahba and received the patronage of its commander, al-Mansur Ibrahim. When al-Mansur succeeded his father as ruler of Hims, Ibn Nazif went with him, where he received a pension from al-Mansur. It was in Hims that Ibn Nazif wrote his history, dedicated to his patron, and called it *The Victorious History*; the term victorious in the title is a double entendre, meant as an homage to his patron al-Mansur, which in Arabic means "the victorious." Ibn Nazif's *The Victorious History* is exceptionally valuable for contemporary events in northern Mesopotamia and northeastern Syrian.[11]

- *Ta'rikh al-malik al-Zahir (The History of the Monarch al-Zahir Baybars)*—also known as *al-Rawd al-zahir fi ta'rikh al-malik al-Zahir (The Blooming Meadow from the History of the Monarch al-Zahir Baybars)* by 'Izz al-Din Ibn Shaddad (1217–1285): *The History of the Monarch al-Zahir* is a valuable historical biography of the Mamluk Sultan Baybars (r. 1260–1277). 'Izz al-Din Ibn Shaddad was an Ayyubid and Mamluk courtier, and must be differentiated from the other well-known earlier scholar Baha' al-Din Ibn Shaddad, who was Saladin's advisor.

- *Al-A'laq al-khatira fi dhikr umara' al-Sham wa-l-Jazira (The Noteworthy Treasures on the Rulers of Syria and Northern Mesopotamia)* by 'Izz al-Din Ibn Shaddad: *The Noteworthy Treasures* is an extensive historical–geographical source for Syria, northern Mesopotamia, and Mosul from the beginning of time until 1261. A French translation of the parts on Aleppo and northern Syria was made by A.-M. Eddé.

- *Al-Rawd al-zahir fi sirat al-malik al-Zahir (The Blooming Meadow from the Life of the Monarch al-Zahir Baybars)* by Ibn 'Abd al-Zahir (1223–1292):

---

11. See also p. 196.

Appendix C: Bibliographic Overview of the Major Muslim Sources of the Crusader Period

The *Blooming Meadow* is another important historical biography of Sultan Baybars. Ibn 'Abd al-Zahir served in the Mamluk chancery. It has been translated into English by F. Sadeque.

- *Mufarrij al-kurub fi akhbar Bani Ayyub* (*Dissipater of Anxieties on the Reports of the Ayyubids*) by Ibn Wasil (1208–1297): Jamal al-Din Muhammad son of Salim, famously known as Ibn Wasil, was born in Hama to a family that played a prominent role in the civilian elite of the city throughout the thirteenth century. He was a specialist in Islamic law, history, metrics, logic, and poetry. He moved and taught in several cities, including Jerusalem, and was also a frequent figure in Ayyubid and Mamluk courts. In 1261, he was sent on an embassy by the Mamluk Sultan Baybars (r. 1260–1277) to the Hohenstaufen king of Sicily, Manfred (r. 1258–1266). Ibn Wasil's *Dissipater of Anxieties* contains a wealth of historical information on the history of Syria–Palestine and Egypt during the thirteenth century.[12]

- *Kitab al-ta'rikh al-salihi* (*The Upright History*; alternatively, *The History of the Reign of Sultan al-Salih Ayyub*)[13] by Ibn Wasil: *The Upright History* is a universal chronicle from creation to 1239, and was meant as a present to Sultan al-Salih Ayyub (r. 1240–1249).

- *Zubdat al-fikra fi ta'rikh al-hijra* (*The Finest Contemplation on the History of Islam*) by Baybars al-Mansuri (ca. 1245–1325): Rukn al-Din Baybars al-Dawadar al-Mansuri was a slave in the service of the Mamluk Sultan Qalawun (r. 1279–1290), who manumitted him and appointed him governor of Kerak. He was also chief of the chancery for Sultan al-Ashraf Khalil (r. 1290–1293). His *Finest Contemplation* is a universal chronicle that ends just prior to his death, and is thus very valuable for early Mamluk history. It was abbreviated by Baybars al-Mansuri in two subsequent works: (1) *al-Tuhfa al-mulukiyya fi l-dawla al-Turkiyya* (*The Regal Treasure on the Turkic-Mamluk State*), which covers the years 1249–1312 arid 1321–1322; and (2) *Mukhtar al-akhbar* (*Anthology of Noteworthy Events*), which accounts for the Ayyubid and Mamluk periods up to the year 1303.[14]

- *Dhayl Mir'at al-zaman* (*The Continuation of the Mirror of Time*) by al-Yunini (1242–1326): Musa son of Muhammad al-Yunini was a notable

---

12. See also p. 116.

13. In Arabic, *salih* means morally upright; hence, the title is a pun on Sultan al-Salih Ayyub's name.

14. See also p. 144.

Appendix C: Bibliographic Overview of the Major Muslim Sources of the Crusader Period

Hanbali scholar in Syria during the early Mamluk period, and a leading figure in the city of Baalbek. His father was a notable Hanbali scholar during the Ayyubid period. He played an important role in the transmission of Sunni scholarship in Damascus. Al-Yunini's *The Continuation of the Mirror of Time* is a continuation of Sibt Ibn al-Jawzi's *Mirror of Time*, and covers the period between 1256 and 1311.[15]

- *Al-Mukhtasar fi akhbar al-bashar* (*The Concise History of Humankind*) by Abu al-Fida' (1273–1331): Abu al-Fida' was a member of the Ayyubid dynasty and ruler of Hama. He was the last Ayyubid sovereign to survive under the Mamluk Sultanate. His *Concise History* is a short chronicle with a brief section on pre-Islamic history and ends in 1329. It is especially valuable for the early Mamluk history in Syria. The part covering the Crusader period has been translated into English by P. M. Holt.

- *Kanz al-durar wa-jami' al-ghurar* (*The Treasure of Pearls and Container of the Pristine*) by Ibn al-Dawadari (d. after 1336): Little is known about Ibn al-Dawadari. His father Jamal al-Din al-Dawadari (d. 1311) was an influential Mamluk commander. *The Treasure of Pearls* is a historical and literary anthology, and as such is a rich depository of social history. It features valuable information he reported from his father—along with his own eyewitness accounts.

- *Ta'rikh al-islam* (*History of Islam*) by al-Dhahabi (1274–1348): Shams al-Din Muhammad al-Dhahabi was born in Mayyafariqin in northern Mesopotamia. His family relocated to Damascus where his father worked as a goldsmith (hence, the family's nickname *al-Dhahabi*). Following extensive education in Damascus, Baalbek, Cairo, Alexandria, Mecca, Aleppo, and Nablus, he became one of the most respected Shafi'i Hadith scholars, biographers, and historians in Damascus. His *History of Islam* is one of the most important histories composed during the early Mamluk period. It also includes biographical obituaries arranged by year of death, and covers from the Prophet Muhammad until 1301. It also draws on a wide variety of sources, some of which are no longer extant. It is important not only for the historiography of the Crusader period, but even more so for understanding how later historians remembered and commented on the Crusader period.[16]

---

15. See also p. 130.
16. See also p. 184.

Appendix C: Bibliographic Overview of the Major Muslim Sources of the Crusader Period

- *Kitab al-Ilmam bi-l-i'lam fi-ma jarat bihi al-ahkam wa-l-umur al-maqdiyya fi waqi'at al-Iskandariyya* (*The Informative Book on the Ordained Calamities that Befell Alexandria*) by al-Nuwayri al-Iskandarani (d. after 1374): Muhammad son of al-Qasim al-Nuwayri al-Iskandarani hailed from Alexandria in Egypt; hence the name, al-Iskandarani. We do not know the year of his birth nor the precise year of his death, though it was sometime after 1374. We do not know much about him other than that he was a historian. He is most remembered for his *The Informative Book on the Ordained Calamities that Befell Alexandria*, which chronicles the history of his hometown, Alexandria, with a special focus on his eyewitness account of the sack of the city in October 1365 at the hands of King Peter of Cyprus.[17]

- *Al-Tariq al-wadih al-masluk ila ma'rifat tarajim al-khulafa' wa-l-muluk* (*The Clear Treaded Path to Knowing the Lives of Caliphs and Monarchs*)—popularly known as *Ta'rikh Ibn al-Furat* (*History of Ibn al-Furat*)—by Ibn al-Furat al-Misri (1335–1405): Little is known about the life and career of Ibn al-Furat other than that he was a low-level administrator in Egypt. His *Clear Treaded Path* is a general history ranging from creation to 1396. Its value is more as an archive of material taken—often word for word—from other sources, some of which are now lost, than as an original chronicle. A partial translation of the volumes on the Crusader period was made by U. Lyons and M. C. Lyons.

- *Itti'az al-hunafa' bi-akhbar al-a'imma al-fatimiyyin al-khulafa'* (*Lessons to True Believers from the Tales of the Fatimid Caliphs*) by al-Maqrizi (1364–1442): al-Maqrizi was a celebrated and influential scholar. Born in Cairo to a scholarly family that originally came from Baalbek, he had an impressive education that prepared him for an impactful career as a college professor and also as a leading preacher at several prestigious mosques. He also occupied senior posts in the Mamluk administration in Cairo. His *Lessons to True Believers* is a history of the Fatimids, and includes important information about their dealings with the Franks, as well as their relations with the Sunni rulers up to their demise at the hands of Saladin in 1171. Its value is in the way al-Maqrizi retold history for his own Sunni audience.

- *Kitab al-Suluk li-ma'rifat duwal al-muluk* (*The Path to Knowing the History of Monarchs*) by al-Maqrizi: *The Path* is a continuation of the *Lessons*, focusing on Egypt under the Ayyubids up to 1141. Like the *Lessons*,

---

17. See also p. 149.

Appendix C: Bibliographic Overview of the Major Muslim Sources of the Crusader Period

its value is in the way al-Maqrizi employed historical memory for his own day. The section on the Ayyubids has been translated into English by R. J. C. Broadhurst.

Biographical Dictionaries

- *Ta'rikh madinat Dimashq (History of Damascus)* by Ibn 'Asakir (1105–1176): Abu al-Qasim 'Ali son of al-Hasan, famously known as Ibn 'Asakir, was one of the most celebrated Sunni scholars of medieval Damascus, both in his own time and in subsequent centuries. His exceptional prowess in Hadith scholarship and his voluminous literary productivity were two important factors that contributed to his fame. He wrote several books at the request or encouragement of Sultan Nur al-Din, including the massive (74 volumes in a modern edition) *History of Damascus*, which comprises biographies of those worthy of mention who lived in Syria–Palestine, from biblical times to Ibn 'Asakir's own day. The first two volumes of the *History* provide a quasi-historical survey of certain important periods, especially the Islamic conquests of Syria, and also contain a wealth of information on sacred spaces and their association with major biblical or Islamic personalities in and around Damascus.[18]

- *Bughyat al-talab fi ta'rikh Halab (The Pursued Desire on the History of Aleppo)* by Ibn al-'Adim: *The Pursued Desire* is only partially extant. It focuses on Aleppo and its area and the notables who lived there. Its relevance to the Crusader period is in the introductory volume where Ibn al-'Adim covered military encounters with the Franks in the area of Aleppo. We find similar material in the biographies of rulers and commanders who took part in the political and military life of the period.

- *'Uyun al-anba' fi tabaqat al-atibba' (The Best Accounts on the Generations of Physicians)* by Ibn Abu Usaybi'a (1203–1270): Muwaffaq al-Din Ahmad son of al-Qasim al-Khazraji, famously known as Ibn Abu Usaybi'a (i.e., son of the man with a little finger), was a Damascene who hailed from a family of physicians who had served at the courts of various Ayyubid sultans and sovereigns, including Saladin. He studied medicine in Damascus and in Cairo with some of the most influential physicians of his day and practiced at the Nur al-Din

---

18. See also pp. 41–42.

Appendix C: Bibliographic Overview of the Major Muslim Sources of the Crusader Period

Hospital in Damascus. Ibn Abu Usaybi'a's *Best Accounts* is the earliest biographical dictionary of its kind in Arabic, and contains some 440 biographies of physicians spanning from ancient Greece to the thirteenth century. It also includes material on practical medicine in his day. As such, it is a valuable and detailed source for the history of science and medicine during the Crusader period.[19] *The Best Accounts* is now available in an English translation by E. Savage-Smith et al.

- *Wafayat al-a'yan wa-anba' abna' al-zaman (Death-dates of Notables and Accounts of People of the Past)* by Ibn Khallikan (1211–1282): This influential biographical dictionary of rulers, statesmen, and notable scholars contains rich details about the Crusader period. Ibn Khallikan occupied the post of deputy chief judge of Cairo (1249–1261), and then became chief judge of Damascus (1261–1271 and 1280–1281). An English translation of the *Death-dates* was made in 1843 by M. G. de Slane with the title *Ibn Khallikan's Biographical Dictionary*.

- *Siyar a'lam al-nubala' (The Lives of Eminent Notables)* by al-Dhahabi: *The Lives* is essentially a replica of the biographical obituaries that we find in al-Dhahabi's *History of Islam*.

- *Tabaqat al-shafi'iyya al-kubra (The Great Generations of Shafi'i Scholars)* by al-Subki (1327–1370): Taj al-Din son of Takiy al-Din 'Ali al-Subki was born in Cairo to a notable Shafi'i family who originated from the town of Subk al-Dahhak in the southwest Nile delta of Egypt; hence the name al-Subki. He studied in Cairo and Damascus and served as a professor and judge in Damascus as well as preacher at the Umayyad Mosque. He was a passionate advocate for Shafi'i jurisprudence and Ash'ari theology, which by his day was embraced by most Shafi'i scholars. His *Great Generations* is a biographical dictionary of Shafi'i scholars from the ninth century until his day. The biographies of Shafi'i scholars who lived during the Crusader period are rich with details about scholarly life, relations between rulers and scholars, as well as the influence these Shafi'i scholars had on some members of the general public and their pronouncements on different aspects of Muslim–Frankish relations, such as wars, alliances, truces, trade, and so on.[20]

- *Kitab al-Muqaffa al-kabir (The Great Book of Generations)* also known as *al-Ta'rikh al-kabir al-muqaffa li-Misr (The Great History of Generations of Egypt)* by al-Maqrizi: *The Great Book* is a biographical dictionary of

---

19. See also p. 186.
20. See also p. 50.

Appendix C: Bibliographic Overview of the Major Muslim Sources of the Crusader Period

the notable figures who inhabited Egypt throughout history. Little in terms of original information on the period under discussion is found in this work.

Literary Anthologies, Collections of Poems, and Folktales

- *Diwan (Poems)* of al-Abiwardi (d. 1113): Al-Abiwardi was a specialist in the genealogies of Arab tribes but is most renowned as a poet. He was born near Abiward in Khurasan. As a young man he moved to Baghdad, where he worked in the service of the Seljuk grand vizier, Nizam al-Mulk (r. 1063–1092), and gained favor at the court because of his skills as a poet. At some point he was appointed head of the library at the great Nizamiyya College there. He wrote several works on history, genealogy, and other subjects, which are now lost. All that has survived are some of his poems, which were collected after his death.[21]

- *Diwan (Poems)* of Ibn al-Khayyat (1058–1123): Ibn al-Khayyat was a court poet for the ruler of Tripoli before it was captured by the Franks. He then moved to Damascus and stayed there until his death. He composed some of the fieriest jihad poetry of the period.

- *Maqamat (Rhymed Verses)* of Ahmad son of Abu Bakr al-Razi (fl. late twelfth century): Very little is known about him, other than that he was a court poet in Aleppo. The *Rhymed Verses* was written there in the period between 1178 and 1179, and the poems therein echo clear anti-Crusader and anti-Shi'i sentiments. They can be classified as part of the jihad propaganda at the time.

- *Kharidat al-qasr wa-jaridat al-'asr (The Pearl-Like Virgin of the Palace, Being the Register of the Age)* by 'Imad al-Din al-Isfahani: *The Pearl-Like Virgin* is an anthology of poetry and prose from the twelfth century. The volume on Damascene and Ayyubid poets is most relevant to the Crusader period. The work also furnishes valuable information about 'Imad al-Din's career.

- *Dhayl al-Kharida wa-sayl al-Jarida (The Continuation of the Pearl-Like Virgin and of the Register)* by 'Imad al-Din al-Isfahani: *The Continuation* is an addendum of the *Pearl-Like Virgin*.

- *Diwan (Poems)* of Jamal al-Din Ibn Matruh (1196–1251): Jamal al-Din Yahya son of 'Isa Ibn Matruh was born in Asyut, where he studied

---

21. See also p. 66.

Hadith and poetry. In 1228, he entered the service of al-Salih Ayyub, who was then governor of Egypt for his father Sultan al-Kamil, and accompanied him on several military campaigns. When al-Salih became sultan (r. 1240–1249), Ibn Matruh was promoted and attained the rank of commander, occupying such important posts as head of the treasury in Cairo and after that governor of Damascus (1245–1248).[22]

- *Nihayat al-arab fi funun al-adab* (*The Coveted Desire on the Arts of Good Manners*) by al-Nuwayri (1279–1333): *The Coveted Desire* is an encyclopedia that touches on various topics relating to the universe and Earth, humans and world history, as well as fauna and flora. It targets an educated citizenry. It has been translated into English by E. Muhanna.

- *Sirat al-Zahir Baybars* (*Life of al-Zahir Baybars*): The *Life* is a fictional biography that mythologizes the career of the Mamluk Sultan Baybars (r. 1260–1277), who became an iconic figure in anti-Crusader activism. It represents the kind of popular storytelling (often presented in quasi-theatrical performances) that became very fashionable in the Mamluk period (1250–1517) as a medium to revisit the Crusader period by focusing on specific personalities. As such, this type of folktale must be seen as one of the ways Muslims remembered the period and passed that memory to later generations. The *Life* has been partially translated into French by G. Bohas and J.-P. Guillaume.

- *Sirat Dhat al-Himma* (*Life of Dhat al-Himma*): Similar in purpose to the *Life of al-Zahir Baybars*, this is also a fictional work that celebrates the early Islamic conquests against the Byzantines by casting them in the context of the romantic exploits of a legendary Muslim woman named Dhat al-Himma (Woman of Noble Resolve) or Dalhama (She-Wolf). Such rethinking of the early Islamic conquests was very common during the Crusader period.

Memoirs, Correspondences, and Travel Literatures

- *Kitab al-I'tibar* (*The Book of Contemplation*) by Usama Ibn Munqidh (1095–1188): Usama belonged to the powerful Munqidh clan from Shayzar, between Hims and Hama in Syria. They played an important role in political and military life down to the 1180s, especially under Nur al-Din and Saladin. Usama was involved in many Muslim

---

22. See also p. 132.

Appendix C: Bibliographic Overview of the Major Muslim Sources of the Crusader Period

courts (Nur al-Din's, the Fatimids', Saladin's), and even the Frankish courts of Antioch, Jerusalem, and Acre. He was also well connected to the Islamic scholarly communities in Syria and Egypt, which gave him tremendous access to information found nowhere else. His *Book of Contemplation* is a memoir in which Usama related his experiences, observations, and exploits throughout his life. It remains one of the most important sources for social relations between Muslims and Franks and political intrigues of the period. It is available in a recent English translation by P. M. Cobb.

- *Rasa'il (Letters)* of al-Qadi al-Fadil (1135–1200): Al-Qadi al-Fadil was Saladin's vizier and secretary. This key resource for the life of the sultan remains only partially edited and the texts available are very difficult to use given that they employ an excessively ornate language. Nevertheless, some of the letters have details about battles, campaigns, alliances and political conditions, and propaganda. They can help reconstitute the involvement of scholarly elites in the politics of their day as well as the dynamics of the Ayyubid court and its interaction with the caliph of Baghdad and other notable players in the Muslim Near East and beyond.

- *Kitab al-Isharat ila ma'rifat al-ziyarat (A Lonely Wayfarer's Guide to Pilgrimage)* by al-Harawi (d. 1215): Abu al-Hasan 'Ali son of Abu Bakr al-Harawi was born sometime in the mid-twelfth century in Mosul to a family that hailed from Herat in modern Afghanistan. He was a celebrated traveler who moved throughout the Islamic world and Byzantine lands. His *Guide* is a geographical guide to Islamic sacred sites and shrines, many of which were shared with Jews and Christians. The parts that deal with sites and shrines in Syria–Palestine are very useful for scholars of the Crusades as they furnish important information about social and religious life at the time, the conditions of many Islamic sacred places under Crusader control, as well as interrelations between Muslims and Franks in some localities. The *Guide* is available in an English translation by J. W. Meri.[23]

- *Rihla (Travels)* of Ibn Jubayr (1145–1217): Ibn Jubayr was born in Valencia, Spain. He was a judge and an administrator in Granada under the Almohads. His pilgrimage journey, which he recounts in his *Travels*, lasted from 1183 to 1185. The book describes in detail his experiences and keen observations of daily life while on his journey

---

23. See also p. 1.

from Granada to Mecca and back to Spain. The sections on Crusader territories in Palestine and Norman Sicily are rich with details about Crusader–Muslim encounters. The *Travels* is available in an English translation by R. J. C. Broadhurst.[24]

- *Muʿjam al-buldan (Dictionary of Countries)* by Yaqut al-Hamawi (d. 1229): Yaqut al-Hamawi was a renowned traveler and scholar. Born somewhere in the Byzantine territories, Yaqut was enslaved at the age of six and taken to Baghdad. His master provided him with an Islamic education, which allowed Yaqut to meet many notable scholars. Yaqut's *Dictionary of Countries* is an extremely valuable compendium of geographical and toponymic information on cities, towns, and villages in the Islamic Near East. He also included some biographical details on important scholars who hailed from these places. His remarks and comments on the status of cities and towns occupied by the Franks are very telling. He died in Aleppo.

- *Subh al-aʿsha fi sinaʿat al-insha (The Guiding-Light for the Dim-Sighted in the Profession of Chancery)* by al-Qalqashandi (1355–1418): Shihab al-Din al-Qalqashandi was a Shafiʿi legal scholar and secretary in the chancery of the Mamluk court in Cairo. His *Guiding-Light* is a massive encyclopedia of chancery records, and preserves correspondences and records from the Crusader period found nowhere else. A few selections from *The Guiding-Light* have been translated into English by H. El-Toudy and T. G. Abdelhamid.[25]

Jihad Books, Juridical Directives, and Religious Merits of Jerusalem

- *Kitab al-Jihad (Book of Jihad)* by al-Sulami (1040–1106): *Book of Jihad* is a historical and legal treatise on jihad authored in reaction to the First Crusade. The role of al-Sulami and his book has been exceedingly exaggerated in recent decades by scholars of the Crusades. Some have even compared him to Pope Urban II. However, the evidence shows that he was a marginal scholar; his peers and later scholars did not consider him worthy of mention; and in all medieval Muslim sources, his book did not have a single case of proven impact. Al-Sulami's sentiments surely reflected the views of some

---

24. See also p. 15.
25. See also p. 191.

Appendix C: Bibliographic Overview of the Major Muslim Sources of the Crusader Period

people in Damascus. Yet, given the indifference shown to him and his book, it is not an exaggeration to say that the majority of the Damascene society and its political and religious elite did not seem to share his enthusiasm. The *Book of Jihad* is available in an English translation by N. Christie.

- *Al-Arba'in hadithan fi al-hathth 'ala al-jihad* (*The Forty Hadiths for Inciting Jihad*) by Ibn 'Asakir: A very influential treatise on jihad, *The Forty Hadiths* includes forty hadiths attributed to the Prophet Muhammad on the virtues and rewards of jihad. It was written by Ibn 'Asakir in the 1160s at the request of Sultan Nur al-Din, and was intended for propaganda. It was used several times for preaching, especially around the time when Emperor Frederick II was in the Holy Land in 1228–1229. *The Forty Hadiths* is available in an English translation by S. A. Mourad and J. E. Lindsay.

- *Fada'il al-quds* (*Merits of Jerusalem*) by Ibn al-Jawzi: The *Merits* was written by the influential Ibn al-Jawzi, and is important as it shows the participation of Muslim scholars outside Syria and Palestine in preaching and authoring on topics that were very religiously and emotionally impactful to many Muslim audiences at the time.

- *Al-Mustaqsa fi ziyarat al-masjid al-aqsa* (*The Exhaustive Treatise on the Pilgrimage to the Aqsa Sanctuary in Jerusalem*) by al-Qasim Ibn 'Asakir (1133–1203): Al-Qasim Ibn 'Asakir was the son of the famous Ibn 'Asakir of Damascus and followed in his father's footsteps. His *Exhaustive Treatise* was one of the most important works on Jerusalem written at the time. It was heavily used and paraphrased in Syria and Egypt by several scholars shortly after its compilation. It survives as quoted in similar works from the fourteenth century.

- *Fada'il bayt al-maqdis* (*Merits of Jerusalem*) by Diya' al-Din al-Hanbali (1173–1245): Diya' al-Din was a very influential Hanbali scholar of Damascus, whose family originally came from the region of Jerusalem (they moved because they refused to live under Frankish rule). The *Merits* provides a new articulation of the religious significance of Jerusalem in Islam that rejects biblical history. It was very popular in Damascus during the thirteenth century, as it was taught close to fifty times in Hanbali mosques there.

- *Ahkam al-jihad wa-fada'iluh* (*On the Laws of Jihad and Its Merits*) by al-'Izz son of 'Abd al-Salam (1182–1262): 'Izz al-Din 'Abd al-'Aziz son of 'Abd al-Salam al-Shafi'i was born in Damascus. His family came originally from North Africa. In Damascus, al-'Izz studied Hadith and jurisprudence with some of the leading Shafi'i and Ash'ari scholars of the city. As a fanatic theologian, he had a very confrontational and bullying personality toward those who differed with him on matters of religious observance and doctrine. He was also a vocal voice against normalization of relations with the Franks, which was the main reason that got him jailed and then fired from his prestigious post as preacher of the Umayyad Mosque. He moved to Jerusalem and from there to Cairo, where Sultan al-Salih Ayyub appointed him as preacher and judge at the historically significant Mosque of 'Amr son of al-'As in the adjacent town of Fustat. His reputation as a notorious propagandist against the Franks became the material of legends in later centuries. *On the Laws of Jihad* is a long treatise on what he considered to be Islam's position on jihad and warfare.[26]

- *Majmu' al-fatawa (Collected Juridical Directives)* by Ibn Taymiyya (1263–1328): Taqiy al-Din Ahmad Ibn Taymiyya was born in Harran in southeastern modern Turkey just north of the Syrian border. His family relocated to Damascus in the wake of the Mongol advances against northern Mesopotamia. It was in Damascus that he made a name for himself as a prominent Hanbali jurist and theologian. Ibn Taymiyya's arguments and rhetoric in his juridical directives and other writings echo normative beliefs in his day that reflected what some among the Sunni religious establishment believed to be the true teachings of God in the Qur'an and the Sunna of his Prophet Muhammad, especially his utter rejection of Shi'ism and what he considered errant Sunni practices. He was occasionally imprisoned due to his controversial theological views.[27] Ibn Taymiyya issued several juridical directives that are relevant to Crusades history, especially the post-1290 period when fear prevailed among some Muslim scholars of the possibility that the Franks might return to coastal Syria and Palestine.

---

26. See also p. 48.
27. See also p. 54.

APPENDIX D

GLOSSARY OF DYNASTIES, PERSONS, SECTS, TERMS, ETC.

'Abbasids. The 'Abbasid dynasty came to power by manipulating a Shi'i revolt against their predecessors, the Umayyads, in the late 740s, but once the 'Abbasids took power, they began to follow the Sunni paradigm for the caliphate. The 'Abbasids ruled primarily from Baghdad (est. 762). In 945, Baghdad was sacked by the Buyids—a group of Shi'i soldiers of fortune from the region of Daylam on the southern shores of the Caspian Sea. From that point forward, the 'Abbasid caliphs became subordinate to a series of Muslim warlord regimes, most notably the Buyids (945–1055) and the Sunni Seljuks (1055–1194), until the invading Mongol armies sacked Baghdad in 1258 and, for all intents and purposes, brought an end to the 'Abbasid Caliphate. A version of the 'Abbasid Caliphate continued under Mamluk tutelage in Cairo, but it amounted to little more than a means to provide a veneer of legitimacy for the Mamluk sultans. The Ottoman conquest of Egypt in 1517 resulted in the dissolution of the 'Abbasid caliphal line.

Almohads. The Almohads (*al-Muwahhidun*) were a dynasty of militant Berber caliphs in North Africa who toppled their predecessors—fellow Berber Almoravids (1062–1147)—and took over their empire. Almohad rule was effectively reduced to Marrakesh and eliminated in 1269. The Almohads were Sunnis, following a minor branch of jurisprudence called the Zahiri school.

Amir. See Commander.

Amir al-Mu'minin. See Commander of the Faithful.

Al-Ash'ari. A Sunni theologian who established a school of theology named after him (Ash'arism), which became dominant in Sunni Islam. He died in 936.

Al-Ashraf Khalil. Al-Ashraf Salah al-Din Khalil son of Qalawun (r. 1290–1293) succeeded his father, Qalawun, as Mamluk sultan. Under al-Ashraf Khalil the last of the Crusader outposts in coastal Syria were defeated and destroyed in 1291. He was assassinated in 1293.

Appendix D: Glossary of Dynasties, Persons, Sects, Terms, etc.

Atabeg. See Chief Commander.

Ayyubids. The Ayyubids were a Sunni Kurdish dynasty established by Saladin, protégé of Nur al-Din. Named after Saladin's father, Ayyub (Job), the Ayyubid family confederation ruled Syria, northern Mesopotamia, Egypt, the Hijaz, and Yemen from Saladin's death in 1193 until the Egyptian branch of the family was overthrown in 1250 by some of its military slaves (*mamluks*). Ten years later, the Mamluk Sultanate defeated the Mongols at 'Ayn Jalut in northern Palestine, absorbed the Ayyubid holdings in Syria, and began the process of driving the Franks from the region.

Baybars. The triumphant (al-Zahir), pillar of the religion (Rukn al-Din), the monarch Baybars al-Bunduqdari was one of the most important Mamluk sultans of Egypt during the Crusader period (r. 1260–1277). He seized the throne in the aftermath of 'Ayn Jalut (1260) by ambushing and assassinating Sultan Qutuz (r. 1259–1260) on their return journey to Egypt—a fine reward for Qutuz after having saved Egypt and Palestine from the Mongol invaders. After spending the first few years of his sultanate consolidating his position in Egypt, Baybars began an intense series of campaigns that left the Frankish states in near ruins. Because Egypt with its Mediterranean ports was the Mamluk Sultanate's center of gravity, he and his successors pursued an aggressive policy of destroying the Frankish ports along the Syrian coast to prevent Frankish reinforcements from the sea. Highlights include: Caesarea, Arsuf, Haifa (1265–1266); Jaffa, Antioch (1268); Ascalon (1270). Baybars's military activities were not limited to the coast; he conquered important Frankish fortresses at Safed, Beaufort, Crac des Chevaliers, Montfort; reinforced the Fortress of Subayba (Nimrod's Fortress); and embarked on a number of campaigns against Cilician Armenia and Isma'ili strongholds in Syria. Baybars died in Damascus and is buried in the Zahiriyya Mausoleum, which became a major library in Damascus.

Al-Bukhari. A scholar of Hadith who compiled one of the most important Hadith collections. He died in 870.

Burids. The Burids were a Sunni Turkic dynasty that ruled Damascus from 1104 to 1154. Zahir al-Din Tughtakin seized control of Damascus in 1104 after the death of his patron, Duqaq (the Seljuk ruler of Damascus). Tughtakin served as chief commander (*atabeg*) of Damascus until his own death in 1128. The dynasty takes its name from Tughtakin's son, Taj al-Muluk Buri, who succeeded his father (r. 1128–1132). In

Appendix D: Glossary of Dynasties, Persons, Sects, Terms, etc.

order to maintain their control over the important strategic position of Damascus, the Burids occasionally allied with the Kingdom of Jerusalem against Seljuk and Zangid forces; they also occasionally allied themselves with Seljuk and Zangid forces against the Crusaders. The Burids are most noted for their defense of Damascus and defeat of the Second Crusade in 1148 under the leadership of Muʻin al-Din Unur, who served as regent (r. 1140–1149) for the last Burid ruler and sometime ally of Nur al-Din Zangi, Mujir al-Din Abaq (r. 1140–1154). Nur al-Din occupied Damascus and incorporated it into his Syrian domains in 1154.

Caliph (*khalifa*). Derived from *Khalifat rasul Allah* (Deputy of the Messenger of God); alternatively, *Khalifat Allah* (God's deputy). One of the titles used for the head of the Muslim community (*umma*). This title is generally used to refer to the political leadership role of the head of the Muslim community. See Commander of the Faithful, Imam.

Chief Commander (*atabeg*). A title used by members of the Seljuk ruling dynasty and their senior commanders who were appointed to rule major districts. It literally means "fatherly master." We have translated *atabeg* as "chief commander" to distinguish it from *amir*, which we have translated as "commander."

College (*madrasa*). A college often had a main professor, several assistants, and specialized in a specific field. They were generally endowed to ensure their survival beyond the life of the benefactor. They also ranged from a single-room structure to a large compound with a courtyard, rooms for study and lodging, a prayer room, and a garden.

Commander (*amir*). A title used to designate a high-ranking military officer.

Commander of the Faithful (*Amir al-Muʼminin*). One of the titles used for the head of the Muslim community (*umma*). This title is generally used to refer to the military leadership role of the head of the Muslim community as commander in chief. See also Caliph, Imam.

Companions (*sahaba*). The Companions were the early converts to Islam who knew Muhammad personally. Hence, they were considered the best generation of Muslims. The Companions played important roles in the preservation and transmission of Hadith, one of the foundations of Islamic thought and practice.

Cubit (*dhiraʻ*). A cubit in the medieval Arab world was a unit of length, which equaled approximately 51 centimeters or 20 inches.

Appendix D: Glossary of Dynasties, Persons, Sects, Terms, etc.

Dhimmi. The term used to designate the contract status by which members of other revealed religions (e.g., Jews, Christians, Zoroastrians) were afforded certain protections in exchange for paying an annual *jizya* tax and acquiescing to a range of disabilities imposed on them as inferior persons in the Islamic social order. Conversion to Islam changed one's status from Dhimmi to Muslim and removed the obligation to pay the *jizya*. See Jizya.

Dinar. The common gold coin at the time.

Dirham. The common silver coin at the time. See Qirat.

Diwan. The Arabic term for a collection of poetry or prose. It is also used for a register of persons or accounts as well as for a state administrative office where correspondences and chancery documents are written or stored.

Druzes. An esoteric sect that has its origins in Isma'ili Shi'ism during the reign of the sixth Fatimid caliph, al-Hakim bi-Amr Allah (r. 996–1021). During the Crusader period, Druze communities in the mountains of Lebanon and northern Palestine fought against the Franks as allies of the various Sunni rulers of Damascus. After the Franks were driven from coastal Syria, the Druzes were suspected of collaborating with the Franks, and the Sunni Mamluks tried to displace them from their villages.

End-of-Days Guide (*mahdi*). According to Muslim beliefs, the End-of-Days Guide will appear before the Day of Judgment to rule the world and reestablish justice. Whereas in the Sunni tradition the specific identity of the Guide is contested, according to the Shi'i tradition, the Guide is the twelfth imam, Muhammad al-Mahdi, who has been in a state of occultation since the late ninth century.

Fatimids. Named after Fatima, the daughter of the Prophet Muhammad, the Fatimid Caliphate belonged to the Isma'ili branch of Shi'i Islam, which was openly hostile to the Sunni 'Abbasid Caliphate in Baghdad. Established in North Africa in 909, they conquered Egypt in 969. Almost immediately, the Fatimid general, Jawhar, began laying the foundations for the new palace city, al-Qahira (Old Cairo). From Egypt, the Fatimids expanded into Syria and the Hijaz (Mecca and Medina). Under their tutelage, Egypt and its new capital became one of the wealthiest and most important cosmopolitan way stations for international trade and culture in the Mediterranean world, southwest Asia, and the Indian Ocean. Saladin brought an end to the Fatimid Caliphate in 1171.

Appendix D: Glossary of Dynasties, Persons, Sects, Terms, etc.

Fatwa. See Juridical directive.

Ghaznawids. A dynasty of Sunni Turkic warlords who established themselves in Afghanistan, eastern Iran, parts of Central Asia, and what is today Pakistan between 977 and 1186. They were notorious for pillaging Hindu and Buddhist temples, a policy that was extensively pursued under their most notorious ruler, Mahmud of Ghazna (d. 1030).

Hadith. The corpus of statements or traditions attributed to or anecdotes about Muhammad and his deeds. Hadith is also the name of the individual statement or tradition. They were transmitted by many of Muhammad's Companions and are preserved in a wide variety of books. They form one of the foundations of Islamic law and practice.

Hadith memorizer (*hafiz*). A person who has memorized a great deal of hadiths and can recite them without the aid of books or memory prompts. It should be noted that Hadith scholarship was the principal field of Islamic scholarship open to women, some of whom achieved high standing and great renown—*hafiza* is the feminine form of *hafiz*. In modern times the honorific title *hafiz* has come to be applied to someone who has memorized the entire Qur'an whereas in the Crusader period memorization of the entire Qur'an was the foundation of all Islamic education. Hence, any Islamic scholar in any discipline would have memorized the entire Qur'an as part of his/her elementary education.

Hanafis. A branch (*madhhab*) of Sunni Islamic jurisprudence named after Abu Hanifa (d. 767). It was very popular among Turkic peoples, especially the Seljuks. It had few followers in Syria and Egypt until the Seljuk invasion.

Hanbalis. A branch (*madhhab*) of Sunni Islamic jurisprudence named after Ahmad Ibn Hanbal (d. 855). The Hanbali school is the strictest in terms of adherence to the Sunna of Muhammad with a significant degree of literalism in their interpretation of the Qur'an and Hadith. They were the second largest community in Damascus during the Crusader period and represented a serious challenge to the Shafi'i community there.

Hijra. Hijra means the migration of the Prophet Muhammad and his followers from Mecca to Medina in 622. The move to Medina triggered major transformations in the movement that he was forming and reshaped its religious message. Hijra also refers to the Islamic calendar (see Appendix A).

Hulegu. Mongol general (d. 1265) who conquered much of western Asia. Under his leadership, Mongol forces laid siege to and destroyed Baghdad in 1258, marking the end to the ʿAbbasid Caliphate and the establishment of Mongol Il-Khan rule in Iraq and Iran.

Husayn. Son of the fourth caliph, ʿAli, and grandson of the Prophet Muhammad. He was killed by an Umayyad army in Karbala (Iraq) in 680. He is the most influential religious figure for Shiʿis (in some ways comparable to Jesus).

Imam. One of the titles for the head of the Muslim community (*umma*). It is generally used to refer to the religious leadership role of the head of the Muslim community. According to the Shiʿi tradition, the rightful Imam must be a lineal descendant of Muhammad, specifically through the line of ʿAli and Muhammad's daughter, Fatima. Imam is also the term used for a local religious leader or the person who leads others in ritual prayer (*salat*). See also Commander of the Faithful, Caliph, Shiʿism.

Ismaʿilis. Sect of Shiʿism, named after the seventh Imam, Ismaʿil son of Jaʿfar al-Sadiq. Also known as Seveners. It was the official version of Islam advocated by the Fatimid caliphs (909–1171). In the eleventh century, the sect split in two as a result of a schism over the succession among two Fatimid brothers, which gave rise to the Nizari Ismaʿilis, who started as a minority and counted among their ranks a militant group (famously known in English as Assassins). After the fall of the Fatimid Caliphate in 1171, their version of Ismaʿilism lost official patronage, which allowed the Nizaris to become the predominant force in Ismaʿilism until today.

Jihad. According to the celebrated thirteenth-century lexicographer Ibn Manzur (1232–1311), the basic meaning of the word jihad (from the root *j-h-d*) is to struggle against something or to exert one's effort toward an objective. In a specifically religious context, and as understood and articulated by nearly every Muslim religious scholar past and present, including Ibn Manzur, jihad has one meaning: to exert one's effort in fighting the enemies of God by deeds or by words. The rather obvious parallelism between two quranic phrases—*jihad fi sabil Allah* (waging jihad in the path of God) and *qital fi sabil Allah* (fighting/slaying in the path of God)—cemented the equation in Islamic religious thought between jihad and religious warfare. In fact, the phrase *jihad fi sabil Allah* came to mean "warfare against infidels." It is important to note that it has become common practice among modern

Appendix D: Glossary of Dynasties, Persons, Sects, Terms, etc.

apologists to argue that the traditional Islamic position on jihad is that the "greater" spiritual jihad is superior to the "lesser" military jihad and that it is sufficient in and of itself—even to the exclusion of military jihad. Such a position is without foundation in the classical sources (e.g., Qur'an, canonical Hadith collections, treatises on jihad, etc.). When the authors of the Muslim sources in this anthology used the word jihad they invariably meant warfare against the enemies of God and the Muslims.

Jizya. Tax paid by members of revealed religions (e.g., Jews, Christians, Zoroastrians) in exchange for certain protections and limited freedoms and the acceptance of a range of disabilities imposed on them as inferior persons in the Islamic social order. The quranic basis for this tax is verse 9:29: ❦*Fight against such of those to whom the Scriptures were given as believe neither in God nor the Last Day, who do not forbid what God and His apostle have forbidden, and do not embrace the true Faith, until they pay tribute* (jizya) *out of hand and are utterly subdued*❦. Some jurists extended it to members of other religious communities, such as Hindus. See Dhimmi.

Juridical directive (*fatwa*). A nonbinding juridical directive on a point of Islamic law given by a qualified jurist in response to a question posed by an individual, a judge, or a sovereign. Depending on the status of or respect for a particular jurist, the juridical directive may or may not have received wide acceptance by the public. In principle, a juridical directive was non-binding because the jurist who issued it did not have state enforcement powers to compel acceptance. Of course, sovereigns from time to time chose to use a juridical directive by a respected jurist to legitimate a policy for pragmatic reasons of state.

Al-Kamil. The Monarch al-Kamil Nasir al-Din Muhammad was the fourth Ayyubid sultan of Egypt (r. 1218–1238). During his tenure as sultan, the Ayyubids defeated the Fifth Crusade (1217–1221). In the context of the Sixth Crusade (1228–1229), al-Kamil negotiated a 10-year peace with Frederick II and returned most of Jerusalem and other holy sites in Palestine to the Crusader kingdom.

Khalifa. See Caliph.

Khatib. Preacher; that is, the person who delivers the sermon (*khutba*) at the Friday congregational prayers in the mosque.

Khatun. An honorific title for wives and daughters of sultans and other local sovereigns of Turkoman and Kurdish origin.

Madhhab. *Madhhab* or branch of jurisprudence was a term used to designate the practice of Islamic law according to the teachings of the

Appendix D: Glossary of Dynasties, Persons, Sects, Terms, etc.

branch's founder. Individually and collectively, they form Sunni Shari'a law. See also Hanafis, Hanbalis, Malikis, Shafi'is, and Shi'is.

Madrasa. See College.

Mahdi. See End-of-Days Guide.

Malik. See Monarch.

Malikis. A branch (*madhhab*) of Sunni Islamic jurisprudence named after Malik son of Anas (d. 795). During the Crusader period, they were a visible minority in Damascus and Egypt.

Mamluk. Military slave. Usually used to describe slaves from Central Asia and the Caucasus Mountains who were bought for the Muslim armies and trained as cavalry. Some of them were later manumitted, and many rose in rank to become commanders, generals, viziers, and even sultans.

Mamluk Sultanate. The Sunni Mamluk Sultanate began shortly after the death of the Ayyubid Sultan al-Salih Ayyub in 1249. Dissatisfied with the policies of his son and successor, Turanshah, al-Salih Ayyub's military slaves (*mamluks*) assassinated him on 2 May 1250 in a palace coup. It would take another decade of at times bloody palace intrigues and the defeat of the Mongols at 'Ayn Jalut (3 September 1260) before the Mamluk Sultanate was firmly established in Egypt and Syria under Sultan Baybars (r. 1260–1277) and his successors, who handed the Crusaders their final defeat in Syria (1291). They sponsored a renaissance that left its mark on learning, architecture, culture, religion, and commerce in the Islamic Near East and the Mediterranean world. The Mamluk Dynasty was overthrown by the Ottoman Sultan Selim I in 1517.

Mihrab. See Prayer niche.

Mile. The medieval Arab mile measured between 1.8 and 2 kilometers (1.2 miles).

Monarch (*malik*). One of the titles used for Ayyubid and Mamluk sovereigns. While the title *al-Malik* can be translated as "the King," we have translated it as "the Monarch" throughout in order to avoid the impression that the Ayyubid and Mamluk sovereigns were kings in the fashion of the European kings. When a ruler is referred to by both titles—*al-Sultan al-Malik*—we have translated them as "the Sultan and Monarch." For example, we have rendered *al-Sultan al-Malik al-Kamil* as "the Sultan and Monarch al-Kamil."

Appendix D: Glossary of Dynasties, Persons, Sects, Terms, etc.

Muʿawiya son of Abu Sufyan. The first Umayyad caliph (r. 661–680). He embraced Islam before Muhammad conquered Mecca in 630. He served as one of Muhammad's scribes after his conversion. He was related to Muhammad by marriage—one of Muhammad's wives was Muʿawiya's widowed sister, Umm Habiba. During the reign of ʿUmar son of al-Khattab (r. 634–644), Muʿawiya participated in the first wave of Islamic conquests in Syria. After the commanders in Syria died in the Plague of Emmaus (638–639), ʿUmar appointed him head of the Muslim armies in Syria.

Al-Muʿazzam ʿIsa. Sharaf al-Din al-Muʿazzam ʿIsa was the Ayyubid ruler of Damascus (r. 1200–1227) and Palestine (r. 1218–1227). He was the nephew of Saladin, and brother of al-Kamil, the Ayyubid sultan in Egypt.

Muezzin (*muʾadhdhin*). The person who performs the call to prayer (*adhan*).

Noble Sanctuary (*al-Haram al-Sharif*). The Noble Sanctuary in Jerusalem refers to the entire esplanade where the Dome of the Rock and the Aqsa Mosque are located. In the Jewish and Christian traditions, the area is known as the Temple Mount.

Nur al-Din. Nur al-Din was the ruler of Aleppo and northern Syria following the death of his father Zangi in 1146; his elder brother Sayf al-Din took Mosul and northern Mesopotamia. After Sayf al-Din died in 1149, Nur al-Din launched his ambitious plan to bring the Sunni territories in Syria under his control. In April 1154, he captured Damascus from the Burids, and then turned his attention to Egypt, which finally fell to his general Shirkuh and protégé Saladin, in 1169. He was considered the champion who laid the foundations for Saladin's main achievements: the defeat of the Franks at the battle of Hattin and the reconquest of Jerusalem in 1187.

Nusayris (ʿAlawis). An esoteric sect named after Muhammad son of Nusayr (d. 868), a disciple of the eleventh Shiʿi Imam, Hasan al-ʿAskari (d. 873). Nusayri religious practices are a mixture of Shiʿi, Christian, and gnostic practices. Because the Nusayris ascribe to the first Shiʿi Imam, ʿAli son of Abu Talib, a kind of divine status, they are also known as ʿAlawis. Twelver Shiʿi scholars did not consider Nusayris to be Shiʿis, referring to them as extremists. Sunni scholars such as Ibn Taymiyya deemed Nusayris to be infidels (*kuffar*) and polytheists (*mushrikun*). During the Crusader period, Nusayris resided primarily in northwestern Syria and often allied themselves with Franks. After

Appendix D: Glossary of Dynasties, Persons, Sects, Terms, etc.

the Franks were driven from coastal Syria, the Sunni Mamluks turned their attention to rooting out the Isma'ili, Nusayri, and Druze communities in Syria.

Ottomans. A dynasty of Sunni (Hanafi) sultans who ruled an empire that stretched from the Adriatic Sea to Iraq, and from Ukraine to Yemen and Sudan. They originally came from Central Asia, and were among the Turkic tribes that joined the Seljuk invasion of the Muslim world. They inhabited Anatolia and emerged in the fifteenth century as a major power, capturing Constantinople in 1453 and occupying Syria in 1516 and Egypt in 1517. The nineteenth century witnessed major disintegration of the Ottoman empire, and the First World War reduced it to what is today Turkey.

Parasang. A parasang was a unit of distance similar to the English league. There is no exact measure for it, because it is based on the distance a person could cover on foot over a specific period of time. Medieval calculations range between 3 and 5 miles or 5–7 kilometers.

Prayer Niche (*mihrab*). The niche or some other marking in the wall of a mosque that indicates the direction (*qibla*) of ritual prayer toward the Ka'ba in Mecca. See Qibla.

Qalawun. Mamluk Sultan of Egypt during the Crusader period (r. 1279–1290). He played a key role in weakening the Frankish position in Syria, capturing the fortress of Marqab (Margat) in 1285; Latakia in 1287; and Tripoli in 1289, which ended the Crusader County of Tripoli. He was succeeded by his son, al-Ashraf Khalil, under whose leadership the last of the Crusader outposts in Syria were destroyed.

Qibla. Direction of ritual prayer toward the Ka'ba in Mecca. It is believed that Jerusalem was the original direction of prayer during Muhammad's early career in Medina, and that it was changed from Jerusalem to Mecca in 624. See Prayer niche.

Qirat. A qirat is a silver coin generally worth one-twenty-fourth of a dinar. Qirat is also the word used for the unit of weight itself. The English word carat is likely derived from qirat. See also Dinar.

Rashidun Caliphs. The first four caliphs in Islam—Abu Bakr (r. 632–634), 'Umar (r. 634–644), 'Uthman (r. 644–656), and 'Ali (r. 656–661). They were close Companions of Muhammad and after his death in 632 ruled in succession from Medina until 'Ali moved the capital to Kufa in Iraq. Each was related to Muhammad by marriage—Abu Bakr and 'Umar as fathers-in-law, 'Uthman and 'Ali as sons-in-law. 'Ali was also a paternal cousin of Muhammad. All but the first caliph, Abu

Appendix D: Glossary of Dynasties, Persons, Sects, Terms, etc.

Bakr, met their demise at the hand of an assassin. The term Rashidun means "rightly guided," reflecting later Sunni dogmas and religious myths about them and their age, not historical reality. The Shi'i tradition rejects this designation, and considers the first three caliphs to be illegitimate usurpers of 'Ali's rightful position as Muhammad's successor. See Shi'is.

Royal cubit (*dhira'malaki*). The royal cubit was approximately 60 centimeters or 23.5 inches. It is longer than the common cubit (*dhira'*), which is six-sevenths of the former.

Saladin (Salah al-Din). Protégé of Nur al-Din, Saladin seized control of Egypt after the death of the last Fatimid caliph, al-'Adid, in 1171, and restored Egypt to Sunni rule. After Nur al-Din's death in 1174, Saladin (r. 1174–1193) turned his attention to incorporating the Zangid territories of Syria and northern Mesopotamia into his realm. By the mid-1180s, he was in a strong enough position to turn his attention to the Crusaders. Under Saladin's leadership, Egypt and Syria were ruled as a family confederation, with members of his extended family administering various provinces throughout the realm. See also Ayyubids.

Seljuks. A Sunni Turkic dynasty, the Seljuks had converted to Islam in the late tenth century and served as irregular cavalry forces in a number of frontier regimes during the early decades of the eleventh century. In 1040, the Seljuks under the leadership of two brothers—Toghril Beg and Chagri Beg—defeated the Ghaznawids at the Battle of Dandanqan in Afghanistan and established themselves in Afghanistan and eastern Iran. Leaving his younger brother, Chagri, to administer the family lands in the east, Toghril turned his attention westward. In 1055, Toghril and his ardently Sunni Seljuk Turkoman tribesmen overthrew the equally ardently Shi'i Buyids in Baghdad. The 'Abbasid caliph conferred on Toghril the title of Sultan, and he and his house ruled from Baghdad in the name of the 'Abbasid caliphs. In their heyday, the Seljuk sultans ruled an empire that stretched from eastern Iran to the Mediterranean. Although their position in Syria had all but disappeared by the late eleventh century, they did control Baghdad until 1194. They were great champions of Sunni Islam.

Shafi'is. A branch (*madhhab*) of Sunni Islamic jurisprudence named after al-Shafi'i (d. 820). Since the tenth century, it was the major branch of Sunni jurisprudence in Syria and Egypt with an extensive network of legal scholars and judges.

Appendix D: Glossary of Dynasties, Persons, Sects, Terms, etc.

Sharif. An honorific title indicating that the person in question is a male descendant of the Prophet Muhammad. We have translated it as "honorable member of the prophetic household."

Shi'is. An Islamic sect. Shi'is believe that Muhammad designated his cousin and son-in-law, 'Ali, to be his successor on 16 March A.D. 632 at Ghadir Khumm. Hence, their name, Shi'i, is derived from the formal title of this group—*shi'at 'Ali* (the faction of 'Ali). There are three basic doctrines that distinguish Shi'is from Sunnis. First, the rightful imam had to be a lineal descendant of Muhammad, in particular through the line of 'Ali and Muhammad's daughter, Fatima. The second is that the caliph or imam was not only the political head of the community, but an infallible religious teacher—guaranteed to be without error in matters of faith and morals. The third is that the suffering and martyrdom of the imams, especially 'Ali (d. 661) and Husayn (d. 680), have salvific value for the faithful. The majority of Shi'is are known as Ithna 'Asharis or Twelvers as they are followers of the twelfth Imam (Muhammad al-Mahdi) who disappeared around 874. See also Druzes, Isma'ilis, Nusayris.

Successors (*tabi'un*). The Successors belonged to the second generation of early Muslims, who did not receive their teachings about Islam from Muhammad directly, but from one of his Companions (*sahaba*). Companions and Successors played important roles in the transmission of Hadith, one of the foundations of Islamic thought and practice, and in the consolidation of Islamic dogma and rituals.

Sultan. Arabic for sovereign. An Ayyubid regional ruler was referred to as "sultan," but this is different from the sultan who was the head of the Ayyubid realm. In order to avoid confusion, in all cases in which the term does not refer to the actual sultan, it has been translated as "sovereign."

Sunna. The proper conduct established by the Prophet Muhammad as set forth in the whole body of Hadith literature. Sometimes it is used interchangeably with Hadith.

Sunnis. An Islamic sect. The Sunnis represent the majority of Muslims in the premodern and modern worlds. The name "Sunni" is derived from the formal title of this group—*ahl al-sunna wa al-jama'a* (people of tradition and community consensus). In the dispute over who was qualified to succeed Muhammad as the head of the Muslim community upon his death, the Sunnis reject the Shi'i position that Muhammad had designated his cousin and son in-law, 'Ali, to be his successor

Appendix D: Glossary of Dynasties, Persons, Sects, Terms, etc.

and that successive caliphs/imams must be a descendant of 'Ali and Muhammad's daughter, Fatima. The Sunnis also reject the Shi'i doctrines that the caliph/imam is an infallible religious teacher and that the suffering and martyrdom of the imams have salvific value for the believer. At the risk of oversimplification, one of the highest values of the Sunni community was the maintenance of the broad unity of the Muslim community (*umma*). As such, the general position that developed among Sunni theorists was one of pragmatism—that the caliph needed only to be good enough politically to do the job and maintain the unity of the entire community. Hence, the Sunnis are often referred to as "caliphal loyalists." In the medieval period, Sunnis generally prioritized religious practice over religious doctrine, and were divided into five branches of jurisprudence: Hanafis, Malikis, Shafi'is, Hanbalis, and Zahiris.

Tughtakin. Zahir al-Din Tughtakin seized control of Damascus in 1104 after the death of his patron, Duqaq (the Seljuk ruler of Damascus). Tughtakin is the first of the Sunni Burids and served as chief commander (*atabeg*) of Damascus until his own death in 1128.

Turkoman. The term to designate pastoral nomadic Turkic peoples, originally from Central Asia, who had converted to Islam. The most prominent example of Turkomans during the Crusader period were the Seljuks.

'Umar son of al-Khattab. The second caliph in Islam. It was during the reign of 'Umar (634–644) that the first wave of Islamic conquests, including Syria, Egypt, and Mesopotamia, occurred.

Umayyads. A dynasty of caliphs who ruled the Muslim world from their capital in Damascus (661–750). They introduced major religious reforms and dogmatic initiatives that transformed Islam and made it a global religion. During the Crusader period, the Umayyad Caliphate was viewed as the golden age of Islamic history in Syria, a view held by many Syrians until today. After they were overthrown by the 'Abbasids in 750, the dynasty survived in Muslim Spain until 1031.

Zangi. A Seljuk chief commander (*atabeg*), who in the late 1120s gained control of Mosul in northern Iraq, Aleppo in northern Syria, and most of the territory in between. He is most remembered for capturing Edessa from the Crusaders in 1144, the first major Islamic military victory against the Crusaders, which began to turn the tide in favor of the Muslims in northern Syria and northern Mesopotamia. His

Appendix D: Glossary of Dynasties, Persons, Sects, Terms, etc.

victory against Edessa transformed him into a great jihad fighter and hero of Islam. Zangi was killed in 1146.

Zawiya. A designated corner inside a building, typically inside a mosque or in a mosque courtyard, which became known as a meeting place for the teaching of certain subjects.

Ziyara. Arabic for visitation. In the Islamic tradition, *ziyara* refers to a pious visitation or pilgrimage to a holy place, tomb, or shrine other than the Pilgrimage (*Hajj*) to Mecca.

BIBLIOGRAPHY

Classical Sources

Abu al-Fida'. *Al-Mukhtasar fi akhbar al-bashar*. 2 vols. Baghdad: Maktabat al-Muthanna, 1968.

———. *The Memoirs of a Syrian Prince: Abu al-Fida', Sultan of Hamah (672–732/1273–1331)*. Trans. P. M. Holt. Wiesbaden: Franz Steiner, 1983.

Abu al-Ma'ali Ibn al-Murajja. *Fada'il bayt al-maqdis wa-l-khalil wa-fada'il al-sham*. Ed. O. Livne-Kafri. Shafa 'Amr: Dar al-Mashriq, 1995.

Abu Shama. *Tarajim rijal al-qarnayn al-sadis wa-l-sabi'—Dhayl 'ala al-Rawdatayn*. Ed. 'I. al-'Attar. Cairo: Dar al-Kutub al-Malikiyya, 1947.

———. *Kitab al-Rawdatayn fi akhbar al-dawlatayn al-Nuriyya wa-l-Salahiyya*. 5 vols. Ed. I. al-Zaybaq. Beirut: Mu'assasat al-Risala, 1997.

al-'Azimi. "La chronique abrégée d'al-'Azimi." Ed. C. Cahen. *Journal Asiatique* 230 (1938): 353–448.

———. *Ta'rikh Halab*. Ed. I. Za'rur. Damascus: No publisher, 1984.

Baybars al-Mansuri. *Al-Tuhfa al-mulukiyya fi al-dawla al-Turkiyya*. Ed. 'A.-H. Hamdan. Cairo: al-Dar al-Misriyya al-Lubnaniyya, 1987.

———. *Mukhtar al-akhbar*. Ed. 'A.-H. Hamdan. Cairo: al-Dar al-Misriyya al-Lubnaniyya, 1993.

———. *Zubdat al-fikra fi ta'rikh al-hijra*. Ed. D. S. Richards. Beirut: German Orient Institute, 1998.

———. *Zubdat al-fikra fi ta'rikh al-hijra—hawadith 501–538 H. wa 621–649 H.: nusus tarikhiyya lam tunshar min qabl*. Ed. 'U. Tadmuri. Beirut: al-Maktaba al-'Asriyya, 2016.

al-Dhahabi. *Siyar a'lam al-nubala'*. 28 vols. Eds. Sh. al-Arna'ut et al. Beirut: Mu'assasat al-Risala, 1996.

———. *Ta'rikh al-islam*. 47 vols. Ed. 'U. Tadmuri. Beirut: Dar al-Kitab al-'Arabi, 1987–1998.

Diya' al-Din al-Hanbali. *Fada'il bayt al-maqdis*. Ed. M. M. al-Hafiz. Damascus: Dar al-Fikr, 1988.

Haji Khalifa. *Sullam al-wusul ila tabaqat al-fuhul*. 6 vols. Ed. M. Arna'ut. Istanbul: Markaz al-Abhath li-l-Tarikh wa-l-Funun wa-l-Thaqafa al-Islamiyya, 2010.

al-Harawi. *A Lonely Wayfarer's Guide to Pilgrimage: 'Ali ibn Abi Bakr al-Harawi's Kitab al-Isharat ila Ma'rifat al-Ziyarat*. Ed. and trans. J. W. Meri. Princeton: Darwin Press, 2004.

Ibn 'Abd al-Salam. *Ahkam al-jihad wa-fada'iluh*. Ed. N. Hammad. Jidda: Maktabat Dar al-Wafa', 1986.

Ibn 'Abd al-Zahir. *Baybars I of Egypt*. Trans. F. Sadeque. Dacca: Oxford University Press, 1956.

———. *Al-Rawd al-zahir fi sirat al-malik al-Zahir*. Ed. 'A. al-Khuwaytir. Riyad: Mu'assasat Fu'ad, 1976.

Ibn Abi Usaybi'a. *'Uyun al-anba' fi tabaqat al-atibba'*. 4 vols. Ed. Q. Wahab. Damascus: Wizarat al-Thaqafa, 1997.

———. *A Literary History of Medicine: The* 'Uyun al-anba' fi tabaqat al-atibba' *of Ibn Abi Usaybi'ah*. 5 vols. Ed. and trans. E. Savage-Smith et al. Leiden: Brill, 2020.

Ibn al-'Adim. *Bughyat al-talab fi ta'rikh Halab*. 12 vols. Ed. S. Zakkar. Damascus: Dar al-Fikr, 1988.

———. *Zubdat al-halab min ta'rikh Halab*. 2 vols. Ed. S. Zakkar. Damascus: Dar al-Kitab al-'Arabi, 1997.

Ibn 'Asakir. *Ta'rikh madinat Dimashq*. 80 vols. Eds. 'U. al-'Amrawi and 'A. Shiri. Beirut: Dar al-Fikr, 1995–2001.

———. *Sirat al-Sayyid al-Masih li-Ibn 'Asakir al-Dimashqi*. Ed. S. A. Mourad. Amman: Dar al-Shuruq, 1996.

———. *Mu'jam al-shuyukh*. 3 vols. Ed. W. Taqiy al-Din. Damascus: Dar al-Basha'ir, 2000.

———. *al-Arba'un fi al-hathth 'ala al-jihad*. Ed. and trans. S. A. Mourad and J. E. Lindsay. *The Intensification and Reorientation of Sunni Jihad Ideology in the Crusader Period*. Leiden: Brill, 2013. Pp. 130–203.

Ibn al-Athir. *Al-Ta'rikh al-bahir fi al-dawla al-atabakiyya bi-l-Mawsil*. Ed. 'A.-Q. Talimat. Cairo: Dar al-Kutub al-Haditha, 1963.

———. *Al-Kamil fi al-Tarikh*. 10 vols. Ed. 'U. Tadmuri. Beirut: Dar al-Kitab al-'Arabi, 1997.

———. *The Annals of the Saljuq Turks: Selections from* al-Kamil fi'l-Ta'rikh *of Ibn al-Athir*. Trans. D. S. Richards. Abingdon: Routledge, 2002.

———. *The Chronicle of Ibn al-Athir for the Crusading Period from* al-Kamil fi'l-Ta'rikh. 3 parts. Trans. D. S. Richards. Farnham: Ashgate, 2006–2008.

Ibn al-Dawadari. *Kanz al-durar wa-jami' al-ghurar*. 7 vols. (1, 3, 5–9). Eds. B. Radtke et al. Wiesbaden: Franz Steiner, 1960–1994.

Ibn al-Furat al-Misri. *Tarikh Ibn al-Furat*. Vols. 7–9: ed. Q. Zurayq. Beirut: The American Press, 1936–1942. Vols. 4–5.1, ed. H. M. al-Shamma'. Basra: Dar al-Tiba'a al-Haditha, 1967–1969.

———. *Ayyubids, Mamlukes and Crusaders: Selections from the Tarikh al-duwal wa'l-muluk of Ibn al-Furat*. 2 vols. Trans. U. Lyons and M. C. Lyons. Ed. J. Riley-Smith. Cambridge: Heffer, 1971.

Ibn al-Jawzi. *Fada'il al-quds*. Ed. J. S. Jabbur. Beirut: Dar al-Afaq al-Jadida, 1980.

———. *Al-Muntazam fi ta'rikh al-muluk wa-l-umam*. 18 vols. Eds. M. 'Ata and M. 'Ata. Beirut: Dar al-Kutub al-'Ilmiya, 1995.

———. *Kitab Fada'il al-jihad*. In *Arba'at kutub fi al-jihad min 'asr al-hurub al-salibiyya*. Ed. S. Zakkar. Damascus: al-Takwin li-l-Tiba'a wa-l-Nashr, 2007.

Ibn Jubayr. *Rihlat Ibn Jubayr*. Beirut: Dar Sadir, 1988.

———. *The Travels of Ibn Jubayr*. Trans. R. J. C. Broadhurst, with a new introduction by Robert Irwin. London: I. B. Tauris, 2020 [1952].

Ibn Khallikan. *Ibn Khallikan's Biographical Dictionary*. 4 vols. Trans. M. G. de Slane. New York: Johnson Reprint, 1971 [1843].

———. *Wafayat al-a'yan wa-anba' abna' al-zaman*. 7 vols. Ed. I. 'Abbas. Beirut: Dar Sadir, 1977.

Ibn Manzur. *Lisan al-'arab*. 15 vols. Beirut: Dar Sadir, 1990.

Ibn Matruh. *Diwan*. In 'Awad M. al-Salih, *Jamal al-Din Ibn Matruh: Hayatuh wa-shi'ruh*. Benghazi: Qar Yunus University, 1995.

Ibn Nazif al-Hamawi. *al-Ta'rikh al-mansuri: talkhis al-Kashf wa-l-bayan fi hawadith al-zaman*. Ed. A.-'I. Dudu. Damascus: Matba'at al-Hijaz, 1981. Pp. 189–193.

Ibn Qadi Shuhba. *Tabaqat al-shafi'iyya*. 4 vols. Ed. 'A.-'A Khan. Beirut: 'Alam al-Kutub, 1986.

Ibn al-Qalanisi. *Dhayl Ta'rikh Dimashq*. Ed. H. F. Amedroz. Beirut: Matba'at al-Aba' al-Yasu'iyyin, 1908.

———. *The Damascus Chronicle of the Crusades: Extracted and Translated from the Chronicle of Ibn al-Qalanisi*. Trans. H. A. R. Gibb. London: Luzac, 1932.

———. *Damas de 1075 à 1154: Traduction annotée d'un fragment de l'Histoire de Damas d'Ibn Al-Qalansi*. Trans. R. le Tourneau. Damascus: Institut Français de Damas, 1952.

Ibn Shaddad. *al-Nawadir al-sultaniyya wa-l-mahasin al-yusufiyya*. Ed. J.-D. al-Shayyal. Cairo: Maktabat al-Khanji, 1994.

Ibn Shaddad (Baha' al-Din). *The Rare and Excellent History of Saladin*. Trans. D. S. Richards. Aldershot: Ashgate, 2002.

———. *Sirat al-sultan al-nasir Salah al-Din al-Ayyubi: al-Nawadir al-sultaniyya wa-l-mahasin al-yusufiyya*. Ed. A. Ibish. Damascus: Matba'at al-Awa'il, 2003.

Ibn Taymiyya. *Majmu' al-fatawa*. 22 vols. (36 parts). Ed. M. 'Ata. Beirut: Dar al-Kutub al-'Ilmiyya, 2000.

Ibn Wasil. *Mufarrij al-kurub fi akhbar bani Ayyub*. 6 vols. Vols. 1–3: ed. J.-D. al-Shayyal. Cairo: Idarat Ihya' al-Turath al-Qadim, 1953–1957. Vols. 4–5: ed. H. M. Rabi'. Cairo: Matba'at Dar al-Kutub, 1974–1977. Vol. 6: ed. 'U. 'A.-S. Tadmuri. Beirut: al-Maktaba al-'Asriyya, 2004.

———. *Die Chronik des ibn Wasil—Ğamal al-Din Muhammad ibn Wasil*, Mufarriğ al-kurub fi aḫbar Bani Ayyub—*Kritische Edition des letzten Teils (646/1248–659/1261) mit Kommentar: Untergang der Ayyubiden und Beginn der Mamlukenherrschaft*. Ed. M. Rahim. Wiesbaden: Harrassowitz, 2010.

———. *Kitab al-Ta'rikh al-salihi*. 2 vols. Ed. 'U. Tadmuri. Sayda: al-Maktaba al-'Asriyya, 2010.

'Imad al-Din al-Isfahani. *Kharidat al-qasr wa-jaridat al-'asr: Qism Shu'ara' al-Sham*. 4 vols. Ed. Sh. Faysal. Damascus: al-Matba'a al-Hashimiyya, 1955–1968.

———. *Kitab al-Fath al-qussi fi al-fath al-qudsi*. Ed. M. M. Subh. Cairo: al-Dar al-Qawmiyya, 1965.

———. *'Imâd al-Dîn al-Isfahânî (519–597/1125–1201): La conquête de la Syrie et de la Palestine par Saladin (al-Fath al-qussî fi l-fath al-qudsî)*. Trans. H. Massé. Paris: Librairie orientaliste Paul Geuthner, 1972.

———. *Al-Barq al-shami*. 5 vols. Ed. F. S. Husayn et al. Amman: Mu'assasat Shuman, 1987.

———. *Dhayl Kharidat al-qasr wa-jaridat ahl al-'asr*. Ed. 'A. A. 'Abd al-Ghani and M. Kh. al-Badi. Damascus: Dar Kinan, 2010.

———. *Nusrat al-fatra wa-'usrat al-fitra*. 2 vols. Ed. I. M. Okleh. London: al-Furqan Islamic Heritage Foundation, 2019.

'Izz al-Din Ibn Shaddad. *Al-A'laq al-khatira fi dhikr umara' al-Sham wa-l-Jazira*. 3 vols. Ed. S. al-Dahhan et al. Damascus: Institut français de Damas, 1953–1991.

———. *Ta'rikh al-malik al-Zahir*. Ed. A. Hutayt. Wiesbaden: Franz Steiner, 1983.

———. *Description de la Syrie du nord: traduction annotée de al-A'laq al-hatira fi dikr umara' al-Sam wa l-Gazira*. Trans. A.-M. Eddé. Damascus: Institut français de Damas, 1984.

al-Maqrizi. *Kitab al-Suluk li-ma'rifat duwal al-muluk*. 4 vols. Eds. M. M. Ziyada and S. 'Ashur. Cairo, 1934–1973.

———. *A History of the Ayyubid Sultans of Egypt*. Trans. R. J. C. Broadhurst. Boston: Twayne Publishers, 1980.

———. *Kitab al-Muqaffa al-Kabir*. 8 vols. Ed. M. al-Ya'lawi. Beirut: Dar al-Gharb al-Islami, 1991–2006.

———. *Itti'az al-hunafa bi-akhbar al-a'imma al-fatimiyyin al-khulafa*. 4 vols. Ed. A.F. Sayyid. Cairo: Dar al-Kutub wa-l-Watha'iq al-Qawmiyya, 2016.

al-Nuwayri. *Nihayat al-arab fi funun al-adab*. 33 vols. Cairo: al-Mu'assasa al-Misriyya al-'Amma li-l-Ta'lif, 1964–2004.

———. *The Ultimate Ambition in the Arts of Erudition: A Compendium of Knowledge from the Classical Islamic World*. Trans. E. Muhanna. New York: Penguin Books, 2016.

al-Nuwayri al-Iskandarani. *Kitab al-Ilmam bi-l-i'lam fima jarat bih al-ahkam wa-l-umur al-maqdiyya fi waq'at al-Iskandariyya*. 7 vols. Ed. A. S. Atiya. Hyderabad: Matba'at Majlis Da'irat al-Ma'arif al-'Uthmaniyya, 1968–1976.

al-Qadi al-Fadil. *Rasa'il al-Qadi al-Fadil*. Ed. 'A. N. 'Isa. Beirut: Dar al-Kutub al-'Ilmiyya, 2005.

al-Qalqashandi. *Subh al-a'sha fi sina'at al-insha*. 14 vols. Cairo: Dar al-Kutub al-Misriyya, 1913–1919.

———. *Selections from Subh al-A'sha by al-Qalqashandi, Clerk of the Mamluk Court*. Ed. and trans. H. El-Toudy and T. G. Abdelhamid. Abingdon: Routledge, 2017.

al-Raba'i. *Fada'il al-Sham wa-Dimashq*. Ed. S.-D. al-Munajjid. Damascus: al-Majma' al-'Ilmi al-'Arabi, 1950.

Sibt Ibn al-Jawzi. *Mir'at al-zaman fi ta'rikh al-a'yan*. 2 vols. Hyderabad: Da'irat al-Ma'arif al-'Uthmaniyya, 1951.

al-Shayzari. *The Book of the Islamic Market Inspector: Niyayat al-rutba fi talab al-hisba (The Utmost Authority in the Pursuit of Hisba) by 'Abd al-Rahman b. Nasr al-Shayzari*. Trans. R. P. Buckley. New York: Oxford University Press, 1999.

Sirat al-amira Dhat al-Himma wa-waladiha 'Abd al-Wahhab. 7 vols. Beirut: al-Maktaba al-Thaqafiyya, 1980–1981.

Sirat al-Zahir Baybars. 5 vols. Cairo: al-Hay'a al-Misriyya al-'Amma li-l-Kitab, 1996.

———. *Roman de Baibars*. Trans. G. Bohas and J.-P. Guillaume. Paris: Sindbad, 1985.

al-Subki. *Tabaqat al-shafi'iyya al-kubra*. 5 vols. Ed. M. 'Ata. Beirut: Dar al-Kutub al-'Ilmiyya, 1999.

al-Sulami. *The Book of the Jihad of 'Ali ibn Tahir al-Sulami (d. 1106)*. Ed. and trans. N. Christie. Farnham: Ashgate, 2015.

Usama Ibn Munqidh. *Kitab al-I'tibar*. Ed. Q. al-Samarra'i. Riyadh: Dar al-Asala, 1987.

———. *The Book of Contemplation: Islam and the Crusades*. Trans. P. M. Cobb. London: Penguin, 2008.

al-Wasiti (Abu Bakr). *Fadaʾil al-bayt al-muqaddas*. Ed. I. Hasson. Jerusalem: Magness Press, 1978.

al-Wasiti (Abu al-Faraj). *Kitab al-Arbaʿin fi al-Jihad wa-l-mujahidin*. Ed. B. al-Badr. Beirut: Dar Ibn Hazm, 1992.

Yaqut al-Hamawi. *Muʿjam al-buldan*. Beirut: Dar Ihyaʾ al-Turath al-ʿArabi, 1979.

al-Yunini. *Dhayl Mirʾat al-zaman*. 4 vols. Cairo: Dar al-Kitab al-Islami, 1992.

———. *Dhayl Mirʾat al-zaman*. In *Early Mamluk Syrian Historiography: al-Yunini's Dhayl Mirʾat al-zaman*, Vol. 2. Ed. L. Guo. Leiden: Brill, 1998.

Modern Scholarship

Amitai, Reuven. "Notes on the Ayyubid Inscriptions at al-Subayba (Qalʿat Nimrod)." *Dumbarton Oaks Papers* 43 (1989): 113–119.

Andrea, Alfred J. and Andrew Holt, eds. *Seven Myths of the Crusades*. Indianapolis: Hackett Publishing, 2015.

Antrim, Zayde. "Ibn ʿAsakir's Representations of Syria and Damascus in the Introduction to the *Taʾrikh madinat Dimashq*." *International Journal of Middle East Studies* 38 (2006): 109–29.

Atiya, Aziz S. *A Fourteenth Century Encyclopedist from Alexandria: A Critical and Analytical Study of al-Nuwairy al-Iskandarani's "Kitab al-Ilmam."* Salt Lake City: Middle East Center at the University of Utah, 1977.

Bauden, Frédéric. "Taqi al-Din Ahmad ibn ʿAli al-Maqrizi." In *Medieval Muslim Historians of the Franks in the Levant*. Ed. A. Mallett. Leiden: Brill, 2014. Pp. 161–200.

Campbell, Sandra. "Millennial Messiah or Religious Restorer: Reflections on the Early Islamic Understanding of the Term Mahdi." *Jusur: The UCLA Journal of Middle Eastern Studies* 11 (1995): 1–11.

Canard, Michel. "Les principaux personnages du roman de chevalerie arabe *Ḏat al-Himma wa-l-Battal*." *Arabica* 8 (1961): 158–173.

Chevedden, Paul E. "The View of the Crusades from Rome and Damascus: The Geo-Politics and Historical Perspectives of Pope Urban II and ʿAli ibn Tahir al-Sulami." *Oriens* 39 (2011): 257–329.

Christie, Niall. "Motivating Listeners in the *Kitab al-Jihad* of ʿAli ibn Tahir al-Sulami (d. 1106)." *Crusades* 6 (2007): 1–14.

———. *Muslims and Crusaders: Christianity's Wars in the Middle East: 1095–1382, from the Islamic Sources*. Farnham: Routledge, 2014.

———. "Ibn al-Qalanisi." In *Medieval Muslim Historians of the Franks in the Levant*. Ed. A. Mallett. Leiden: Brill, 2014. Pp. 7–28.

———. *The Book of the Jihad of 'Ali ibn Tahir al-Sulami (d. 1106): Text, Translation and Commentary*. Farnham: Ashgate, 2015.

Christie, Niall and Deborah Gerish. "Parallel Preaching: Urban II and al-Sulami." *Al-Masaq* 15.2 (2003): 139–148.

Cline, Eric H. *Jerusalem Besieged: From Ancient Canaan to Modern Israel*. Ann Arbor: University of Michigan Press, 2005.

Cobb, Paul M. *Usama ibn Munqidh: Warrior-Poet in the Age of the Crusades*. Oxford: Oneworld, 2006.

———. *The Race for Paradise: An Islamic History of the Crusades*. Oxford: Oxford University Press, 2014.

———. "Hamdan al-Atharibi's *History of the Franks* Revisited, Again." In *Syria in Crusader Times: Conflict and Coexistence*. Ed. C. Hillenbrand. Edinburgh: Edinburgh University Press, 2020. Pp. 3–20.

Constable, Giles. "The Second Crusade as Seen by Contemporaries." *Traditio* 9 (1953): 213–279.

Cook, David. *Studies in Muslim Apocalyptic*. Princeton: Darwin Press, 2002.

———. *Contemporary Muslim Apocalyptic Literature*. Syracuse: Syracuse University Press, 2005.

———. *Understanding Jihad*. Berkeley: University of California Press, 2015.

Cornell, Rkia Elaroui. *Rabi'a from Narrative to Myth: The Many Faces of Islam's Most Famous Woman Saint, Rabi'a al-'Adawiyya*. Oxford: Oneworld, 2019.

Crawford, Paul F. "The First Crusade: Unprovoked Offense or Overdue Defense?" In *Seven Myths of the Crusades*. Eds. A. J. Andrea and A. Holt. Indianapolis: Hackett Publishing, 2015. Pp. 1–28.

Dejugnat, Yann. "La Méditerranée comme frontière dans le récit de voyage (rihla) d'Ibn Jubayr: modalités et enjeux d'une perception." *Mélanges de la Casa de Velázquez* 38.2 (2008): 149–170.

Determann, Matthias. "The Crusades in Arab School Textbooks." *Islam and Christian-Muslim Relations* 19.2 (2008): 199–214.

Eddé, Anne-Marie. *La principauté ayyoubide d'Alep (579/1183–658/1260)*. Wiesbaden: Franz Steiner, 1999.

———. "Kamal al-Din 'Umar Ibn al-'Adim." In *Medieval Muslim Historians of the Franks in the Levant*. Ed. A. Mallett. Leiden: Brill, 2014. Pp. 109–135.

———. *Saladin*. Trans. J. M. Todd. Cambridge: Harvard University Press, 2014.

Elisséeff, Nikita. *La description de Damas d'Ibn 'Asakir*. Damascus: Institut Français de Damas, 1959.

———. *Nur ad-Din: Un grand prince musulman de Syrie au temps des croisades (511–569 H./1118–1174)*. 3 vols. Damascus: Institut Français de Damas, 1967.

Forey, Alan J. "The Second Crusade: Scope and Objectives." *Durham University Journal* 55 (1994): 165–175.

Gabrieli, Francesco. *Arab Historians of the Crusades*. Berkeley: University of California Press, 1997.

Guinle, Francis. *Les stratégies narratives dans la recension damascene de Sirat al-Malik al-Ẓahir*. Damascus: Institut français du Proche-Orient, 2011.

Guo, Li. *Early Mamluk Syrian Historiography: al-Yunini's Dhayl Mir'at al-zaman*. 2 vols. Leiden: Brill, 1998.

Halwani, Ahmad 'A. *Ibn 'Asakir wa-dawruh fi al-jihad didd al-salibiyyi fi 'ahd al-dawlatayn al-nuriyya wa-l-ayyubiyya*. Damascus: Dar al-Fida', 1991.

Hillenbrand, Carole. *The Crusades: Islamic Perspectives*. Edinburgh: Edinburgh University Press, 1999.

———. "'Abominable Acts': The Career of Zengi." In *The Second Crusade: Scope and Consequences*. Eds. J. Phillips and M. Hoch. Manchester: Manchester University Press, 2001. Pp. 111–132.

———. *Turkish Myth and Muslim Symbol: The Battle of Manzikert*. Edinburgh: Edinburgh University Press, 2007.

———, ed. *Syria in Crusader Times: Conflict and Coexistence*. Edinburgh: Edinburgh University Press, 2020.

Hirschler, Konrad. *Medieval Arabic Historiography: Authors as Actors*. Abingdon: Routledge, 2006.

———. "The Jerusalem Conquest of 492/1099 in the Medieval Arabic Historiography of the Crusades: from Regional Plurality to Islamic Narrative." *Crusades* 13 (2014): 37–76.

———. "Ibn Wasil: An Ayyubid Perspective on Frankish Lordships and Crusades." In *Medieval Muslim Historians of the Franks in the Levant*. Ed. A. Mallett. Leiden: Brill, 2014. Pp. 136–160.

———. *Medieval Damascus: Plurality and Diversity in an Arabic Library. The Ashrafiya Library Catalogue*. Edinburgh: Edinburgh University Press, 2016.

Hoch, Martin. "The Crusaders' Strategy Against Fatimid Ascalon and the 'Ascalon Project' of the Second Crusade." In *The Second Crusade and the Cistercians*. Ed. M. Gervers. New York: St. Martin's Press, 1992. Pp. 119–128.

———. "The Choice of Damascus as the Objective of the Second Crusade: A Re-evaluation." In *Autour de la Première Croisade: Actes du Colloque de la Society for the Study of the Crusades and the Latin East—Clermont-Ferrand, 22–25 Juin 1995*. Ed. M. Balard. Paris: Sorbonne, 1996. Pp. 359–369.

———. "The Price of Failure: The Second Crusade as a Turning-Point in the History of the Latin East?" In *The Second Crusade: Scope and Consequences*. Eds. J. Phillips and M. Hoch. Manchester: Manchester University Press, 2001. Pp. 180–200.

Housley, Norman. *Contesting the Crusades*. Malden: Blackwell, 2006.

Humphreys, R. Stephen. *From Saladin to the Mongols: The Ayyubids of Damascus, 1193–1260*. Albany: SUNY Press, 1977.

———. *Islamic History: A Framework for Inquiry*. Princeton: Princeton University Press, 1991.

———. "Ayyubids, Mamluks, and the Latin East in the Thirteenth Century." *Mamluk Studies Review* 3 (1998): 1–17.

———. "Adapting to Muslim Rule: The Syrian Orthodox Community in Twelfth-Century Northern Syria and the Jazira." In *Syria in Crusader Times: Conflict and Coexistence*. Ed. C. Hillenbrand. Edinburgh: Edinburgh University Press, 2020. Pp. 63–85.

Jotischky, Andrew. *Crusading and the Crusader States*. Harlow: Pearson, 2004.

Kedar, Benjamin Z. "The Subjected Muslims of the Frankish Levant." In *Muslims under Latin Rule, 1100–1300*. Ed. J. M. Powell. Princeton: Princeton University Press, 1990. Pp. 135–174.

Khalek, Nancy. *Damascus after the Muslim Conquest: Text and Image in Early Islam*. Oxford: Oxford University Press, 2011.

———. "Early Islamic History Reimagined: The Biography of ʿUmar ibn ʿAbd al-ʿAziz in Ibn ʿAsakir's *Tarikh madinat Dimashq*." *Journal of the American Oriental Society* 134.3 (2014): 431–452.

Khalidi, Tarif. *Arabic Historical Thought in the Classical Period*. New York: Cambridge University Press, 1996.

———. *The Muslim Jesus: Sayings and Stories in Islamic Literature*. Cambridge: Harvard University Press, 2001.

———. *The Qurʾan: A New Translation*. New York: Penguin, 2009.

Khayat, Henri M. "The Šiʿite Rebellions in Aleppo in the 6th A.H./12th A.D. Century." *Rivista degli Studi Orientali* 46 (1971): 167–195.

Köhler, Michael A. *Alliances and Treatises between Frankish and Muslim Rulers in the Middle East: Cross Cultural Diplomacy in the Period of the Crusades*. Trans. P. M. Holt. Revised, edited and introduced by K. Hirschler. Leiden: Brill, 2013.

Landau-Tasseron, Ella. "Jihad." In *Encyclopaedia of the Qurʾan*. 6 vols. Ed. J. D. McAuliffe. Leiden: Brill, 2001–2006. 3: 35–43.

Lane, E.W. *An Account of the Manners and Customs of the Modern Egyptians*. Cairo: The American University in Cairo Press, 2012 (reprint of the 1860 edition).

Latiff, Osman. *The Cutting Edge of the Poet's Sword: Muslim Poetic Responses to the Crusades*. Leiden: Brill, 2018.

Lev, Yaacov. "The Jihad of Sultan Nur al-Din of Syria (1146–1174): History and Discourse." *Jerusalem Studies in Arabic and Islam* 35 (2008): 227–284.

Lindsay, James E. "Ibn 'Asakir as a Preserver of *Qisas al-Anbiya*': The Case of David B. Jesse." *Studia Islamica* 82 (1995): 45–82.

———. "Caliphal and Moral Exemplar? 'Ali Ibn 'Asakir's Portrait of Yazid b. Mu'awiya." *Der Islam* 74 (1997): 250–78.

———, ed. *Ibn 'Asakir and Early Islamic History*. Princeton: Darwin Press, 2001.

———. "Sarah and Hagar in Ibn 'Asakir's *Ta'rikh madinat Dimashq*." *Medieval Encounters: Jewish, Christian and Muslim Culture in Confluence and Dialogue* 10 (2008): 1–14.

———. *Daily Life in the Medieval Islamic World*. Indianapolis: Hackett Publishing, 2008.

Lyons, Malcolm. *The Arabian Epic: Heroic and Oral Story-telling*. 3 vols. Cambridge: Cambridge University Press, 2005.

Lyons, Malcolm and D. E. P. Jackson. *Saladin: The Politics of Holy War*. Cambridge: Cambridge University Press, 1999.

Madden, Thomas F. *The New Concise History of the Crusades*. New York: Rowman & Littlefield, 2014.

Mallet, Alex. "Ibn Nazif al-Hamawi." In *Christian–Muslim Relations, 600–1500*. Ed. D. Thomas. Leiden: Brill, 2010. P. 245.

———. "Sibt Ibn al-Jawzi." In *Medieval Muslim Historians of the Franks in the Levant*. Ed. A. Mallett. Leiden: Brill, 2014. Pp. 84–108.

———, ed. *Medieval Historians and the Franks in the Levant*. Leiden: Brill, 2014.

Mayer, Hans E. "Latins, Muslims and Greeks in the Latin Kingdom of Jerusalem." *History* 63 (1978): 175–192.

Meri, Josef W. *The Cult of Saints among Muslims and Jews in Medieval Syria*. New York: Oxford University Press, 2002.

Micheau, Françoise. "Ibn al-Athir." In *Medieval Muslim Historians of the Franks in the Levant*. Ed. A. Mallett. Leiden: Brill, 2014. Pp. 52–83.

Mourad, Suleiman A. "Jesus According to Ibn 'Asakir." In *Ibn 'Asakir and Early Islamic History*. Ed. J. E. Lindsay. Princeton: Darwin Press, 2001. Pp. 24–43.

———. "From Hellenism to Christianity and Islam: The Origin of the Palm Tree Story concerning Mary and Jesus in the Gospel of Pseudo-Matthew and the Qur'an." *Oriens Christianus* 86 (2002): 206–216.

———. "Jihad Propaganda in Early Crusader Syria: A Preliminary Examination of the Role of Displaced Scholars in Damascus." *Al-'Usur al-Wusta: Bulletin of Middle East Medievalists* 20.1 (2008): 1–7.

———. "Mary in the Qur'an: A Reexamination of Her Presentation." In *The Qur'an in Its Historical Context*. Ed. Gabriel Said Reynolds. London: Routledge, 2008. Pp. 163–174.

———. "Did the Crusades Change Jerusalem's Religious Symbolism in Islam?" *Al-ʿUsur al-Wusta: Bulletin of Middle East Medievalists* 22:1–2 (2010): 3–8 (volume published in 2014).

———. "Why Did Ibn Taymiyya Hate Mount Lebanon? An Inquiry into the Medieval Ideology of Muslim-on-Muslim Violence." In *In the House of Understanding: Histories in Memory of Kamal Salibi*. Eds. A. R. Abu Husayn, T. Khalidi, and S. A. Mourad. Beirut: American University of Beirut Press, 2017. Pp. 373–388.

———. "The Shahada and the Creation of an Islamic Identity." In *Geneses: Comparative Study of the Historiographies of the Rise of Christianity, Rabbinic Judaism and Islam*. Ed. J. Tolan. London: Routledge, 2019. Pp. 216–237.

———. "A Critique of the Scholarly Outlook of the Crusades: The Case for Tolerance and Coexistence." In *Syria in Crusader Times: Conflict and Coexistence*. Ed. C. Hillenbrand. Edinburgh: Edinburgh University Press, 2020. Pp. 144–160.

———. *Ibn ʿAsakir of Damascus: Champion of Sunni Islam in the Time of the Crusades*. Oxford: Oneworld, 2021.

———. "Crusader-Muslim Relations: The Power of Diplomacy in a Troubling Age." In *The Palgrave Handbook in International Political Theory*. Ed. H. Williams. London: Palgrave Macmillan, 2022 (in press).

———. "Arabic-Islamic Sources for the Crusades." In *The Cambridge History of the Crusades*, Vol. 2: *Expansion, Impact and Decline*. Eds. J. Phillips and A. Jotischky. Cambridge: Cambridge University Press, 2022. Chapter 5 (in press).

———. "War and Peace in the Medieval Islamic World, 622–1453." In *The Cambridge History of International Law*, Vol. 8. Ed. I. Rabb. Cambridge: Cambridge University Press, 2022 (in press).

Mourad, Suleiman A. and James E. Lindsay. *The Intensification and Reorientation of Sunni Jihad Ideology in the Crusader Period: Ibn ʿAsakir (1105–1176) of Damascus and His Age; with an edition and translation of Ibn ʿAsakir's* The Forty Hadiths for Inciting Jihad. Leiden: Brill, 2013.

Mouton, Jean-Michel. "Yusuf al-Fandalawi, cheikh des malékites de Damas sous les bourides." *Revue des Études Islamiques* 51 (1983): 63–75.

Muhanna, Elias. *The World in a Book: Al-Nuwayri and the Islamic Encyclopedic Tradition*. Princeton: Princeton University Press, 2018.

Nicholson, Helen. *The Crusades*. Indianapolis: Hackett Publishing, 2009.

Northrup, Linda. *From Slave to Sultan: The Career of Al-Mansur Qalawun and the Consolidation of Mamluk Rule in Egypt and Syria (678–689 A.H./1279–1290 A.D.)*. Stuttgart: Franz Steiner, 1998.

Peacock, A. C. S. *The Great Seljuk Empire*. Edinburgh: Edinburgh University Press, 2015.

Peters, Edward. *The First Crusade: The Chronicle of Fulcher of Chartres and Other Source Materials*. Philadelphia: University of Pennsylvania Press, 1998.

———. "The *Firanj* Are Coming—Again." *Orbis* 48.1 (2004): 3–17.

Phillips, Jonathan. *The Second Crusade: Extending the Frontiers of Christendom*. New Haven: Yale University Press, 2010.

———. *The Life and Legend of the Sultan Saladin*. London: The Bodley Head, 2019.

Rapoport, Yossef and Shahab Ahmed, eds. *Ibn Taymiyya and His Times*. Karachi: Oxford University Press, 2010.

Richards, D. S. "Consideration of Two Sources for the Life of Saladin." *Journal of Semitic Studies* 25 (1980): 45–65.

———. "'Imad al-Din al-Isfahani: Administrator, Littérateur and Historian." In *Crusaders and Muslims in Twelfth-Century Syria*. Ed. M. Shatzmiller. Leiden: Brill, 1993. Pp. 133–146.

Richter-Bernburg, Lutz. "'Imad al-Din al-Isfahani." In *Medieval Muslim Historians of the Franks in the Levant*. Ed. A. Mallett. Leiden: Brill, 2014. Pp. 29–51.

———. "Ayyubid Realpolitik and Political-Military Vicissitudes versus Counter-crusading Ideology in the Memoirist-Chronicler al-Katib al-Isfahani." In *Syria in Crusader Times: Conflict and Coexistence*. Ed. C. Hillenbrand. Edinburgh: Edinburgh University Press, 2020. Pp. 265–284.

Rikabi, Jawdat. *La poésie profane sous les ayyûbides et ses principaux représentants*. Paris: Maisonneuve, 1949.

Riley-Smith, Jonathan. "Islam and the Crusades in History and Imagination, 8 November 1898–11 September 2001." *Crusades* 2 (2003): 151–167.

———. *The Crusades: A Short History*. New Haven: Yale University Press, 2005.

———. *The Crusades, Christianity, and Islam*. New York: Columbia University Press, 2008.

———. *The First Crusade and the Idea of Crusading*. Philadelphia: University of Pennsylvania Press, 2009.

Sayeed, Asma. *Women and the Transmission of Religious Knowledge in Islam*. Cambridge: Cambridge University Press, 2013.

Sharon, Moshe. *Corpus Inscriptionum Arabicarum Palaestinae*. Leiden: Brill, 1997–2016.

Sharon, Moshe and Ami Schraeger. "Frederick II's Arabic Inscription from Jaffa (1229)." *Crusades* 11 (2012): 139–158.

Sivan, Emmanuel. *L'islam et la croisade: idéologie et propagande dans les réactions musulmanes aux croisades*. Paris: Librairie d'Amérique et d'Orient, 1968.

———. *Radical Islam: Medieval Theology and Modern Politics*. New Haven: Yale University Press, 1985.

Smarandache, Bogdan C. "Assessing the Evidence for a Turning Point in Ayyubid-Frankish Relations in a Letter by al-Qadi al-Fadil." In *Syria in Crusader Times: Conflict and Coexistence*. Ed. C. Hillenbrand. Edinburgh: Edinburgh University Press, 2020. Pp. 285–304.

Spellberg, Denise A. *Politics, Gender, and the Islamic Past: The Legacy of 'A'isha bint Abi Bakr*. New York: Columbia University Press, 1996.

Stewart, Devin J. "The *Maqamat* of Ahmad b. Abi Bakr b. Ahmad al-Razi al-Hanafi and the Ideology of the Counter-Crusade in Twelfth-Century Syria." *Middle Eastern Literatures* 11.2 (2008): 211–232.

Tabbaa, Yasser. "Monuments with a Message: Propagation of *Jihad* under Nur al-Din." In *The Meeting of Two Worlds: Cultural Exchange between East and West during the Period of the Crusades*. Eds. V. P. Gross and C. V. Bornstein. Kalamazoo: Medieval Institute, 1986. Pp. 223–240.

———. *The Transformation of Islamic Art during the Sunni Revival*. Seattle: University of Washington Press, 2001.

Talmon-Heller, Daniella. *Islamic Piety in Medieval Syria: Mosques, Cemeteries and Sermons under the Zangids and Ayyubids (1146–1260)*. Leiden: Brill, 2007.

Taylor, Julie A. *Muslims in Medieval Italy: The Colony at Lucera*. Lanham: Lexington Books, 2003.

Tolan, John V. *Saracens: Islam in the Medieval European Imagination*. New York: Columbia University Press, 2002.

———. *Saint Francis and the Sultan: The Curious History of a Christian-Muslim Encounter*. Oxford: Oxford University Press, 2009.

Tolan, John V. and Philippe Josserand. *Les relations entre le monde arabo-musulman et le monde latin (milieu du Xe - milieu du XIII siècle)*. Rosny: Bréal, 2000.

Yarbrough, Luke. "Symbolic Conflict and Cooperation in the Neglected Chronicle of a Syrian Prince." In *Syria in Crusader Times: Conflict and Coexistence*. Ed. C. Hillenbrand. Edinburgh: Edinburgh University Press, 2020. Pp. 125–143.

INDEX A
HONORIFIC TITLES

Many of the sovereigns, commanders, and scholars in this anthology were known by honorific titles indicating they were supporters of the religion (*Din*) or the realm (*Dawla*), for example, Salah al-Din (Righteousness of the Religion), Asad al-Din (Lion of the Religion), Iftikhar al-Dawla (Pride of the Realm), Sayf al-Dawla (Sword of the Realm), and so on.

It should be noted as well that it was common to give sons theophoric names, that is, names that begin with "Servant of" ('*Abd*) and conclude with one of the names of God, for example 'Abd Allah (Servant of God), 'Abd al-Malik (Servant of the King), 'Abd al-Rahman (Servant of the Merciful), 'Abd al-Wahid (Servant of the One), and so on.

It should be emphasized that any honorific title in the anthology or a name that begins with *'Abd, Abu,* or *Ibn* must be treated as an indivisible unit. *Nur al-Din* does not mean that *Nur* is the first name and *al-Din* is the last name, *'Abd al-Malik* does not mean that *'Abd* is the first name and *al-Malik* is the last name, and so on.

Certain terms (e.g., Muslim, Christian, Frank, Syria, Egypt, etc.) occur frequently throughout the anthology. For the most part, we have only indexed these terms in connection with relevant persons and events.

'Alam al-Din (Banner of the Religion), 122, 130, 141, 194, 211, 212
'Asab al-Dawla (Spine of the Realm), 72, 72n37
Asad al-Din (Lion of the Religion), 56, 170, 170n50, 202n18
Asil al-Din (Foundation of the Religion), 143
Badr al-Din (Full Moon of the Religion), 146–147, 176n69, 212
Baha' al-Din (Magnificence of the Religion), 99, 229, 231
Burhan al-Din (Proof of the Religion), 84

Diya' al-Din (Brightness of the Religion), 84, 84n86, 184n93, 241
Fakhr al-Din (Glory of the Religion), xxi, 48, 117, 121–122, 126, 133n174, 174, 196–197, 197n13, 199
Faris al-Din (Knight of the Religion), 141
Fath al-Din (Triumph of the Religion), 200
Ghiyath al-Din (Rescuer of the Religion), 71n28
Hujjat al-Din (Proof of the Religion), 85n89, 163, 163n30

Index A: Honorific Titles

Hujjat al-Islam (Proof of Islam), 85, 85n89, 163n30
Husam al-Dawla (Sword of the Realm), 73
Husam al-Din (Sword of the Religion), 129, 194
Iftikhar al-Dawla (Pride of the Realm), 67
'Imad al-Din (Pillar of the Religion), xvii n12, 71, 94, 96, 106, 181n89, 226, 227, 228, 237
'Ismat al-Din (Chastity of the Religion), 167
'Izz al-Din (Glory of the Religion), 48, 48n12, 87, 104, 107, 139, 141n202, 194, 231, 241
Jalal al-Din (Splendor of the Religion), 117, 178n76
Jamal al-Din (Beauty of the Religion), 48, 116, 123, 132, 232, 233, 237
Kamal al-Din (Perfection of the Religion), 135–136
Karim al-Din (Benefactor of the Religion), 179
Mu'ayyid al-Din (Supporter of the Religion), 56n27
Muhadhdhab al-Din (Refinement of the Religion), 187, 187n98
Muhyi al-Din (Revivifier of the Religion), 181n87, 200n20
Mu'in al-Din (Helper of the Religion), 81–87, 245
Mujir al-Din (Shield of the Religion), 85, 245
Mukhtar al-Din (Favorite of the Religion), 192
Muwaffaq al-Din (Fortunate of the Religion), 186, 235
Najm al-Din (Star of the Religion), 50, 73, 124, 128–129, 147, 178
Nasih al-Islam (Counsel of Islam), 83
Nasir al-Din (Champion of the Religion), 55n25, 110–111, 110n139, 114, 249

Nasr al-Din (Victory of the Religion), 147
Nur al-Din (Light of the Religion), xix, xxi–xxii, 17–18, 24–25, 41–42, 56, 62, 83, 83n84, 84, 84n87, 86, 86n91, 87–90, 94, 130, 158, 165–173, 186, 206, 226–228, 230, 235, 238–239, 241, 244, 245, 251, 253
Qasim al-Dawla (Beauty of the Realm), 165
Qutb al-Din (Pole of the Religion), 101–102, 169, 169n49
Rashid al-Din (Guidance of the Religion), xvii n12, 97–98
Rukn al-Din (Pillar of the Religion), 117, 142n206, 144, 232, 244
Sabiq al-Din (Trailblazer of the Religion), 194
Sa'd al-Din (Felicity of the Religion), 178
Salah al-Din (Righteousness of the Religion), xxii, 16n76, 147n217, 243, 253
Sarim al-Din (Rigorousness of the Religion), 95
Sayf al-Dawla (Sword of the Realm), 197n15
Sayf al-Din (Sword of the Religion), 74, 83, 83n84, 85–87, 104, 104n128, 124, 139, 143, 149, 151, 165, 169n49, 206, 207–208, 207n5, 251
Sayf al-Islam (Sword of Islam), 56n30
Shams al-Dawla (Sun of the Realm), 140
Shams al-Din (Sun of the Religion), 74, 83–84, 107, 119, 122–123, 176n68, 184, 209, 229, 233
Shams al-Muluk (Sun of the Monarchs), 113, 163, 163n26
Sharaf al-Din (Eminence of the Religion), 135n180, 251
Shihab al-Din (Shooting Star of the Religion), 28, 74n60, 134, 191, 230, 240

271

Index A: Honorific Titles

Siraj al-Din (Lamp of the Religion), 124
Taj al-Dawla (Crown of the Realm), 66
Taj al-Din (Crown of the Religion), 50, 174, 174n57, 236
Taj al-Muluk (Crown of the Monarchs), 78, 244
Taqiy al-Din (Pious of the Religion), 54, 91, 242
Zahir al-Din (Triumphant of the Religion), 244, 255
Zahr al-Dawla (Radiance of the Realm), 35

INDEX B

NAMES

Abaq (Burid ruler of Damascus), 85, 167n42, 245
al-'Abbas son of al-Walid al-Khallal, 33
'Abbasids, 6n33, 33nn130–131, 35n136, 55, 56n27, 69n24, 74n56, 83, 84, 97, 98n107, 103n125, 165n33, 170, 174n61, 181n87, 243, 246, 248, 253, 255
'Abd al-Ghani son of Sa'id al-Misri, 36
'Abd al-Karim (muezzin in Jerusalem during Frederick II's visit), 119–120
'Abd Allah (North African merchant), 151, 152
'Abd Allah son of al-'Abbas son of 'Ali son of Abu Talib, 3
'Abd Allah son of Abu Bakr, 154
'Abd Allah son of 'Amr son of al-'As, 157
'Abd Allah son of al-Hasan al-Misri, 7
'Abd Allah son of Ilyas, 130
'Abd Allah son of 'Umar, 29
'Abd Allah son of Zayd al-Azraq, 46
'Abd al-'Aziz al-Mughith son of al-Mu'azzam, 183
'Abd al-Malik (Umayyad caliph), 138n191
'Abd al-Malik al-Qahir son of al-Mu'azzam, 183
'Abd al-Rahman (master architect), 212
'Abd al-Rahman al-Halhuli (mystic), 81
'Abd al-Samad son of al-Hakam, 35
'Abd al-Wahhab (cleric), 78
'Abd al-Wahhab (master builder), 212

al-Abiwardi, 66, 68, 70, 237
Abraham (Friend of God), xxii, 9, 9n47, 10, 10n57, 11–12, 12n64, 13–14, 25n95, 65, 200n23, 212–213
Abu al-'Abbas al-Yafuni, 30
Abu 'Abd Allah al-Bashshari, 33–34
Abu 'Abd Allah al-Damaghani, 37, 37n146
Abu 'Abd Allah al-Musabbihi, 30
Abu 'Abd Allah al-Suri, 36–37
Abu 'Abd Allah son of Abu Kamil, 36
Abu 'Ali 'Abd al-Wahid son of Ahmad, 32
Abu 'Ali al-Farisi, 174
Abu Bakr (first caliph in Islam), 160, 252
Abu Bakr al-Banna' al-Bashshari, 33
Abu Bakr al-Khara'iti, 32
Abu Bakr al-Shashi, 68
Abu Bakr son of al-Tayyib, 55
Abu Bakr al-Tamimi, 30
Abu al-Durr Yaqut (Damascene merchant), 24–25
Abu al-Fida', 233
Abu Ghalib al-Ma'arri, 37
Abu Hamid al-Isfarayini, 55, 55n22
Abu Hanifa, 174, 175n56, 177, 247. *See also* Hanafis.
Abu al-Hasan 'Ali son of al-Musallam, 163
Abu al-Hasan al-Arsufi, 32
Abu al-Hasan Muhammad son of Ahmad, 32
Abu al-Hasan son of Abu Jarada, 76–77

Index B: Names

Abu al-Hasan al-Qabisi, 162
Abu al-Hasan al-Zafiri, 205
Abu Hirmas Shuja' (muezzin), 135
Abu Hurayra (Companion), xxii, 2, 2n10, 43
Abu al-Husayn al-Quduri, 55, 177, 178n75
Abu al-Husayn son of Jami', 36
Abu al-Majd al-'Asqalani, 205
Abu Mansur (physician), 188, 190
Abu Mansur Yaqut, 205
Abu Muhammad al-Battal, 31, 31n117
Abu Muhammad al-Damaghani, 68
Abu Muhammad al-Nasihi, 174n55
Abu Muhammad son of Abu Zayd, 55, 55n24
Abu Musa al-Fakhuri, 30
Abu al-Qasim 'Ali son of Ahmad, 7
Abu al-Qasim al-Tabarani, 30
Abu al-Qasim al-Zanjani, 68
Abu Sa'd al-Hulwani, 68
Abu Shama, 134, 136, 142, 226, 230–231
Abu Tahir al-Silafi, 11, 11n62
Abu Tahir al-Yafuni, 30
Abu Turab al-Ba'labakki, 162
Abu 'Ubayda son of al-Jarrah (Companion), 2, 2n7, 138
Abu Ya'la Ibn al-Farra', 55, 55n23
Abu Yusuf, 177n74
Abu al-Yusur al-Ma'arri (Nur al-Din's secretary), 165
Adam, xvii; and Acre 4, 20; and Hebron 11; and Jerusalem, 9–10, 9–10n54
al-'Adil (Ayyubid sultan), 30, 124, 194–195, 208, 209
al-Afdal son of Badr al-Jamali (Fatimid vizier), 35, 35n139, 56n30, 63–65, 63n10, 66–67, 69–70
al-Afdal (son of Saladin), 92
'Afrun son of Suhar al-Hitti (Ephron son of Zohar the Hittite), 12
Agnes of Courtenay, 17

Ahmad son of Abu Bakr al-Razi, 237
Ahmad son of Abu al-Hawari, 9
Ahmad son of Muhammad al-Qayrawani, 163, 164
'A'isha (wife of Muhammad), 160, 160n14
'Akk (prophet), 5, 33
'Alam al-Din al-Birzali, 130
'Alam al-Din Qaysar, 122
'Alam al-Din Sulayman, 194
'Ali son of Abu Talib (fourth caliph in Islam), 4–5, 4n26, 31, 31n116
'Ali son of Ahmad al-Mashtub (Scarface) (Ayyubid commander), 104–5, 104n128, 206–207, 207n5
'Ali son of Aybak (Mamluk sultan), 141
Almohads, 15, 239, 243
Alp Arslan son of Sultan Mahmud (Seljuk commander), 165
Alphonse Jordan of Toulouse, 80, 83, 87, 169
Amalric I, xxi, 169, 192
Amir al-Mu'minin. *See* Commander of the Faithful.
'Amr son of al-'As (Companion), 34, 34n133, 48, 157, 242
'Amr son of al-Jamuh (Companion), 153–154
'Amr son of Thawr al-Qaysarani, 32
Anas son of Malik (Companion), 45
Aq-Sunqur al-Bursuqi (Seljuk commander), 71, 165
Aq-Sunqur (Zangi's father), 165
Armenians, 35n139, 56, 56n30, 63, 63n10, 73, 99, 100, 100n115, 101–103, 101nn118–119, 169
'Asab al-Dawla Abaq, 72, 72n37
Asad al-Din Shirkuh (Saladin's uncle), 56, 166n38, 170, 170n50, 212n18, 251
al-A'sha, 38, 38n152
al-Ash'ari, 243
Ash'arism (Ash'ari theological school), 41, 41n3, 48, 50, 236, 242–243

Index B: Names

Asher (Jacob's son), 4
al-Ashraf Khalil (Mamluk sultan), xiii, 144, 147, 147n217, 148, 200n20, 203, 232, 243, 252
al-Ashraf Musa (Ayyubid sovereign), 50, 110–113, 113n148, 114, 115, 119, 121
al-Ashraf Sha'ban (Mamluk sultan), 151
Asil al-Din Khawaja, 143
Atabeg. *See* Chief commander.
al-'Attafi, 24
al-Awza'i, 33
Ayyubids, xxi, 30n112, 31n15, 59, 107, 110, 113nn146–147, 114, 116, 122, 130, 133n174, 134, 135n179, 141n205, 144, 146, 176n71, 179n78, 181n87, 186, 187n98, 193, 196, 214, 229–231–235, 237, 239, 244, 249–251, 253–254
al-Azhari, 38
al-'Azimi, 71, 72n37, 73, 73n52, 75, 227–228
Badr al-Din Baktut, 212
Badr al-Din Baylik al-Khazindar, 146
Badr al-Din al-Salamish, 147
Badr al-Jamali (Fatimid vizier), 35, 56n30, 63n10, 66
al-Ba'labakki, 162, 162n22
Balaban son of 'Abd Allah, 211
Baldwin I (king of Jerusalem), 35, 60
Baldwin II (king of Jerusalem), 12n66
Baldwin III (king of Jerusalem), 207n6
Baldwin IV (king of Jerusalem), xxi, 17, 25, 191, 193
al-Battani (Albategnius), 32n120
Baybars (Mamluk sultan), 116–117, 125, 139n198, 141n201, 142n206, 143, 148, 203, 210, 231–232, 238, 244; capture and renovation of the Crac des Chevaliers, 144–145, 211, 211n16; death of, 145–147; capture and renovation of Subayba castle, 208n9, 211, 211n17, 212; inscriptions in Hebron and Jerusalem, 212–213

Baybars al-Mansuri, 144, 146, 147n217, 148, 232
Bedouins, 65, 146, 151, 153, 155, 168, 175
Bertrand son of Alphonse Jordan of Toulouse, 83, 87, 169n48
Bohemond III, 166
al-Bukhari, 56, 244
Burhan al-Din al-Hanafi, 84
Burids, 62, 74n60, 78, 163n26, 167n42, 244–245, 251, 255
Buri Khan, 72
Buyids, 243, 253
Byron (knight), 12
Byzantines, xv, xix, 1, 11, 28, 31n117, 32, 37–38, 61, 68n22, 72, 75, 75n69, 98n107, 101, 124, 138n192, 147n218, 161, 169, 219, 238–240. *See* Byzantium.
Caliph (*khalifa*), xxii, 4n26, 7, 33, 55–56, 74, 83–84, 103, 111, 125–126, 129, 170, 181, 239, 243, 245, 247, 253–254; 'Abbasid caliph, 6n33, 35n136, 56n27, 69n24, 97, 98n107, 165, 243; Fatimid caliph, 6n37, 36n141, 54n20, 56nn29–30, 63n10, 205, 246, 248, 253; Rashidun caliph, 6n36, 29, 34n134, 56n31, 137, 215, 247, 252, 255; Umayyad caliph, 15, 34n135, 137n187, 138, 138n191, 138n194, 158, 250
Catholicos (Armenian), 99–103, 125n160
Charles of Anjou, 125n163
Chief commander (*atabeg*), 71n29, 72, 72n31, 73, 73n48, 74, 83–84, 86, 141, 244–245, 255
Children of Israel, 8, 12n65, 160n16
Christ, 125, 126, 158. *See also* Jesus; Messiah.
Christians. *See* Nazarenes.
Commander of the Faithful (*Amir al-Mu'minin*), 6–7, 137, 161, 165, 205–208, 210–213, 243, 245

275

Index B: Names

Companions (*sahaba*), xvi n7, 2n7, 2nn10–11, 9nn50–52, 29, 29n107, 42, 47, 84, 137n188, 138n189, 157, 162n20, 210, 210n13, 210n15, 219, 245, 247, 252, 254
Conrad (king of Germany), xxiii, 80, 80n80, 81, 85, 87
Conrad (son of Frederick II), 125
Constance of Hauteville, 166
David (king of Israel), 2, 6, 8, 10, 13, 200n23
al-Dhahabi, xxi, 130, 184–185, 190, 233, 236
Dhu al-Asabiʿ al-Tamimi, 9, 9n52
Diʿbil son of ʿAli al-Khuzaʿi, 123, 123n158
Disciples (*al-Hawariyyun*) of Jesus, 1n3, 8, 157, 159, 198, 201
Diyaʾ al-Din al-Hanbali, 184n93, 241
Diyaʾ al-Din al-Husayni, 84n86
Druzes, xx, 3n18, 54–55, 57, 246, 252
Duqaq (Seljuk ruler), 244, 255
Ephron. *See* ʿAfrun.
Eschiva of Bures, 95n102
Fadala son of ʿUbayd, 46
Fakhr al-Din al-Hasiri, 174
Fakhr al-Din son of Luqman, 133n174
Fakhr al-Din son of Shaykh al-Shuyukh, xxi, 117, 121–122, 126, 196–197, 199, 197n13
Faris al-Din Aqtay al-Mustaʿrib, 141
al-Farraʾ, 35, 35n137
Fatimids, xxii, 6n37, 13nn71–72, 35n139, 36n141, 41n2, 54n20, 55n26, 56nn28–30, 57, 60, 60n6, 62, 63n10, 65, 73n47, 110n139, 129, 170n51, 205, 205nn1–2, 214, 234, 239, 246, 248, 253
al-Findalawi, xx, 81, 85, 85n89, 86–88, 162–164, 220
Franks, capture of Jerusalem, 64–70; Battle of the Field of Blood, 71–75; defeat at Hattin, 91–96; Third Crusade and capture of Acre, 99–106; Fifth Crusade, 109–114; loss of coastal Syria in 1291, 147–148; Second Crusade, 80–88, 163; Seventh Crusade, 132–133
Frederick I, 99, 99n111, 103
Frederick II, xxi, 107, 115–118, 119–120, 121, 126, 127, 129, 143, 177, 196–199, 241, 249
Frederick VI, 100
Fudayq al-Qaysarani, 32–33
Galen, 186–188, 186n96, 190
Germans, 80, 81, 85–87, 99–103, 117, 126, 198
al-Gharz Khalil, 179, 179n82
Ghayth, 37
Ghaznawids, 247, 253
Godfrey, 12
Gospel, 3, 9, 60, 81n82, 123, 201–203, 220
Gregory IV, 99–103
Guibert of Nogent, 158
Guy of Lusignan, 104
Habib al-Najjar (Habib the Carpenter), 1, 1n3
al-Hakam son of ʿAbd al-Rahman al-Firaʿi, 32
Hamdan al-Atharibi, xvii n13, 76–77
Hamdanids, 197n15
Hanafis (branch of Sunni jurisprudence), 54–55, 247, 249, 254–255. *See also* Abu Hanifa.
Hanbalis (branch of Sunni jurisprudence), xix, 48, 54–55, 130, 163, 174n57, 175n62, 180n84, 184, 228, 233, 241, 242, 247, 250, 255. *See also* Ibn Hanbal.
al-Harawi, xix, 1, 2n4, 6n32, 6n34, 8n46, 10n55, 12, 14, 14n73, 33n129, 39, 239
al-Harawi, Abu Saʿid, 68
al-Hariri, 97
al-Harith al-Ashʿari, 44
al-Hasan son of Ibrahim al-ʿAkki, 35
al-Hasan son of Jarir al-Suri, 35
Hashwiyya, 162n23

Index B: Names

Hebron (al-Khalil), 1, 10n57, 11–12, 12n64, 13n68, 14, 180n85, 207–208, 212, 213n21
Henry IV, 100
al-Hilli, 113–114
Hims, 38, 51, 74, 83, 86–87, 111, 111n143, 112, 112n145, 128, 137n188, 168, 196, 210, 212n18, 231, 238
Hippocrates, 187, 187n97
Hisham son of 'Abd al-Malik (Umayyad caliph), 15, 34
Hospitallers, 93, 95–96, 128, 145, 194, 200–201, 203
Hulegu, 55n25, 135, 181n87, 248
Humphrey II, 93n99
Humphrey IV, 93, 93n99, 96
Husam al-Din Bishara, 194
Husam al-Din son of Abu 'Ali, 129
Husayn (vendor), 155
al-Husayn son of 'Ali (Shi'i Imam), 3n14, 13, 13n72, 31n116, 180, 248, 254
Ibn 'Abd al-Zahir, 200n20, 231–232
Ibn Abu 'Awn, 33, 33n130
Ibn Abu Usaybi'a, xxi, xxiin21, 186, 190, 235–236
Ibn al-'Adim, 230, 235
Ibn al-'Alqami, 56, 56n27
Ibn 'Ammar (ruler of Tripoli), 72, 72n35, 73
Ibn 'Aqil, 68
Ibn 'Asakir, xvi n9, xvi n11, xix, xx–xxi, xxii, 30n113, 41–42, 44n6, 45n7, 47, 49, 81n82, 84n87, 85n89, 86–87, 87n92, 89–90, 160n12, 163n25, 164, 235, 241; on al-Findalawi, 162–164; on Jesus, 157–161; on jihad, 41–47; on Nur al-Din, 89–90, 165–173
Ibn 'Asakir, Fakhr al-Din, 48
Ibn 'Asakir, al-Qasim, 241
Ibn al-Athir, xvin11, 59, 61, 63n11, 66, 70, 85, 87–88, 91, 93, 96, 104, 106, 163n30, 226, 229

Ibn al-Bayni, 176
Ibn al-Dawadari, 233
Ibn al-Furat al-Misri, 234
Ibn Hanbal, 174–175, 247. *See also* Hanbalis.
Ibn Hisham, 175
Ibn Husam al-Dawla, 73, 73n48
Ibn al-Jawzi, 107, 123, 180n84, 228–230, 241
Ibn al-Jawzi, Muhyi al-Din, 181n87
Ibn Jubayr, xvii n15 xix, xxii, 15, 17 18n83, 19n84, 23n91, 26n99 26n101, 27, 39, 193, 239–240
Ibn Khallikan, 236
Ibn al-Khayyat, 237
Ibn Luqman, 133, 133n174
Ibn Matruh, 132–133, 237–238
Ibn Munqidh, Usama, xvii, xxii 75n65, 189, 238–239
Ibn al-Musajjif, 176, 176n69
Ibn al-Nahhal, 195
Ibn Nazif al-Hamawi, 196, 231
Ibn al-Qalanisi, xvi n10, 62, 64n13, 65, 70, 80, 83n83, 84, 87, 227
Ibn Qufl (mystic), 109
Ibn Sallam, Muhammad, 154–155
Ibn Shaddad, Baha' al-Din, xvi n10, xvii n12, 99, 99n109, 103, 103n125, 125n160, 194–195, 229, 231
Ibn Shaddad, 'Izz al-Din, 231
Ibn al-Shahrazuri, 75
Ibn Simmak, 68
Ibn Sulayman Malik Shah, 72, 72n42
Ibn Tabarzad, 175
Ibn Taymiyya, xvi, xix n19, xx, xxii, 54, 55n26, 57, 184, 242, 251
Ibn Tulun, 33, 33n131, 34, 129n167
Ibn Wasil, xvin10, xviin14, 2n7, 116, 117n153, 118, 121, 125n160, 127, 128, 134n178, 137, 137n185, 139–142, 143, 226, 232
Ibrahim al-Qaysarani, 32
Ibrahim son of al-Walid son of Salama, 33

277

Il-Ghazi son of Urtuq (Seljuk commander), 63, 66, 67, 73, 73n47, 110n139
'Imad al-Din Ibn al-Mashtub (Ayyubid commander), 181n89
'Imad al-Din al-Isfahani, xviin12, 94, 96, 106, 226, 228, 237
Imam, 55–56, 81, 84, 134, 197, 207, 248, 254; Shi'i Imam, 3n14, 4n26, 6, 31n116, 130, 205, 246, 248, 251, 254–255
'Imran, ancestor of Mary, 4, 4n23
'Imran son of Harun al-Ramli, 30
'Imran son of Husayn, 45
'Isa Abu Talib (shaykh), 130–131
Isaac (son of Abraham), 4n21, 11, 12, 180n85, 207
Ishmael (son of Abraham), 8n44
Isma'il al-Arsufi, 30
Isma'il al-Maqdisi, 30
Isma'il (Burid ruler of Damascus), 163n26
Isma'il (son of Abu Shama), 134
Isma'ilis, xxii, 54, 54n20, 55, 55n26, 56n29, 57, 84, 170n51, 214, 244, 246, 248, 252, 254
'Ismat al-Din (daughter of Unur), 167, 167n42
'Izz al-Din 'Abd al-'Aziz son of 'Abd al-Salam. *See* al-'Izz son of 'Abd al-Salam.
'Izz al-Din Arsal al-Asadi, 104
'Izz al-Din Aybak (commander under al-Mu'azzam), 107
'Izz al-Din Aybak (Mamluk sultan), 141n202
'Izz al-Din al-Dubaysi, 87
'Izz al-Din Jawili, 104
'Izz al-Din son of Muqaddam, 194
al-'Izz son of 'Abd al-Salam, xix–xx, 48–53, 241–242
Jacob (son of Isaac), 4, 8n41, 10n55, 11, 12, 12n65, 26n97
Jacobites, 8, 159

Ja'far son of Abu Talib al-Tayyar (cousin of Muhammad), 181, 181n86
Jalal al-Din Khwarazm Shah (Seljuk sultan), 117, 178n76
Jamal al-Din al-Dawadari, 233
Jamal al-Din al-Harastani, 48
Jangara, 151, 152
Jesus, xx, 1n3, 2–3, 8, 9n54, 10, 44, 92, 113, 119, 132–133, 138n193, 147, 157–161, 176n70, 198n16, 202, 207n6, 210n15, 248. *See also* Christ; Messiah.
Jethro (father-in-law of Moses), 3, 3n18, 26
Jews, xix, 1, 14, 18n83, 23n91, 25n94, 32, 56, 65, 139, 158, 158n3, 159, 215–216, 222, 239, 246, 249, 251
John of Brienne (king of Jerusalem), 113n146, 198n17
John the Baptist (John son of Zachariah), 44, 202; Basilica of, 137n187, 138n192, 138n196
Joscelin I, 166n37, 169
Joseph of Arimathea, 10n55
Joseph the Righteous (son of Jacob), 10, 12, 99n109, 229n6
Judah (son of Jacob), 26, 26n97
Kamal al-Din al-Tiflisi, 135–136, 135n182
al-Kamil (Ayyubid sultan), 30n112, 50, 209, 238, 249–250; and Fifth Crusade, 107, 107n131, 109–114, 113n148; and Frederick II, 107, 115, 116–127, 129, 132, 196; and al-Mu'azzam, 143, 175, 178, 181, 181n89, 251
Karim al-Din al-Khilati, 179
Khalid son of al-Walid (Companion), 137, 210
Khalifa. *See* Caliph.
al-Khatib al-Baghdadi, 37, 37n145, 175n65
Khaythama son of Sulayman, 32

Index B: Names

Khudayr al-Rikabi, 163
Kumashtakin al-Taji, 72, 72n45, 74
Kurds, 74n60, 104n128, 106, 135, 177, 207n5, 244, 249
Kutbugha (Mongol general), 141
al-Layth son of al-Muzaffar, 33, 33n128
Leo II (Levon), 100n115
Leopold VI, 113
Luqman the Wise, 2, 2n6
Mahmud (Burid ruler of Damascus), 74n60
Mahmud (Seljuk sultan), 74, 74n55, 165, 165n34
Majd al-Mulk al-Balasani, 68, 68n20
al-Makin al-Harrani, 74
Malik Shah (Seljuk sultan), 72n42, 165
Malik son of Anas, 55n24, 162n20, 250. *See also* Malikis.
Malikis (branch of Sunni jurisprudence), 54–55, 55n24, 162, 249, 250. *See also* Malik son of Anas.
Mamluk Sultanate, xiii, xxi, 30, 54, 116, 117n153, 130, 139n198, 141nn201–203, 143–144, 151n223, 184, 191, 200n20, 208n9, 214, 231–234, 238, 240, 243–244, 246, 250–252
Manfred (son of Frederick II), 116–117, 124–125, 127, 143, 232
al-Mansur Ibrahim of Hims (Ayyubid sovereign), 51, 128, 196, 231
al-Mansur Muhammad II of Hama (Ayyubid sovereign), 139–141
al-Maqrizi, xviii, 225–226, 234–235, 236–237
Martha, 202
Mary (mother of Jesus), 3–4, 4n23, 8, 44, 119, 159–161, 202. *See also* Church of Mary.
Mary Magdalen, 202

Maslama son of ʿAli al-Khushani, 33
Masʿud son of Aq-Sunqur al-Bursuqi (Seljuk commander), 165, 165n35
Masʿud (sultan of Anatolia), 75
Mawdud, 72, 72n41
Mazawirs, 72, 72n34
Melisende, 207n6
Messiah, 6, 8–9, 176, 176n70, 201–203. *See also* Christ; Jesus.
Mongols, xx, 54–56, 111, 111n141, 134n178, 135n179, 137n185, 138n196, 141n204, 208n9, 211n17, 242, 243, 244, 248, 250; capture of Damascus, 134–139; battle of ʿAyn Jalut, 139–142
Moses, 3, 3n18, 4, 13, 13n68, 26, 113, 113n148, 200n23
Muʿawiya son of Abu Sufyan (Umayyad caliph), 29, 32, 34, 158, 161, 251
al-Muʿazzam ʿIsa (Ayyubid sovereign), xxi, 97, 107n131, 113n148, 117, 121, 124, 176n70, 177n73, 178n77, 179nn81–82, 180n85, 181n89, 182n90, 185, 187–189, 190, 207–208, 230, 251; and Fifth Crusade, 109–114; biography by al-Dhahabi, 184; biography by Sibt Ibn al-Jawzi, 174–183; deal with Frederick II, 115; destruction of the wall of Jerusalem, 107–108
al-Muʿazzam Turanshah (Ayyubid sultan), 124, 250
al-Mughith (brother of al-Muʿazzam ʿIsa), 179, 180
Muhadhdhab al-Din ʿAbd al-Rahim son of ʿAli, 187, 187n98
Muhammad (prophet), 3n14, 4n26, 5, 13n72, 23, 19, 31n116, 54, 54n20, 66, 69, 69n24, 83n85, 126, 137n188, 153–154, 158, 161, 162nn20–21, 168n46, 175n64, 184, 200n23, 206, 215, 233, 241–242, 246–247, 253–254

Muhammad al-Sharif (butcher), 153
Muhammad son of al-Hanafiyya, 31, 31n116
Muhammad son of al-Taffal (schoolmaster), 153
Muhammad son of Hamdan al-Ansari, 209
Muhammad son of Muhammad al-Qaysarani, 32
Muʿin al-Din Unur. *See* Unur, Muʿin al-Din.
al-Muqtadir (ʿAbbasid caliph), 35
al-Mustarshid bi-Allah (ʿAbbasid caliph), 165
al-Mutanabbi, xxi, 197n15
Najm al-Din Ibn Sallam, 178–179
Najm al-Din son of Baybars, 147
al-Najm Khalil, 179
Naphtali (Jacob's son), 4
al-Nasir Dawud (Ayyubid sovereign), 51, 115, 123, 128–129, 146, 179, 183, 189
Nasir al-Din Urtuq, 63, 66, 110, 110n139, 111, 114
Nasr son of Qawwam (Damascene merchant), 24
Nazarenes (*Nasara*), 4, 4n24, 159
Nebuchadnezzar, 8
Nizam al-Mulk (Seljuk vizier), 66, 237
Noah, 11, 39
al-Nuʿman son of Bashir (Companion), 43
Nur al-Din, xix, xxi–xxii, 17–18, 24, 41–42, 83, 83n84, 84, 84n87, 86, 86n91, 94, 130, 158, 186, 228, 230, 235, 238–239, 241, 244, 251; capture of al-ʿUrayma castle, 87–88; capture of Egypt, 89–90; capture of Damascus, 62, 227, 245, 251, 253; Ibn ʿAsakir's biography of, 165–173; pulpit for the Aqsa Mosque, 206
al-Nusayr al-Tusi, 55, 55n25
Nusayris, 54–55, 57, 251–252
al-Nuwayri, 238

al-Nuwayri al-Iskandarani, xvii n15, xx, 149, 155, 234
Ottomans, 243, 250–252
Pelagius, 113
Philip the Greek (of Macedon), 202
Pope, xiii, 125–127, 125n160, 133, 158, 197n12, 198, 240
Ptolemy, 31, 32n120, 33
al-Qadi al-Fadil, 191, 239
al-Qaʾim bi-Amr Allah (ʿAbbasid caliph), 6
Qalawun (Mamluk sultan), xxi, 144, 200–203, 212–213, 232, 243, 252
al-Qalqashandi, 191, 191n5, 193, 200, 203, 240
Qandil (bandit), 182
Qarmatis, 55
Qasim son of al-Muhanna al-ʿAlawi, 168n46
al-Qaysarani (poet), xvii n13, 78–79
Qilij Arslan (Seljuk sultan), 31, 31n115, 72n42, 75n67, 99–102
Quraysh, 69n24, 153n224, 216, 220
Qutb al-Din son of Qilij Arslan, 101–102
Qutb al-Din son of Zangi, 169
Qutuz (Mamluk sultan), 139–142, 244
Rabiʿa al-ʿAdawiyya, 9, 9n48
Rachel (mother of Joseph), 10
Rashid al-Din al-Nabulusi, xvii n12, 97–98
Rashidun caliphs, 56, 56n31, 137, 252. *See also* Caliphs.
Raymond III of Tripoli, 25, 91n97, 95n102
Raymond IV of Toulouse, 87
Raymond of Poitiers, 166, 166n38
Raymond of Toulouse, 80n81
Rebecca (wife of Isaac), 180n85, 207
Reuben (son of Jacob), 26, 26n97
Reynald of Châtillon (lord of Kerak), 92–93, 166
Richard the Lionheart, and Khuwaylifa, 11n63; and Saladin, 194–195

Rightly guided caliphs. *See* Rashidun caliphs.
Roger I of Sicily, 60, 61
Roger II of Sicily, xv n5
Roger of Salerno, 73n53
Sabiq al-Din, 194
Saʻd al-Din Masʻud, 178
al-Saʻid son of Baybars (Mamluk sultan), 147
Safwan son of Salih, 30
Sahl, 130
Saladin (Salah al-Din), 1, 11n63, 16n76, 25, 35, 42, 48, 57, 59, 134, 135n179, 141n205, 145, 147, 166n38, 166n41, 177n73, 181n88, 186, 202n18, 226, 228–231, 234–235, 238–239, 244, 246, 251, 253; and Acre, 104–106; and al-Ashraf Khalil, 147n217, 148; and Ascalon, 29; and Atlit, 33; and Baldwin IV, 191–193; and Cairo, 52, 56; and Catholicos (Gregory IV), 99–103; and Hattin, 91–96; and Jaffa, 30; and Jerusalem, 26n101, 29, 97–98, 118, 121–122, 206–207, 217; and Kerak, 16; and Richard the Lionheart, 194–195
Salah al-Din. *See* Saladin.
Salamish son of Baybars (Mamluk sultan), 147
Salih (prophet), 5, 5n28
al-Salih Ayyub son of al-Kamil (Ayyubid sultan), 48, 50, 52, 113, 116, 128, 132, 141, 210, 211, 212, 213, 232, 238, 242, 250
al-Salih Ismaʻil (Ayyubid monarch), 50–52, 52n16, 53, 124, 128–129
Samaritans, 4n21, 32
Sanjar (brother of the Seljuk Sultan Muhammad), 74
Sanjar al-Halabi, 141, 212
Sarah (wife of Abraham), 11–12, 12n64, 213
Sarim al-Din al-Najmi, 95

Sarnard (chancellor of Manfred), 124
Sayf al-Din al-Akuzz, 149, 151
Sayf al-Din Ghazi (Zangid ruler of Mosul), 83, 83n84, 85–87, 251
Sayf al-Din Suwar, 74
Seljuks, 31, 31n15, 60, 60n6, 66, 68n20, 71nn27–29, 72n31, 72nn41–42, 72n45, 73n47, 74n55, 165n32, 165nn34–35, 196, 237, 243–245, 247, 252–253, 255
Shaddad son of Aws al-Khazraji (Companion), 9
al-Shafʻi, 207, 253
Shafiʻis (branch of Sunni jurisprudence), 41, 41n2, 48, 50, 54–55, 55n22, 75, 99, 134, 135n82, 163n25, 184, 191, 207, 230, 233, 236, 240–242, 247, 253, 255
Shams al-Din al-Husayni, 83–84
Shams al-Din son of Kumushtakin, 74
Shams al-Din Sunqur, 209
Shams al-Muluk (nephew of al-Kamil), 113
Sharif, 83n85, 253
Shawar al-Saʻdi, 169
Shaybani, 174n56, 177n74, 178
Shem, 11
Shiʻi rejectionists, 55–57
Shiʻis (Shiʻism), xx, xxi, 3n14, 4n26, 31n116, 54–57, 63n10, 68n20, 84, 130, 166, 237, 242–243, 246, 248, 251, 253–255
Shirkuh. *See* Asad al-Din Shirkuh.
Shuʻayb. *See* Jethro.
Sibawayh, 174, 176
Sibt Ibn al-Jawzi, xvin11, xviin15, xxi, 100n114, 107–111, 114–115, 119–120, 123, 127, 130, 174, 181n87, 185, 226, 229–230, 233
al-Sirafi, 174, 174n59
Siraj al-Din al-Urmawi, 124

281

Index B: Names

Solomon (king of Israel), 2, 6, 8, 10, 13n70, 26
al-Subki, xvii n12, 50, 52–53, 236
Successors (*tabi'un*), 9, 9n50, 14, 29, 254
Sufism (Islamic mysticism), 15, 96, 109n136, 154–155, 168
Sukayna daughter of al-Husayn, 3
al-Sulami, xvii, 240–241
Sulayman son of Ahmad al-Tabarani, 30
Sunnis, xv, xx, xxi, 41, 48n9, 54–55, 56, 84, 130, 162, 166, 173, 175n62, 175n65, 176n71, 177n74, 214, 233–235, 242–244, 246, 247, 250–251, 253–255
Sunqur al-Jakurmushi (Zangid commander), 74
Suqman son of Urtuq (Seljuk commander), 63, 66, 67, 73n47
Suwanj (Seljuk commander), 66
Taj al-Din al-Kindi, 174
Tamim (ruler of Tunis), 60n5
Tancred, 72
Taqiy al-Din 'Umar, 91
al-Tatar. *See* Mongols.
Templars, 93, 95–96, 105–106, 119, 194, 201
Torah, 12, 81n82, 160n16, 220
Tughtakin (Seljuk ruler of Damascus), 72n31, 73, 73n48, 85, 244, 255
Turkomans, 61, 63, 65–66, 73n47, 74nn60–61, 74n64, 81–83, 99, 101, 107, 110n139, 210, 249, 253, 255
'Ubayd Allah son of Maymun al-Qaddah (Fatimid caliph), 54, 54n20
Ugo III, 92n98, 96
'Umar son of 'Abd al-'Aziz (Umayyad caliph), 138
'Umar son of al-Khattab (second caliph in Islam), 6, 10, 29, 34n134, 36, 43, 137, 215, 250, 255
'Umar son of Tamim son of Warqa', 32
Umayyads, 15, 31n117, 34nn134–135, 137n187, 138n191, 138n194, 243, 248, 251, 255
Unur, Mu'in al-Din (Burid commander), 81–88, 163, 167, 167n42, 245
'Uqba son of 'Amir, 46
Urtuq, 63, 66, 110n139
Usama Ibn Munqidh. *See* Ibn Munqidh, Usama.
'Utba son of 'Abd al-Salami, 47
'Uthman (third caliph in Islam), 252
Venetians, 149
al-Walid son of 'Abd al-Malik (Umayyad caliph), 138, 138n191
al-Wasiti, 32
Yaghi Siyan, 62, 65
Yaman (Burid commander), 74
Ya'qub son of Siqlab, 179n79, 186–190
Yaqut al-Hamawi, xix, 28, 37n143, 38–39, 132n171, 240
Yaquti, 66
Yazid son of Khalid son of 'Abd Allah son of Mawhab, 30
Yazid son of Khalid son of Murashshal, 30
Yazid son of Samura, 32
al-Yunini, 130, 232–233
Zachariah (prophet), 5, 44
al-Zafir bi-Amr Allah (Fatimid caliph), 205
al-Zahir li-I'zaz Din Allah (Fatimid caliph), 6
al-Zahir son of Saladin, 1, 97, 99, 181
Zahr al-Dawla Bana' al-Juyushi, 35
Zangi, 'Imad al-Din son of Aq-Sunqur, xxii, 71, 74, 74n58, 74n60, 83, 85–87, 165, 206, 251, 255
Zangids, xix, xxi, 59, 62, 134, 214, 229–230, 245, 253
Zipporah (wife of Moses), 3–4, 26
Zoroastrian, 18n83, 23n91, 102n123, 158, 246, 249
Zumurrud (wife of Zangi), 74

INDEX C
PLACE NAMES

al-'Abbasa, 129, 129n167
Acre ('Akka), 14, 16–17, 28–30, 36, 67, 78, 80, 83, 99, 100n117, 113, 114, 121–123, 126, 128, 157, 161, 176–177, 193–194, 207n5, 229, 239; al-Harawi's descriptions of, 4–5; Ibn Jubayr's descriptions of, 19–21, 22–23, 25–27; Yaqut's descriptions of, 33–35; Franks' capture of in 1191, 104–106; Frederick II's arrival in 1228, 118–120; oaths of truce regarding, 200–203; Sultan al-Ashraf Khalil's capture of in 1291, 147
Aleppo, 1, 28, 59, 71, 72n40, 73nn50–51, 74–76, 78, 83–84, 86, 89, 99, 135–136, 163, 165–167, 169n49, 181, 184, 197n15, 227–231, 233, 235, 237, 240, 251, 255
Alexandria, xx, 11, 11n62, 15, 26, 175, 184, 233–234; Peter of Cyprus's sack of, 149–155
'Amman, 13, 175n67, 180
Andalusia, 59, 59n3, 125
Antartus. *See* Tartus.
Antioch, 37, 37n148, 61, 66, 71, 72n32, 72n40, 73, 73n53, 76 137n187, 166, 166nn38–40, 167n44, 169, 239, 244; al-Harawi's description of, 1–2; al-Qaysarani on the Frankish women in, 78–79; Ibn al-Qalanisi on the capture of in 1098, 62–63
Apamea, 166

Apollonius (Balynias), 31, 31n118
Apulia, 117, 125
al-'Aqiq, 2
Aqsa Mosque, 6–8, 7n39, 14, 67, 89, 108, 119n154, 121, 123, 128, 138n191, 206, 251
al-Aqsis, 60, 60n6
Armanaz, 63, 63n9
Armenia, 73, 210, 244
Ascalon, xxi–xxii, 1, 11n63, 30n110, 62, 65, 66, 67, 69–70, 128, 194, 209n10, 244; al-Harawi's description of, 13, 13n72, 14; Fatimid inscription, 205; Yaqut's description of, 28–29
al-Atharib, 73, 76, 76n72, 77
Atlit, xxi, 28, 33, 144, 147, 200, 201, 202
'Ayn Jalut, 135n179, 137, 139–142, 208n9, 244, 250
'Ayntab (fortress), 166
A'zaz, 166
Baalbek, 39, 72, 87, 130, 168, 184, 196, 233–234
Badr (battle), 220
Baghdad, xix, 28, 36–37, 37nn144–146, 38n151, 55, 55nn22–23, 56, 59, 66, 68, 68n19, 73n53, 76, 78, 84, 94, 99, 107, 111, 116, 123n158, 174n57, 175, 178n75, 228–230, 237, 239, 240, 243, 246, 248, 253
Balata, 12
Balatunus (fortress), 72
Balis (Barbalissos), 71, 74, 74n59

283

Index C: Place Names

Balkh, 29n108
al-Balqa', 39, 175
Baniyas (Balanea), 17n79, 37, 37n148, 145n211, 167, 167n44, 169
Banyas (Belinas), 17, 17n79, 37n148, 86, 162, 167n44, 208
al-Baqi', 2
al-Bara (castle), 166
Bari, 125n161. *See also* Apulia.
Barletta, 199
Basarfut (castle), 166
Baysan. *See* Beit Shean.
Bayt Jibrin, 13, 29
Beaufort (*al-Shaqif*), 50, 244
Beirut, 33n124, 72, 144, 147, 203
Beit Shean (Baysan), 2, 182
Belda, 145, 145n212
Bethlehem, 1, 2, 10, 12
Bijaya, 20, 25
Bikisra'il (fortress), 72, 72n39
Bilbis, 56, 170
Biqa', 82
al-Bira, 121
Buna, 25
Byblos (Jubayl), 92, 96
Byzantium, 61, 80, 165. *See also* Byzantines.
Caesarea, 28, 30, 30n110, 31–33, 78, 110, 182, 244; Mu'awiya's conquest of, 32
Calabria, 197
Canaan, 13n68, 67n17, 201n26
Capharda. *See* Kafartab.
Casal. *See* al-Zab.
Cave of the Spirits, 6, 7
Chastel Neuf. *See* Hunin.
Church of Mary (Cathedral of St. Mary), 137, 137n187, 138
Church of Refuse (*Kanisat al-Qumama*), 9, 9n53. *See also* Church of the Resurrection.
Church of the Ascension, 8
Church of the Holy Sepulchre. *See* Church of the Resurrection.
Church of the Nativity, 10
Church of the Resurrection (*Kanisat al-Qiyama*), 9n53, 10n55
Church of St. Anne, 207
Church of the Tree, 3
Cilicia. *See* Armenia.
College of Hadith (Damascus), 41, 130
College, Khatuniyya (Damascus), 167n42
College, Nizamiyya (Baghdad), 66, 99, 229, 237
College, Saladin (Cairo), 48, 52
College, Saladin (Jerusalem), 116, 207
Constantinople, 20, 61, 75, 80, 86, 113n146, 161, 169, 198n17, 252
Crac des Chevaliers (*Husn al-Akrad*), 203, 211, 211n16, 244; capture of by Baybars in 1271, 144–145
Cyprus, xx, 34, 55, 234; Peter of Cyprus's sack of Alexandria, 149–155
Damascus, early Muslim conquest of, 2n7, 137–138; Franks purchasing arms in, 50; Mongols' capture of, 134–136; Nur al-Din's siege of, 167; retaliations against the Christians of, 137–139; Second Crusade's siege of, xxi, 80–88, 163, 220
Damietta, and Fifth Crusade, 107, 109–114, 181n89; capture of King Louis IX in 1250, 132
Darayya, 137
Da'uq, 182
Dawsar (fortress), 171
Dome of the Chain, 6, 6n35, 7
Dome of the Rock, 5–8, 14, 67, 108, 119, 119n154, 121–123, 128, 134, 251. *See also* Noble Sanctuary.
Duluk, 166
Dunaysir, 111
Dura, 208
Edessa, 67, 72, 75n68, 101n119, 165, 166, 166n37, 168, 255–256

Index C: Place Names

Egypt, Nur al-Din's occupation of, 56, 89–90, 169–170, 253; Amalric I's attack against, 169–170; Fatimid conquest of, 170n51, 246; and Fifth Crusade, 109–114; King Louis IX's attack against, 124, 132–133; Ottoman conquest of, 243, 252
Eilat (Ayla), 39
Gaza, 14, 29, 60, 128–129, 141, 209n11
Germany, 197
Ghuta, 135, 159. *See* Damascus.
Gibelin. *See* Bayt Jibrin.
Gizre, 59, 87n94, 229. *See also* Jazirat Ibn 'Umar.
Granada, xix, 15, 239–240
Green Field (*al-Midan al-akhdar*), 86, 86n91, 135–136
Haifa, 144, 147, 244
Hama, 24, 74n64, 116, 139–140, 168, 196, 231–233, 238
Harim, 166, 169
Harran, 54, 75, 110–111, 168, 196, 242
Hattin, 3, 91–96, 106, 228, 251
Hawran, 177
Hazrama, 135
Hijaz, 16, 139, 162, 180, 244, 246
Hulwan, 68
Hunin (Chastel Neuf), 17
Husn al-Akrad. *See* Crac des Chevaliers.
Ifriqiya, 60n4. *See also* North Africa.
Innib, 166, 166n38; castle of, 166
Irbil, 117
Iskandaruna (Iscandelion), 20
al-Istil, 17
Italy, xv, 125n161, 197
Jabala, 37, 72, 72n39, 145n212
Ja'bar (fortress), 165, 196, 231
Jaffa, 3n13, 26nn99–100, 115, 194, 244; Frederick II in, 119; Saladin's conquest of, 30; Yaqut's description of, 28, 30, 30n110

Jaffa Gate (Jerusalem), 158
Jazira. *See* Northern Mesopotamia.
Jazirat Ibn 'Umar, 59, 87, 229
Jericho, 13, 182, 188n100, 202n26
Jerusalem, xiii–xiv, xxii, 16, 26, 26nn99–101, 27, 33, 35, 38–39, 48, 51–52, 60n6, 67nn17–18, 71, 80, 89, 94, 100, 102–103, 113, 128–129, 134, 138n191, 158, 180, 182, 188, 188n100, 190–192, 194, 197, 198n17, 202, 206, 206n3, 207, 210n14, 213, 213n21, 216–217, 227–228, 230, 232, 239–242, 245, 249, 251; al-Harawi's description of, 1, 5–9, 9n52, 10, 12–14; as *qibla*, 210n14, 252; destruction of the walls of by al-Mu'azzam, 107–108, 184; Fatimids' conquest of, 63, 66–67, 73n47, 110n139; Frederick II's visit to, 119–124, 127; Ibn al-Qalanisi on the conquest of in 1099, 62–65; Ibn al-Athir's on the conquest of, 66–70; negotiations over, 114–115; Rashid al-Din's poem on, 97–98; Saladin's conquest of, 3, 26n101, 38, 97–98, 122, 251
Jordan, district of (*al-Urdunn*), 2, 2n8, 33–34, 36
Jordan, modern country of, 3n18, 28n102, 39n154, 175n67, 181n86
Jordan River, 115, 128n166, 141, 201
Jubayl. *See* Byblos.
Ka'ba, 5n27, 252
Kafar Burayk, 208
Kafar Latha (castle), 166
Kafar Manda, 3
Kafartab, 64, 165
Karbala, 13n72, 247
al-Karmil (Mount Carmel), 176–177
Kerak, 16, 92–93, 108, 144, 232; Yaqut's description of, 28, 28n102, 39
Khalid (fortress), 166
al-Khalil. *See* Hebron.
Khurasan, 55n22, 66, 84, 237

285

Khuwaylifa, 11, 11n63
Kidron Valley, 8, 8n46, 188n100
Konya, 101–102, 124
La'at 'Adan (town in Yemen), 2
Lake Tiberias, 2, 2n8, 17n79, 26, 37n148, 91, 167n44
Latakiya, 37n148, 167n44
Lebanon, xx, 3n18, 15, 32, 54, 246
Longobardy, 197
Lucera, 125
al-Lukamiyya, 72, 72n43
Lydda, 210n15
Ma'arrat al-Nu'man, 62–64, 165
Ma'arrat Misrin, 63, 63n9
Mada'in, 210n15
Manbij, 168
Mar Saba. *See* al-Siq.
Mar'ash, 166
Mardin, 73n47, 110–111, 135
Margat, 28, 37, 145n211, 252. *See also* al-Marqab.
al-Marqab, 37, 145n211, 203, 252
al-Masiyya, 17
al-Massisa (Mopsuestia), 32, 102
Mayyafariqin, 135, 138n183, 184, 233
Mecca, xix, 3, 5, 5n27, 5n29, 8, 8n44, 15, 37n143, 44n6, 74, 93, 99, 112, 122, 144, 162, 168, 168n45, 180–181, 184, 201, 210n14, 215–216, 220, 223, 233, 240, 246–247, 250, 252, 255
Medina, 2nn11–12, 69, 93, 112, 138n191, 138n194, 168, 168nn45–47, 210n14, 215, 246–247, 252
Mediterranean, xiii, xiv, xiv n2, xv, xviii n18, xx, 28n102, 29–30, 33, 36, 36n142, 37, 115, 244, 246, 250, 253
Midian, 3, 4n20
Mir'ish, 74
Mizza, 81
Montfort, 244
Mosul, xix, 1, 59, 71n29, 72n41, 83n84, 84, 89, 94, 99, 135, 144, 163, 165–166, 169, 169n49, 228–229, 231, 239, 251, 255
Mount Carmel. *See* al-Karmil.
Mount Gerizim. *See* al-Tur.
Mount of Olives, 8n46, 9, 210n15
Mount Silpius, 2
Mount Zion. *See* Zion; Church of Zion.
al-Mu'alla, 181
al-Munaytra, 167
Nablus, 8n41, 12, 51, 97, 110, 118, 122, 176–177, 184, 233. *See also* Shechem.
Nahr al-Jawz, 166
Najran, 38
al-Naqar, 182
al-Nayrab, 85, 163
Nazareth, 3n13, 4, 159n10
Nile River, 50, 112, 129, 236
Nimrod's Fortress. *See* Subayba.
Noble Sanctuary (Jerusalem), 118–119, 121, 123, 128, 251. *See also* Aqsa Mosque and Dome of the Rock.
North Africa (North Africans), xv, xx, 15, 18, 23–25, 48, 54n20, 55n24, 60, 87n93, 139, 151–152, 242–243, 246
Northern Mesopotamia (*al-Jazira*), xiv n3, xv, 59, 71, 110n139, 115, 135n183, 136, 169n49, 181n89, 184, 196, 225, 228–229, 231, 233, 242, 244, 251, 253, 255
Nudar, 175
Orontes valley, 73
Palestine, xvii, xix, 9, 11n63, 15–16, 29, 30–32, 39, 41n2, 110, 115, 116, 129n167, 134, 135n179, 209n11, 210n15, 231–232, 235, 239–242, 244, 246, 249, 251
Palmyra, 111n143, 168
Qarawa, 182
Qasyun, 179, 180
Qaymun, 182
Qayniya, 163, 163n28

Index C: Place Names

Qusayr, 112, 112n45
Ra'ban, 130–131
al-Rabwa, 81, 83, 158, 159n5, 163
Ramla, 11n63, 64, 182n90
Raqqa, 165, 168
al-Ra's, 130
al-Rawandan (fortress), 166
Rome, 31n118, 38, 125, 125n160, 126, 161, 197
Safed, 244
Salamiyya, 111
Saleph River (Göksu), 100n116
al-Salihiyya, 140, 141
Saône (*Sihyawn*), 28, 38
Sarkhad, 168
al-Shaqif. *See* Beaufort.
Shayzar, 75, 75n65, 165, 168, 171, 238
Shechem, 8n41, 12n65. *See also* Nablus.
Sicily, xv, xv n5, 15, 22, 59–60, 118–119, 125, 194, 197, 229, 232, 240
Sidon, xxi, 14, 36, 50, 198, 200–202; Baybars's capture of, 144, 147
Siloam, Pool of, 8, 8n43
Sinjar, 168
al-Siq (Mar Saba Monastery), 188
Siwas, 147
Soldiers' Camps (outside Damascus), 81
Spain, xv, xix, 15, 59, 59n3, 229, 239–240, 255
Subayba (Nimrod's Fortress), 208, 208n9, 209, 211, 211n17, 244
Syria, Saladin's conquest of, 56; Nur al-Din's conquest of, 56
Tabuk, 181
Tall 'Afrin, 73
Tall al-'Ujul, 121
Tall Bashir, 166

Tartus, 37n148, 145n210, 167n44
Tawq, 182
Temple Mount, 4n21, 6n35, 31n119, 44, 118n154, 251. *See also* Noble Sanctuary.
Tiberias, 2–4, 25–26, 31, 94–95, 128, 128n166
Tibnin (Toron), 17–18, 26, 93n99
Toledo, 59
Toron. *See* Tibnin.
Tortosa. *See* Tartus.
Tower of David (Jerusalem), 63, 65, 67
Tripoli, 25, 32, 36, 72, 72n35, 73n54, 83, 87, 87n94, 91n97, 93, 95, 95n102, 111–112, 130, 144, 151, 161, 178, 237, 252; Franks' capture of, 71
al-Tur (Mount Gerizim), 4
Tuscany, 197
Tyre, xxii, 14, 80, 93, 105, 157, 161; Baybars's capture of, 144, 147; Ibn Jubayr's visit and description of, 17, 20–22, 25–27; Yaqut's description of, 28, 33–36, 36n142, 37, 37n145
Uhud, 168; Battle of, 153, 155
Umayyad Mosque (Damascus), 13n72, 41, 48, 50, 78, 138, 138n193, 138n196, 236, 242
al-'Urayma (castle), 83, 87, 88
Valencia, xix, 15, 239
Yaman, 74
Yemen, 2, 5n28, 112n144, 139, 149, 244, 251
Yunin, 130
al-Zab (Casal), 20
Zamzam, 8, 8n44
Zion, 38; Mount of, 8n46, 67, 67n17; Church of, 8, 38

287

INDEX D
TERMS AND EVENTS

Aries (*al-Hamal*), 31, 75
Calendar (Gregorian/solar), xxii, 19n84, 202n27, 215–217
Calendar (Islamic/lunar), xxii, 19n84, 37n143, 63n12, 189n101, 215–217
Calendar (Jewish/lunar), 215–216
Calendar (Seleucid/Greek), 202n27
Cancer (*al-Saratan*), 31
Capricorn (*al-Jadi*), 31
Cassiopeia (*Dhat al-Kursi*), 31
Cross, 10n54, 20, 64, 95, 151, 153, 158, 177; Holy Cross, 104–106, 194, 201–202; majestic Cross, 92, 94–95; True Cross, 92–95, 96
Cubit (*dhira'*), 5, 5n31, 7, 245; royal cubit (*dhira' malaki*), 7, 7n38, 252
Day of Assembly, 42, 42n5
Day of Judgment, 42n5, 138n193, 158, 160n12
Day of Resurrection, 42, 42n5, 46, 89, 108, 171n52
Dhimmi, 23, 23n91, 246
Dinar, 17–18, 17n82, 24, 34, 56, 65, 70, 95, 105, 106, 119, 130–131, 154, 178, 246, 252
Dirham, 246
Diwan, 66, 66n15, 76, 237, 246
Easter, 10n56, 94, 189, 216
End-of-Days Guide (*Mahdi*), 157, 160, 246
Exigency (*maslaha*), 151
Fatwa. *See* Juridical directive.
Garden, 10, 81n82, 85, 163, 220, 222, 245; Gardens of Delight, 46n7, 87, 164. *See also* Heaven; Paradise.
Gemini (*al-Taw'am*), 31, 80
Hadith (corpus of hadiths), xvi n7, 11nn61–62, 15, 24n93, 29n107, 33n124, 35–36, 37n145, 41, 48, 99, 132, 170–171, 174n54, 175, 184, 219, 233, 235, 238, 242, 244–245, 247–248, 254
Hadith (specific report), xvi n7, 13, 35, 43–47, 159n6, 171n52, 179, 247
Hadith memorizer, 11, 11n61, 30, 36–37, 86, 247
Hafiz. *See* Hadith memorizer.
Heaven, 5, 6, 8, 42, 57, 153–154, 159, 161, 172, 201, 211, 213, Heavenly confirmed, 211, 216; Heavenly fire, 4; Heavenly table, 3n13, 8n45. *See also* Garden; Paradise.
Hell, 25, 45, 47, 57, 179, 221
Hijra, 200, 207, 215, 247
Jihad, xv-xx; al-'Izz son of 'Abd al-Salam on, 48–49; 56, 60, 64, 80, 82–84, 89, 94, 107, 110, 114, 153–154, 157; and al-Findalawi, 163–164; and Nur al-Din, 166, 169, 206; and al-Mu'azzam, 174, 179–183; and al-'Adil, 209; and Sunqur, 209; and Baybars, 211, 219, 221–222, 223n2, 227, 237, 240–242; and Zangi, 255; definition of, 248–249; Ibn 'Asakir on, 41–47

288

Index D: Terms and Events

Jizya tax, 18, 18n83, 23n91, 158, 222–223, 246, 249
Juridical directive (*fatwa*), xix, xx, 50, 52–54, 57, 249
Libra (*al-Mizan*), 31
Madrasa. *See* College.
Mahdi. *See* End-of-Days Guide.
Mile, 21n90, 250
Muezzin, 118, 135, 251
Necessity (*darura*), 108, 151n222
Night of Completion, 162, 162n24
Orion (*al-Jawza'*), 31
Paradise, 46, 47, 155, 179. *See also* Garden; Heaven.
Parasang, 17, 17n81, 19, 26, 36, 85, 252
Pascha. *See* Easter.
Pilgrimage (Hajj), 5n29, 37n143, 74, 180, 255
Plague of Emmaus (*'Amwas*), 2, 2n9, 34n134, 138n189, 251
Prayer niche (*mihrab*), 5, 5n27, 6, 8, 8n42, 10, 20, 123, 250, 252
Qibla, 5n27, 210, 210n14, 252
Qirat, 17–18, 17n82, 252
Royal cubit. *See* Cubit.
Shahada (Islamic credo), 157, 159n6, 161
Virgo (*al-Sammak al-A'zal*), 31
Vizier, 7, 35n139, 55–56, 63n10, 66, 68n20, 181n87, 191n4, 237, 239
Ziyara, 5n29, 255. *See also* Pilgrimage.

289

Index E

Quranic and Biblical References

Qur'an

2:135	25	9:111	81n82, 85, 163, 220
2:216	220		
2:255	6	12:1–111	10n55
3:4	25n96	12:21	23
3:169–170	220	12:90	24
3:195	154, 220	13:18	25
3:199	222	17:1	6
4:74	221	17:16	109
4:84	220	18:29	45
4:95–96	221	19:25	10, 10n59
4:125–126	213	19:34	119
4:157	159	19:40	208
5:21–22	13, 13n68	20:102	36
5:112–115	3n13, 8n45	20:127	25
6:17–18	178	21:89	208
7:155	19	23:50	158
8:12	221	23:91	119
8:15–18	221	24:61	154
8:45	221	27:17–19	13n70
8:60	221	28:23–24	4n20
8:61	222	31:11–19	2n6
9:5	221, 223	36:20	1, 2n4
9:18	209, 210	36:69	175
9:20	44, 221	37:43–44	87, 164
9:29	222, 223	38:21	8n42
9:36–37	216	47:4	222
9:39	222	55:24	20n86
9:41	222	61:6	160n16
9:88	222	78:22	25
		112:1–4	6

Index E: Quranic and Biblical References

Hebrew Bible/Old Testament

Genesis 23:1–20	12n64
Genesis 37–50	10n55
Exodus 2:16–21	4n20
Exodus 2:18	3n18
Numbers 10:29	3n18
Numbers 20:1–8	4n20
Numbers 13:1–13	13n68
Deuteronomy 1:22–40	13n68
Joshua 3:15–16	202n26
Joshua 24:32	12n65
1 Kings 18:20–40	176n72
2 Chronicles 20:7	10n57
Isaiah 41:8	10n57

New Testament

Matthew 25:57–61	10n55
Mark 15:42–47	10n55
Luke 10:1–24	1n3
Luke 23:50–16	10n55
John 2:1–11	3n13
John 4:1–42	8n41
John 5:1–15	8n40
John 9:1–12	8n43
John 19:38–42	10n55
Acts 10:9–16	3n13
Acts 11:27–28	1n3
Acts 21:10–12	1n3
Romans 5:12–21	9n54
1 Corinthians 15:21–22	9n54
James 2:23	10n57